Achieving Success

MW01124280

A Guide for College and Life

Second Edition

◆ *Edited by*
Chris Heavey
Dan Gianoutsos

Kendall Hunt
publishing company

Cover image © University of Nevada, Las Vegas

Kendall Hunt
publishing company

www.kendallhunt.com
Send all inquiries to:
4050 Westmark Drive
Dubuque, IA 52004-1840

Copyright © 2012, 2013 by Chris Heavey and Dan Gianoutsos

ISBN 978-1-4652-2989-2

Kendall Hunt Publishing Company has the exclusive rights to reproduce this work,
to prepare derivative works from this work, to publicly distribute this work,
to publicly perform this work and to publicly display this work.

All rights reserved. No part of this publication may be reproduced,
stored in a retrieval system, or transmitted, in any form or by any
means, electronic, mechanical, photocopying, recording, or otherwise,
without the prior written permission of the copyright owner.

Printed in the United States of America
10 9 8 7 6 5 4 3 2

Contents

Getting Started

Welcome! We are delighted to have you here at the University of Nevada, Las Vegas (UNLV) and as a student in this First-Year Seminar. This course serves a unique role in your college education, because its primary purpose is to help you succeed in college. College is a lot different than high school. First, UNLV is a much larger place than your high school. There are many more offices and divisions and resources and students than in even the largest high school. Second, college offers you a lot more freedom and more choices than you had in high school; but, along with this freedom comes responsibility, and sometimes unanticipated challenges. The goal of this course is to help you successfully navigate this freedom and make well-informed decisions that help you reach your goals in this large and complex environment.

There are two different ways in which this course is designed to help you succeed here at UNLV. First, it's a course where your instructor or section leader will have a chance to get to know you. You will also have a chance to get to know at least some of your classmates. Building relationships is an important part of being successful in college, and this is designed to be at least one course where you can build relationships during your first year at UNLV. Hopefully you will have the chance to build lots of friendships in your other courses, too.

Second, this course will teach you about UNLV, and many resources, tools, and strategies to help you be successful in college. For example, in this course you will learn how UNLV is organized and where you can go to get help and advice, and we'll talk about how to manage your time and set appropriate goals.

One way to think about the goal of this course is that it is to make you an "intentional" college student: in other words, one who takes ownership of your own college path by making thoughtful, well-informed decisions that are designed to help you reach your personal, social, and academic goals. To make well-informed decisions and move purposely toward your goal of a college degree and a career, you will need an understanding of the university and its procedures and requirements, as well as an understanding of how to succeed in your courses. We will cover these topics in the pages that follow. We will also start teaching you the basic knowledge and skills expected of all UNLV graduates, such as how to think critically and write effectively, and what it means to be an ethical and engaged citizen in a diverse, rapidly changing world.

Before we plunge in, let's take a moment to learn about the history of UNLV. Although UNLV is a young institution compared to most universities its size, it is a dynamic university in a vibrant city. The first seeds of UNLV began when the University of Nevada, Reno (UNR) offered extension classes in some spare rooms of what was then Las Vegas High School. The year was 1951. As the city of Las Vegas grew rapidly, so did demand for university-level education. Three years later, the Southern Regional Division of the University of Nevada was formally established. The Nevada Southerners, as they were known, chose the Rebel as a mascot to reflect their desire to gain independence from the north. Soon thereafter, the Regents selected an 80-acre parcel to establish our campus along what was then a dirt road, Maryland Parkway. In 1957, the first classes were held on our current campus. Shortly thereafter, we received our own accreditation as an institution of higher education. Still under the control of UNR, we held our first graduation in 1964. Finally, in 1968 the university won its independence, and in 1969 it was officially renamed the University of Nevada, Las Vegas.

From the beginning we have grown rapidly, along with the city around us. We've gone from being a remote outpost along a dirt road to being a large urban university in a city of almost 2 million people. After existing for only 10 years, UNLV became the largest university in the state by enrollment. We've now grown to a university of more than 27,000 students, with more than 2,700 faculty and staff, 220 degree programs, and more than 100,000 alumni! As we hope you'll experience for yourself, UNLV is an exciting place to be. Welcome aboard!

◆ Your Undergraduate Degree

As a student here at UNLV, you will choose a major that represents your focused interest. It's what you most want to learn about; perhaps it relates directly to the career you want to pursue, or perhaps it is a pathway into further education at the post-graduate level. Some of you have already chosen majors, but others are currently undecided—what we call "Exploring Majors." Either way, at some point before you graduate, you will choose a major and fulfill a list of specific requirements for that degree.

In addition to completing the requirements for your major, you will also fulfill a list of General Education Requirements. This course fulfills the first of your General Education Requirements—the First-Year Seminar requirement. This course and the 11 or so remaining courses that you take to fulfill the General Education Requirements are designed to, in combination with the courses you complete for your major, ensure that you develop the skills and knowledge expected of all UNLV graduates. The specific skills and knowledge you are expected to have as a graduate of UNLV are listed in the University Undergraduate Learning Outcomes, or UULOs for short. There are five broad UULOs, each with six more specific objectives.

The University Undergraduate Learning Outcomes are:

Intellectual Breadth and Lifelong Learning—Graduates are able to understand and integrate basic principles of the natural sciences, social sciences, humanities, fine arts, and health sciences, and develop skills and a desire for lifelong learning. Specific outcomes for all students include:

1. Demonstrate in-depth knowledge and skills in at least one major area.
2. Identify the fundamental principles of the natural and health sciences, social sciences, humanities, and fine arts.
3. Apply the research methods and theoretical models of the natural and health sciences, social sciences, humanities, and fine arts to define, solve, and evaluate problems.

4. Transfer knowledge and skills gained from general and specialized studies to new settings and complex problems.
5. Demonstrate lifelong learning skills, including the ability to place problems in personally meaningful contexts; reflect on one's own understanding, demonstrate awareness of what needs to be learned; articulate a learning plan; and act independently on the plan, using appropriate resources.
6. Achieve success in one's chosen field or discipline, including applying persistence, motivation, interpersonal communications, leadership, goal setting, and career skills.

Inquiry and Critical Thinking—Graduates are able to identify problems, articulate questions, and use various forms of research and reasoning to guide the collection, analysis, and use of information related to those problems. Specific outcomes for all students include:

1. Identify problems, articulate questions or hypotheses, and determine the need for information.
2. Access and collect the needed information from appropriate primary and secondary sources.
3. Use quantitative and qualitative methods, including the ability to recognize assumptions, draw inferences, make deductions, and interpret information to analyze problems in context, and then draw conclusions.
4. Recognize the complexity of problems, and identify different perspectives from which problems and questions can be viewed.
5. Evaluate and report on conclusions, including discussing the basis for and strength of findings, and identify areas where further inquiry is needed.
6. Identify, analyze, and evaluate reasoning, and construct and defend reasonable arguments and explanations.

Communication—Graduates are able to write and speak effectively to both general and specialized audiences, create effective visuals that support written or spoken communication, and use electronic media common to one's field or profession. Specific outcomes for all students include:

1. Demonstrate general academic literacy, including how to respond to needs of audiences and to different kinds of rhetorical situations, analyze and evaluate reasons and evidence, and construct research-based arguments using Standard Written English.
2. Effectively use the common genres and conventions for writing within a particular discipline or profession.
3. Prepare and deliver effective oral presentations.
4. Collaborate effectively with others to share information, solve problems, or complete tasks.
5. Produce effective visuals using different media.
6. Apply the up-to-date technologies commonly used to research and communicate within one's field.

Global/Multicultural Knowledge and Awareness—Graduates will have developed knowledge of global and multicultural societies, and an awareness of their place in and effect on them. Specific outcomes for all students include:

1. Demonstrate knowledge of the history, philosophy, arts, and geography of world cultures.

2. Respond to diverse perspectives linked to identity, including age, ability, religion, politics, race, gender, ethnicity, and sexuality; both in American and international contexts.
3. Apply the concept of social justice.
4. Demonstrate familiarity with a non-native language, or experience living in a different culture.
5. Function effectively in diverse groups.
6. Demonstrate awareness of one's own place in and effect on the world.

Citizenship and Ethics—Graduates are able to participate knowledgeably and actively in the public life of our communities and make informed, responsible, and ethical decisions in their personal and professional lives. Specific outcomes for all students include:

1. Acquire knowledge of political, economic, and social institutions.
2. Identify the various rights and obligations that citizens have in their communities.
3. Apply various forms of citizenship skills such as media analysis, letter writing, community service, and lobbying.
4. Explain the concept of sustainability as it impacts economic, environmental, and social concerns.
5. Examine various concepts and theories of ethics, and how to deliberate and assess claims about ethical issues.
6. Apply ethical concepts and theories to specific ethical dilemmas students will experience in their personal and professional lives.

Encountering these UULOs for the first time may seem intimidating. It is a long list of things you are expected to know and be able to do. Remember, however, that you will have your entire college career to master these skills. In this course you will be introduced to all of the UULOs. Other courses, such as your required composition courses, your constitutions course, or the distribution courses, focus on specific UULOs. You will revisit all of the UULOs, with more expected of you, during your Second-Year Seminar. And within your major, as you progress from the lower-level courses all the way to your culminating experience, you will have the opportunity to further refine and enhance your performance for each one of the five UULOs. Think of your education here at UNLV as an intentional, progressive sequence designed to help you become a well-educated, well-rounded person able to achieve your goals.

Before we leave this topic, we want to say one more thing about the interrelationship between your major, general education, and the UULOs. Students (hopefully) choose a major because it aligns most closely with their passions and their goals. Majors are about what we want to be. Some majors open doors to careers that require specialized skills and knowledge. But, the UULOs define more generally what it means to be an educated person. Although the UULOs are more general, they are *not* less important. In fact, when employers describe what they want in employees, the list looks pretty much like the UULOs you just read. Also, when we look later at who is most successful after college, again it is those who have mastered *both* the specific skills and knowledge required for their chosen field, *and* the general skills and knowledge described by the UULOs. So, think of your major and general education as partners working to prepare you to be successful in whatever you choose to pursue.

◆ Your Commitment as a Student at UNLV

It is important to note one final thing before closing this chapter. We've discussed the goals of this course, the basic structure of your undergraduate education at UNLV, and what resources the campus has to support you in your journey. What we haven't discussed is your commitment to UNLV. By coming to UNLV, you become part of our community, and commit yourself to behave in a manner that is consistent with our intellectual community. This commitment is spelled out in the UNLV Student Conduct Code. The first two paragraphs of the Student Conduct Code explain its basic goal and your role in helping us achieve this goal:

UNLV Student Conduct Code

The aim of education is the intellectual, personal, social, and ethical development of the individual. The educational process is ideally conducted in an environment that encourages reasoned discourse, intellectual honesty, openness to constructive change, and respect for the rights of all individuals. Self-discipline and a respect for the rights of others within the University of Nevada, Las Vegas ("University" or "UNLV") community are necessary for the fulfillment of such goals.

The UNLV Student Conduct Code ("Code") is designed to promote this environment and sets forth standards of conduct expected of students/student organizations who choose to join the University community. When students choose to accept admission to the University, they accept the rights and responsibilities of membership in the University's academic and social community. Students/student organizations that are found to violate these standards will be subject to conduct sanctions in order to promote their own personal development, to protect the University community, and to maintain order and stability on campus.

As members of this university, we are all responsible for creating the environment described above. Those who fail to uphold this responsibility can be sanctioned, as specified in the remainder of the Student Conduct Code.

There is also a separate code focused on academic misconduct. Academic misconduct by students undermines the fundamental values of the university. As stated in the Student Academic Misconduct Policy:

UNLV Student Academic Misconduct Policy

Integrity is a concern for every member of the campus community; all share in upholding the fundamental values of honesty, trust, respect, fairness, responsibility, and professionalism. By choosing to join the UNLV community, students accept the Student Academic Misconduct Policy and are expected to always engage in ethical decision making. Students enrolling in UNLV assume the obligation to conduct themselves in a manner compatible with UNLV's function as an educational institution.

You can download the entire Student Conduct Code and the Student Academic Misconduct Policy from the Office of Student Conduct website at: http://studentconduct.unlv.edu/. Hopefully, the need for these policies is self-evident.

We close this introduction by wishing you the best as you pursue your personal, social, and academic goals here at UNLV. It is our hope that this course and the resources available at UNLV will provide you with the tools you need to achieve academic excellence and become an actively engaged citizen on and off campus.

Touching All the Bases

An Overview and Preview of the Most Powerful
Principles of College Success

ACTIVATE YOUR THINKING — Journal Entry — 2.1

1. How do you think college will be different from high school?

_____

_____

_____

2. What do you think it will take to be successful in college? (What personal
   characteristics, qualities, or strategies do you feel are most important for
   college success?)

_____

_____

_____

3. How well do you expect to do in your first term of college? Why?

_____

_____

_____

LEARNING GOAL

To equip you with a set of
powerful success strategies
that you can use imme-
diately to get off to a fast
start in college and can
use continually throughout
your college experience to
achieve success.

The Most Powerful Research-Based Principles of College Success

Research on human learning and student development indicates four powerful
principles of college success:

1. Active involvement;
2. Use of campus resources;
3. Interpersonal interaction and collaboration; and
4. Personal reflection and self-awareness (Astin, 1993; Kuh, 2000; Light,
   2001; Pascarella & Terenzini, 1991, 2005; Tinto, 1993).

From "Thriving in College and Beyond" by Cuseo, Fecas, Thompson. © Kendall Hunt Publishing.

These four principles represent the bases of college success. They are introduced and examined carefully in this opening chapter for two reasons:

1. You can put them into practice to establish good habits for early success in college.
2. These principles represent the foundational bases for the success strategies recommended throughout this book.

The four bases of college success can be represented visually by a baseball diamond (see **Figure 2.1**).

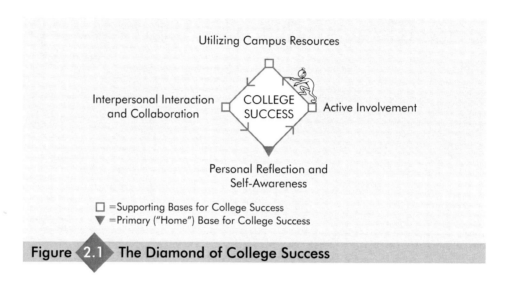

Figure **2.1**   The Diamond of College Success

Touching the First Base of College Success: Active Involvement

Research indicates that active involvement may be the most powerful principle of human learning and college success (Astin, 1993; Kuh, 2000). The bottom line is this: To maximize your success in college, you cannot be a passive spectator; you need to be an active player in the learning process.

The principle of active involvement includes the following pair of processes:

- The amount of personal time you devote to learning in the college experience;
- The degree of personal effort or energy (mental and physical) you put into the learning process.

Think of something you do with intensity, passion, and commitment. If you were to approach academic work in the same way, you would be faithfully implementing the principle of active involvement.

One way to ensure that you're actively involved in the learning process and putting forth high levels of energy or effort is to act on what you are learning. You can engage in any of the following actions to ensure that you are investing a high level of effort and energy:

- **Writing.** Express what you're trying to learn in print.
  Action: Write notes when reading rather than passively underlining sentences.

Tell me and I'll listen.
Show me and I'll understand.
Involve me and I'll learn.

–Teton Lakota Indian saying

Student Perspective

"You don't have to be smart to work hard."

–24-year-old, first-year student who has returned to college

- **Speaking.** Express what you're trying to learn orally.
  Action: Explain a course concept to a study-group partner rather than just looking over it silently.
- **Organizing.** Group or classify ideas you're learning into logical categories.
  Action: Create an outline, diagram, or concept map (e.g., see Figure 2.1) to visually connect ideas.

The following section explains how you can apply both components of active involvement—spending time and expending energy—to the major learning challenges that you will encounter in college.

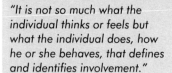

"It is not so much what the individual thinks or feels but what the individual does, how he or she behaves, that defines and identifies involvement."

–Alexander Astin, professor emeritus at University of California, Los Angeles, identified as the "most frequently cited author" in higher education and the person "most admired for creative insightful thinking"

Time Spent in Class

Since the total amount of time you spend on learning is associated with how much you learn and how successfully you learn, this association leads to a straightforward recommendation: Attend all class sessions in all your courses. It may be tempting to skip or cut classes because college professors are less likely to monitor your attendance or take roll than your teachers were in high school. However, don't let this new freedom fool you into thinking that missing classes will have no effect on your grades. Over the past 75 years, many research studies in many types of courses have shown a direct relationship between class attendance and course grades—as one goes up or down, so does the other (Anderson & Gates, 2002; Devadoss & Foltz, 1996; Grandpre, 2000; Launius, 1997; Moore, 2003, 2006; Moore et al., 2003; Shimoff & Catania, 2001; Wiley, 1992; Wyatt, 1992). **Figure 2.2** represents the results of a study conducted at the City Colleges of Chicago, which shows the relationship between students' class attendance during the first 5 weeks of the term and their final course grades.

© GreenstockCreative, 2010. Under license from Shutterstock, Inc.

Student Perspective

"My biggest recommendation: GO TO CLASS. I learned this the hard way my first semester. You'll be surprised what you pick up just by being there. I wish someone would have informed me of this before I started school."

–Advice to new students from a college sophomore (Walsh, 2005)

Figure 2.2 Relationship Between Class Attendance Rate and Final Course Grades

Time Spent on Coursework Outside the Classroom

You will spend fewer hours per week sitting in class than you did in high school. However, you will be expected to spend more time on your own on academic work. Studies clearly show that when college students spend more time on academic work outside of class the result is better learning and higher grades (National Survey of Student Engagement, 2003). For example, one study of more than 25,000 college students found that the percentage of students receiving mostly A grades was almost three times higher for students who spent 40 or more hours per week on academic work than it was for students who spent between 20 and 40 hours. Among students who spent 20 or fewer hours per week on academic work, the percentage receiving grades that were mostly Cs or below was almost twice as high as it was for students who spent 40 or more hours on academic work (Pace, 1990a, 1990b).

Unfortunately, more than 80 percent of beginning college students report having studied 10 or fewer hours per week during their final year in high school and just 3 percent report studying more than 20 hours per week (Sax, Lindholm, Astin, Korn, & Mahoney, 2004). In addition, only 20 percent expect to spend more than 25 hours per week studying throughout college (National Survey of Student Engagement, 2005). This has to change if new college students are to earn good grades.

If you need further motivation to achieve good grades, keep in mind that higher grades during college result in higher chances of career success after college. Research on college graduates indicates that the higher their college grades, the higher

- The status (prestige) of their first job;
- Their job mobility (ability to change jobs or move into different positions); and
- Their total earnings (salary).

Thus, the more you learn, the more you'll earn. This relationship between college grades and career success exists for students at all types of colleges and universities regardless of the reputation or prestige of the institution (Pascarella & Terenzini, 1991, 2005). In other words, how well you do academically in college matters more to your career success than where you go to college and what institutional name appears on your diploma.

Active Listening and Note Taking

You'll find that college professors rely heavily on the lecture method—they profess their knowledge by speaking for long stretches of time, and the students' job is to listen and take notes on the knowledge they dispense. This method of instruction places great demands on the ability to listen carefully and take notes that are both accurate and complete.

Remember

Research shows that, in all subject areas, most test questions on college exams come from the professor's lectures and that students who take better class notes get better course grades (Brown, 1988; Kiewra, 2000).

The best way to apply the principle of active involvement during a class lecture is to engage in the physical action of writing notes. Writing down

Student Perspective

"In high school, you were a dork if you got good grades and cared about what was going on in your class. In college, you're a dork if you don't."

—College sophomore (Appleby, 2008)

Pause for Reflection

In high school, how many hours per week did you spend on schoolwork outside of class during your senior year?

Student Perspective

"I thought I would get a better education if the school had a really good reputation. Now, I think one's education depends on how much effort you put into it."

—First-year college student (Bates, 1994)

Student Perspective

"I never had a class before where the teacher just stands up and talks to you. He says something and you're writing it down, but then he says something else."

—First-year college student (Erickson & Strommer, 1991)

what your instructor is saying in class "forces" you to pay closer attention to what is being said and reinforces your retention of what was said. By taking notes, you not only hear the information (auditory memory) but also see it on paper (visual memory) and feel it in the muscles of your hand as you write it (motor memory).

> **Remember**
>
> Your role in the college classroom is not to be a passive spectator or an absorbent sponge that sits back and simply soaks up information through osmosis. Instead, your role is more like an aggressive detective or investigative reporter who's on a search-and-record mission. You need to actively search for information by picking your instructor's brain, picking out your instructor's key points, and recording your "pickings" in your notebook.

See **Box 2.1** for top strategies on classroom listening and note taking, which you should put into practice immediately.

> "All genuine learning is active, not passive. It is a process in which the student is the main agent, not the teacher."
>
> —Mortimer Adler, American professor of philosophy and educational theorist

Take Action!

Listening and Note Taking   2.1

One of the tasks that you will be expected to perform at the start of your first term in college is taking notes in class. Studies show that professors' lecture notes are the number one source of test questions (and test answers) on college exams. Get off to a fast start by using the following strategies to improve the quality of your note taking:

1. **Get to every class.** Whether or not your instructors take roll, you're responsible for all material covered in class. Remember that a full load of college courses (15 units) only requires that you be in class about 13 hours per week. If you consider your classwork to be a full-time job that only requires you to show up about 13 hours a week, that's a sweet deal, and it's a deal that allows more educational freedom than you had in high school. To miss a session when you're required to spend so little time in class per week is an abuse of your educational freedom. It's also an abuse of the money you, your family, or taxpaying American citizens pay to support your college education.

2. **Get to every class on time.** The first few minutes of a class session often contain valuable information, such as reminders, reviews, and previews.

© Joanne Harris and Daniel Bubnich, 2010. Under license from Shutterstock, Inc.

3. **Get organized.** Arrive at class with the right equipment; get a separate notebook for each class, write your name on it, date each class session, and store all class handouts in it.
4. **Get in the right position.**
   - The ideal place to sit—front and center of the room, where you can hear and see most effectively;
   - The ideal posture—upright and leaning forward, because your body influences your mind; if your body is in an alert and ready position, your mind is likely to follow;
   - The ideal position socially—near people who will not distract your focus of attention or detract from the quality of your note taking.

!
Remember

These attention-focusing strategies are particularly important during the first year of college, when class sizes tend to be larger. In a large class, individuals tend to feel more anonymous, which can reduce their sense of personal responsibility and their drive to stay focused and actively involved. Thus, in large-class settings, it's especially important to use effective strategies that eliminate distractions (such as those described in Chapter 5) and attention drift.

5. **Get in the right frame of mind.** Get psyched up; come to class with attitude—an attitude that you're going to pick your instructor's brain, pick up answers to test questions, and pick up your grade.
6. **Get it down (in writing).** Actively look, listen, and record important points at all times in class. Pay special attention to whatever information instructors put in writing, whether it is on the board, on a slide, or in a handout.
7. **Don't let go of your pen.** When in doubt, write it out; it's better to have it and not need it than to need it and not have it.

!
Remember

Most college professors do not write all important information on the board for you; instead, they expect you to listen carefully to what they're saying and write it down for yourself.

8. **Finish strong.** The last few minutes of class often contain valuable information, such as reminders, reviews, and previews.
9. **Stick around.** As soon as class ends, don't immediately bolt; instead, hang out for a few moments to briefly review your notes (by yourself or with a classmate). If you find any gaps, check them out with your instructor before he or she leaves the classroom. This quick end-of-class review will help your brain retain the information it just received.

Note: For more detailed information on listening and note taking, see Chapter 6.

Active Class Participation

You can become actively involved in the college classroom by arriving at class prepared (e.g., having done the assigned reading), by asking relevant questions, and by contributing thoughtful comments during class discussions. When you communicate orally, you elevate the level of active involvement you invest in the learning process because speaking requires you to exert both mental energy (thinking about what you are going to say) and physical energy (moving your lips to say it). Thus, class participation will increase your ability to stay alert and attentive in class. It also sends a clear message to the instructor that you are a motivated student who takes the course seriously and wants to learn. Since class participation accounts for a portion of your final grade in many courses, your attentiveness and involvement in class can have a direct, positive effect on your course grade.

Pause for Reflection

When you enter a classroom, where do you usually sit?

Why do you sit there? Is it a conscious choice or more like an automatic habit?

Do you think that your usual seat places you in the best possible position for listening and learning in the classroom?

Active Reading

Writing not only promotes active listening in class but also can promote active reading out of class. Taking notes on information that you're reading, or on information you've highlighted while reading, helps keep you actively involved in the reading process because it requires more mental and physical energy than merely reading the material or passively highlighting sentences. (See **Box 2.2** for top strategies for reading college textbooks that you should put into practice immediately.)

Take Action!

2.2

Top Strategies: Improving Textbook-Reading Comprehension and Retention

If you haven't already acquired textbooks for your courses, get them immediately and get ahead on your reading assignments. Information from reading assignments ranks right behind lecture notes as a source of test questions on college exams. Your professors are likely to deliver class lectures with the expectation that you have done the assigned reading and can build on that knowledge when they're lecturing. If you haven't done the reading, you'll have more difficulty following and taking notes on what your instructor is saying in class. Thus, by not doing the reading you pay a double penalty. College professors also expect you to relate or connect what they talk about in class to the reading they have assigned. Thus, it's important to start developing good reading habits now. You can do so by using the following strategies to improve your reading comprehension and retention.

1. **Come fully equipped.**
   - Writing tool and storage—Always bring a writing tool (pen, pencil, or keyboard) to record important information and a storage space (notebook or computer) in which you can save and retrieve information acquired from your reading for later use on tests and assignments.
   - Dictionary—Have a dictionary nearby to quickly find the meaning of unfamiliar words that may interfere with your ability to comprehend what you're reading. Looking up definitions of unfamiliar words does more than help you understand what you're reading; it's also an effective way to build your vocabulary. Building your vocabulary will improve your reading comprehension in all college courses, as well as your performance on standardized tests, such as those required for admission to graduate and professional schools.

Student Perspective

"I recommend that you read the first chapters right away because college professors get started promptly with assigning certain readings. Classes in college move very fast because, unlike high school, you do not attend class five times a week but two or three times a week."

–Advice to new college students from a first-year student

   - Glossary of terms—Check the back of your textbook for a list of key terms included in the book. Each academic subject or discipline has its own vocabulary, and knowing the meaning of these terms is often the key to understanding the concepts covered in the text. Don't ignore the glossary; it's more than an ancillary or afterthought to the textbook. Use it regularly to increase your comprehension of course concepts. Consider making a photocopy of the glossary of terms at the back of your textbook so that you can have a copy of it in front of you while you're reading, rather than having to repeatedly stop, hold your place, and go to the back of the text to find the glossary.

2. **Get in the right position.** Sit upright and have light coming from behind you, over the side of your body opposite your writing hand. This will reduce the distracting and fatiguing effects of glare and shadows.

3. **Get a sneak preview.** Approach the chapter by first reading its boldface headings and any chapter outline, summary, or end-of-chapter questions that may be provided. This will supply you with a mental map of the chapter's important ideas before you start your reading trip and provide an overview that will help you keep track of the chapter's major ideas (the "big picture"), thereby reducing the risk that you'll get lost among the smaller, more details you encounter along the way.

4. **Use boldface headings and subheadings.** Headings are cues for important information. Turn them into questions, and then read to find their answers. This will launch you on an answer-finding mission that will keep you mentally active while reading and enable you to read with a purpose. Turning headings into questions is also a good way to prepare for tests because you're practicing exactly what you'll be expected to do on tests—answer questions.

5. **Pay attention to the first and last sentences.** Absorb opening and closing sentences in sections beneath the chapter's major headings and subheadings. These sentences often contain an important introduction and conclusion to the material covered within that section of the text.

6. **Finish each of your reading sessions with a short review.** Recall what you have highlighted or noted as important information (rather than trying to cover a few more pages). It's best to use the last few minutes of reading time to "lock in" the most important information you've just read because most forgetting takes place immediately after you stop processing (taking in) information and start doing something else.

Source: Underwood (1983).

Remember

Your goal while reading should be to discover or uncover the most important information contained in what you're reading; when you finish reading, your final step should be to reread (and lock in) the key information you discovered while reading.

Note: More detailed information on reading comprehension and retention is provided in Chapter 6.

◆ Touching the Second Base of College Success: Use of Campus Resources

Your campus environment contains multiple resources designed to support your quest for educational and personal success. Studies show that students who use campus resources report higher levels of satisfaction with college and get more out of the college experience (Pascarella & Terenzini, 1991, 2005).

! Remember

Involvement with campus services is not just valuable but also "free"; the cost of these services has already been covered by your college tuition. By investing time and energy in campus resources, you not only increase your prospects for personal success but also maximize the return on your financial investment in college—that is, you get a bigger bang for your buck.

"Do not be a PCP (Parking Lot→ Classroom→ Parking Lot) student. The time you spend on campus will be a sound investment in your academic and professional success."

–Drew Appleby, professor of psychology

Your Campus Resources

Using your campus resources is an important, research-backed principle of college success, and it is a natural extension of the principle of active involvement. Successful students are active learners inside and outside the classroom, and this behavior extends to active use of campus resources. An essential first step toward putting this principle into practice is to become fully aware of all key support services that are available on campus.

"The impact of college is not simply the result of what a college does for or to a student. Rather, the impact is a result of the extent to which an individual student exploits the people, programs, facilities, opportunities, and experiences that the college makes available."

–Earnest Pascarella and Patrick Terenzini, *How College Affects Students*

◆ Academic Resources at UNLV

Academic Success Center

The Academic Success Center (ASC) is a resource and service hub that partners with the UNLV campus community to welcome, guide, and support students through their college experience. The ASC is committed to helping students overcome academic challenges they may encounter. The ASC offers a range of student services that include academic success coaching, campus-wide tutoring services, academic advising, student-athlete academic services, testing services, bridge programs, and first-year programs for Exploring Majors. Below are highlights of four of these programs:

Academic Success Coaching. Academic Success Coaching helps students negotiate the rigors of college life through one-on-one sessions by addressing various academic and personal issues such as time management, study skills, motivation, and setting goals. The Academic Success Coaches are select graduate students who are highly trained in academic success matters, and possess substantial experience working with undergraduate students. To request a Coach, stop by the Academic Success Center and fill out a request form.

Tutoring Services. The ASC offers free tutoring for a variety of UNLV courses throughout the academic school year. The ASC also provides Supplemental Instruction for an assortment of courses, as well as exam review sessions. The mission of the tutoring program is to enhance the student's overall academic experience by providing a respectful and safe educational environment for learning. The free tutoring services are located on the second floor of Lied Library. An active UNLV student ID is required. A current schedule of courses tutored, times, and location is updated on Facebook (http://www. facebook.com/unlvtutoring).

Bridge Program. The ASC Bridge Program is for students who are admitted to UNLV and have placed into developmental college math courses (MATH 95 and MATH 96), or students who have taken MATH 95 or MATH 96 and have not received a passing grade. The program uses online math software to help students review the concepts needed to be successful in 100-level math. Students will go through segments of the online program with the guidance of a tutor. At the end of the program, students retake the math placement test with the hope that they test into 100-level math, saving them both the time and money needed to complete developmental math. Additionally, the program provides tutorials on key math concepts and other college success tips. Registration information, and more, are available at: academicsuccess. unlv.edu/learningsupport/bridge.

Academic Advising. The ASC Academic Advising unit provides comprehensive academic advising services to all Exploring Majors students. The Academic Advisors assist Exploring students in charting courses for success and achieving degree progress. Academic Advisors help students plan a sequence of course schedules to efficiently complete their degrees, explore the relationship between UNLV's majors/minors and career goals to instill confidence upon major/minor declaration, and interpret university, college, and center policies and procedures.

The ASC also offers exciting scholarship programs like Hixson-Lied Success Scholars, which targets Nevada students who have overcome financial, academic, and/or personal challenges. The ASC is located on the southwest side of the main campus, in between the Student Services Center and the Dining Commons. For more information, visit the ASC website at: http:// academicsuccess.unlv.edu/. To contact the ASC, call 702-895-3177 or email at: asc@unlv.edu.

Academic Advising Centers

Each of the ten colleges and schools at UNLV, as well as the Academic Success Center, has an advising center to serve its students. Each advising center is eager to help you get answers to your questions and to support your success as a student. They will help you understand your degree requirements and to plan your program of study. They also can connect you with other campus resources as needed. You should contact the advising center for the college within which your degree program resides. If you're still exploring which major to choose, you will be advised by the Academic Success Center. You can find out more about academic advising at UNLV and find contact information for all of the advising centers across campus at: http://www.unlv.edu/advising.

Disability Resource Center

As a commitment to provide equal access to academic programs and campus services, UNLV established the Disability Resource Center (DRC) to support students who experience disabilities through the appropriate use of accommodations, supportive services, and advocacy. The DRC collaborates with the campus community to provide eligible students (on a case-by-case basis) with services such as note-taking assistance, various testing accommodations, assistive technologies, adapted print material, workshops, and much more. Students interested in obtaining DRC accommodations must apply online and provide current and appropriate documentation for review. The DRC is located in the Student Services Complex A (SSC-A), Room 143, and can be contacted at 702-895-0866, or by email at: drc@unlv.edu. For more information, visit: http://drc.unlv.edu/.

International Programs

We live in a complex, global world. The increasing interconnectedness of our world makes it ever more important to be able understand issues from an international perspective. Speaking other languages is also an increasingly valuable skill. One way to enhance your understanding of the world beyond our borders, and perhaps to learn another language, is to study abroad. The Office of International Programs provides resources and support for international study. They offer for-credit study abroad programs in 25 different countries across the globe. Courses span a wide range that can be a part of any degree program. Financial aid and scholarships are also available to support your adventure. The Office of International Programs is located in CBC B325 and can be contacted at 702-895-3896 or by email at: international.programs@ unlv.edu. Their website is http://internationalprograms.unlv.edu/.

Student Conduct

The Office of Student Conduct serves as a central resource for helping students prevent academic dishonesty and behavior misconduct as defined by the UNLV Student Academic Misconduct Policy and Student Conduct Code. The Office also promotes awareness of student rights and responsibilities, as well as the process of policy enforcement and opportunities to be involved in the process. The Office is located in the Central Desert Complex (CDC), Building 1, Room 188, and can be contacted at 702-895-2308 or by email at: officeofstudentconduct@ unlv.edu. To explore more of the Office's resources and services, visit http://student conduct.unlv.edu/

Writing Center

The UNLV Writing Center offers free assistance to students with any writing project, which may range from research papers to curricula vitae, during any stage of the writing process. Within the Center, students can meet one on one with a writing consultant, or utilize the computer lab with consultant assistance available on hand. Although the consultants do not proofread or edit papers, they can help students brainstorm, construct outlines, work on drafts, or simply serve as a soundboard for ideas. Walk-in opportunities are occasionally available, but the Center strongly recommends scheduling an appointment by calling 702-895-3908, emailing at writingcenter@unlv.edu, or stopping in at the Center (located in the Central Desert Complex, Building 3). Students can also receive some writing services on the second floor of the Lied Library. Further, the Writing Center offers scheduled workshops on various writing issues, including structure, style, grammar, usage, and documentation formats. For more information, visit http://writingcenter.unlv.edu/.

University Libraries

The University Libraries include five libraries on the UNLV campus: the Lied Library (main), the Curriculum Materials Library, the Architecture Student Library, the Music Library, and the Law Library. For more information on the materials and services of these libraries, see *Chapter 9: Information Literacy and the UNLV Libraries*. The University Libraries' main contact number is 702-895-2286, and librarians can be contacted directly through the "Ask a Librarian" program, which includes online chat, text messaging, or an email online form. See the University Libraries main website for more information at: http://library.unlv.edu/.

◆ Other Resources at UNLV

Career Services

Career Services can assist you with transitioning to the world of work and career. They can help you develop a career plan aligned with your major, build your resume, network, search for a job, and even prepare for an interview. They offer career and guidance counseling as well as personality and career interest tools. Career Services is located in Student Services Complex, Building A, room 201, and can be contacted at 702-895-3495. For more information, visit http://hire.unlv.edu/.

Financial Aid and Scholarships

Financial Aid and Scholarships supports student access and persistence by providing financial aid to eligible students. Opportunities include scholarships, loans, reduced-tuition programs, and monthly payment plans. For more information, visit http://finaid.unlv.edu/.

Jean Nidetch Women's Center

The Jean Nidetch Women's Center is a resource center that offers programs to educate, support, and promote student wellness, equality, and diversity with an emphasis on women's concerns and current issues. The Women's Center is located on the second floor of the Student Services Complex, Room 225, and can be contacted at 702-895-4475. For more information, visit http://unlv.edu/srwc/womens-center/.

Student Engagement and Diversity

The Office of Civic Engagement and Diversity (OCED) serves as the nexus for student involvement on campus. Students can get involved in a wide range of student activities, including student organizations, fraternities and sororities, multicultural programs, international student programs, service programs, and leadership opportunities. OCED is located on the third floor of the Student Union. For more information, visit the website at: http://getinvolved.unlv.edu, or call 702-895-5631. Below are highlights of several of their programs:

Student Organizations. There are over 300 student organizations at UNLV, including academic, civic engagement, multicultural, international, spiritual/ faith-based, sport clubs, and special interests. Students can browse a list of student organizations on the UNLV website, or attend the Involvement Fair at the start of each semester. The SORCE (Student Organization Resource Center), located in the Student Union, Room 305, provides resources to Registered Student Organizations and supports students in exploring involvement opportunities.

Campus Programs. Campus programming and the Rebel Pride Council provide activities and entertainment for students at UNLV to help them enjoy their experience on campus. Programs include PREMIER UNLV, Homecoming, the Film Series, Rebels After Dark, and many other special events throughout the semester.

Service Programs. Service programs assist students in developing a sense of civic engagement in their community through the act of service. A student-led programming board, the Rebel Service Council, offers service opportunities such as Delivering and Serving Hope, Adopt-a-School, Make a Difference Day, Alternative Spring Break, and much more.

Multicultural Programs. Multicultural endeavors at UNLV provide opportunities for students to explore cultural identity in a safe and inclusive environment. The student-led programming board, Students Organizing Diversity Activities (SODA), plans monthly programs to celebrate diversity on the UNLV campus.

Leadership and Civic Engagement Minor. The Leadership and Civic Engagement Minor is an academic program available to undergraduate students who are interested in developing their skills as leaders in their field of study, or as student leaders within the University community. Students are welcome to enroll in the 200-level classes without pursuing the minor.

Student Counseling and Psychological Services
Located in the Student Recreation and Wellness Center, Student Counseling and Psychological Services (CAPS) provides students with individual, family, and group counseling through a variety of clinical services. As personal and social concerns can interfere with academic work and emotional well-being, CAPS services can help students increase self-understanding and develop the skills necessary to overcome their concerns and make the most of their college experience. The CAPS clinicians are highly trained and have experience with students of all ages and different backgrounds. For more information, visit http://unlv.edu/srwc/caps, or call 702-895-3627.

Student Government

Students have the opportunity to practice student advocacy and enhance their leadership skills by getting involved in UNLV's student government: Consolidated Students of the University of Nevada, Las Vegas (CSUN). For more information, visit http://unlvcsun.com/.

Student Recreation and Wellness Center

Over 184,000 square feet in size, the Student Recreation and Wellness Center (SRWC) is the only facility on campus dedicated specifically to recreation and total student wellness. The SRWC houses some of the latest recreation and fitness equipment, including a four-court gym, circuit training machines, free weights, a cardio theatre, an indoor jogging track, a lap pool, a spa and leisure pool, and much more. The SRWC offers a full schedule of recreation and fitness classes and programs. The SRWC also houses intramural sports programs and outdoor activities. In addition, the SRWC provides "The Rebel Wellness Zone," which includes resources, programs, and events geared toward helping students achieve their goals for a healthy, well-balanced life. For more information on the SRWC, visit http://srwc.unlv.edu/srwc, or call 702-774-7100.

Student Health Center

The Student Health Center allows registered and enrolled students to utilize health services without having to pay office visit co-pays. Students can receive treatment for minor illnesses and injuries, receive vaccines, and utilize the pharmacy. While routine appointments are free, there are fees for some services. The Center offers same-day appointments for convenience. The Student Health Center is located in the SRWC and can be contacted at 702-895-3370. For more information, visit http://srwc.unlv.edu/srwc/health-center.

◆ Touching the Third Base of College Success: Interpersonal Interaction and Collaboration

Learning is strengthened when it takes place in a social context that involves interpersonal interaction. As some scholars put it, human knowledge is socially constructed, or built through interaction and dialogue with others. According to these scholars, your interpersonal conversations become mentally internalized (represented in your mind) and are shaped by the dialogue you've had with others (Bruffee, 1993). Thus, by having frequent, intelligent conversations with others, you broaden your knowledge and deepen your thinking.

Four particular forms of interpersonal interaction have been found to be strongly associated with student learning and motivation in college:

1. Student–faculty interaction
2. Student–advisor interaction
3. Student–mentor interaction
4. Student–student (peer) interaction

Pause for Reflection

Look back at the major campus resources that have been mentioned in this section. Which two or three of them do you think you should use immediately?

Why have you identified these resources as your top priorities at this time?

Consider asking your course instructor or academic advisor for recommendations about what campus resources you should consult during your first term on campus.

Interaction with Faculty Members

Studies repeatedly show that college success is influenced heavily by the quality and quantity of student–faculty interaction *outside the classroom*. Such contact is positively associated with the following positive outcomes for college students:

- Improved academic performance;
- Increased critical thinking skills;
- Greater satisfaction with the college experience;
- Increased likelihood of completing a college degree; and
- Stronger desire to seek education beyond college (Astin, 1993; Pascarella & Terenzini, 1991, 2005).

These positive results are so strong and widespread that we encourage you to seek interaction with college faculty outside of class time. Here are some of the most manageable ways to increase your out-of-class contact with college instructors during the first year of college.

1. Approach your instructors immediately after class.

If you are interested in talking about something that was just discussed in class, your instructor will likely be most interested in discussing it with you as soon as the class session ends. Furthermore, interaction with your instructor immediately after class can help the professor get to know you as an individual, which should increase your confidence and willingness to seek subsequent contact.

2. Seek interaction with your course instructors during their office hours.

One of the most important pieces of information on a course syllabus is your instructor's office hours. Make note of these office hours, and make an earnest attempt to capitalize on them. College professors spend most of their professional time outside the classroom preparing for class, grading papers, conducting research, and serving on college committees. However, some of their out-of-class time is reserved specifically for office hours during which they are expected to be available.

You can schedule an office visit with your instructor during the early stages of the course. You can use this time to discuss course assignments, term-paper topics, and career options in your instructor's field. Try to make at least one visit to the office of each of your instructors, preferably early in the term, when quality time is easier to find, rather than at midterm, when major exams and assignments begin to pile up.

Even if your early contact with instructors is only for a few minutes, it can be a valuable icebreaker that helps your instructors get to know you as a person and helps you feel more comfortable interacting with them in the future.

3. Contact your instructors through e-mail.

Electronic communication is another effective way to interact with an instructor, particularly if that professor's office hours conflict with your class

Student Perspective

"I wish that I would have taken advantage of professors' open-door policies when I had questions, because actually understanding what I was doing, instead of guessing, would have saved me a lot of stress and re-doing what I did wrong the first time."

—College sophomore (Walsh, 2005)

schedule, work responsibilities, or family commitments. If you are a commuter student who does not live on campus, or if you are an adult student who is juggling family and work commitments and your academic schedule, e-mail communication may be an especially effective and efficient mode of interaction for you. If you're shy or hesitant about "invading" your professor's office space, e-mail can provide a less threatening way to interact and may give you the self-confidence to seek face-to-face contact with an instructor. In one national survey, almost half of college students reported that e-mail has allowed them to communicate their ideas with professors on subjects that they would not have discussed in person (Pew Internet & American Life Project, 2002).

Interaction with an Advisor

An academic advisor can be an effective referral agent who can direct you to, and connect you with, campus support services that best meet your needs. An advisor can also help you understand college procedures and navigate the bureaucratic maze of college policies and politics.

> ### Remember
> An academic advisor is not someone you see just once per term when you need to get a signature for class scheduling and course registration. An advisor is someone you should visit more regularly than your course instructors. Your instructors will change from term to term, but your academic advisor may be the one professional on campus with whom you have regular contact and a stable, ongoing relationship throughout your college experience.

Your academic advisor should be someone whom you feel comfortable speaking with, someone who knows your name, and someone who's familiar with your personal interests and abilities. Give your advisor the opportunity to get to know you personally, and seek your advisor's input on courses, majors, and personal issues that may be affecting your academic performance.

If you have been assigned an advisor and you find that you cannot develop a good relationship with this person, ask the director of advising or academic dean if you could be assigned to someone else. Ask other students about their advising experience and whether they know any advisors they can recommend to you.

Pause for Reflection

Do you have a personally assigned advisor?

If yes, do you know who this person is and where he or she can be found?

If no, do you know where to go if you have questions about your class schedule or academic plans?

If your college does not assign you a personal advisor but offers drop-by or drop-in advising, you may see a different advisor each time you visit the center. If you are not satisfied with this system of multiple advisors, find one advisor with whom you feel most comfortable and make that person your personal advisor by scheduling your appointments in advance. This will enable you to consistently connect with the same advisor and develop an ongoing relationship.

Interaction with a Mentor

A mentor may be described as an experienced guide who takes personal interest in you and the progress you're making toward your goals. (For example, in the movie *Star Wars*, Yoda served as a mentor for Luke Skywalker.) Research in higher education demonstrates that a mentor can make first-year students feel significant and enable them to stay on track until they complete their college degree (Campbell & Campbell, 1997; Knox, 2008). A mentor can assist you in troubleshooting difficult or complicated issues that you may not be able to resolve on your own and is someone with whom you can share good news, such as your success stories and personal accomplishments. Look for someone on campus with whom you can develop this type of trusting relationship. Many people on campus have the potential to be outstanding mentors, including the following:

- Your instructor in a first-year seminar or experience course
- Faculty in your intended major
- Juniors, seniors, or graduate students in your intended field of study
- Working professionals in careers that interest you
- Academic support professionals (e.g., professional tutors in the Learning Center)
- Career counselors
- Personal counselors
- Learning assistance professionals (e.g., from the Learning Center)
- Student development professionals (e.g., the director of student life or residential life)
- Campus minister or chaplain
- Financial aid counselors or advisor

Interaction with Peers (Student–Student Interaction)

Studies of college students repeatedly point to the power of the peer group as a source of social and academic support (Pascarella, 2005). One study of more than 25,000 college students revealed that when peers interact with one another while learning they achieve higher levels of academic performance and are more likely to persist to degree completion (Astin, 1993). In another study that involved in-depth interviews with more than 1,600 college students, it was discovered that almost all students who struggled academically had one particular study habit in common: They always studied alone (Light, 2001).

Peer interaction is especially important during the first term of college. At this stage of the college experience, new students have a strong need for belongingness and social acceptance because many of them have just left the lifelong security of family and hometown friends. As a new student, it may be useful to view your early stage of the college experience and academic performance in terms of the classic hierarchy model of human needs, developed by American psychologist Abraham Maslow (see **Figure 2.3**).

According to Maslow's model, humans cannot reach their full potential and achieve peak performance until their more basic emotional and social needs have been met (e.g., their

Pause for Reflection

Four categories of people have the potential to serve as mentors for you in college:

1. Experienced peers (to be discussed in the next section)

2. Faculty (instructors)

3. Administrators (e.g., office and program directors)

4. Staff (e.g., student support professionals and administrative assistants)

Think about your first interactions with faculty, staff, and administrators on campus. Do you recall anyone who impressed you as being approachable, personable, or helpful? If you did, make a note of that person's name in case you would like to seek out the person again. (If you haven't met such a person yet, when you do, be sure you remember that person because he or she may be an effective mentor for you.)

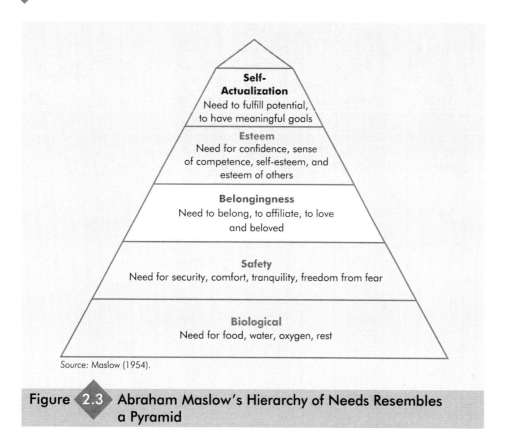

Self-
Actualization
Need to fulfill potential,
to have meaningful goals

Esteem
Need for confidence, sense
of competence, self-esteem, and
esteem of others

Belongingness
Need to belong, to affiliate, to love
and beloved

Safety
Need for security, comfort, tranquility, freedom from fear

Biological
Need for food, water, oxygen, rest

Source: Maslow (1954).

Figure 2.3   Abraham Maslow's Hierarchy of Needs Resembles a Pyramid

needs for personal safety, social acceptance, and self-esteem). Making early connections with your peers helps you meet these basic human needs, provides you
with a base of social support to ease your integration into the college community,
and prepares you to move up to higher levels of the need hierarchy (e.g., achieving
educational excellence and fulfilling your potential).

Studies repeatedly show that students who become socially integrated
or connected with other members of the college community are more likely
to complete their first year of college and continue on to complete their
college degree (Tinto, 1993). (For effective ways to make these interpersonal
connections, see **Box 2.3.**)

© Monkey Business Images, 2010. Under license from
Shutterstock, Inc.

Take Action!

Making Connections with Members of Your College Community

Consider 10 tips for making important interpersonal connections in college. Start making these connections now so that you can begin constructing a base of social support that will strengthen your performance during your first term and, perhaps, throughout your college experience.

1. Connect with a favorite peer or student development professional that you may have met during orientation.
2. Connect with peers who live near you or who commute to school from the same community in which you live. If your schedules are similar, consider carpooling together.
3. Join a college club, student organization, campus committee, intramural team, or volunteer-service group whose members may share the same personal or career interests as you.
4. Connect with a peer leader who has been trained to assist new students (e.g., peer tutor, peer mentor, or peer counselor) or with a peer who has more college experience than you (e.g., sophomore, junior, or senior).
5. Look for and connect with a motivated classmate in each of your classes, and try working as a team to take notes, complete reading assignments, and study for exams. (Look especially to team up with a peer who may be in more than one class with you.)
6. Connect with faculty members in a field that you're considering as a major by visiting them during office hours, conversing briefly with them after class, or communicating with them via e-mail.
7. Connect with an academic support professional in your college's Learning Center for personalized academic assistance or tutoring related to any course in which you'd like to improve your performance.
8. Connect with an academic advisor to discuss and develop your educational plans.
9. Connect with a college librarian to get early assistance and a head start on any research project that you've been assigned.
10. Connect with a personal counselor or campus minister to discuss any college-adjustment or personal-life issues that you may be experiencing.

2.3

Getting involved with campus organizations or activities is one way to connect you with other students. Also, try to interact with students who have spent more time at college than you. Sophomores, juniors, and seniors can be valuable social resources for a new student. You're likely to find that they are willing to share their experiences with you because you have shown an interest in hearing what they have to say. You may even be the first person who has bothered to ask them what their experiences have been like on your campus. You can learn from their experiences by asking them which courses and instructors they would recommend or what advisors they found to be most well informed and personable.

! **Remember**

Your peers can be more than competitors or a source of negative peer pressure; they can also be collaborators, a source of positive social influence, and a resource for college success. Be on the lookout for classmates who are motivated to learn and willing to learn with you, and keep an eye out for advanced students who are willing to assist you. Start building your social-support network by surrounding yourself with success-seeking and success-achieving students. They can be a stimulating source of positive peer power that drives you to higher levels of academic performance and heightens your motivational drive to complete college.

Collaboration with Peers

Simply defined, collaboration is the process of two or more people working interdependently toward a common goal (as opposed to working independently or competitively). Collaboration involves true teamwork, in which teammates support one another's success and take equal responsibility for helping the team move toward its shared goal. Research on students from kindergarten through college shows that when students collaborate in teams their academic performance and interpersonal skills improve dramatically (Cuseo, 1996).

To maximize the power of collaboration, use the following guidelines to make wise choices about teammates who will contribute positively to the quality and productivity of your learning team:

1. Observe your classmates with an eye toward identifying potentially good teammates. Look for fellow students who are motivated and who will likely contribute to your team's success, rather than those whom you suspect may just be hitchhikers looking for a free ride.

2. Don't team up exclusively with peers who are similar to you in terms of their personal characteristics, backgrounds, and experiences. Instead, include teammates who differ from you in age; gender; ethnic, racial, cultural or geographical background; learning style; and personality characteristics. Such variety brings different life experiences, styles of thinking, and learning strategies to your team, which enrich not only its diversity but its quality as well. If your team consists only of friends or classmates whose interests and lifestyles are similar to your own, this familiarity can interfere with your team's focus and performance because your common experiences can get you off track and on to topics that have nothing to do with the learning task (e.g., what you did last weekend or what you are planning to do next weekend).

"TEAM = Together Everyone Achieves More"

–Author unknown

"Surround yourself with only people who are going to lift you higher."

–Oprah Winfrey, actress and talk-show host

! **Remember**

Seek diversity; capitalize on the advantages of collaborating with peers with varied backgrounds and lifestyles. Simply stated, studies show that we learn more from people who are different from us than we do from people who are similar to us (Pascarella, 2001).

Keep in mind that learning teams are not simply study groups formed the night before an exam. Effective learning teams collaborate more regularly and work on more varied academic tasks than late-night study groups. For example, you can form note-taking teams, reading teams, or test results-reviews teams.

◆ Touching the Fourth (Home) Base of College Success: Personal Reflection and Self-Awareness

The final steps in the learning process, whether it be learning in the classroom or learning from experience, are to step back from the process, thoughtfully review it, and connect it to what you already know. Reflection may be defined as the flip side of active involvement; both processes are necessary for learning to be complete. Learning requires not only effortful action but also thoughtful reflection. Active involvement gets and holds your focus of attention, which enables information to reach your brain, and personal reflection promotes consolidation, which locks that information into your brain's long-term memory (Bligh, 2000; Broadbent, 1970). Brain research reveals that two brain-wave patterns are associated with the mental states of involvement and reflection (Bradshaw, 1995). The brain-wave pattern on the left in **Figure 2.4** reveal faster activity, indicating that the person is actively involved in the learning task and attending to it. The slower brain-wave pattern on the right in the figure indicates that the person is thinking deeply about information taken in, which will help consolidate or lock that information into long-term memory. Thus, effective learning combines active mental involvement (characterized by faster, shorter brain waves) with thoughtful reflection (characterized by slower, longer brain waves).

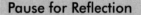

Pause for Reflection

Think about the students in your classes this term. Are there any students who you might want to join with to form learning teams?

Do you have any classmates who are in more than one class with you and who might be good peer partners for the courses you have in common?

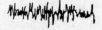

Faster Brain-Wave Pattern Associated with a Mental State of *Active Involvement*

Slower Brain-Wave Pattern Associated with a Mental State of *Reflective Thinking*

Figure ◄ 2.4 ►

Personal reflection involves introspection—turning inward and inspecting yourself to gain deeper self-awareness of what you've done, what you're doing, or what you intend to do. Two forms of self-awareness are particularly important for success in college:

1. Self-assessment
2. Self-monitoring

"We learn to do neither by thinking nor by doing; we learn to do by thinking about what we are doing."

–George Stoddard, former professor of psychology and education at the University of Iowa

Self-Assessment

Simply defined, self-assessment is the process of reflecting on and evaluating your personal characteristics, such as your personality traits, learning habits, and strengths or weaknesses. Self-assessment promotes self-awareness, which is the critical first step in the process of self-improvement, personal planning, and effective decision making. The following are important target areas for self-assessment and self-awareness because they reflect personal characteristics that play a pivotal role in promoting success in college and beyond:

- **Personal interests.** What you like to do or enjoy doing;
- **Personal values.** What is important to you and what you care about doing;
- **Personal abilities or aptitudes.** What you do well or have the potential to do well;
- **Learning habits.** How you go about learning and the usual approaches, methods, or techniques you use to learn;
- **Learning styles.** How you prefer to learn; that is, the way you like to:
  - Receive information—which learning format you prefer (e.g., reading, listening, or experiencing);
  - Perceive information—which sensory modality you prefer (e.g., vision, sound, or touch);
  - Process information—how you mentally deal with information once you have taken it in (e.g., think about it on your own or discuss it with others).
- **Personality traits.** Your temperament, emotional characteristics, and social tendencies (e.g., whether you lean toward being outgoing or reserved);
- **Academic self-concept.** What kind of student you think you are and how you perceive yourself as a learner (e.g., your level of self-confidence and whether you believe success is within your control or depends on factors beyond your control).

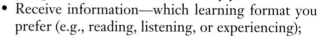
Pause for Reflection

How would you rate your academic self-confidence at this point in your college experience? (Circle one.)

very confident   somewhat confident
somewhat unconfident   very unconfident

Why did you make this choice?

Self-Monitoring

Research indicates that one characteristic of successful learners is that they monitor or watch themselves and maintain self-awareness of:

- Whether they are using effective learning strategies (e.g., they are aware of their level of attention or concentration in class);
- Whether they are comprehending what they are attempting to learn (e.g., they're understanding it at a deep level or merely memorizing it at a surface level); and
- How to regulate or adjust their learning strategies to meet the demands of different tasks or subjects (e.g., they read technical material in a science textbook more slowly and stop to test their understanding more often than when they're reading a novel; Pintrich, 1995; Weinstein, 1994; Weinstein & Meyer, 1991).

! Remember

Successful students are self-aware learners who know their learning strategies, styles, strengths, and shortcomings.

You can begin to establish good self-monitoring habits by getting in the routine of periodically pausing to reflect on how you're going about learning and how you're "doing" college. For instance, consider these questions:

- Am I listening attentively to what my instructor is saying in class?
- Do I comprehend what I am reading outside of class?
- Am I effectively using campus resources that are designed to support my success?
- Am I interacting with campus professionals who can contribute to my current success and future development?
- Am I interacting and collaborating with peers who can contribute to my learning and increase my level of involvement in the college experience?
- Am I effectively implementing the success strategies identified in this book?

> "Successful students know a lot about themselves."
>
> –Claire Weinstein and Debra Meyer, professors of educational psychology at the University of Texas

◆ Summary and Conclusion

Research reviewed in this chapter points to the conclusion that successful students are:

1. **Involved.** They invest time and effort in the college experience;
2. **Resourceful.** They capitalize on their surrounding resources;
3. **Interactive.** They interact and collaborate with others; and
4. **Reflective.** They are self-aware learners who assess and monitor their own performance.

Successful students are students who could honestly check almost every box in the following self-assessment checklist of success-promoting principles and practices.

A Checklist of Success-Promoting Principles and Practices

1. **Active Involvement**

   Inside the classroom:
   - ☑ **Get to class.** Treat it like a job; if you cut, your pay (grade) will be cut.
   - ☑ **Get involved in class.** Come prepared, listen actively, take notes, and participate.

   Outside the classroom:
   - ☑ **Read actively.** Take notes while you read to increase attention and retention.
   - ☑ **Double up.** Spend twice as much time on academic work outside the classroom than you spend in class—if you're a full-time student, that makes it a 40-hour academic workweek (with occasional "overtime").

© Rudyanto Wijaya, 2010. Under license from Shutterstock, Inc.

Pause for Reflection

How would you rate your academic self-confidence at this point in your college experience? (Circle one.)

very confident   somewhat confident
somewhat unconfident   very unconfident

Why?

Pause for Reflection

Before exiting this chapter, look back at the Checklist of Success-Promoting Principles and Practices and see how these ideas compare with those you recorded at the start of this chapter, when we asked you how you thought college would be different from high school and what it would take to be successful in college.

What ideas from your list and our checklist tend to match?

Were there any ideas on your list that were not on ours, or vice versa?

2. Use of Campus Resources

Capitalize on academic and student support services:

- ☑ Learning Center
- ☑ Writing Center
- ☑ Disability Services
- ☑ College library
- ☑ Academic Advisement Center
- ☑ Office of Student Life
- ☑ Financial Aid Office
- ☑ Counseling Center
- ☑ Health Center
- ☑ Career Development Center
- ☑ Experiential Learning Resources

3. Interpersonal Interaction and Collaboration

Interact with the following people:

- ☑ **Peers.** Join student clubs and participate in campus organizations.
- ☑ **Faculty members.** Connect with professors and other faculty members immediately after class, in their offices, or via e-mail.
- ☑ **Academic advisors.** See an advisor for more than just a signature to register; find an advisor you can relate to and with whom you can develop an ongoing relationship.
- ☑ **Mentors.** Try to find experienced people on campus who can serve as trusted guides and role models.

Collaborate by doing the following:

- ☑ **Form learning teams.** Join not only last-minute study groups but also teams that collaborate more regularly to work on such tasks as taking lecture notes, completing reading and writing assignments, conducting library research, and reviewing results of exams or course assignments.
- ☑ **Participate in learning communities.** Enroll in two or more classes with the same students during the same term.

4. Personal Reflection and Self-Awareness

- ☑ **Self-Assessment.** Reflect on and evaluate your personal traits, habits, strengths and weaknesses.
- ☑ **Self-Monitoring.** Maintain self-awareness of how you're learning, what you're learning, and whether you're learning.

Learning More Through the World Wide Web

Internet-Based Resources for Further Information on Liberal Arts Education

For additional information related to the ideas discussed in this chapter, we recommend the following Web sites:

Learning Strategies: **www.dartmouth.edu/~acskills/success/index.html**

Academic Success Strategies: **www.uni.edu/walsh/linda7.html**

www.lifehack.org/articles/lifehack/from-a-freshman-five-tips-for-success-in-college.html

2.1 Constructing a Master List of Campus Resources

1. Use each of the following sources to gain more in-depth knowledge about the support services available on your campus:

- Information published in your college catalog and student handbook

- Information posted on your college's Web site

- Information gathered by speaking with a professional in different offices or centers on your campus

2. Using the preceding sources of information, construct a master list of all support services that are available to you on your campus. Your final product should be a list that includes the following:

- The names of different support services your campus offers

- The types of support each service provides

- A short statement indicating whether you think you would benefit from each particular type of support

- The name of a person whom you could contact for support from each service

Notes

- You can pair up with a classmate to work collaboratively on this assignment. Working together with a peer on any research task can reduce your anxiety, increase your energy, and generate synergy—which results in a final product that is superior to what could have been produced by one person working alone (independently).
- After you complete this assignment, save your master list of support services for future use. You might not have an immediate need for some of these services during your first term in college, but all of them are likely to be useful to you at some point in your college experience.

2.2 Support Services

Learning Center
Types of Support

_____

Will I benefit?   Contact Person:

_____

Will I benefit?   Contact Person:

_____

Will I benefit?   Contact Person:

Writing Center
Types of Support

_____

Will I benefit?   Contact Person:

_____

Will I benefit?   Contact Person:

_____

Will I benefit?   Contact Person:

Disability Services
Types of Support

_____

Will I benefit?   Contact Person:

_____

Will I benefit?   Contact Person:

_____

Will I benefit?   Contact Person:

College Library
Types of Support

_____

Will I benefit?   Contact Person:

_____

Will I benefit?   Contact Person:

_____

Will I benefit?   Contact Person:

Academic Advisement Center
Types of Support

_____

Will I benefit?   Contact Person:

_____

Will I benefit?   Contact Person:

_____

Will I benefit?   Contact Person:

Office Of Student Life
Types of Support

_____

Will I benefit?   Contact Person:

_____

Will I benefit?   Contact Person:

_____

Will I benefit?   Contact Person:

Financial Aid Office
Types of Support

_____

Will I benefit?   Contact Person:

_____

Will I benefit?   Contact Person:

_____

Will I benefit?   Contact Person:

Counseling Center
Types of Support

_____

Will I benefit?   Contact Person:

_____

Will I benefit?   Contact Person:

_____

Will I benefit?   Contact Person:

Health Center
Types of Support

_____

Will I benefit?   Contact Person:

_____

Will I benefit?   Contact Person:

_____

Will I benefit?   Contact Person:

Career Development Center
Types of Support

_____

Will I benefit?   Contact Person:

_____

Will I benefit?   Contact Person:

_____

Will I benefit?   Contact Person:

Experiential Learning Resources
Types of Support

_____

Will I benefit?   Contact Person:

_____

Will I benefit?   Contact Person:

_____

Will I benefit?   Contact Person:

Other
Types of Support

_____

Will I benefit?   Contact Person:

_____

Will I benefit?   Contact Person:

_____

Will I benefit?   Contact Person:

Alone and Disconnected: Feeling Like Calling It Quits

Josephine is a first-year student in her second week of college. She doesn't feel like she's fitting in with other students on her campus. She also feels guilty about the time she's taking time away from her family and her old high school friends who are not attending college, and she fears that her ties with them will be weakened or broken if she continues spending so much time at school and on schoolwork. Josephine is feeling so torn between college and her family and old friends that she's beginning to have second thoughts about whether she should have gone to college.

Reflection and Discussion Questions

1. What would you say to Josephine that might persuade her to stay in college?

2. Could the college have done more during her first 2 weeks on campus to make Josephine (and other students) feel more connected with college and less disconnected from family?

3. Do you see anything that Josephine could do now to minimize the conflict she's experiencing between her commitment to college and her commitment to family and old friends?

Liberal Arts

The Meaning, Purpose, and Value of General Education

ACTIVATE YOUR THINKING   **Journal Entry**   **3.1**

Before you launch into this chapter, do your best to answer the following question:

Which one of the following statements represents the most accurate meaning of the term *liberal arts*?

1. Learning to be less politically conservative
2. Learning to be more artistic
3. Learning ideas rather than practical skills
4. Learning to spend money more freely
5. Learning skills for freedom

◆LEARNING GOAL

To appreciate the meaning, purpose, and benefits of the liberal arts and to develop a strategic plan for making the most out of general education.

Personal Story

I was once advising a first-year student (Laura) who intended to major in business. While helping her plan the courses she needed to complete her degree, I pointed out to Laura that she still needed to take a course in philosophy. Here's how our conversation went after I made this point.

Laura (in a somewhat irritated tone): Why do I have to take philosophy? I'm a business major.

Dr. Cuseo: Because philosophy is an important component of a liberal arts education.

Laura (in a very agitated tone): I'm not liberal and I don't want to be a liberal. I'm conservative and so are my parents; we all voted for Ronald Reagan in the last election!

—Joe Cuseo

◆ The Meaning and Purpose of a Liberal Arts Education

If you're uncertain about what the term "liberal arts" means, you're not alone. Most first-year students don't have the foggiest idea what a liberal arts education represents (Hersh, 1997). If they were to guess, they may mistakenly say that it's something impractical or related to liberal politics.

From *"Thriving in College and Beyond"* by Cuseo, Fecas, Thompson. © Kendall Hunt Publishing.

Laura probably would have picked option 1 as her answer to the multiple-choice question posed at the start of this chapter. That would not have been the right choice; option 5 is the correct answer. Literally translated, the term "liberal arts" derives from the Latin words liberales—meaning to "liberate" or "free," and artes—meaning "skills." Thus, "skills for freedom" is the most accurate meaning of the term "liberal arts."

The roots of the term "liberal arts" date back to the origin of modern civilization—to the ancient Greeks and Romans, who argued that political power in a democracy rests with the people because they choose (elect) their own leaders. In a democracy, people are liberated from uncritical dependence on a dictator or autocrat. To preserve their political freedom, citizens in a democracy must be well educated and critical thinkers so that they can make wise choices about whom they elect as their leaders and lawmakers (Bishop, 1986; Cheney, 1989).

The political ideals of the ancient Greeks and Romans were shared by the founding fathers of the United States who also emphasized the importance of an educated citizenry for preserving America's new democracy. As Thomas Jefferson, third president of the United States, wrote in 1801 (Ford, 1903, p. 278):

I know of no safe depository of the ultimate powers of a society but the people themselves; and if we think them not enlightened enough to exercise control with a wholesome discretion [responsible decision-making], the remedy is not to take power from them, but to inform their discretion by education.

Thus, the liberal arts are rooted in the belief that education is the essential ingredient for preservation of democratic freedom. When people are educated in the liberal arts, they gain the breadth of knowledge and depth of thinking to vote wisely, preserve democracy, and avoid autocracy (dictatorship).

The importance of a knowledgeable, critical-thinking citizenry for making wise political choices is still relevant today. Contemporary political campaigns are using more manipulative media advertisements. These ads rely on short sound bites, one-sided arguments, and powerful visual images that are intentionally designed to appeal to emotions and discourage critical thinking (Goleman, 1992).

Over time, the term "liberal arts" has acquired the more general meaning of liberating or freeing people to be self-directed individuals who make personal choices and decisions that are determined by their own, well-reasoned ideas and values, rather than blind conformity to the ideas and values of others (Gamson, 1984). Self-directed critical thinkers are empowered to resist manipulation by politicians and other societal influences, including:

- Authority figures (e.g., they question excessive use or abuse of authority by parents, teachers, or law enforcers);
- Peers (e.g., they resist peer pressure that's unreasonable or unethical); and
- Media (e.g., they detect and reject forms of advertisements designed to manipulate their self-image and material needs).

A liberal arts education encourages you to be your own person and to ask "Why?" It's the component of your college education that supplies you with the mental tools needed to be an independent thinker with an inquiring mind that questions authority and resists conformity.

"Knowledge will forever govern ignorance; and a people who mean to be their own governors must arm themselves with the power which knowledge gives."

—James Madison, fourth president of the United States and cosigner of the American Constitution and first author of the Bill of Rights

"It is such good fortune for people in power that people do not think."

—Adolf Hitler, German dictator

"In a nation whose citizens are to be led by persuasion and not by force, the art of reasoning becomes of the first importance."

—Thomas Jefferson

Student Perspective

"I want knowledge so I don't get taken advantage of in life."

—First-year college student

The Liberal Arts Curriculum

The first liberal arts curriculum (collection of courses) was designed with the belief that individuals who experienced these courses would be equipped with (a) a broad base of knowledge that would ensure they would be well informed in various subjects and (b) a range of mental skills that would enable them to think deeply and critically. Based on this educational philosophy of the ancient Greeks and Romans, the first liberal arts curriculum was developed during the Middle Ages and consisted of the following subjects: logic, language, rhetoric (the art of argumentation and persuasion), music, mathematics, and astronomy (Ratcliff, 1997; Association of American Colleges & Universities, 2002).

The purpose of the original liberal arts curriculum has withstood the test of time. Today's colleges and universities continue to offer a liberal arts curriculum designed to provide students with a broad base of knowledge in multiple subject areas and equip them with critical skills. The liberal arts curriculum today is often referred to as general education—representing skills and knowledge that are general rather than narrowly specialized. General education is what all college students learn, no matter what their major or specialized field of study may be (Association of American Colleges & Universities, 2002).

On some campuses, the liberal arts are also referred to as the core curriculum, with "core" standing for what is central or essential for all students to know and do because of their importance for effective performance in any field, or as breadth requirements, referring the their broad scope that spans a range of subject areas.

! Remember

Whatever term is used to describe the liberal arts, the bottom line is that they are the foundation of a college education upon which all academic specializations (majors) are built; they are what all college graduates should be able to know and do for whatever occupational path they choose to pursue; they are what distinguishes college education from vocational preparation; and they define what it means to be a well-educated person.

Major Divisions of Knowledge and Subject Areas in the Liberal Arts Curriculum

The divisions of knowledge in today's liberal arts curriculum have expanded to include more subject areas than those included in the original curriculum that was based on the work of the ancient Greeks and Romans. The liberal arts' divisions, and the courses that make up each division, vary somewhat from campus to campus. Campuses also vary in terms of the nature of courses required within each division of knowledge and the range of courses from which students can choose to fulfill their general educational requirements.

Pause for Reflection

For someone to be successful in any major and career, what do you think that person should:

1. Know; and

2. Be able to do?

On average, about one-third of a college graduate's course credits were required general education courses selected from the liberal arts curriculum (Conley, 2005).

Despite campus-to-campus variation in the number and nature of courses required, the liberal arts curriculum on every college campus represents the areas of knowledge and the types of skills that all students should possess, no matter what their particular major may be. It allows you to stand on the shoulders of intellectual giants from a range of fields and capitalize on their collective wisdom.

On most campuses today, the liberal arts curriculum typically consists of general divisions of knowledge and related subject areas similar to those listed in the sections that follow. As you read through these divisions of knowledge, highlight any subjects in which you've never had a course.

Humanities

Courses in the humanities division of the liberal arts curriculum focus on the human experience and human culture, asking the important questions that arise in the life of humans, such as "Why are we here?" "What is the meaning or purpose of our existence?" "How should we live?" "What is the good life?" and "Is there life after death?"

The following are the primary subject areas in the humanities division:

- **English Composition.** Writing clearly, critically, and persuasively;
- **Speech.** Speaking eloquently and persuasively;
- **Literature.** Reading critically and appreciating the artistic merit of various literary genres (forms of writing), such as novels, short stories, poems, plays, and essays;
- **Languages.** Listening, speaking, reading and writing languages other than the student's native tongue;
- **Philosophy.** Thinking rationally, developing wisdom (the ability to use knowledge prudently), and living an ethically principled life;
- **Theology.** Understanding how humans conceive of and express their faith in a transcendent (supreme) being.

"Never mistake knowledge for wisdom.

One helps you make a living; the other helps you make a life."

—Sandra Carey, lobbyist to the California State Assembly

"Dancing is silent poetry."

—Simonides, ancient Greek poet

Fine Arts

Courses in the fine arts division focus largely on the art of human expression, asking such questions as "How do humans express, create, and appreciate what is beautiful?" and "How do we express ourselves aesthetically (through the senses) with imagination, creativity, style, and elegance?"

The primary subject areas of the fine arts division are as follows:

- **Visual Arts.** Creating and appreciating human expression through visual representation (drawing, painting, sculpture, photography, and graphic design);
- **Musical Arts.** Appreciating and creating rhythmical arrangements of sounds;
- **Performing Arts.** Appreciating and expressing creativity through drama and dance.

Mathematics

Courses in the mathematics division are designed to promote skills in numerical calculation, quantitative reasoning and problem solving.

Mathematics has the following primary subject areas:

- **Algebra.** Mathematical reasoning involving symbolic representation of numbers in a language of letters that vary in size or quantity;
- **Statistics.** Mathematical methods for summarizing; estimating probabilities; representing and understanding numerical information depicted in graphs, charts, and tables; and drawing accurate conclusions from quantitative data;
- **Calculus.** Higher mathematical methods for calculating the rate at which the quantity of one entity changes in relation to another and for calculating the areas enclosed by curves.

© El Greco, 2010. Under license from Shutterstock, Inc.

Natural Sciences

Courses in the natural sciences division of the liberal arts curriculum are devoted to systematic observation of the physical world and the explanation of natural phenomena, asking such questions as "What causes physical events that take place in the natural world?" "How can we predict and control these events?" and "How do we promote symbiotic interaction between humans and the natural environment that sustains the survival of both?"

The following are the primary subject areas of the natural sciences division:

- **Biology.** Understanding the structure and underlying processes of all living things;
- **Chemistry.** Understanding the composition of natural and synthetic (manmade) substances and how these substances may be changed or developed;
- **Physics.** Understanding the properties of physical matter, the principles of energy and motion, and electrical and magnetic forces;
- **Geology.** Understanding the composition of the earth and the natural processes that have shaped its development;
- **Astronomy.** Understanding the makeup and motion of celestial bodies that comprise the universe.

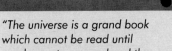

"The universe is a grand book which cannot be read until one learns to comprehend the language and become familiar with the characters of which it is composed. It is written in the language of mathematics."

–Galileo Galilei, seventeenth-century Italian physicist, mathematician, astronomer, and philosopher

Social and Behavioral Sciences

Courses in the division of social and behavioral sciences focus on the observation of human behavior, individually and in groups, and ask such questions as "What causes humans to behave the way they do?" and "How can we predict, control, or improve human behavior and human interaction?"

This division has the following primary subject areas:

- **Psychology.** Understanding the human mind, its conscious and subconscious processes, and the underlying causes of human behavior;
- **Sociology.** Understanding the structure, interaction, and collective behavior of organized social groups and institutions or systems that comprise human society (e.g., families, schools, and social services);
- **Anthropology.** Understanding the cultural and physical origin, development, and distribution the human species;

© Laurence Gough, 2010. Under license from Shutterstock, Inc.

The natural sciences division of the liberal arts curriculum focuses on the observation of the physical world and the explanation of natural phenomena.

"Science is an imaginative adventure of the mind seeking truth in a world of mystery."

–Cyril Herman Hinshelwood, Nobel Prize–winning English chemist

"Man, the molecule of society, is the subject of social science."

–Henry Charles Carey, nineteenth-century American economist

"To eat is a necessity, but to eat intelligently is an art."

–La Rochefoucauld, seventeenth-century French author

- **History.** Understanding past events, their causes, and their influence on current events;
- **Political Science.** Understanding how societal authority is organized and how this authority is exerted to govern people, make collective decisions, and maintain social order;
- **Economics.** Understanding how the monetary needs of humans are met through allocation of limited resources and how material wealth is produced and distributed;
- **Geography.** Understanding how the place (physical location) where humans live influences their cultural and societal development and how humans have shaped and been shaped by their surrounding physical environment.

Physical Education and Wellness

Courses in the physical education and wellness division of the liberal arts curriculum focus on the human body, how to best maintain health, and how to attain peak performance levels of performance. They ask such questions as "How does the body function most effectively?" and "What can we do to prevent illness, promote wellness, and improve the physical quality of our lives?"

These primary subject areas fall under this division:

- **Physical Education.** Understanding the role of human exercise for promoting health and peak performance;
- **Nutrition.** Understanding how the body uses food as nourishment to promote health and generate energy;
- **Sexuality.** Understanding the biological, psychological, and social aspects of sexual relations;
- **Drug Education.** Understanding how substances that alter the body and mind affect physical health, mental health, and human performance.

Most of your liberal arts requirements will be taken during your first 2 years of college. Don't be disappointed if some of these requirements seem similar to courses you recently had in high school, and don't think you'll be bored because these are subjects you've already studied. College courses will not be videotape replays of high school courses because you will examine these subjects in greater depth and breadth and at a higher level of thinking (Conley, 2005). Research shows that most of the higher-level thinking gains that students make in college take place during their first 2 years—the years during which they're taking most of their liberal arts courses (Pascarella & Terenzini, 2005).

◆ Transferable Learning Skills That Last a Lifetime

A liberal arts education promotes success in your major, career, and life by equipping you with a set of lifelong learning skills with two powerful qualities:

- **Transferability.** These skills can be transferred and applied to a range of subjects, careers, and life situations.
- **Durability.** These skills are long lasting and can be continually used throughout your lifetime.

To use an athletic analogy, what the liberal arts do for the mind is similar to what cross-training does for the body. Cross-training engages the body in a range of exercises to promote total physical fitness and develop a range of physical skills (e.g., strength, endurance, flexibility, and agility), which can be applied to improve performance in any sport or athletic endeavor. Similarly, the liberal arts engage the mind in a range of subject areas (e.g., arts, sciences, and humanities), which develop a range of mental skills that can be applied to improve performance in any academic field or professional career.

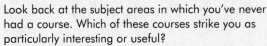

Pause for Reflection

Look back at the subject areas in which you've never had a course. Which of these courses strike you as particularly interesting or useful?

Why?

! Remember

The liberal arts not only provide you with academic skills needed to succeed in your chosen major but also equip you with skills to succeed in whatever career or careers you decide to pursue. Don't underestimate the importance of these transferable and durable skills. Work hard at developing them, and take seriously the general education courses that promote their development.

> "You know you've got to exercise your brain just like your muscles."
>
> –Will Rogers, Native American humorist and actor

A major difference exists between learning factual knowledge and learning transferable skills. A transferable skill can be applied to different situations or contexts. The mental skills developed by the liberal arts are transportable across academic subjects you'll encounter in college and work positions you'll assume after college. It could be said that these lifelong learning skills are a mental gift that keeps on giving.

The transferable skills developed by the liberal arts are summarized in **Box 3.1**.

As you read them, rate yourself on each of the skills using the following scale:

4 = very strong, 3 = strong, 2 = needs some improvement, 1 = needs much improvement

> "If you give a man a fish, you feed him for a day.
>
> If you teach a man how to fish, you feed him for life."
>
> –Author unknown

Students often see general education as something to get out of the way and get behind them so they can get into their major and career (Association of American Colleges & Universities, 2007). Don't take the view that general education as a series of obstacles along the way to a degree; instead, view it as a learning process from which you can take a set of powerful skills that are:

1. **Portable.** Travel well across work situations and life roles; and
2. **Stable.** Remain relevant and useful across changing times.

! Remember

When you acquire lifelong *learning* skills, you're also acquiring lifelong *earning* skills.

Pause for Reflection

Reflect on the four skill areas developed by a liberal arts education (communication, information literacy, computation, and higher-level thinking). Which one do you think is most important or most relevant to your future success?

Write a one-paragraph explanation about why you chose this skill.

The skills developed by a liberal arts education are strikingly similar to the types of skills that employers seek in new employees. In numerous national surveys and in-depth interviews, employers and executives in both industry and government consistently report that they seek employees with skills that fall into the following three categories:

Take Action!

Transferable Lifelong Learning Skills Developed by the Liberal Arts

1. Communication Skills. Accurate comprehension and articulate expression of ideas. Five particular types of communication skills are essential for success in any specialized field of study or work:

- **Written communication skills.** Writing in a clear, creative, and persuasive manner;
- **Oral communication skills.** Speaking concisely, confidently, and eloquently;
- **Reading skills.** Comprehending, interpreting, and evaluating the literal meaning and connotations of words written in various styles and subject areas;
- **Listening skills.** Comprehending spoken language accurately and sensitively;
- **Electronic communication skills.** Using computer and technology-mediated communication skills effectively.

2. Information literacy skills. Effectively and efficiently accessing, retrieving, and evaluating information from various sources, including in-print and online (technology-based) systems.

"Ability to recognize when information is needed and have the ability to locate, evaluate, and use it effectively."

–Definition of "information literacy," American Library Association Presidential Committee on Information Literacy

3. Computation skills. Accurate calculation, analysis, summary, interpretation, and evaluation of quantitative information or statistical data.

4. Higher-level thinking skills. Learning deeply and thinking at a more advanced level than simply acquisition and memorization of factual information.

3.1

Student Perspective

"They asked me during my interview why I was right for the job and I told them because I can read well, write well and I can think. They really liked that because those were the skills they were looking for."

–English major hired by a public relations firm (*Los Angeles Times*, 2004)

1. **Communication skills** (e.g., listening, speaking, writing, and reading; Business–Higher Education Forum, 1999; National Association of Colleges & Employers, 2003; Peter D. Hart Research Associates, 2006):

    "There is such a heavy emphasis on effective communication in the workplace that college students who master these skills can set themselves apart from the pack when searching for employment." Marilyn Mackes, executive director of the National Association of Colleges and Employers (Mackes, 2003, p. 1).

2. **Thinking skills** (e.g., problem solving and critical thinking; Business–Higher Education Forum, 1999; Peter D. Hart Research Associates, 2006; Van Horn, 1995):

    "We look for people who can think critically and analytically. If you can do those things, we can teach you our business." Paul Dominski, store recruiter for the Robinson-May Department Stores Company (Indiana University, 2004, p. 1).

3. **Lifelong learning skills** (e.g., learning how to learn and how to continue learning; Conference Board of Canada, 2000):

    "Employers are virtually unanimous that the most important knowledge and skills the new employee can bring to the job are problem solving, communication, and 'learning to learn' skills. The workers of the future need to know how to think and how to continue to learn." David Kearns, former chief executive officer (CEO) for the Xerox Corporation (Kearns, 1989, p. 8).

The remarkable resemblance between the work skills sought by employers and the academic skills developed by a liberal arts education isn't surprising when you think about the typical duties or responsibilities of working professionals. They need good communication skills because they must listen, speak, describe, and explain ideas to co-workers and customers. They read and critically interpret written and statistical reports, and they write letters, memos, and reports. They need highly developed thinking skills to analyze problems, construct well-organized plans, generate innovative ideas and solutions to problems (creative thinking), and evaluate whether their plans and strategies will be effective (critical thinking).

"At State Farm, our [employment] exam does not test applicants on their knowledge of finance or the insurance business, but it does require them to demonstrate critical thinking skills and the ability to calculate and think logically. These skills plus the ability to read for information, to communicate and write effectively need to be demonstrated."

–Edward B. Rust Jr., chairman and chief executive officer of State Farm Insurance Companies (Association of American Colleges & Universities, 2007)

A Liberal Arts Education Is Preparation for Your Major

Don't assume that liberal arts courses you're taking as general education requirements have nothing to do with your specialized field of interest. Liberal arts courses provide a relevant foundation for success in your major. Recall our story at the start of the chapter about Laura, the first-year student with a business major who questioned why she had to take a course in philosophy. Laura needed to take philosophy because she will encounter topics in her business major that relate either directly or indirectly to philosophy. In her business courses, she will likely encounter philosophical issues relating to (a) the logical assumptions and underlying values of capitalism, (b) business ethics (e.g., hiring and firing practices), and (c) business justice (e.g., how profits should be fairly or justly distributed to workers and shareholders). Philosophy will equip her with the fundamental logical thinking and ethical reasoning skills to understand these issues deeply and respond to them humanely.

Pause for Reflection

During your college experience, you might hear students say that they need to get their general education (liberal arts) courses out of the way so that they can get into courses that relate to their major and career. Would you agree or disagree with this argument?

Why?

As with the field of business, liberal arts subjects are relevant to successful performance in any major and career. For example, historical and ethical perspectives are needed for all fields because all of them have a history and none of them are value free.

Learning from the collective wisdom of diverse disciplines provides you with a broad base of knowledge that enables you to view issues and solve problems from multiple angles or vantage points. Although you may specialize in a particular field of study in college (your major), real-life issues and challenges are not divided neatly into specialized majors. Important and enduring issues, such as effective leadership, improving race relations, and preventing international warfare, can neither be fully understood nor effectively solved by using the thinking tools of a single academic discipline. Approaching multidimensional issues such as these from the perspective of a single, specialized field of study is likely to result in single-minded and over-simplified attempt to solve a complex problem.

"The unexamined life is not worth living."

–Socrates, classic Greek philosopher and one of the founding fathers of Western philosophy

The Liberal Arts Promote Self-awareness and Development of the Whole Person

One of the most emphasized intended outcomes of a liberal arts education is to "know thyself" (Cross, 1982). The ability to turn inward and become aware

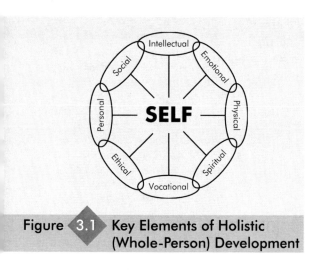

Figure 3.1 Key Elements of Holistic (Whole-Person) Development

Student Perspective

"I want to see how all the pieces of me come together to make me, physically and mentally."

–College sophomore

of your self is a form of intelligence that has been referred to as intrapersonal intelligence (Gardner, 1999), and it's essential for beginning any quest for personal growth and self-fulfillment.

To become self-aware requires awareness of all elements that comprise the self. As illustrated in **Figure 3.1**, the human self is composed of multiple dimensions that join together to form the whole person.

Key Dimensions of the Self

Each of the following elements of self plays an influential role in promoting human health, success, and happiness:

1. **Intellectual.** Knowledge, perspectives, and ways of thinking;
2. **Emotional.** Feelings, self-esteem, emotional intelligence, and mental health;
3. **Social.** Interpersonal relationships;
4. **Ethical.** Values, character, and moral convictions;
5. **Physical.** Bodily health and wellness;
6. **Spiritual.** Beliefs about the meaning or purpose of life and the hereafter;
7. **Vocational.** Occupational or career development and satisfaction;
8. **Personal.** Identity, self-concept, and self-management.

Research strongly suggests that quality of life depends on attention to and development of all elements of the self. It's been found that people who are healthy (physically and mentally) and successful (personally and professionally) are those who attend to and integrate dimensions of their self, enabling them to lead well-rounded and well-balanced lives (Covey, 1990; Goleman, 1995; Heath, 1977).

In Figure 3.1, these diverse dimensions of the self are joined or linked to represent how they are interrelated and work not independently but interdependently to affect an individual's development and well-being (Love & Love, 1995).

These elements are discussed separately in this chapter to keep them clear in your mind. In reality, they do not operate independently of one another; they are interconnected and influence one another. (This is why the elements the self in Figure 3.1 are depicted as links in an interconnected chain.) Thus, the self is a diverse, multidimensional entity that has the capacity to develop along various interdependent dimensions.

One of the primary goals of the liberal arts is to provide a well-rounded education that promotes development the whole person (Kuh, Shedd, & Whitt, 1987). Research on college students confirms that their college experience affects them in multiple ways and promotes the development of multiple dimensions of self (Bowen, 1997; Feldman & Newcomb, 1994; Pascarella & Terenzini, 1991).

Since wholeness is essential for wellness, success, and happiness, carefully read the following descriptions and skills associated with each of the eight elements of holistic development. As you are read the skills and qualities listed beneath each of the eight elements, place a checkmark in the space next to any skill that is particularly important to you. You may check more than one skill within each area.

Student Perspective

"Being successful is being balanced in every aspect of your life."

–First-year college student

◆ Skills and Qualities Associated with Each Element of Holistic (Whole-Person) Development

1. **Intellectual development.** Acquiring knowledge and learning how to learn deeply and think at a higher level.
   Goals and skills:
   - ☑ Becoming aware of your intellectual abilities, interests, and learning styles
   - ☑ Maintaining attention and concentration
   - ☑ Improving your ability to retain knowledge (long-term memory)
   - ☑ Moving beyond memorization to higher levels of thinking
   - ☑ Acquiring effective research skills for accessing information from various sources and systems
   - ☑ Viewing issues from multiple angles or viewpoints (psychological, social, political, economic, etc.) to attain a balanced, comprehensive perspective
   - ☑ Evaluating ideas critically in terms of their truth and value
   - ☑ Thinking creatively or imaginatively
   - ☑ Responding constructively to differing viewpoints or opposing arguments
   - ☑ Detecting and rejecting persuasion tactics that appeal to emotions rather than reason

"The research portrays the college student as changing in an integrated way, with change in any one area appearing to be part of a mutually reinforcing network or pattern of change in other areas."

–Ernest Pascarella and Pat Terenzini, *How College Affects Students* (2005)

2. **Emotional development.** Strengthening skills for understanding, controlling, and expressing emotions.
   Goals and skills:
   - ☑ Dealing with personal emotions in an honest, nondefensive manner
   - ☑ Maintaining a healthy balance between emotional control and emotional expression
   - ☑ Responding with empathy and sensitivity to emotions experienced by others
   - ☑ Dealing effectively with depression
   - ☑ Dealing effectively with anger
   - ☑ Using effective stress-management strategies to control anxiety and tension
   - ☑ Responding effectively to frustrations and setbacks
   - ☑ Dealing effectively with fear of failure and poor performance
   - ☑ Accepting feedback in a constructive, nondefensive manner
   - ☑ Maintaining optimism and enthusiasm

"Intellectual growth should commence at birth and cease only at death."

–Albert Einstein, Nobel Prize–winning physicist

3. **Social development.** Enhancing the quality and depth of interpersonal relationships.
   Goals and skills:
   - ☑ Developing effective conversational skills
   - ☑ Becoming an effective listener
   - ☑ Relating effectively to others in one-to-one, small-group, and large-group situations
   - ☑ Collaborating effectively with others when working in groups or teams
   - ☑ Overcoming shyness

"It's not stress that kills us, it is our reaction to it."

–Hans Selye, Canadian endocrinologist and author of *Stress Without Distress*

☑ Developing more meaningful and intimate relationships
☑ Resolving interpersonal conflicts assertively, rather than in aggressively or passively
☑ Providing feedback to others in a constructive and considerate manner
☑ Relating effectively with others from different cultural backgrounds and lifestyles
☑ Developing leadership skills

4. **Ethical development.** Developing a clear value system for guiding life choices and decisions and building moral character, or the ability to make and act on ethical judgments and to demonstrate consistency between convictions (beliefs) and commitments (actions).

Goals and skills:
☑ Gaining deeper self-awareness of personal values and ethical assumptions
☑ Making personal choices and life decisions based on a meaningful value system
☑ Developing the capacity to think and act with personal integrity and authenticity
☑ Using electronic technology in an ethical and civil manner
☑ Resisting social pressure to act in ways that are inconsistent with personal values
☑ Treating others in an ethical manner
☑ Knowing how to exercise individual freedom without infringing on the rights of others
☑ Developing concern and commitment for human rights and social justice
☑ Developing the courage to confront those who violate the rights of others
☑ Becoming a responsible citizen

Chi rispetta sara rippetato.

("Respect others and you will be respected.")

–Italian proverb

5. **Physical development.** Applying knowledge about how the human body functions to prevent disease, preserve wellness, and promote peak performance.

Goals and skills:
☑ Maintaining awareness of your physical condition and state of health
☑ Applying knowledge about exercise and fitness training to promote physical and mental health
☑ Understanding how sleep patterns affect health and performance
☑ Maintaining a healthy balance among work, recreation and relaxation
☑ Applying knowledge of nutrition to reduce the risk of illness and promote optimal performance
☑ Becoming knowledgeable about nutritional imbalances and eating disorders
☑ Developing a positive physical self-image
☑ Becoming knowledgeable about the effects of drugs and their impact on physical and mental well-being
☑ Being knowledgeable about human sexuality and sexually transmitted diseases
☑ Understanding how biological differences between the sexes affect male–female relationships and gender orientation

"The moral challenge is simply to abide by the knowledge we already have."

–Soren Kierkegaard, nineteenth-century Danish philosopher and theologian

6. **Spiritual development.** Searching for answers to the big questions, such as the meaning or purpose of life and death, and exploring nonmaterial issues that transcend human life and the physical world.

"If you don't stand for something you will fall for anything."

–Malcolm X, African American Muslim minister, public speaker, and human rights activist

Goals and skills:
- ☑ Developing a personal philosophy or worldview about the meaning and purpose of human existence
- ☑ Appreciating what cannot be completely understood
- ☑ Appreciating the mysteries associated with the origin of the universe
- ☑ Searching for the connection between the self and the larger world or cosmos
- ☑ Searching for the mystical or supernatural—that which transcends the boundaries of the natural world
- ☑ Being open to examining questions relating to death and life after death
- ☑ Being open to examining questions about the possible existence of a supreme being or higher power
- ☑ Being knowledgeable about different approaches to spirituality and their underlying beliefs or assumptions
- ☑ Understanding the difference and relationship between faith and reason
- ☑ Becoming aware and tolerant of religious beliefs and practices

7. **Vocational development.** Exploring career options, making career choices wisely, and developing skills needed for lifelong career success.
   Goals and skills:
   - ☑ Understanding the relationship between college majors and careers
   - ☑ Using effective strategies for exploring and identifying potential careers
   - ☑ Selecting career options that are consistent with your personal values, interests, and talents
   - ☑ Acquiring work experience in career fields that relate to your occupational interests
   - ☑ Developing an effective résumé and portfolio
   - ☑ Adopting effective strategies for identifying individuals to serve as personal references and for improving the quality of personal letters of recommendation
   - ☑ Acquiring effective job-search strategies
   - ☑ Using effective strategies for writing letters of inquiry and applications to potential employers
   - ☑ Developing strategies for performing well in personal interviews
   - ☑ Acquiring effective networking skills for developing personal contacts with potential employers

8. **Personal development.** Developing positive self-beliefs, personal attitudes, and personal habits.
   Goals and skills:
   - ☑ Developing a strong sense of personal identity and a coherent self-concept (e.g., "Who am I?")
   - ☑ Finding a sense of purpose direction in life (e.g., "Who will I become?")
   - ☑ Developing self-respect and self-esteem
   - ☑ Increasing self-confidence
   - ☑ Developing self-efficacy, or the belief that events and outcomes in life are influenced or controlled by personal initiative and effort

"A man too busy to take care of his health is like a mechanic too busy to take care of his tools."

–Spanish proverb

Student Perspective

"You may think I'm here, living for the 'now' . . . but I'm not. Half of my life revolves around the invisible and immaterial. At some point, every one of us has asked the Big Questions surrounding our existence: What is the meaning of life? Is my life inherently purposeful and valuable?"

–College student (Dalton, Eberhardt, Bracken, & Echols, 2006)

"Everyone is a house with four rooms: a physical, a mental, an emotional, and a spiritual. Most of us tend to live in one room most of the time but unless we go into every room every day, even if only to keep it aired, we are not complete."

–Native American proverb

"Your work is to discover your work and then with all your heart to give yourself to it."

–Hindu Siddhartha Prince Gautama Siddharta, a.k.a. Buddha, founder of the philosophy and religion of Buddhism

☑ Setting realistic personal goals and priorities
☑ Becoming self-motivated and self-disciplined
☑ Developing the perseverance and persistence to reach long-range goals
☑ Acquiring practical skills for managing personal affairs effectively and efficiently
☑ Becoming independent and self-reliant

"I'm a great believer in luck and I find the harder I work, the more I have of it."

—Thomas Jefferson

 **The Cocurriculum: Using the Whole Campus to Develop the Whole Person**

To maximize the impact of a liberal arts education, you need to take advantage of the total college environment. This includes not only the courses you take in the college curriculum, but also the learning experiences you have outside the classroom, known as the cocurriculum. Cocurricular experiences include all educational discussions you have with your peers and professors outside the classroom, as well as your participation in the various events and programs offered on your campus. As mentioned in Chapter 2, research clearly indicates that out-of-class learning experiences are as important to your overall development as the course curriculum (Kuh, 1995; Kuh, Douglas, Lund, & Ramin-Gyurnek, 1994), hence the term "co"-curriculum.

The learning that takes place in college courses is primarily vicarious—that is, you learn from or through somebody else—by listening to professors in class and by reading outside of class. While this type of academic learning is valuable, it needs to be complemented by experiential learning (i.e., learning directly through firsthand experiences). For example, leadership cannot be developed solely by listening to lectures and reading books about leadership. To fully develop your leadership skills, you need to have leadership experiences, such as those developed by "leading a [discussion] group in class, holding office in student government or by being captain of a sports team" (Association of American Colleges & Universities, 2002, p. 30). Fully using campus resources is one of the keys to college success, so take advantage of your whole college to develop yourself as a whole person.

Listed in **Snapshot Summary 3.1** are some programs and services included in a cocurriculum, accompanied by the primary dimension of the self that they are designed to develop.

Pause for Reflection

Look back and count the number of checkmarks you've placed by each of the eight areas of self-development. Did you find that you placed roughly the same number of checkmarks in all eight areas, or were there large discrepancies across the eight areas?

Based on the checkmarks that you placed in each area, would you say that your interests in self-development are balanced across elements of the self, or do they suggest a strong interest in certain dimensions of yourself, with little interest in others?

Do you think you will eventually develop a more balanced set of interests across these different dimensions of self-development?

"To educate liberally, learning experiences must be offered which facilitate maturity of the whole person. These are goals of student development and clearly they are consistent with the mission and goals of liberal education."

—Theodore Berg, "Student Development and Liberal Education"

!
Remember

A liberal arts education includes both the curriculum and the cocurriculum; it involves strategic use of the total college environment, both inside and outside the classroom.

Snapshot Summary

3.1

Cocurricular Programs and Services Promoting Dimensions of Holistic Development

Intellectual Development
- Academic advising
- Learning center services
- College library
- Tutoring services
- Information technology services
- Campus speakers
- Concerts, theater productions, and art shows

Emotional and Social Development
- Student activities
- Student clubs and organizations
- Counseling services
- Peer counseling
- Peer mentoring
- Residential life programs
- Commuter programs

Ethical Development
- Judicial Review Board
- Student government
- Integrity committees and task forces

Physical Development
- Student health services
- Wellness programs
- Campus athletic activities and intramural sports

Spiritual Development
- College chaplain
- Campus ministry
- Peer ministry

Vocational Development
- Career development services
- Internships programs
- Service learning experiences
- Work–study programs
- Major and career fairs

Personal Development
- Financial aid services
- Campus workshops on self-management (e.g., managing time or money)

Note: This list represents just a sample of the total number of programs and services that may be available on your campus. As you can see from the list's length, colleges and universities are organized to promote your development in multiple ways. The power of the liberal arts is magnified when you combine coursework and cocurricular experiences to create a college experience that contributes to your development as a whole person.

◆ Broadening Your Perspective of the World Around You

Student Perspective

"College was not something I deemed important in order to be really rich later on in life. It was something I considered fundamental to learning about myself and the world around me."

–First-year college student (Watts, 2005)

"

"A quality liberal education leads students to reflect on their place in the world and locate themselves historically and socially."

–Nancy Thomas, "In Search of Wisdom: Liberal Education for a Changing World"

You should know more than yourself; you should know your world. The liberal arts education helps you move beyond yourself and expands your perspective to include the wider world around you (Braskamp, 2008). The components of this larger perspective are organized and illustrated in **Figure 3.2**.

In Figure 3.2, the center circle represents the self. Fanning out to the right of the self is a series of arches that encompasses the *social–spatial perspective*; this perspective includes increasingly larger social groups and more distant places, ranging from the narrowest perspective (the individual) to the widest perspective (the universe). The liberal arts liberate you from the narrow tunnel vision of a self-centered (egocentric) perspective, providing a panoramic perspective of the world that enables you to move outside yourself and see yourself in relation to other people and other places.

To the left of the self in Figure 3.2 are three arches labeled the *chronological perspective*; this perspective includes the three dimensions of time: past (historical), present (contemporary), and future (futuristic). The liberal arts not only widen your perspective but also lengthen it by stretching your vision beyond the present—enabling you to see yourself in relation to humans who've lived before you and will live after you. The chronological perspective gives you hindsight to see where the world has been, insight into the world's current condition, and foresight to see where the world may be going.

It could be said that the chronological perspective provides you with a mental time machine for flashing back to the past and flashing forward to the future, and the social–spatial perspective provides you with a conceptual telescope for viewing people and places that are far away. Together, these two broadening perspectives of the liberal arts enable to you to appreciate the experience of anyone living anywhere at any time.

The elements that comprise each of these broadening perspectives are provided in the next sections.

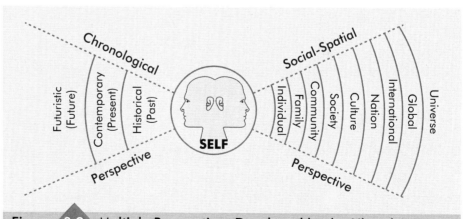

Figure 3.2 Multiple Perspectives Developed by the Liberal Arts

◆ Elements of the Social–Spatial Perspective

The Family Perspective

Moving beyond the perspective of your individual self, you are part of a larger social unit—your family. The people with whom you were raised have almost certainly influenced the person you are today and how you got to be that way. Moreover, your family hasn't only influenced you; you've also influenced your family. For example, your decision to go to college may make your parents and grandparents proud and may influence the decision of other members of your family to attend college. In addition, if you have children, graduating from college will have a positive influence on their future welfare. As mentioned in the introduction to this book, children of college graduates experience improved intellectual development, better physical health, and greater economic security (Bowen, 1977, 1997; Pascarella & Terenzini, 1991, 2005).

The Community Perspective

Moving beyond the family, you are also a member of a larger social unit—your community. This wider social circle includes friends and neighbors at home, at school, and at work. These are communities where you can begin to take action to improve the world around you. If you want to make the world a better place, this is the place to start—through civic engagement in your local communities.

Civically responsible people also demonstrate civic concern by stepping beyond their narrow self-interests to selflessly volunteer time and energy to help members of their community, particularly those in need. They demonstrate their humanity by being humane (they show genuine compassion for others who are less fortunate than they are) and by being humanitarian (they work to promote the welfare of other humans).

The Societal Perspective

Moving beyond our local communities, we are also members of a larger society that includes people from different regions of the country, cultural backgrounds, and social classes.

In human societies, groups of people are typically stratified into social classes with unequal levels of resources, such monetary wealth. According to U.S. Census (2000) figures, the wealthiest 20 percent of the American population controls approximately 50 percent of the total American income, while the 20 percent with the lowest level of income controls 4 percent of the nation's wealth. Sharp differences in income level exist among people of different race, ethnicity, and gender. A recent survey revealed that Black households had the lowest median income in 2007 ($33,916), compared to a median income of $54,920 for non-Hispanic White households (Current Population Survey Annual Social and Economic Supplement, 2008).

The Cultural Perspective

Culture can be broadly defined as a distinctive pattern of beliefs and values that are learned by a group of people who share the same social heritage and tradi-

"Think globally, act locally."

–Patrick Geddes, Scottish urban planner and social activist

"Get involved. Don't gripe about things unless you are making an effort to change them. You can make a difference if you dare."

–Richard C. Holbrooke, former director of the Peace Corps and American ambassador to the United Nations

"[Liberal arts education] shows you how to accommodate yourself to others, how to throw yourself into their state of mind, how to come to an understanding of them. You are at home in any society; you have common ground with every class."

–John Henry Newman

Pause for Reflection

What would you say is the factor that is most responsible for poverty in human societies?

tions. In short, culture is the whole way in which a group of people has learned to live (Peoples & Bailey, 2008); it includes their customary style of speaking (language), fashion, food, art, music, values, and beliefs.

Intercultural awareness is one of the outcomes of a liberal arts education (Wabash National Study, 2007). Being able to step outside of your own culture and see issues from a broader worldview enables you to perceive reality and evaluate truth from diverse vantage points. This makes your thinking more comprehensive and less ethnocentric (centered on your own culture).

"It is difficult to see the picture when you are inside the frame."

–Author unknown

The National Perspective

Besides being a member of society, you're also a citizen of a nation. Having the privilege of being a citizen in a free nation brings with it the responsibility of participating in your country's governance through the process of voting. As a democracy, the United States is a nation that has been built on the foundation of equal rights and freedom of opportunity, which are guaranteed by its constitution.

Exercise your right to vote, and when you do vote, be mindful of political leaders who are committed to ensuring equal rights, social justice, and political freedom. When the personal rights and freedom of any of our fellow citizens are threatened by prejudice and discrimination, the political stability and survival of any democratic nation is threatened.

"A progressive society counts individual variations as precious since it finds in them the means of its own growth. A democratic society must, in consistency with its ideal, allow intellectual freedom and the play of diverse gifts and interests."

–John Dewey, U.S. educator, philosopher, and psychologist

The International Perspective

Moving beyond your particular country of citizenship, you are also a member of an international world that includes close to 200 nations (Rosenberg, 2009). Communication and interaction among citizens of different nations is greater today than at any other time in world history, largely because of rapid advances in electronic technology (Dryden & Vos, 1999; Smith, 1994). The World Wide Web is making today's world a small one indeed, and success in today's world requires an international perspective. Our lives are increasingly affected by events beyond our national borders because boundaries between nations are breaking down as a result of international travel, international trading, and multinational corporations. Employers of college graduates are placing higher value on prospective employees with international knowledge and foreign language skills (Fixman, 1990; Office of Research, 1994). By learning from and about different nations, you become more than a citizen of your own country: you become cosmopolitan—a citizen of the world.

"A liberal [arts] education frees a person from the prison-house of class, race, time, place, background, family, and nation."

–Robert Hutchins, former dean of Yale Law School and president of the University of Chicago

The Global Perspective

Broader than an international perspective is the global perspective. It extends beyond the relations among citizens of different nations to include all life forms that inhabit the earth and the relationships between these diverse life forms and the earth's natural resources (minerals, air, and water). Humans share the earth and its natural resources with approximately 10 million animal species (Myers, 1997) and more than 300,000 forms of vegetative life (Knoll, 2003). As inhabitants of this planet and as global citizens, we have an environmental responsibility to address global warming and other issues that require balancing our industrial–technological progress with the need to sustain the earth's natural resources and preserve the life of our planet's cohabitants.

"Treat the Earth well. It was not given to you by your parents. It was loaned to you by your children."

–Kenyan proverb

The Universal Perspective

Beyond the global perspective is the broadest of all perspectives—the universe. The earth is just one planet that shares a solar system with seven other planets and is just one celestial body that shares a galaxy with millions of other celestial bodies, including stars, moons, meteorites, and asteroids (Encrenaz et al., 2004).

Just as we should guard against being ethnocentric (thinking that our culture is the center of humanity), we should guard against being geocentric (thinking that we are at the center of the universe). All heavenly bodies do not revolve around the earth; our planet revolves around them. The sun doesn't rise in the east and set in the west; our planet rotates around the sun to produce our earthly experiences of day and night.

"In astronomy, you must get used to viewing the earth as just one planet in the larger context of the universe."

–Physics professor (Donald, 2002)

◆ Elements of the Chronological Perspective

The Historical Perspective

A historical perspective is critical for understanding the root causes of our current human condition and world situation. Humans are products of both a social and a natural history. Don't forget that the earth is estimated to be more than 4.5 billion years old and our human ancestors date back more than 250,000 years (Knoll, 2003). Thus, our current lives represent a small frame of time in a long chronological reel. Every modern convenience we now enjoy reflects the collective efforts and cumulative knowledge of diverse human groups that have accumulated over thousands of years of history. By studying the past, we can build on our ancestors' achievements and avoid their mistakes. For example, by understanding the causes and consequences of the Holocaust, we can reduce the risk that an atrocity of that size and scope will ever happen again.

"The sun, with all those planets revolving around it and dependent on it, can still ripen a bunch of grapes as if it had nothing else in the universe to do."

–Galileo Galilei

Pause for Reflection

Look back at the broadening perspectives developed by a liberal arts education. What college course would develop each perspective? If you're unsure or cannot remember whether a course is designed to develop any of these perspectives, look at the course's goals described in your college catalog (in print or online).

The Contemporary Perspective

The contemporary perspective focuses on understanding the current world situation and the events that comprise today's news. One major goal of a liberal arts education is to increase your understanding the contemporary human condition so that you may have the wisdom to improve it (Miller, 1988). For example, despite historical progress in the nation's acceptance and appreciation of different ethnic and racial groups, the Unites States today remains a nation that is deeply divided with respect to culture, religion, and social class (Brooking Institute, 2008).

The current technological revolution is generating information and new knowledge at a faster rate than at any other time in human history (Dryden & Vos, 1999). Knowledge quickly becomes obsolete when there is rapid creation and communication of new information (Naisbitt, 1982). Workers in the today's complex, fast-changing world need to continually update their skills to perform their jobs and advance in their careers (Niles & Harris-Bowlsbey, 2002). This creates a demand for workers who have learned how to learn, a hallmark of the liberal arts.

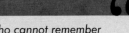

"Those who cannot remember the past are damned to repeat it."

–George Santayana, Spanish-born American philosopher

"Yesterday is gone. Tomorrow has not yet come. We have only today. Let us begin."

–Mother Teresa of Calcutta, Albanian, Catholic nun and winner of the Nobel Peace Prize

> "The only person who is educated is the one who has learned how to learn and change."
>
> –Carl Rogers, humanistic psychologist and Nobel Peace Prize nominee

> "In times of change, learners inherit the Earth . . . [they] find themselves beautifully equipped to deal with a world that no longer exists."
>
> –Eric Hoffer, author of *The Ordeal of Change* (XXXX) and recipient of the Presidential Medal of Freedom

> "The future is literally in our hands to mold as we like. But we cannot wait until tomorrow. Tomorrow is now."
>
> –Eleanor Roosevelt

> "We all inherit the past. We all confront the challenges of the present. We all participate in the making of the future."
>
> –Ernest Boyer and Martin Kaplan, *Educating for Survival*

Pause for Reflection

In light of the information you've read in this chapter, how would you interpret the following statement: "We can't know where we're going until we know where we've been"?

> "A truly great intellect is one which takes a connected view of old and new, past and present, far and near, and which has an insight into the influence of all these on one another, without which there is no whole, and no center."
>
> –John Henry Newman, *The Idea of a University* (1852)

The Futuristic Perspective

The futuristic perspective allows us to flash forward and envision what our world will be like years from now. This perspective focuses on such questions as "Will we leave the world a better or worse place for humans who will inhabit after our departure, including our children and grandchildren?" and "How can humans living today avoid short-term, shortsighted thinking and adopt a long-range vision that anticipates the consequences of their current actions on future generations of humans?"

To sum up, a comprehensive chronological perspective brings the past, present, and future into focus on a single screen. It enables us to see how the current world is a single segment of a temporal sequence that's been shaped by events that preceded it and will shape future events.

Remember

By embracing the perspectives of different times, places, and people, you're embracing the diversity promoted by a liberal arts education. These diverse perspectives liberate or emancipate you from the here and now and empower you to see things long ago and far away.

The Synoptic Perspective: Integrating Diverse Perspectives to Form a Unified Whole

A liberal arts education helps you not only appreciate multiple perspectives but also integrate them into a meaningful whole (King, Brown, Lindsay, & VanHencke, 2007). Understanding of how the perspectives of time, place, and person interrelate to form a unified whole is sometimes referred to as a synoptic perspective (Cronon, 1998; Heath, 1977). The word derives from a combination of two roots: syn, meaning "together" (as in the word "synthesize"), and optic, meaning "to see." Thus, a "synoptic" perspective literally means to "see things together" or "see the whole." It enables you to see how all the trees come together to form the forest.

A liberal arts education helps you step beyond yourself to see the wider world and connects you with it. By seeing yourself as an integral part of humankind, you become integrated with the whole of humanity; you're able to see how you, as an individual, fit into the big picture—the larger scheme of things (Heath, 1968). When we view ourselves as nested within a web of interconnections with other places, cultures, and times, we become aware of the common humanity we all share. This increased sense of connection with humankind decreases our feelings of personal isolation or alienation (Bellah, Madsen, Sullivan, Swidler, & Tipton, 1985). In his book The Perfect Education, Kenneth Eble (1966, pp. 214–215) skillfully describes this benefit of a liberal arts education:

It can provide that overarching life of a people, a community, a world that was going on before the individual came onto the scene and that will continue on after [s]he departs. By such means we come to see the world not alone. Our joys are more intense for being shared. Our sorrows are less destructive for our knowing universal sorrow. Our fears of death fade before the commonness of the occurrence.

! Remember

A liberal arts education launches you on a quest for two forms of wholeness: (a) an *inner* wholeness in which elements of self become connected to form a *whole person*, and (b) an *outer* wholeness in which your individual self becomes connected with the *whole world*. This inner and outer quest will enable you to lead a richer, more fulfilling life that's filled with greater breadth, balance, and wholeness.

> *"Without exception, the observed changes [during college] involve greater breadth, expansion, and appreciation for the new and different. These changes are eminently consistent with values of a liberal [arts] education, and the evidence for their presence is compelling."*
>
> —Ernest Pascarella and Pat Terenzini, *How College Affects Students*

◆ Educating You for Life

Research shows that the primary reasons students go to college are to prepare for a career and get a better job (Sax, Lindholm, Astin, Korn, & Mahoney, 2004). While these are important reasons and your career is an important element of your life, a person's vocation or occupation represents just one element of the self. It also represents just one of many roles or responsibilities that you are likely to have in life.

Similar to global issues, personal issues and challenges that individuals face in their everyday lives are multidimensional, requiring perspectives and skills that go well beyond the boundaries of a single academic field or career specialization. Your occupational role represents just one of many roles you assume in life, which include the roles of family member, friend, co-worker, community member, citizen, and possibly, mother or father. A liberal arts education provides you with the breadth of knowledge and the variety skills needed to successfully accommodate the multiple roles and responsibilities you face in life.

Pause for Reflection

In light of the knowledge you've acquired thus far in this chapter, what points or arguments would you make to counter the claim that the liberal arts are impractical?

> *"Virtually all occupational endeavors require a working appreciation of the historical, cultural, ethical, and global environments that surround the application of skilled work."*
>
> —Robert Jones, "Liberal Education for the Twenty-First Century: Business Expectations"

> *"The finest art, the most difficult art, is the art of living."*
>
> —John Albert Macy, American author, poet, and editor of Helen Keller's autobiography

Personal Story

One life role that a liberal arts education helped prepare me for was the role of parent. Courses that I took in psychology and sociology proved to be useful in helping me understand how children develop and how a parent can best support them at different stages of their development. Surprisingly, however, there was one course I took in college that I never expected would ever help me as a parent. That course was statistics, which I took to fulfill a general education requirement in mathematics. It was not a particularly enjoyable course; some of my classmates sarcastically referred to it as "sadistics" because they felt it was a somewhat painful or torturous experience. However, what I learned in that course became valuable to me many years later when, as a parent, my 14-year-old son (Tony) developed a life-threatening disease, leukemia, which is a form of cancer that attacks blood cells. Tony's form of leukemia was a particularly perilous one because it had only a 35 percent average cure rate; in other words, 65 percent of those who develop the disease don't recover and eventually die from it. This statistic was based on patients that received the traditional treatment of chemotherapy, which was the type of treatment that my son began receiving when his cancer was first detected.

Another option for treating Tony's cancer was a bone-marrow transplant, which involved using radiation to destroy all of his own bone marrow (that was making the abnormal blood cells) and replace it with bone marrow donated to him by another person. My wife and I got opinions from doctors at two major cancer centers—one from a center that specialized in chemotherapy, and one from a center that specialized in bone-marrow transplants. The chemotherapy doctors felt strongly that drug treatment would be the better way to treat and cure Tony, and the bone-marrow transplant doctors felt strongly that his chances of survival would be much better if he had a transplant. So, my wife and I had to decide between two opposing recommendations, each made by a respected group of doctors.

To help us reach a decision, I asked both teams of doctors for research studies that had been done on the effectiveness of chemotherapy and bone-marrow transplants for treating my son's particular type of cancer. I read all of these studies and carefully analyzed their statistical findings. I remembered from my statistics course that when an average is calculated for a general group of people (e.g., average cure rate for people with leukemia), it tends to lump together individuals from different subgroups (e.g., males and females or young children and teenagers). Sometimes, when separate statistics are calculated for different subgroups, the results may be different from the average statistic for the whole group. So, when I read the research reports, I looked for any subgroup statistics that may have been calculated. I found two subgroups of patients with my son's particular type of cancer that had a higher rate of cure with chemotherapy than the general (whole-group) average of 35 percent. One subgroup included people with a low number of abnormal cells at the time when the cancer was first diagnosed, and the other subgroup consisted of people whose cancer cells dropped rapidly after their first week of chemotherapy. My son belonged to both of these subgroups, which meant that his chance for cure with chemotherapy was higher than the overall 35 percent average. Furthermore, I found that the statistics showing higher success rate for bone-marrow transplants were based only on patients whose body accepted the donor's bone marrow and did not include those who died because their body rejected the donor's bone marrow. So, the success rates for bone-marrow patients were not actually as high as they appeared to be, because the overall average did not include the subgroup of patients who died because of transplant rejection. Based on these statistics, my wife and I decided to go with chemotherapy and not the transplant operation.

Our son has now been cancer free for more than 5 years, so we think we made the right decision. However, I never imagined that a statistics course, which I took many years ago to fulfill a general education requirement, would help me fulfill my role as a parent and help me make a life-or-death decision about my own son.

—Joe Cuseo

! Remember

The liberal arts education not only prepares you for a career but also prepares you for life.

◆ Summary and Conclusion

General education represents the foundation of a college education upon which all academic majors are built. It promotes success in any major and career by supplying students with a set of lifelong learning skills that can be applied in multiple settings and that can be continually used throughout life.

General education promotes development of the whole person (intellectual, emotional, social, physical, spiritual, etc.) and broadens your perspective on the world by expanding (a) your social–spatial perspective to include increasingly larger social groups and more distant places, from the individual to the universe; and (b) your chronological perspective to include the past, present, and future.

Despite popular beliefs the contrary, the liberal arts have many practical benefits, including promoting career mobility and career advancement. Most importantly, a liberal arts education prepares you for life roles other than an occupation, including roles such as family member, community member, and citizen. In short, a liberal arts education prepares you for than a career; it prepares you for life.

Learning More Through the World Wide Web

Internet-Based Resources for Further Information on Liberal Arts Education

For additional information related to the ideas discussed in this chapter, we recommend the following Web sites:

Liberal Arts Education: www.aacu.org/resources/liberaleducation/index.cfm

Liberal Arts Resources: www.eace.org/networks/liberalarts.html

3.1 Planning Your Liberal Arts Education

Since general education is an essential component of your college experience, it should be intentionally planned. This exercise will leave you with a flexible plan that capitalizes on your educational interests while ensuring that your college experience has both breadth and balance.

1. Use your course catalog (bulletin) to identify the general education requirements at your college. The requirements should be organized into general divisions of knowledge similar to those discussed in this chapter (humanities, fine arts, natural sciences, etc.) Within each of these liberal arts divisions, you'll find specific courses listed that fulfill the general education requirements for that particular division. (Catalogs can sometimes be difficult to navigate; if you encounter difficulty or doubt about general education requirements, seek clarification from an academic advisor on campus).

2. You'll probably have some freedom to choose courses from a larger group of courses that fulfill general education requirements within each division. Use your freedom of choice to choose courses whose descriptions capture your curiosity or pique your interest. You can take liberal arts courses not only to fulfill general education requirements but also to test your interest and talent in fields that you may end up choosing as a college major or minor.

3. Highlight the courses in the catalog that you plan to take to fulfill your general education requirements in each division of the liberal arts, and use the form that follows to pencil in the courses you've chosen. (Use pencil because you will likely make some adjustments to your plan.) Remember that the courses you're taking this term may be fulfilling certain general education requirements, so be sure to list them on your planning form.

3.2 General Education Planning Form

Division of the Liberal Arts Curriculum: _____

General education courses you're planning to take to fulfill requirements in this division (record the course number and course title):

_____   _____

_____   _____

_____   _____

Division of the Liberal Arts Curriculum: _____

General education courses you're planning to take to fulfill requirements in this division (record the course number and course title):

_____   _____

_____   _____

_____   _____

Division of the Liberal Arts Curriculum: _____

General education courses you're planning to take to fulfill requirements in this division (record the course number and course title):

_____   _____

_____   _____

_____   _____

Division of the Liberal Arts Curriculum: _____

General education courses you're planning to take to fulfill requirements in this division (record the course number and course title):

_____   _____

_____   _____

_____   _____

Division of the Liberal Arts Curriculum: _____

General education courses you're planning to take to fulfill requirements in this division (record the course number and course title):

_____   _____

_____   _____

_____   _____

4. Look back at the general education courses you've listed and identify the broadening perspectives developed by the liberal arts that each course appears to be developing. (See **pp. 54–57** for a description of these perspectives.) Use the form that follows to ensure that your overall perspective is comprehensive and that you have no blind spots in your liberal arts education. For any perspective that's not covered in your plan, find a course in the catalog that will enable you to address the missing perspective.

Broadening Social–Spatial Perspectives

Perspective	Course Developing This Perspective
(See **pp. 54–57** for further descriptions of these perspectives.)	
Self	_____
Family	_____
Community	_____
Society	_____
Culture	_____
Nation	_____
International	_____
Global	_____
Universe	_____

Broadening Chronological Perspectives

Perspective	Course Developing This Perspective
(See **pp. 57–58** for detailed description of these perspectives.)	
Historical	_____
Contemporary	_____
Futuristic	_____

5. Look back at the general education courses you've listed and identify what element of holistic (whole-person) development each course appears to be developing. (See **pp. 49–52** for a description of each of these elements.) Use the form that follows to ensure that your course selection didn't overlook any element of the self. For any element that's not covered in your plan, find a course in the catalog or a cocurricular experience program that will enable you to address the missing area. For cocurricular learning experiences (e.g., leadership and volunteer experiences), consult your student handbook or contact someone in the Office of Student Life.

Dimensions of Self
(See **pp. 49–52** for further description of these dimensions.)

Course or Cocurricular Experience Developing This Dimension of Self
(Consult your student handbook for cocurricular experiences.)

Intellectual _____

Emotional _____

Social _____

Ethical _____

Physical _____

Spiritual _____

Vocational _____

Personal _____

Remember

This general education plan is not set in stone; it may be modified as you gain more experience with the college curriculum and campus life. Its purpose is not to restrict your educational exploration or experimentation but to give it some direction, breadth, and balance.

Dazed and Confused: General Education versus Career Specialization

Joe Tech was really looking forward to college because he thought he would have freedom to select the courses he wanted and the opportunity to get into the major of his choice (computer science). However, he's shocked and disappointed with his first-term schedule of classes because it consists mostly of required general education courses that do not seem to relate in any way to his major. He's frustrated further because some of these courses are about subjects that he already took in high school (English, history, and biology). He's beginning to think he would be better off quitting college and going to a technical school where he could get right into computer science and immediately begin to acquire the knowledge and skills he'll need to prepare him for his intended career.

Reflection and Discussion Questions

1. Can you relate to this student, or do you know of students who feel the same way as Joe does?

2. If Joe decides to leave college for a technical school, how do you see it affecting his future: (a) in the short run and (b) in the long run?

3. Do you see any way Joe might strike a balance between pursuing his career interest and obtaining his college degree so that he could work toward achieving both goals at the same time?

Goal Setting, Motivation, and Character

4

1. How would you define the word "successful"?

_____

_____

_____

LEARNING GOAL

To develop meaningful goals to strive for, along with strategies for maintaining motivation and building character to achieve those goals.

◆ What Does Being "Successful" Mean to You?

The word "success" means to achieve a desired outcome; it derives from the Latin root *successus*, which means "to follow or come after" (as in the word "succession"). Thus, by definition, success involves an order or sequence of actions that lead to a desired outcome. The process starts with identifying an end (goal) and then finding a means (sequence of steps) to reach that goal (achieving success). Goal setting is the first step in the process of becoming successful because it gives you something specific to strive for and ensures that you start off in the right direction. Studies consistently show that setting goals is a more effective self-motivational strategy than simply telling yourself that you should try hard or do your best (Boekaerts, Pintrich, & Zeidner, 2000; Locke & Latham, 1990).

By setting goals, you show initiative—you initiate the process of gaining control of your future and taking charge of your life. By taking initiative, you demonstrate what psychologists call an internal locus of control—you believe that the locus (location or source) of control for events in your life is *internal*, and thus inside of you and within your control, rather than *external*, or outside of you and beyond your control (controlled by such factors as luck, chance, or fate; Rotter, 1966).

Research has revealed that individuals with a strong internal locus of control display the following characteristics:

1. Greater independence and self-direction (Van Overwalle, Mervielde, & De Schuyer, 1995);
2. More accurate self-assessment (Hashaw, Hammond, & Rogers, 1990; Lefcourt, 1982);
3. Higher levels of learning and achievement (Wilhite, 1990); and
4. Better physical health (Maddi, 2002; Seligman, 1991).

> "You've got to be careful if you don't know where you're going because you might not get there."
>
> –Yogi Berra, Hall of Fame baseball player

> "There is perhaps nothing worse than reaching the top of the ladder and discovering that you're on the wrong wall."
>
> –Joseph Campbell, American professor and writer

> "Success is getting what you want. Happiness is wanting what you get."
>
> –Dale Carnegie, author of the best-selling book *How to Win Friends and Influence People* (1936) and founder of The Dale Carnegie Course, a worldwide program for business based on his teachings

> "The future is literally in our hands to mold as we like. But we cannot wait until tomorrow. Tomorrow is now."
>
> –Eleanor Roosevelt, UN diplomat and humanitarian

From "Thriving in College and Beyond" by Cuseo, Fecas, Thompson. © Kendall Hunt Publishing.

> "What lies behind us and what lies in front of us are small matters compared to what lies within us."
>
> –Ralph Waldo Emerson, nineteenth-century American essayist and lecturer

Pause for Reflection

You are not required by law or by others to attend college; you've made the decision to continue your education. Do you believe you are in charge of your educational destiny?

Why or why not?

> "When we have begun to take charge of our lives, to own ourselves, there is no longer any need to ask permission of someone."
>
> –George O'Neil, American poet and playwright

> "The price of greatness is responsibility."
>
> –Winston Churchill, British prime minister during World War II and Nobel Prize winner in literature

> "Man who stand on hill with mouth open will wait long time for roast duck to drop in."
>
> –Confucius, Chinese philosopher who emphasized sincerity and social justice

> "The cynic knows the price of everything and the value of nothing."
>
> –Oscar Wilde, Irish playwright, poet, and author of numerous short stories

An internal locus of control also contributes to the development of another positive trait that psychologists call self-efficacy—the belief that you have power to produce a positive effect on the outcomes of your life (Bandura, 1994). People with low self-efficacy tend to feel helpless, powerless, and passive; they think (and allow) things to happen to them rather than taking charge and making things happen for them. College students with a strong sense of self-efficacy believe they're in control of their educational success, regardless of their past or current circumstances.

If you have a strong sense of self-efficacy, you initiate action, put forth effort, and sustain that effort until you reach your goal. If you encounter setbacks or bad breaks along the way, you don't give up or give in; you persevere or push on (Bandura, 1986, 1997).

Students with a strong sense of academic self-efficacy have been found to:

1. Put great effort into their studies;
2. Use active-learning strategies;
3. Capitalize on campus resources; and
4. Persist in the face of obstacles (Multon, Brown, & Lent, 1991; Zimmeman, 1995).

Students with self-efficacy also possess a strong sense of personal responsibility. As the breakdown of the word "responsible" implies, they are "response" "able"—that is, they think they're able to respond effectively to personal challenges, including academic challenges.

Students with self-efficacy don't have a false sense of entitlement. They don't feel they're entitled to, or owed, anything; they believe that success is earned and is theirs for the taking. For example, studies show that students who convert their college degree into a successful career have two common characteristics: personal initiative and a positive attitude (Pope, 1990). They don't take a passive approach and assume a good position will fall into their lap; nor do they believe they are owed a position simply because they have a college degree or credential. Instead, they become actively involved in the job-hunting process and use various job-search strategies (Brown & Krane, 2000).

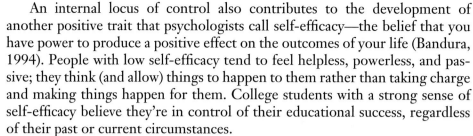

Strategies for Effective Goal Setting

Motivation begins with goal setting. Studies show that people who neglect to set and pursue life goals are prone to feelings of "life boredom" and a belief that one's life is meaningless (Bargdill, 2000).

Goals may be classified into three general categories: long range, midrange, and short range, depending on the length of time it takes to reach them and the order in which they are to be achieved. Short-range goals need to be completed before a mid-range goal can be reached, and mid-range goals must be reached before a long-range goal can be achieved. For example, if your long-range goal is a successful career, you must complete the courses required for a degree that will allow you entry into a career (mid-range goals); to reach your mid-range goal of a college degree, you need to successfully complete the courses you're taking this term (short-range goals).

Setting Long-Range Goals

Setting effective long-range goals involves two processes: (a) self-awareness, or insight into who you are now, and (b) self-projection, or a vision of what you

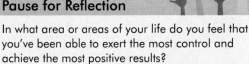

want to become. When you engage in both of these processes, you're able to see a connection between your short- and your long-range goals.

Long-range goal setting enables you to take an approach to your future that is proactive—acting beforehand to anticipate and control your future life rather than putting it off and being forced to react to it without a plan. Research shows that people who neglect to set goals for themselves are more likely to experience boredom with life (Bargdill, 2000). Setting long-range goals and planning ahead also help reduce feelings of anxiety about the future because you've given it forethought, which gives you greater power to control it (i.e., it gives you a stronger sense of self-efficacy). As the old saying goes, "To be forewarned is to be forearmed."

Remember that setting long-range goals and developing long-range plans doesn't mean you can't adjust or modify them. Your goals can undergo change as you change, develop skills, acquire knowledge, and discover interests or talents. Finding yourself and discovering your path in life are among the primary purposes of a college education. Don't think that the process of setting long-range goals means you will be locked into a premature plan and reduced options. Instead, it will give you something to reach for and some momentum to get you moving in the right direction.

Pause for Reflection

In what area or areas of your life do you feel that you've been able to exert the most control and achieve the most positive results?

In what area or areas of your life do you wish you had more control and were achieving better results?

What have you done in those areas of your life in which you've taken charge and gained control that might be transferred or applied to those areas in which you need to gain more control?

"To fail to plan is to plan to fail."

–Robert Wubbolding, internationally known author, psychologist, and teacher

Steps in the Goal-Setting Process

Effective goal setting involves a four-step sequence:

1. **Awareness of yourself.** Your personal interests, abilities and talents, and values;
2. **Awareness of your options.** The choices available to you;
3. **Awareness of the options that best fit you.** The goals most compatible with your personal abilities, interests, values, and needs;
4. **Awareness of the process.** The steps that you need to take to reach your chosen goal.

Discussed in the next sections are strategies for taking each of these steps in the goal-setting process.

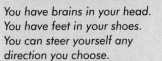

You have brains in your head. You have feet in your shoes. You can steer yourself any direction you choose.

–Theodore Seuss Giesel, a.k.a. Dr. Seuss, author of children's books including *Oh the Places You'll Go*

Step 1. Gain Awareness of Yourself

The goals you choose to pursue say a lot about who you are and what you want from life. Thus, self-awareness is a critical first step in the process of goal setting. You must know yourself before you can choose the goals you want to achieve. While this may seem obvious, self-awareness and self-discovery are often overlooked aspects of the goal-setting process. Deepening your self-awareness puts you in a better position to select and choose goals and to pursue a personal path that's true to who you are and what you want to become.

"Know thyself, and to thine own self be true."

–Plato, ancient Greek philosopher

> **Remember**
>
> Self-awareness is the first, most important step in the process of making any important life choice or decision. Good decisions are built on a deep understanding of one's self.

No one is in a better position to know who you are, and what you want to be, than *you*. One effective way to get to know yourself more deeply is through self-questioning. You can begin to deepen your self-awareness by asking yourself questions that can stimulate your thinking about your inner qualities and priorities. Effective self-questioning can launch you on an inward quest or journey to self-discovery and self-insight, which is the critical first step to effective goal setting. For example, if your long-range goal is career success, you can launch your voyage toward achieving this goal by asking yourself thought-provoking questions related to your personal:

- **Interests.** What you like to do;
- **Abilities and talents.** What you're good at doing; and
- **Values.** What you believe is worth doing.

The following questions are designed to sharpen your self-awareness with respect to your interests, abilities, and values. As you read each question, briefly note what thought or thoughts come to mind about yourself.

> "In order to succeed, you must know what you are doing, like what you are doing, and believe in what you are doing."
>
> –Will Rogers, Native American humorist and actor

Your Personal Interests

1. What tends to grab your attention and hold it for long periods?

2. What sorts of things are you naturally curious about or tend to intrigue you?

3. What do you enjoy and do as often as you possibly can?

4. What do you look forward to or get excited about?

5. What are your favorite hobbies or pastimes?

6. When you're with your friends, what do you like to talk about or spend time doing together?

7. What has been your most stimulating or enjoyable learning experience?

8. If you've had previous work or volunteer experience, what jobs or tasks did you find most enjoyable or stimulating?

9. When time seems to fly by for you, what are you usually doing?

10. What do you like to read about?

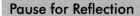

11. When you open a newspaper or log on to the Internet, what do you tend to read first?

12. When you find yourself daydreaming or fantasizing about your future life, what do you most find yourself doing?

Pause for Reflection

From your responses to the preceding questions, identify a long-range goal you could pursue that's compatible with your personal interests. In the space that follows, note the goal and the interests that are compatible with it.

Your Personal Abilities and Talents

1. What seems to come easily or naturally to you?

2. What would you say is your greatest or talent or personal gift?

3. What do you excel at when you apply yourself and put forth your best effort?

4. What are your most advanced or well-developed skills?

5. What would you say has been the greatest accomplishment or achievement in your life thus far?

6. What about yourself are you most proud of or do you take the most pride in doing?

7. When others come to you for advice or assistance, what is it usually for?

"Never desert your line of talent. Be what nature intended you for and you will succeed."

–Sydney Smith, eighteenth-century English writer and defender of the oppressed

8. What would your best friend or friends say is your best quality, trait, or characteristic?

9. When you had a strong feeling of being successful after you had done something, what was it that you did?

10. If you've received awards or other forms of recognition, what have you received them for?

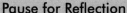

Pause for Reflection

From your responses to the preceding questions, identify a long-range goal you could pursue that's compatible with your personal abilities and talents. In the space that follows, note the goal and the abilities and talents that are compatible with it.

11. On what types of learning tasks or activities have you experienced the most success?

12. In what types of courses do you tend to earn the highest grades?

Your Personal Values

1. What matters most to you?

2. If you were to single out one thing you stand for or believe in, what would it be?

3. What would you say are your highest priorities in life?

4. What makes you feel good about what you're doing when you're doing it?

5. If there were one thing in the world you could change, improve, or make a difference in, what would it be?

6. When you have extra spending money, what do you usually spend it on?

7. When you have free time, what do you usually find yourself doing?

8. What does living a "good life" mean to you?

9. How would you define success? (What would it take for you to feel that you were successful?)

10. How would you define happiness? (What would it take for you to feel happy?)

11. Do you have any heroes or anyone you admire, look up to, or feel has set an example worth following? If yes, who and why?

> "Do what you value; value what you do."
>
> –Sidney Simon, author of *Values Clarification* (XXXX) and *In Search of Values*

Pause for Reflection

From your responses to the preceding questions, identify a long-range goal you could pursue that's compatible with your personal values. In the space that follows, note the goal and the values that are compatible with it.

12. How would you like others to see you? Rank these characteristics in the order of their priority for you (1 = highest, 4 = lowest).

- Smart _____

- Wealthy _____

- Creative _____

- Caring _____

Step 2. Gain Awareness of Your Options

The second critical step in the goal-setting process is to become aware of your long-range goal choices. For example, to effectively choose a career goal, you need to be aware of the careers options available to you and have a realistic understanding of the type of work done in these careers. To gain this knowledge, you'll need to capitalize on available resources, such as by doing the following:

1. Reading books about different careers
2. Taking career development courses
3. Interviewing people in different career fields
4. Observing (shadowing) people working in different careers

One characteristic of effective goal setting is to create goals that are realistic. In the case of careers, getting firsthand experience in actual work settings (e.g., shadowing, internships, volunteer services, and part-time work) would allow you to get a realistic view of what work is like in certain careers—as opposed to the idealized or fantasized way careers are portrayed on TV and in the movies.

"Students [may be] pushed into careers by their families, while others have picked one just to relieve their anxiety about not having a career choice. Still others may have picked popular or lucrative careers, knowing nothing of what they're really like or what it takes to prepare for them."

–Lee Upcraft, Joni Finney, and Peter Garland, student development specialists

Step 3. Gain Awareness of the Options That Best Fit You

In college, you'll have many educational options and career goals from which to choose. To deepen your awareness of what fields may be a good fit for you, take a course in that field to test out how well it matches your interests, values, talents, and learning style. Ideally, you want to select a field that closely taps into, or builds on, your strongest skills and talents. Choosing a field that's compatible with your strongest abilities should enable you to master the skills required by that field more deeply and efficiently. You're more likely to succeed or excel in a field that draws on your talents, and the success you experience will, in turn, strengthen your self-esteem, self-confidence, and drive to continue with it. You've probably heard of the proverb "If there's a will, there's a way" (i.e., when you're motivated, you're more likely to succeed). However, it's also true that "If there's a way, there's a will" (i.e., when you know how to do something well, you're more motivated to do it).

Student Perspective

"Making good grades and doing well in school helps my ego. It gives me confidence, and I like that feeling."

–First-year college student (Franklin, 2002)

Step 4. Gain Awareness of the Process

The fourth and final step in an effective goal-setting process is becoming aware of the steps needed to reach your goal. For example, if you've set the goal of achieving a college degree in a particular major, you need to be aware of the course requirements for a degree in that major. Similarly, to set a career goal, you need to know what major or majors lead to that career because some careers require a specific major but other careers may be entered through various majors.

Pause for Reflection

Think about a career you're considering and answer the following questions:

1. Why are you considering this career? What led or caused you to become interested in this choice? Why or why not?

2. Would you say that your interest in this career is motivated primarily by intrinsic factors (i.e., factors "inside" of you, such as your personal abilities, interests, needs, and values)? Or would you say that your interest in the career is motivated more heavily by extrinsic factors (i.e., factors "outside" of you, such as starting salary, pleasing parents, and meeting family expectations or societal expectations for your gender or ethnicity)?

Remember

The four-step process for effective goal setting applies to more than just educational goals. It's a strategic process that could and should be applied to any goal you set for yourself in life, at any stage of your life.

◆ Motivation: Moving Toward Your Long-Range Goals

The word "motivation" derives from the Latin *movere*, meaning "to move." Success comes to those who exert effort to move toward their goal. Knowledge of all kinds of success-promoting strategies, such as those discussed this text, provides only the potential for success; turning this potential into reality requires motivation, which converts knowledge into action. If you have all the knowledge, strategies, and skills for being successful but don't have the will to succeed, there's no way you will succeed. Studies show that without a strong personal commitment to attain a goal it will not be reached, no matter how well designed the goal and the plan to reach it are (Locke & Latham, 1990).

Motivation consists of three elements that may be summarized as the "three Ds" of motivation:

1. Drive
2. Discipline
3. Determination

Drive

Drive is the force within you that supplies you with the energy needed to overcome inertia and initiate action. Much like shifting into the drive gear is necessary to move your car forward, it takes personal drive to move forward and toward your goals.

People with drive aren't just dreamers: They're dreamers and doers. They take action to convert their dreams into reality, and they hustle—they go all out and give it their all, all of the time, to achieve their goals. College students with drive approach college with passion and enthusiasm. They don't hold back and work halfheartedly; they give 100 percent and put their whole heart and soul into the experience.

Discipline

Discipline includes such positive qualities as commitment, devotion, and dedication. These personal qualities enable you to keep going over an extended period. Successful people think big but start small—they take all the small steps and diligently do all the little things that need to be done, which in the long run add up to a big accomplishment: the achievement of their long-range goal.

People who are self-disciplined accept the day-to-day sweat, toil, and perspiration needed to attain their long-term aspirations. They're willing to tolerate short-term strain or pain for long-term gain. They have the self-control and self-restraint needed to resist the impulse for instant gratification or the temptation to do what they feel like doing instead of what they need to do. They're willing to sacrifice their immediate needs and desires in the short run to do what is necessary to put them where they want to be in the long run.

"Mere knowledge is not power; it is only possibility. Action is power; and its highest manifestation is when it is directed by knowledge."

–Francis Bacon, English philosopher, lawyer, and champion of modern science

"You can lead a horse to water, but you can't make him drink."

–Author unknown

"Education is not the filling of a pail, but the lighting of a fire."

–William Butler Yeats, Irish poet and playwright

"Success comes to those who hustle."

–Abraham Lincoln, 16th U.S. president and author of the Emancipation Proclamation, which set the stage for the abolition of slavery in the United States

Pause for Reflection

Think about something that you do with drive, effort, and intensity. What thoughts, attitudes, and behaviors do you display when you do it?

Do you see ways in which you could apply the same approach to your college experience?

! Remember

Sacrifices made for a short time can bring benefits lasting a lifetime.

The ability to delay short-term (and short-sighted) gratification is a distinctively human characteristic that differentiates people from other animals. As you can see in **Figure 4.1**, the upper frontal part of the brain that's responsible for long-range planning and controlling emotions and impulses is much larger in humans than it is in one of the most intelligent and human-like animals, the chimpanzee.

> "I long to accomplish some great and noble task, but it is my chief duty to accomplish small tasks as if they were great and noble."
>
> –Helen Keller, seeing- and hearing-impaired author and activist for the rights of women and the handicapped

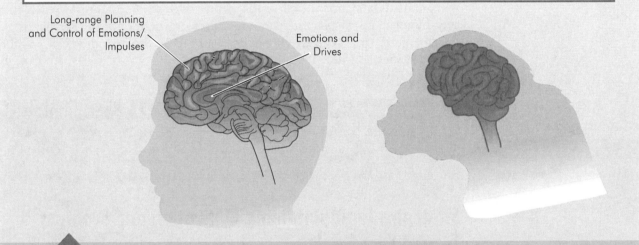

The part of the brain responsible for long-range planning and controlling emotions and impulses is much larger in humans than in other animals, including the highly intelligent chimpanzee.

Long-range Planning and Control of Emotions/ Impulses

Emotions and Drives

Figure 4.1   Where Thoughts, Emotions, and Drives are Experienced in the Brain

! Remember

Sometimes you've got to do what you have to do in order to get to do what you want to do.

Personal Story   When I entered college in the mid-1970s, I was a first-generation student from an extremely impoverished background. Not only did I have to work to pay for part of my education, but I also needed to assist my family financially. I stocked grocery store shelves at night during the week and waited tables at a local county club on the weekends. Managing my life, time, school, and work required full-time effort. However, I always understood that my purpose was to graduate from college and all of my other efforts supported that goal. Thus, I went to class and arrived on time even when I did not feel like going to class. One of my greatest successes in life was to keep my mind and body focused on the ultimate prize of getting a college education. That success has paid off many times over.

—*Aaron Thompson*

Studies show that individuals with dedication—who are deeply committed to what they do—are more likely to report that they are healthy and happy (Maddi, 2002; Myers, 1993).

Determination

People who are determined pursue their goals with a relentless tenacity. They have the fortitude to persist in the face of frustration and the resiliency to bounce back after setbacks. If they encounter something on the road to their goal that's hard to do, they work harder and longer to do it. When they encounter a major bump or barrier, they don't let it stand in their way by giving up or giving in; instead, they dig deeper and keep going.

People with determination are also more likely to seek out challenges. Research indicates that people who continue to pursue opportunities for personal growth and self-development throughout life are more likely to report feeling happy and healthy (Maddi, 2002; Myers, 1993). Rather than remaining stagnant and simply doing what's safe, secure, or easy, they stay hungry and display an ongoing commitment to personal growth and development; they keep striving and driving to be the best they can possibly be in all aspects of life.

Student Perspective

"Why is it so hard when I *have* to do something and so easy when I *want* to do something?"

—First-year college student

"Self-discipline is the ability to make yourself do the thing you have to do, when it ought be done, whether you like it or not."

—Thomas Henry Huxley, nineteenth-century English biologist

"If you are going through hell, keep going."

—Winston Churchill

"SUCCESS is peace of mind which is a direct result of self-satisfaction in knowing you made the effort to become the best that you are capable of becoming."

—John Wooden, college basketball coach and author of the *Pyramid of Success*

! Remember

On the highway to success, you can't be a passive passenger; you're the driver and at the wheel. Your goal setting will direct you there, and your motivation will drive you there.

Strategies for Maintaining Motivation and Progress Toward Your Goals

Reaching your goals requires will and energy; it also requires skill and strategy. Listed here are strategies for maintaining your motivation and commitment to reaching your goals.

Put your goals in writing. When you put your goals in writing, they become visible and memorable. Doing so can provide you with a sense of direction, a source of motivation for putting your plan into action, or a written contract with yourself that makes you more accountable to following through on your commitment.

Create a visual map of your goals. Lay out your goals in the form a flowchart to show the steps you'll be taking from your short- through your mid- to your long-range goals. Visual diagrams can help you "see" where you want to go, enabling you to connect where you are now and where you want to be. Diagramming can be energizing because it gives you a sneak preview of the finish line and a maplike overview of how to get there.

Keep a record of your progress. Research indicates that the act of monitoring and recording progress toward goals can increase motivation to continue pursuing them (Matsui, Okada, & Inoshita, 1983). The act of keeping records of your progress probably increases your motivation by giving you frequent feedback on your progress and positive reinforcement for staying on track and moving toward your target (long-range goal) (Bandura & Cervone, 1983;

Schunk, 1995). For example, you can keep a journal of the goals you've reached. Your entries can keep you motivated by supplying you with concrete evidence of your progress and commitment. You can also chart or graph your progress, which can sometimes provide a powerful visual display of your upward trends and patterns. Place it where you see it regularly to keep your goals in your sight and on your mind.

Develop a skeletal résumé of your goals. Include your goals as separate sections or categories that will be fleshed out as you complete them. Your to-be-completed résumé can provide a framework or blueprint for organizing, building, and tracking progress toward your goals. It can also serve as a visual reminder of the things you plan to accomplish and eventually showcase to potential employers. Furthermore, every time you look at your growing résumé, you'll be reminded of your past accomplishments, which can energize and motivate you to reach your goals. As you fill in and build up your résumé, you can literally see how much you've achieved, which boosts your self-confidence and motivation to continue achieving. (See Chapter 14, for a sample skeletal résumé.)

Reward yourself for making steady progress toward your long-range goals. Reward is already built into reaching your long-range goal because it represents the end of your trip, which lands you at your desired destination (e.g., in a successful career). However, short- and mid-range goals may not be desirable ends in themselves but rather means to a desirable end (your long-range goal). Consequently, you need to intentionally reward yourself for landing on these smaller stepping stones up the path to your long-range goal. When you complete these short- and mid-range goals, record and reward your accomplishments (e.g., celebrate your successful completion of midterms or finals by treating yourself to something you enjoy).

A habit of perseverance and persistence through all intermediate steps needed to reach a long-range goal, like any other habit, is more likely to continue if it's followed by a reward (positive reinforcement). Setting small goals, moving steadily toward them, and rewarding yourself for reaching them are components of a simple but powerful strategy. This strategy will help you maintain motivation over the extended period needed to reach a long-range goal.

Capitalize on available campus resources that can help you stay on track and move toward your goal. Research indicates that college success results from a combination of what students do for themselves (personal responsibility) and what they do to capitalize on the resources available to them (resourcefulness; Pascarella & Terenzini, 1991, 2005). Successful college students are resourceful students; they seek out and take advantage of college resources to help them reach their goals.

For example, a resourceful student who's having trouble deciding what field of study to pursue for a degree will seek assistance from an academic advisor on campus. A resourceful student who's interested in a particular career but is unclear about the best educational path to take toward that career will use the Career Development Center as a resource.

Use your social resources. The power of social support groups for helping people achieve personal goals is well documented by research in various fields (Ewell, 1997; Moeller, 1999). You can use the power of people by surrounding yourself with peers who are committed to successfully achieving their educational goals and by avoiding "toxic" people who are likely to poison your plans or dampen your dreams.

"Life isn't a matter of milestones but of moments."

–Rose Fitzgerald Kennedy, philanthropist and mother of John F. and Robert F. Kennedy

"Willpower is the personal strength and discipline, rooted in strong motivation, to carry out your plans. 'Waypower' is the exertion of willpower that helps you find resources and support."

–Jerry Pattengale, history professor and author of The Purpose-Guided Student: Dream to Succeed

> "Develop an inner circle of close associations in which the mutual attraction is not sharing problems or needs. The mutual attraction should be values and goals."
>
> —Denis Waitley, former mental trainer for U.S. Olympic athletes and author of *Seeds of Greatness*

> "I make progress by having people around who are smarter than I am."
>
> —Henry Kaiser, successful industrialist known as the father of American shipbuilding

Pause for Reflection

What would you say is the biggest setback or obstacle you've overcome in your life thus far?

How did you overcome it? (What enabled you to get past it or prevented you from being blocked by it?)

> "We are what we think."
>
> —Hindu Prince Siddhartha Gautama, a.k.a. Buddha, founder of the philosophy and religion of Buddhism

> "What happens is not as important as how you react to what happens."
>
> —Thaddeus Golas, *Lazy Man's Guide to Enlightenment*

For example, find a supportive and motivating friend and make a mutual pact to help each other reach your respective goals. This step could be taken to a more formal level by drawing up a "social contract" whereby you and your partner are "cowitnesses" or designated social-support agents whose role is to help each other stay on track and move toward long-range goals. Studies show that making a public commitment to a goal increases your commitment to it, probably because it becomes a matter of personal pride and integrity that's seen not only through your own eyes but also through the eyes of others (Hollenbeck, Williams, & Klein, 1989).

Convert setbacks into comebacks. The type of thoughts you have after experiencing a setback can affect your emotional reaction to it and the action you take in response. For instance, what you think about a poor performance (e.g., a poor test grade) can affect your emotional reaction to that grade and what action, or lack of action, you take in response to it. You can react to the poor grade by knocking yourself down with a putdown ("I'm a loser") or by building yourself back up with a positive pep talk ("I'm going to learn from my mistakes on this test and rebound with a stronger performance on the next one").

If a poor past performance is seen not as a personal failure but as learning opportunity, the setback may be turned into a comeback. Here are some notable people who turned early setbacks into successful comebacks:

- Louis Pasteur, famous bacteriologist, who failed his admission test to the University of Paris;
- Albert Einstein, Nobel Prize–winning physicist, who failed math in elementary school;
- Thomas Edison, prolific inventor, who was once expelled from school as "uneducable";
- Johnny Unitas, Hall of Fame football player, who was cut twice from professional football teams early in his career.

In response to their early setbacks, these successful people didn't get bitter; they got better. Getting mad or sad about a setback is likely to make you stressed or depressed and leave you focused on a past event that you can no longer control. By reacting rationally to a poor performance and using the results as feedback to improve your future performance, you gain control of it. You put yourself in the position to convert the setback into a comeback and turn a liability into an opportunity.

This can be a challenging task because when you have an experience, your response to it passes through emotional areas of the brain before it reaches areas of the brain involved in rational thinking and reasoning (see **Figure 4.2**; LeDoux, 1998).

Thus, your brain reacts to events emotionally before it does rationally. If the experience triggers intense emotions (e.g., anger, anxiety, or sadness after receiving a bad test grade), your emotional reaction has the potential to short-circuit or wipe out rational thinking. Thus, if you find yourself beginning to feel overwhelmed by negative emotions following a setback, you need to consciously and quickly block them by rational thoughts (e.g., thinking or saying to yourself, "Before I get carried away emotionally, let me think this through rationally"). This involves more than simply saying, "I have to think positively." Instead, you should develop a set of specific counterthinking strategies ready to use as soon as you begin to think negatively. Described here are thinking strategies that you can use to maintain motivation and minimize negative thinking in reaction to setbacks.

Whatever you do, don't let setbacks make you mad or sad, particularly at early stages in your college experience, because you're just beginning to learn what it takes to be successful in college. A bad

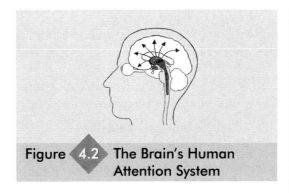

Figure **4.2** The Brain's Human Attention System

Information passes through the emotional center of the brain (lower, shaded area) before reaching the center responsible for rational thinking (upper area). Thus, people need to counteract their tendency to respond emotionally and irrationally to personal setbacks by making a conscious attempt to respond rationally and reflectively.

performance can be turned into a good learning experience by using the results as an error detector for identifying sources or causes of your mistakes and as feedback for improving your future performance.

Remember

Don't let past mistakes bring you down emotionally or motivationally; however, don't ignore or neglect them either. Instead, inspect them, reflect on them, and correct them so that they don't happen again.

"When written in Chinese, the word 'crisis' is composed of two characters. One represents danger, and the other represents opportunity."

–John F. Kennedy, 35th U.S. president

Maintain positive expectations. Just as your thoughts in reaction to something that's already taken place can affect your motivation, so can thoughts about what you expect to happen next affect what will occur. Your expectations of things to come can be either positive or negative. For example, before a test you could think, "I'm poised, confident, and ready to do it." Or you could think, "I know I'm going to fail this test; I just know it."

Expectations can lead to what sociologists and psychologists have called a self-fulfilling prophecy—a positive or negative expectation leads you to act in a way that is consistent with your expectation, which, in turn, makes your expectation come true. For instance, if you expect you're going to fail an exam ("What's the use? I'm going to fail anyway."), you're less likely to put as much effort into studying for the test. During the test, your negative expectation is likely reduce your test confidence and elevate you test anxiety; for example, if you experience difficulty with the first item on a test, you may get anxious and begin to think you're going to have difficulty with all remaining items and flunk the entire exam. All of this negative thinking is likely to increase the probability that your expectation of doing poorly on the exam will become a reality.

In contrast, positive expectations can lead to a positive self-fulfilling prophecy: If you expect to do well on an exam, you're more likely to demonstrate higher levels of effort, confidence, and concentration, all of which combine to increase the likelihood that you'll earn a higher test grade. Research shows that learning and practicing positive self-talk increase a sense of hope—a belief in the ability to reach goals and the ability to actually reach them (Snyder, 1994).

"Whether you think you can or you can't, you're right."

–Henry Ford, founder of Ford Motor and one of the richest people of his generation

Pause for Reflection

Would you consider yourself to be an optimist or a pessimist?

In what situations are you more likely to think optimistically and pessimistically?

Why?

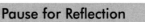

"A pessimist sees the difficulty in every opportunity; an optimist sees the opportunity in every difficulty."

–Winston Churchill

"Many people take no care of their money 'til they come nearly to the end of it, and others do just the same with their time."

–Johann Wolfgang von Goethe, German poet, dramatist, and author of the epic *Faust*

"You've got to think about 'big things' while you're doing small things, so that all the small things go in the right direction."

–Alvin Toffler, American futurologist and author who predicted the future effects of technology on our society

Keep your eye on the prize. Don't lose sight of the long-term consequences of your short-term choices and decisions. Long-range thinking is the key to reaching long-range goals. Unfortunately, however, humans are often more motivated by short-range thinking because it produces quicker results and more immediate gratification. It's more convenient and tempting to think in the short term ("I like it. I want it. I want it now."). Studies show that the later consequences occur, the less likely people are to consider those consequences when they make their decisions (Ainslie, 1975; Elster & Lowenstein, 1992; Lewin, 1935). For example, choosing to do what you feel like doing instead of doing work that needs to be done is why so many people procrastinate, and choosing to use a credit card to get something now instead of saving money to buy it later is why so many people pile up credit-card debt.

To be successful in the long run, you need to keep your focus on the big picture—your long-range goals and dreams that provide your motivation. At the same time, you need to focus on the details—the due dates, to-do lists, and day-to-day duties that require perspiration but keep you on track and going in the right direction.

Thus, setting an important life goal and steadily progressing toward that long-range goal requires two means of focusing. One is a narrow-focus lens that allows you to view the details immediately in front of you. The other is a wide-focus lens that gives you a big-picture view of what's further ahead of you (your long-range goal). Success involves seeing the connection between the small, short-term chores and challenges (e.g., completing an assignment that's due next week) and the large, long-range picture (e.g., college graduation and a successful future). Thus, you need to periodically shift from a wide-focus lens that gives you a vision of the bigger, more distant picture to a narrow-focus lens that shifts your attention to completing the smaller tasks immediately ahead of you and keeping on the path to your long-range goal: future success.

Personal Story

When I was an assistant coach for a youth soccer team, I noticed that many of the less successful players tended to make one of two mistakes when they were trying to move with the ball. Some spent too much time looking down, focusing on the ball at their feet and trying to be sure that they did not lose control of it. By not lifting their head and looking ahead periodically, they often missed open territory, open teammates, or an open goal. Other unsuccessful players made the opposite mistake: They spent too much time with their heads up, trying to see saw where they were headed. By not looking down at the ball immediately in front of them, they often lost control of the ball, moved ahead without it, or sometimes stumbled over it and fell flat on their face. Successful soccer players on the team were in the habit of shifting their focus between looking down to maintain control of the ball immediately in front of them and lifting their eyes to see where they were headed.

The more I thought about how successful players alternate between handling the ball in front of them and viewing the goal further ahead, it struck me that this was a metaphor for success in life. Successful people alternate between both of these perspectives so that they don't lose sight of how completing the short-range tasks in front of them connects with the long-range goal ahead of them.

—Joe Cuseo

> **Remember**
>
> Keep your future dreams and current tasks in clear focus. Integrating these two perspectives will produce an image that can provide you with the inspiration to complete your college education and the determination to complete your day-to-day tasks.

> "Whoever wants to reach a distant goal must take many small steps."
>
> —Helmut Schmidt, former chancellor of West Germany

◆ Personal Character

Reaching your goals depends on acquiring and using effective strategies, but it takes something more. Ultimately, success emerges from the inside out; it flows from positive qualities or attributes found within you, which, collectively, form your personal character.

We become successful and effective humans when our actions and deeds become a natural extension of who we are and how we live. At first, developing the habits associated with achieving success and leading a productive life may require effort and intense concentration because these behaviors may be new to you. However, if these actions occur consistently enough, they're transformed into natural habits.

When you engage in effective habits regularly, they become virtues. A virtue may be defined as a characteristic or trait that is valued as good or admirable, and someone who possesses a collection of important virtues is said to be a person of character (Peterson & Seligman, 2004).

Three virtues in particular are important for success in college and beyond:

1. Wisdom
2. Integrity
3. Civility

> "If you do not find it within yourself, where will you go to get it?"
>
> —Zen saying (Zen is a branch of Buddhism that emphasizes seeing deeply into the nature of things and ongoing self-awareness)

> "We are what we repeatedly do. Excellence, then, is not an act, but a habit."
>
> —Aristotle, ancient Greek philosopher

Wisdom

When you use the knowledge you acquire to guide your behavior toward doing what is effective or good, you demonstrate wisdom (Staudinger & Baltes, 1994). For example, if you apply your knowledge of the four research-based principles found in this book (i.e., active involvement, resourcefulness, collaboration, and reflection) to guide your behavior in college, you are exhibiting wisdom.

> "Sow an act and you reap a habit; sow a habit and you reap a character; sow a character and you reap a destiny."
>
> —Frances E. Willard, nineteenth-century American educator and woman's rights activist

Integrity

The word "integrity" comes from the same root as the word "integrate," which captures a key characteristic of people with integrity: their outer self is integrated or in harmony with their inner self. For example, "outer-directed" people decide on their personal standards of conduct by looking outward to see what others are doing (Riesman, Glazer, & Denney, 2001). In contrast, individuals with integrity are "inner directed"—their actions reflect their inner qualities and are guided by their conscience.

People with character are not only wise but also ethical. Besides doing what effective, they do what is good or right. They don't pursue success at any ethical cost. They have a strong set of personal values that guide them in the right moral direction.

> "As gold which he cannot spend will make no man rich, so knowledge which he cannot apply will make no man wise."
>
> —Dr. Samuel Johnson, famous English literary figure and original author of the *Dictionary of the English Language* (1747)

For example, college students with integrity don't cheat and then rationalize that their cheating is acceptable because "others are doing it." They don't look to other people to determine their own values, and they don't conform to the norm if the norm is wrong; instead, they look inward and let their conscience be their guide.

Civility

People of character are personally and socially responsible. They model what it means to live in a civilized community by demonstrating civility—they respect the rights of other members of their community, including members of their college community. In exercising their own rights and freedoms, they don't step (or stomp) on the rights and freedoms of others. People with civic character not only behave civilly but also treat other members of their community in a sensitive and courteous manner and are willing to confront others who violate the rights of their fellow citizens. They are model citizens whose actions visibly demonstrate to others that they oppose any attempt to disrespect or interfere with the rights of fellow members of their community.

Insensitive Use of Personal Technology in the Classroom: A Violation of Civility

Behavior that interferes with the rights of others to learn or teach in the college classroom represents a violation of civility. Listed here are behaviors illustrating classroom incivility that involve student use of personal technology. These behaviors are increasing in college, as is the anger of college instructors who witness them, so it is wise to avoid engaging in them.

1. **Leave your cell phone off or outside the classroom.** Keeping a cell phone on in class is a clear example of classroom incivility because if it rings it will interfere with the right of others to learn. In a study of college students who were exposed to a cell phone ringing during a class session and were later tested for their recall of information presented in class, they scored approximately 25 percent worse when attempting to recall information that was presented at the time a cell phone rang. This attention loss occurred even when the material was covered by the professor before the cell phone rang and was projected on a slide during the call. This study showed that students were further distracted when classmates frantically searched through a bag or pockets to find and silence a ringing (or vibrating) phone (Shelton, Elliot, Eaves, & Exner, 2009). These findings clearly suggest that the civil thing to do is turn your cell phone off before entering the classroom or keep it out of the classroom altogether.

2. **Save text messaging until after class.** Just as answering a cell phone during class represents a violation of civility because it interferes with the learning of other members of the classroom community, so too does text messaging. Although messaging is often viewed it as a quick and soundless way to communicate, it can momentarily disrupt learning if it takes place when the instructor is covering critical or complex information. Text messaging while driving a car can take your eyes and mind

Pause for Reflection

Thus far in your college experience, which of the following four principles of success have you put into practice most effectively? (Circle one.)

active involvement   resourcefulness
collaboration   reflection

Which of the four principles do you think will be the most difficult for you to put into practice? (Circle one.)

active involvement   resourcefulness
collaboration   reflection

Why?

Student Perspective

"To achieve success through deceitful actions is not success at all. In life, credibility is more important than credentials, and if honesty is not valued personally, others will not value you. Lack of self-respect results in lack of respect from others."

–First-year college student's reflection on an academic integrity violation

"There is no pillow as soft as a clear conscience."

–French proverb

"Our character is what we do when we think no one is looking."

–Henry David Thoreau, American philosopher and lifelong abolitionist who championed the human spirit over materialism and conformity off the road, thereby putting yourself and others in danger. Similarly, messaging in the classroom takes your eyes and mind off the instructor and any visual aids being displayed at the time. It's also discourteous or disrespectful to instructors when you put your head down and turn your attention from them while they're speaking to the class. Finally, it can be distracting or disturbing to classmates who see you messaging instead of listening and learning.

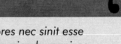

Emollit mores nec sinit esse feros. ("Learning humanizes character and does not permit it to be cruel.")
—Motto of the University of South Carolina

◆ Summary and Conclusion

Goal setting only becomes meaningful if you have motivation to reach the goals you set. Motivation may be said to consist of three Ds: drive, discipline, and determination. Drive is the internal force that gives you the energy to overcome inertia and initiate action. Discipline consists of positive, personal qualities such as commitment, devotion, and dedication that enable you to sustain your effort over time. Determination enables you to relentlessly pursue your goals, persist in the face of frustration, and bounce back after any setback.

Reaching your goals requires all three Ds; it also involves the use of effective self-motivational strategies, such as:

Pause for Reflection

Have you observed an example of personal integrity that you thought was exceptionally admirable or particularly despicable?

What was the situation, and what was done that demonstrated integrity or an integrity violation?

- Visualizing reaching your long-range goals;
- Putting goals in writing;
- Creating a visual map of your goals;
- Keeping a record of your progress;
- Developing a skeletal résumé;
- Rewarding yourself for progress toward long-range goals;
- Capitalizing on available campus and social resources;

Snapshot Summary

4.1

Guidelines for Civil and Responsible Use of Personal Technology in the College Classroom

- Turn your cell phone completely off or leave it out of the classroom. In the rare case of an emergency when you think you need to leave it on, inform you instructor.
- Don't check your cell phone during the class period by turning it on and off.
- Don't text message during class.
- Don't surf the Web during class.
- Don't touch your cell phone during any exam because this may be viewed by the instructor as a form of cheating.

> "The right to do something does not mean that doing it is right."
>
> –William Safire, American author, journalist, and presidential speech writer

- Converting setbacks into comebacks by using positive self-talk, maintaining positive expectations, and avoiding negative self-fulfilling prophecies; and
- Keeping your eye on the long-term consequences of your short-term choices and decisions.

To reach your goals you must acquire and use effective strategies, but you also need character. Three character traits or virtues are particularly important for college and life success:

- **Wisdom.** Using knowledge to guide your behavior toward effective or good actions.
- **Integrity.** Doing what is ethical. Plagiarism, or giving readers the impression (intentionally or not) that someone else's work is your own, is a violation of academic integrity.
- **Civility.** Respecting the rights of other members of your college and larger communities. Violations of civility include insensitive use of personal technology in the classroom (e.g., using cell phones and text messaging).

Studies of highly successful people, whether scientists, musicians, writers, chess masters, or basketball stars, consistently show that achieving high levels of skill and success requires practice (Levitin, 2006). This is true even of people whose success is thought to be to be due to natural gifts or talents. For example, during the Beatles' first 4 years as a band and before they burst into musical stardom, they performed live an estimated 1,200 times, and many of these performances lasted 5 or more hours a night. They performed (practiced) for more hours during those first 4 years than most bands perform during their entire career. Similarly, before Bill Gates became a computer software giant and creator of Microsoft, he logged almost 1,600 hours of computer time during one 7-month period alone, averaging 8 hours a day, 7 days a week (Gladwell, 2008).

What these extraordinary success stories show is that it takes time and practice for effective skills to take hold and take effect. Reaching long-range goals means making small steps; they aren't achieved in one quick, quantum leap. If you are patient and persistent and consistently practice effective strategies, their positive effects will gradually accumulate and eventually have a significant impact on your success in college and beyond.

Remember

Success isn't a short-range goal; it's not a sprint but a long-distance run that takes patience and perseverance to complete. What matters most is not how fast you start but where you finish.

Learning More Through the World Wide Web

Internet-Based Resources for Further Information on Liberal Arts Education

For additional information related to the ideas discussed in this chapter, we recommend the following Web sites:

Goal Setting: www.siue.edu/SPIN/activity.html

Self-Motivational Strategies: www.selfmotivationstrategies.com

Academic Integrity and Character Development: www.academicintegrity.org/useful_links/index.php

4.1 Prioritizing Important Life Goals

Consider the following life goals. Rank them in the order of their priority for you (1 = highest, 5 = lowest).

___ Emotional well-being

___ Spiritual growth

___ Physical health

___ Social relationships

___ Rewarding career

Self-Assessment Questions

1. What were the primary reasons behind your first- and last-ranked choices?

2. Have you established any short- or mid-range goals for reaching your highest-ranked choice? If yes, what are they? If no, what could they be?

4.2 Setting Goals for Reducing the Gap Between the Ideal Scenario and the Current Reality

Think of an aspect of your life with a gap between what you hoped it would be (the ideal) and what it is (the reality). On the lines that follow, identify goals you could purse that would reduce this gap.

Long-range goal: _____

Mid-range goal: _____

Short-range goal: _____

Use the form that follows to identify strategies for reaching each of these three goals. Consider the following areas for each goal:

- Actions to be taken
- Available resources
- Possible roadblocks
- Potential solutions to roadblocks

Long-range goal: _____

- Actions to be taken:

- Available resources:

- Possible roadblocks:

- Potential solutions to roadblocks:

Mid-range goal: _____

- Actions to be taken:

- Available resources:

- Possible roadblocks:

- Potential solutions to roadblocks:

Short-range goal: _____

- Actions to be taken:

- Available resources:

- Possible roadblocks:

- Potential solutions to roadblocks:

4.3 Converting Setbacks into Comebacks: Transforming Pessimism into Optimism

In Hamlet, Shakespeare wrote: "There is nothing good or bad, but thinking makes it so." His point was that experiences have the potential to be positive or negative, depending on how people interpret them and react to them.

Listed here is a series of statements representing negative interpretations and reactions to a situation or experience:

1. "I'm just not good at this."

2. "There's nothing I can do about it."

3. "Things will never be the same."

4. "Nothing is going to change."

5. "This always happens to me."

6. "This is unbearable."

7. "Everybody is going to think I'm a loser."

8. "I'm trapped, and there's no way out."

For each of the preceding statements, replace the negative statement with a statement that represents a more positive interpretation or reaction.

No Goals, No Direction

Amy Aimless decided to go to college because it seemed like that's what she was expected to do. All of her closest friends were going and her parents have talked to her about going to college as long as she can remember.

Now that she's in her first term, Amy isn't sure she made the right decision. She has no educational or career goals, nor does she have any idea about what her major might be. None of the subjects she took in high school and none of the courses she's taking in her first term of college have really sparked her interest. Since she has no goals or sense of purpose, she's beginning to think that being in college is a waste of time and money, so she's considering withdrawing at the end of her first term.

Reflection and Discussion Questions

1. What advice would you give Amy about whether she should remain in college or withdraw?

2. What suggestion would you have for Amy that might help her find some sense of educational purpose or direction?

3. How could you counter Amy's claim that no subjects interest her as a possible college major?

4. Would you agree that Amy is currently wasting her time and her parents' money? Why?

5. Would you agree that Amy shouldn't have begun college in the first place? Why?

Time Management

5

ACTIVATE YOUR THINKING   Journal Entry   5.1

Complete the following sentence with the first thought that comes to your mind:

For me, time is . . .

_____

_____

_____

LEARNING GOAL

To help you appreciate the significance of managing time and supply you with a powerful set of time-management strategies that can be used to promote your success in college and beyond.

The Importance of Time Management

For many first-year students, the beginning of college means the beginning of more independent living and self-management. Even if you've lived on your own for some time, managing time is an important skill to possess because you're likely juggling multiple responsibilities, including school, family, and work.

In college, the academic calendar and your class schedule differ radically from those during high school. You have less "seat time" in class each week and more "free time" outside of class, which you have the freedom to self-manage; it is not closely monitored by school authorities or family members, and you are expected to do more academic work on your own outside of class. Time-management skills grow in importance when a person's time is less structured or controlled by others, leaving the individual with more decision-making power about how to spend personal time. Thus, it is no surprise that research shows the ability to manage time effectively as playing a crucial role in college success (Erickson, Peters, & Strommer, 2006).

Simply stated, college students who have difficulty managing their time have difficulty managing college. In one study, sophomores who had an outstanding first year in college (both academically and socially) were compared with another group of sophomores who struggled during the prior year. Interviews conducted with these students revealed one key difference between the two groups: The sophomores who experienced a successful first year repeatedly brought up the topic of time during the interviews. The successful

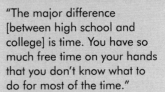

Student Perspective

"The major difference [between high school and college] is time. You have so much free time on your hands that you don't know what to do for most of the time."

–First-year college student (Erickson & Strommer, 1991)

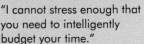

Student Perspective

"I cannot stress enough that you need to intelligently budget your time."

–Advice to new college students from a first-year student

From "Thriving in College and Beyond" by Cuseo, Fecas, Thompson. © Kendall Hunt Publishing.

students said they had to think carefully about how they spent their time and that they needed to budget their time because it was a scarce resource. In contrast, the sophomores who experienced difficulty in their first year of college hardly talked about the topic of time during their interviews, even when they were specifically asked about it (Light, 2001).

Studies also indicate that managing time plays a pivotal role in the lives of working adults. Setting priorities and balancing multiple responsibilities (e.g., work and family) that compete for limited time and energy can be a juggling act and a source of stress for people of all ages (Harriott & Ferrari, 1996).

For these reasons, time management should be viewed not only as a college-success strategy but also as a life-management and life-success skill. Studies show that people who manage their time well report they are more in control of their life and are happier (Myers, 1993). In short, when you gain greater control of your time, you become more satisfied with your life.

Personal Story

I started the process of earning my doctorate a little later in life than other students. I was a married father with a preschool daughter (Sara). Since my wife left for work early in the morning, it was always my duty to get up and get Sara's day going in the right direction. In addition, I had to do the same for me—which was often harder than doing it for my daughter. Three days of my week were spent on campus in class or in the library. (We did not have quick access to research on home computers then as you do now.) The other two days of the workweek and the weekend were spent on household chores, family time, and studying.

I knew that if I was going to have any chance of finishing my Ph.D in a reasonable amount of time and have a decent family life I had to adopt an effective schedule for managing my time. Each day of the week, I held to a strict routine. I got up in the morning, drank coffee while reading the paper, took a shower, got Sara ready for school, and took her to school. Once I returned home, I put a load of laundry in the washer, studied, wrote, and spent time concentrating on what I needed to do to be successful from 8:30 a.m. to 12:00 p.m. every day. At lunch, I had a pastrami and cheese sandwich and a soft drink while rewarding myself by watching *Perry Mason* reruns until 1:00 p.m. I then continued to study until it was time to pick up Sara from school. Each night I spent time with my wife and daughter and prepared for the next day. I lived a life that had a preset schedule. By following this schedule, I was able to successfully complete my doctorate in a decent amount of time while giving my family the time they needed. (By the way, I still watch *Perry Mason* reruns.)

—Aaron Thompson

Strategies for Managing Time

You can use a series of strategies to manage your time:

1. **Analyzing.** Breaking down time into segments and work into specific tasks;
2. **Itemizing.** Identifying what you need to accomplish and when it needs to be done;
3. **Prioritizing.** Organizing your tasks based on their importance.

The following steps can help you discover time you did not know you had and use the time you have more wisely.

1. Break down your time and become more aware about how it's spent.

Have you ever asked yourself "Where did all the time go?" or told yourself "I just can't seem to find the time"? One way to find out where your time went is by taking a time inventory (Webber, 1991). To do this, you conduct a time analysis by breaking down and tracking your time, recording what you do and when you do it. By mapping out how you spend time, you become more aware of how much total time you have available to you and how its component parts are used, including patches of wasted time in which you get little or nothing accomplished. You don't have to do this time analysis for more than a week or two. This should be long enough to give you some sense of where your time is going and allow you to start developing strategies for using your time more effectively and efficiently.

> **Pause for Reflection**
>
> Do you have time gaps between your classes this term? If you do, what have you been doing during those periods?
>
> What would you say is your greatest time waster?
>
> Do you see a need to stop or eliminate it?
>
> If no, why not? If yes, what would you like to see yourself doing instead?

2. Identify which tasks you need to accomplish and when you need to accomplish them.

People make lists to be sure they don't forget items they need from the grocery store or people they want to be sure are invited to a party. You can use the same list-making strategy for work tasks so that you don't forget to do them or forget to do them on time. Studies of effective people show that they are list makers and they write out lists not only for grocery items and wedding invitations but also for things they want to accomplish each day (Covey, 1990).

> *"Doesn't thou love life? Then do not squander time, for that is the stuff life is made of."*
>
> –Benjamin Franklin, eighteenth-century inventor, newspaper writer, and cosigner of the *Declaration of Independence*

You can itemize your tasks by listing them in either of the following time-management tools:

- **Small, portable planner.** List all your major assignments and exams for the term, along with their due dates. By pulling all work tasks from different courses in one place, it is easier to keep track of what you have to do and when you have to do it.
- **Large, stable calendar.** Record in the calendar's date boxes your major assignments for the academic term and when they are due. Place the calendar in a position or location where it's in full view and you can't help but see it every day (e.g., on your bedroom or refrigerator door). If you regularly and literally "look" at the things you have to do, you're less likely to "overlook" them, forget about them, or subconsciously push them out of your mind.

Using a personal planner is an effective way to itemize your academic commitments.

© Gary Woodward, 2010. Under license from Shutterstock, Inc.

3. Rank your tasks in order of their importance.

Once you've itemized your work by listing all tasks you need to do, prioritize them—determine the order in which you will do them. Prioritizing basically involves ranking your tasks in terms of their importance, with the highest-ranked tasks appearing at the top of your list to ensure that they are tackled first. How do you determine which tasks are most important and should be ranked highest? Two criteria or standards of judgment can be used to help determine which tasks should be your priorities:

- **Urgency.** Tasks that are closest to their deadline or due date should receive high priority. For example, finishing an assignment that's due tomorrow should receive higher priority than starting an assignment that's due next month.

Personal Story

My mom was the person who ensured I got up for school on time. Once I got to school the bell would ring to let me know to move on to the next class. When I returned home I had to do my homework and chores. My daily and weekly schedules were dictated by someone else.

When I entered college, I quickly realized that I needed to develop my own system for being organized, focused, and productive without the assistance of my mother. Since I came from a modest background, I had to work my way through college. Juggling schedules became an art and science for me. I knew the things that I could not miss, such as work and school, and the things I could miss—TV and girls. (OK, TV, but not girls.)

After college, I spent 10 years in business—a world where I was measured by being on time and a productive "bottom line." It was during this time that I discovered a scheduling book. When I became a professor, I had other mechanisms to make sure I did what I needed to do when I needed to do it. This was largely based on when my classes were offered. Other time was dedicated to working out and spending time with my family. Now, as an administrator, I have an assistant who keep my schedule for me. She tells me where I am going, how long I should be there, and what I need to accomplish while I am there. Unless you take your parents with you or have the luxury of a personal assistant, it's important to determine which activities are required and to allow time in your schedule for fun. Use a planner!

—Aaron Thompson

Pause for Reflection

Do you have a calendar for the current academic term that you carry with you?

If yes, why? If no, why not?

If you carry neither a calendar nor a work list, why do you think you don't?

Student Perspective

"I like to get rid of my stress by doing what I have to do first, like if it's a paper."

–First-year college student

• **Gravity.** Tasks that carry the heaviest weight (count the most) should receive highest priority. For example, if an assignment worth 100 points and another worth 10 points are due at the same time, the 100-point task should receive higher priority. You want to be sure you invest your work time on tasks that matter most. Just like investing money, you want to invest your time on tasks that yield the greatest dividends or payoff.

One strategy for prioritizing your tasks is to divide them into A, B, and C lists (Lakein, 1973). The A list is for *essential* tasks—what you *must* do now. The B list is for *important* tasks—what you *should* do soon. Finally, the C list is for *optional* tasks—what you *could* or *might* do if there is time remaining after you've completed the tasks on the A and B lists. Organizing your tasks in this fashion can help you decide how to divide your labor in a way that ensures you put first things first. What you don't want to do is waste time doing unimportant things and deceive yourself into thinking that you're keeping busy and getting things done when actually you're doing things that just take your time (and mind) away from the more important things that should be done.

At first glance, itemizing and prioritizing may appear to be rather boring chores. However, if you look at these mental tasks carefully, they require many higher-level thinking skills, such as

1. **Analysis.** Dividing time into component elements or segments and breaking down work into specific tasks;
2. **Evaluation.** Critically evaluating the relative importance or value of tasks; and
3. **Synthesis.** Organizing individual tasks into classes or categories based on their level of priority.

Thus, developing self-awareness about how you spend time is more than a menial, clerical task; when done with thoughtful reflection, it's an exercise in higher-level thinking. It's also a good exercise in values clarification because what people choose to spend their time on is a more accurate indicator of what they truly value rather than what they say they value.

Develop a Time-Management Plan

Humans are creatures of habit. Routines help you organize and gain control of your lives. Doing things by design, rather than leaving them to chance or accident, is the first step toward making things happen for you rather than allowing them to happen you—by chance or accident. By developing an intentional plan for how you're going to spend your time, you're developing a plan to gain greater control of your life.

Don't buy into the myth that you don't have time to plan because it takes too much time that could be spent getting started and getting things done. Time-management experts estimate that the amount of time you spend planning your work reduces your total work time by a factor of three (Lakein, 1973). In other words, for every one unit of time you spend planning, you save three units of work time. Thus, 5 minutes of planning time will typically save you 15 minutes of total work time, and 10 minutes of planning time will save you 30 minutes of work time. This saving of work time probably occurs because you develop a clearer game plan or plan of attack for identifying what needs to be done and the best order in which to get it done. A clearer sense of direction reduces the number of mistakes you may make due to false starts—starting the work but then having to restart it because you started off in the wrong direction. If you have no plan of attack, you're more likely to go off track; when you discover this at some point after you've started, you're then forced to retreat and start over.

As the proverb goes, "A stitch in time saves nine." Planning your time represents the "stitch" (unit of time) that saves you nine additional stitches (units of time). Similar to successful chess players, successful time managers plan ahead and anticipate their next moves.

"Time = Life. Therefore waste your time and waste your life, or master your time and master your life."

–Alan Lakein, international expert on time management and author of the best-selling book *How to Get Control of Your Time and Your Life* (1973)

"Failing to plan is planning to fail."

–Alan Lakein

Elements of a Comprehensive Time-Management Plan

Once you've accepted the notion that taking the time to plan your time saves you time in the long run, you're ready to design a time-management plan. The following are elements of a comprehensive, well-designed plan for managing time.

1. A good time-management plan should have several time frames.

Your academic time-management plan should include:

• A *long-range* plan for the entire academic term that identifies deadline dates for reports and papers that are due toward the end of the term;

- A *mid-range* plan for the upcoming month and week; and
- A *short-range* plan for the following day.

The preceding time frames may be integrated into a total time-management plan for the term by taking the following steps:

- Identify deadline dates of all assignments, or the time when each of them must be completed (your long-range plan).
- Work backward from these final deadlines to identify dates when you plan to begin taking action on these assignments (your short-range plan).
- Identify intermediate dates when you plan to finish particular parts or pieces of the total assignment (your mid-range plan).

This three-stage plan should help you make steady progress throughout the term on college assignments that are due later in the term. At the same time, it will reduce your risk of procrastinating and running out of time.

Here's how you can put this three-stage plan into action this term

a. **Develop a long-range plan for the academic term.**
   - Review the *course syllabus (course outline)* for each class you are enrolled in this term, and highlight all major exams, tests, quizzes, assignments, and papers and the dates on which they are due.

Remember

College professors are more likely than high school teachers to expect you to rely on your course syllabus to keep track of what you have to do and when you have to do it.

   - Obtain a *large calendar* for the academic term (available at your campus bookstore or learning center) and record all your exams, assignments, and so on, for all your courses in the calendar boxes that represent their due dates. To fit this information within the calendar boxes, use creative abbreviations to represent different tasks, such as E for exam and TP for term paper (not toilet paper). When you're done, you'll have a centralized chart or map of deadline dates and a potential master plan for the entire term.

b. **Plan your week.**
   - Make a map of your *weekly schedule* that includes times during the week when you are in class, when you typically eat and sleep, and if you are employed, when you work.
   - If you are a full-time college student, find *at least 25 total hours per week* when you can do academic work outside the classroom. (These 25 hours can be pieced together in any way you like, including time between daytime classes and work commitments, evening time, and weekend time.) When adding these 25 hours to the time you spend in class each week, you will end up with a 40-hour workweek, similar to any full-time job. If you are a part-time student, you should plan on spending at least 2 hours on academic work outside of class for every 1 hour that you're in class.
   - Make good use of your *free time between classes* by working on assignments and studying in advance for upcoming exams. See **Box 5.1** for a summary of how you can use your out-of-class time to improve your academic performance and course grades.

Student Perspective

"The amount of free time you have in college is much more than in high school. Always have a weekly study schedule to go by. Otherwise, time slips away and you will not be able to account for it."

—Advice to new college students from a first-year student (Rhoads, 2005)

c. **Plan your day.**
  • Make a *daily to-do list*.

> **! Remember**
>
> If you write it out, you're less likely to block it out and forget about it.

  • Attack daily tasks in *priority order*.

> **! Remember**
>
> "First things first." Plan your work by placing the most important and most urgent tasks at the top of your list, and work your plan by attacking tasks in the order in which you have listed them.

  • Carry a *small calendar, planner, or appointment book* at all times. This will enable you to record appointments that you may make on the run during the day and will allow you to jot down creative ideas or memories of things you need to do—which sometimes pop into your mind at the most unexpected times.
  • Carry *portable work* with you during the day,—that is, work you can take with you and do in any place at any time. This will enable you to take advantage of "dead time" during the day. For example, carry material with you that you can read while sitting and waiting for appointments or transportation, allowing you to resurrect this dead time and convert it to "live" work time. (This isn't only a good time-management strategy; it's a good stress-management strategy because it puts you in control of "wait time," enabling you use it to save time later rather than making you feel frustrated about losing time or bored about having nothing do with your time while you're waiting.)
  • Wear a *watch* or carry a cell phone that can accurately and instantly tell you what time it is and what date it is. You can't even begin to manage time if you don't know what time it is, and you can't plan a schedule if you don't know what date it is. Set the time on your watch or cell phone slightly ahead of the actual time; this will help ensure that you arrive to class, work, or meetings on time.

2. A good time-management plan should include reserve time to take care of the unexpected.

You should always hope for the best but be prepared for the worst. Your time-management plan should include a buffer zone or safety net, building in extra time that you can use to accommodate unforeseen developments or unexpected emergencies. Just as you should plan to save money in your bank for unexpected extra costs (e.g., emergency medical expenses), you should plan to save time in your schedule for unexpected events that cost you time (e.g., dealing with unscheduled tasks or taking longer than expected to complete already-planned tasks).

> "In high school we were given a homework assignment every day. Now we have a large task assigned to be done at a certain time. No one tells [us] when to start or what to do each day."
>
> —First-year college student (Rhoads, 2005)

Student Perspective

"I was constantly missing important meetings during my first few weeks because I did not keep track of the dates and times. I thought I'd be told again when the time was closer, just as had been done in high school. Something I should have done to address that would have been to keep a well-organized planner for reference."

—College sophomore (Walsh, 2005)

Pause for Reflection

Do you make a to-do list of things you need to get done each day? (Circle one.)

never   seldom   often   almost always

If you circled "never" or "seldom," why don't you?

> Murphy's Laws:
>
> 1. Nothing is as simple as it looks.
> 2. Everything takes longer than it should.
> 3. If anything can go wrong, it will.
>
> —Author unknown (Murphy's Laws were named after Captain Edward Murphy, naval engineer, in 1949)

Take Action!

Making Productive Use of Free Time Outside the Classroom

Unlike high school, homework in college often does not involve turning things in to your instructor daily or weekly. The academic work you do outside the classroom may not even be collected and graded. Instead, it is done for your own benefit as you prepare yourself for upcoming exams and major assignments (e.g., term papers or research reports). Rather than formally assigning work to you as homework, your professors expect that you will do this work on your own and without supervision. Listed here are strategies for working independently and in advance of college exams and assignments, which will increase the quality of your preparation and performance.

Independent Work in Advance of Exams

Use the following strategies to prepare for exams:

- **Complete reading assignments** in advance of lectures that relate to the same topic as the reading. This will make lectures easier to understand and will prepare you to ask intelligent questions and make relevant comments in class.
- **Review your class notes** between class periods so that you can construct a mental bridge from one class to the next and make each upcoming lecture easier to follow. When reviewing your notes before the next class, rewrite any class notes that may be sloppily written. If you find notes related to the same point all over the place, reorganize them by combining them into one set of notes. Lastly, if you find any information gaps or confusing points in your notes, seek out the course instructor or a trusted classmate to clear them up before the next class takes place.
- **Review information** that you have highlighted in your reading assignments to improve your memory of the information. If certain points are confusing to you, discuss them with your course instructor or a fellow classmate.
- **Integrate key ideas** in your class notes with information that you have highlighted in your assigned reading and that is related to the same major point or general category. In other words, put related information from your lecture notes and your reading in the same place.
- **Use a part-to-whole study method** whereby you study material from your class notes and reading in small parts during short, separate study sessions that take place well in advance of the exam (the parts); then make your last study session before the exam a longer review session during which you restudy all the small parts together (the whole). The belief that studying in advance is a waste of time because you will forget it all anyway is a myth. As you'll see in Chapter 6, information studied in advance of an exam remains in your brain and is still there when you later review it. Even if you cannot recall the previously studied information when you first start reviewing it, you will relearn it faster than you did the first time, thus proving that some memory of it was retained.

Independent Work in Advance of Term Papers or Research Reports

Work on large, long-term assignments by breaking them into the following smaller, short-term tasks:

1. Search for and select a topic.
2. Locate sources of information on the topic.
3. Organize the information obtained from these sources into categories.
4. Develop an outline of the report's major points and the order or sequence in which you plan to discuss them.
5. Construct a first draft of the paper (and, if necessary, a second draft).
6. Write a final draft of the paper.
7. Proofread the final draft of your paper for minor mechanical mistakes, such as spelling and grammatical errors, before submitting it to your instructor.

3. A good time-management plan should include a balance of work and recreation.

Don't only plan work time; plan time to relax, refuel, and recharge. Your overall plan shouldn't turn you into an obsessive-compulsive workaholic. Instead, it should represent a balanced blend of work and play, which includes activities that promote your mental and physical wellness—such as relaxation, recreation, and reflection. You could also arrange your schedule of work and play as a self-motivation strategy by using your play time to reward your work time.

Student Perspective

"It is . . . important to allow time for things you enjoy doing because this is what will keep you stable."

–Advice to new college students from a first-year student

Remember

A good time-management plan should help you stress less, learn more, and earn higher grades while leaving you time for other important aspects of your life. A good plan not only enables you to get your work done on time but also enables you to attain and maintain balance in your life.

Pause for Reflection

What activities do you engage in for fun or recreation?

What do you do to relax or relieve stress?

Do you intentionally plan to engage in these activities?

4. A good time-management plan should have some flexibility.

Some people are immediately turned off by the idea of developing a schedule and planning their time because they feel it overstructures their lives and limits their freedom. It's only natural for you to prize your personal freedom and resist anything that appears to restrict your freedom in any way. A good plan preserves your freedom by helping you get done what must be done, reserving free time for you to do what you want and like to do.

A good time-management plan shouldn't enslave you to a rigid work schedule. It should be flexible enough to allow you to occasionally bend it without having to break it. Just as work commitments and family responsibilities can crop up unexpectedly, so, too, can opportunities for fun and enjoyable activities. Your plan should allow you the freedom to modify your schedule so that you can take advantage of these enjoyable opportunities and experiences. However, you should plan to make up the work time you lost. In other words, you can borrow or trade work time for play time, but don't "steal" it; you should plan to pay back the work time you borrowed by substituting it for a play period that existed in your original schedule.

"Some people regard discipline as a chore. For me, it is a kind of order that sets me free to fly."

–Julie Andrews, Academy award–winning English actress who starred in the Broadway musicals *Mary Poppins* and *The Sound of Music*

Remember

When you create a personal time-management plan, remember that it is *your* plan—you own it and you run it. It shouldn't run you.

Converting Your Time-Management Plan into an Action Plan

Once you've planned the work, the next step is to work the plan. A good action plan is one that gives you a preview of what you intend to accomplish and an opportunity to review what you actually accomplished. You can begin to implement an action plan by constructing a daily to-do list, bringing that list with you as the day begins, and checking off items on the list as you get them done. At the end of the day, review your list and identify what was completed and what still needs to be done. The uncompleted tasks should become high priorities for the next day.

At the end of the day, if you find many unchecked items remain on your daily to-do list, this could mean that you're spreading yourself too thin by trying to do too many things in a day. You may need to be more realistic about the number of things you can reasonably expect to accomplish per day by shortening your daily to-do list.

Being unable to complete many of your intended daily tasks may also mean that you need to modify your time-management plan by adding work time or subtracting activities that are drawing time and attention away from your work (e.g., taking phone calls during your planned work times).

Pause for Reflection

By the end of a typical day, how often do you find that you accomplished most of the important tasks you hoped to accomplish? (Circle one.)

never   seldom   often   almost always

Why?

◆ Dealing with Procrastination

Procrastination Defined

The word "procrastination" derives from two roots: *pro* (meaning "forward") plus *crastinus* (meaning "tomorrow.") As these roots suggest, procrastinators don't abide by the proverb "Why put off to tomorrow what can be done today?" Their philosophy is just the opposite: "Why do today what can be put off until tomorrow?" Adopting this philosophy promotes a perpetual pattern of postponing what needs to be done until the last possible moment, which results in rushing frantically to get it done (and compromising its quality), getting it only partially done, or not finishing it.

Research shows that 75 percent of college students label themselves as procrastinators (Potts, 1987), more than 80 percent procrastinate at least occasionally (Ellis & Knaus, 1977), and almost 50 percent procrastinate consistently (Onwuegbuzie, 2000). Furthermore, the percentage of people reporting that they procrastinate is on the rise (Kachgal, Hansen, & Nutter, 2001).

Procrastination is such a serious issue for college students that some colleges and universities have opened "procrastination centers" to provide help exclusively for students who are experiencing problems with procrastination (Burka & Yuen, 1983).

Myths That Promote Procrastination

Before there can be any hope of putting a stop to procrastination, procrastinators need to let go of two popular myths (misconceptions) about time and performance.

Myth 1. "I work better under pressure" (e.g., on the day or night before something is due).

Procrastinators often confuse desperation with motivation. Their belief that they work better under pressure is often just a rationalization to justify or deny the truth, which is that they *only* work when they're under pressure—that is, when they're running out of time and are under the gun to get it done just before the deadline.

It's true that some people will only start to work and will work really fast when they're under pressure, but that does not mean they're working more *effectively* and producing work of better *quality*. Because they're playing "beat the clock," procrastinators' focus no longer is on doing the job *well* but is on doing the job *fast* so that it gets done before they run out of time. This typically results in a product that turns out to be incomplete or inferior to what could have been produced if the work process began earlier.

Student Perspective

"I believe the most important aspect of college life is time management. DO NOT procrastinate because, although this is the easy thing to do at first, it will catch up with you and make your life miserable."

–Advice to new college students from a first-year student

Myth 2. "Studying in advance is a waste of time because you will forget it all by test time."

The misconception that information learned early will be forgotten is commonly used to justify procrastinating with respect to preparing for upcoming exams. Studying that is distributed (spread out) over time is more effective than massed (crammed) studying. Furthermore, last-minute studying that takes place the night before exams often results in lost sleep time due to the need to pull late-nighters or all-nighters. This fly-by-night strategy interferes with retention of information that has been studied and elevates test anxiety because of lost dream sleep (a.k.a. rapid eye movement, or REM), which enables the brain to store memories and cope with stress (Hobson, 1988; Voelker, 2004). Research indicates that procrastinators experience higher rates of stress-related physical disorders, such as insomnia, stomach problems, colds, and flu (McCance & Pychyl, 2003).

Working under time pressure adds to performance pressure because procrastinators are left with no margin of error to correct mistakes, no time to seek help on their work, and no chance to handle random catastrophes that may arise at the last minute (e.g., an attack of the flu or a family emergency).

"Haste makes waste."
–Benjamin Franklin

Psychological Causes of Procrastination

Sometimes, procrastination has deeper psychological roots. People may procrastinate for reasons related not directly to poor time-management habits but more to emotional issues involving self-esteem or self-image. For instance, studies show that procrastination is sometimes used as a psychological strategy to protect self-esteem, which is referred to as self-handicapping. This strategy may be used by some procrastinators (consciously or unconsciously) to give themselves a "handicap" or disadvantage. Thus, if their performance turns out to be less than spectacular, they can conclude (rationalize) that it was because they were performing under a handicap—lack of time (Smith, Snyder, & Handelsman, 1982).

For example, if the grade they receive on a test or paper turns out to be low, they can still "save face" (self-esteem) by concluding that it was because they waited until the last minute and didn't put much time or effort

Although you may work quickly under pressure, you are probably not working better.

© Elena Elisseeva, 2010. Under license from Shutterstock, Inc.

Pause for Reflection

Do you tend to put off work for so long that getting it done turns into an emergency or panic situation?

If your answer is yes, why do you think you find yourself in this position? If your answer is no, what is it that prevents this from happening to you?

"We didn't lose the game; we just ran out of time."

–Vince Lombardi, football coach

"Procrastinators would rather be seen as lacking in effort than lacking in ability."

–Joseph Ferrari, professor of psychology and procrastination researcher

into it. In other words, they had the ability or intelligence to earn a good grade; they just didn't try very hard. Better yet, if they happened to luck out and get a good grade—despite doing it at the last minute—then they can think the grade just shows how intelligent they are. Thus, self-handicapping creates a fail-safe scenario that's guaranteed to protect the procrastinators' self-image: If the work performance or product is less than excellent, it can be blamed on external factors (e.g., lack of time); if it happens to earn them a high grade, then they can attribute the result to themselves—their extraordinary ability enabled them to do so well despite working at the last minute.

In addition to self-handicapping, other psychological factors have been found to contribute to procrastination, including the following:

- **Fear of failure.** Feeling that it's better to postpone the job, or not do it, than to fail at it (Burka & Yuen, 1983; Soloman & Rothblum, 1984);
- **Perfectionism.** Having unrealistically high personal standards or expectations, which leads to the belief that it's better to postpone work or not do it than to risk doing it less than perfectly (Flett, Blankstein, Hewitt, & Koledin, 1992; Kachgal et al., 2001);
- **Fear of success.** Fearing that doing well will show others that the procrastinator has the ability to achieve success and will allow others to expect the procrastinator to maintain those high standards by repeating the performance (Beck, Koons, & Milgram, 2000; Ellis & Knaus, 1977);
- **Indecisiveness.** Having difficulty making decisions, including decisions about what to do or how to begin doing it (Anderson, 2003; Steel, 2003);
- **Thrill seeking.** Enjoying the adrenaline rush triggered by hurrying to get things done just before a deadline (Szalavitz, 2003).

If these or any other issues are involved, their underlying psychological causes must be dealt with before procrastination can be overcome. Because they have deeper roots, it may take some time and professional assistance to uproot them. A good place to get such assistance is the Counseling Center. Personal counselors on college campuses are professional psychologists who are trained to deal with psychological issues that can contribute to procrastination.

Self-Help Strategies for Beating the Procrastination Habit

Once inaccurate beliefs or emotional issues underlying procrastination have been identified and dealt with, the next step is to move from gaining self-insight to taking direct action on the procrastination habit itself. Listed here are our top strategies for minimizing or eliminating the procrastination habit.

1. Continually practice effective time-management strategies.

"Striving for excellence motivates you; striving for perfection is demoralizing."

–Harriet Braiker, psychologist and best-selling author

If effective time-management practices, such as those previously cited in this chapter, are implemented consistently, they can turn into a habit. Studies show that when people repeatedly practice effective time-management strategies these practices gradually become part of their routine and develop into habits. For example, when procrastinators repeatedly practice effective time-

management strategies with respect to tasks that they procrastinate on, their procrastination tendencies begin to fade and are gradually replaced by good time-management habits (Ainslie, 1992; Baumeister, Heatherton, & Tice, 1994).

2. Make the start of work as inviting or appealing as possible.

Getting started can be a stumbling block for many procrastinators. They experience what's called "start-up stress" when they're about to begin a task they expect will be unpleasant, difficult, or boring (Burka & Yuen, 1983). If you have trouble starting your work, one way to give yourself a jump start is to arrange your work tasks in an order that allows you to start on tasks that you're likely to find most interesting or are most likely to experience success with. Once you've overcome the initial inertia and get going, you can ride the momentum you've created to attack the tasks that you find less appealing and more daunting.

You're also likely to discover that the dreaded work wasn't as difficult, boring, or time consuming as it appeared to be. When you sense that you're making some progress toward getting work done, your anxiety begins to decline. Like many experiences in life that are dreaded and avoided, the anticipation of the event turns out to be worse than the event itself. Research on students who hadn't started a project until it was about to be due indicates that these students experience anxiety and guilt about delaying their work but that once they begin working these negative emotions decline and are replaced by more positive feelings (McCance & Pychyl, 2003).

3. Make the work manageable.

Work becomes less overwhelming and less stressful when it's handled in small chunks or pieces. You can conquer procrastination for large tasks by using a "divide and conquer" strategy: Divide the large task into smaller, more manageable units, and then attack and complete them one at a time.

Don't underestimate the power of short work sessions. They can be more effective than longer sessions because it's easier to maintain momentum and concentration for shorter periods. If you're working on a large project or preparing for a major exam, dividing your work into short sessions will enable you to take quick jabs and poke small holes in it, reducing its overall size with each successive punch. This approach will also give you the sense of satisfaction that comes with knowing that you're making steady progress toward completing a big task—continually chipping away at it in short strokes and gradually taking away the pressure associated with having to go for a big knockout punch right before the final bell (deadline).

Pause for Reflection

How often do you procrastinate? (Circle one.)

rarely   occasionally   frequently   consistently

When you do procrastinate, what is the usual reason?

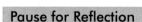

> "Just do it."
>
> —Commercial slogan of Nike, the athletic equipment company named after the Greek goddess of victory

Student Perspective

"Did you ever dread doing something, then it turned out to take only about 20 minutes to do?"

—Conversation between two college students overheard in a coffee shop

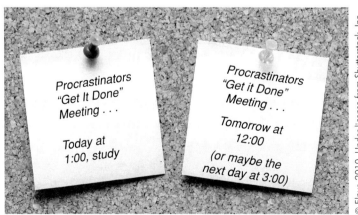

For many procrastinators, getting *started* is often their biggest obstacle.

© Elnur, 2010. Under license from Shutterstock, Inc.

Personal Story

The two biggest projects I've had to complete in my life were writing my doctoral thesis and writing this textbook. The strategy that enabled me to keep going until I competed both of these large tasks was to make up short-term deadlines for myself (e.g., complete 5-10 pages each week). I psyched myself into thinking that these make-believe due dates were real, drop-dead deadlines and that if I didn't meet them by completing these smaller tasks on time I was going to fall so far behind that I'd never get the whole thing done. I think these self-imposed deadlines worked for me because they gave me short, more manageable tasks to work on that allowed me to make steady progress toward my larger, long-term task. It was as if I took a huge, hard-to-digest meal and broke it into small, bite-sized pieces that I could easily swallow and gradually digest over time—as opposed to trying to consume a large meal right before bedtime (the final deadline).

—Joe Cuseo

4. Understand that organization matters.

> "To eat an elephant, first cut it into small pieces."
> –Author unknown

Research indicates that disorganization is a factor that contributes to procrastination (Steel, 2003). How well you organize your workplace and manage your work materials can reduce your risk of procrastination. Having the right materials in the right place at the right time can make it easier to get to and get going on your work. Once you've made a decision to get the job done, you don't want to waste time looking for the tools you need to begin doing it. For procrastinators, this time delay may be just the amount of time they need to change their mind and not start their work.

! Remember

The less effort it takes to start doing something, the more likely you are to do it.

One simple yet effective way to organize your college work materials is by developing your own file system. You can begin to create an effective file system by filing (storing) materials from different courses in different colored folders or notebooks. This will allow you to keep all materials related to the same course in the same place and give you direct and immediate access to the materials you need as soon as you need them. Such a system helps you get organized, reduces stress associated with having things all over the place, and reduces the risk of procrastination by reducing the time it takes for you to start working.

Pause for Reflection

List your two most common sources of distraction while working. Next to each distraction, identify a strategy that you might use to reduce or eliminate it.

Source of Distraction   Strategy for Reducing this Distraction

1.

2.

5. Recognize that location matters.

Where you work can influence when or whether you work. Research demonstrates that distraction is a factor that can contribute to procrastination (Steel, 2003). Thus, it may be possible for you to minimize procrastination by working in an environment whose location and arrangement prevent distraction and promote concentration.

Distractions tend to come in two major forms: social distractions (e.g., people nearby who are not working) and media distractions (e.g., cell phones, e-mails, text messages, CDs, and TV). Research indicates that the number of hours per week that college students spend watching TV is *negatively* associated with academic success, including lower grade point average, less likelihood of graduating with honors, and lower levels of personal development (Astin, 1993).

!

Remember

Select a workplace and arrange your workspace to minimize distraction from people and media. Try to remove everything from your work site that's not directly relevant to your work.

Lastly, keep in mind that you can arrange your work environment in a way that not only disables distraction but also enables concentration. You can enable or empower your concentration by working in an environment that allows you easy access to work-support materials (e.g., class notes, textbooks, and a dictionary) and easy access to social support (e.g., working with a group of motivated students who will encourage you to get focused, stay on task, and keep on track to complete you work tasks).

6. Arrange the order or sequence of your work tasks to intercept procrastination when you're most likely to experience it.

While procrastination often involves difficulty starting work, it can also involve difficulty continuing and completing work (Lay & Silverman, 1996). As previously mentioned, if you have trouble starting work, it might be best to first do tasks that you find most interesting or easiest. However, if you have difficulty maintaining or sustaining your work until it's finished, you might try to schedule work tasks that you find easier and more interesting *in the middle or toward the end* of your planned work time. If you're performing tasks of greater interest and ease at a point in your work when you typically lose interest or energy, you may be able to sustain your interest and energy long enough to continue working until you complete them, which means that you'll have completed your entire list of tasks. Also, doing your most enjoyable and easiest tasks later can provide an incentive or reward for completing your less enjoyable tasks first.

7. Learn that momentum matters.

It's often harder to restart a task than it is to finish a task that you've already started; this occurs because you've overcome come the initial inertia associated with getting started and can ride the momentum that you've already created. Furthermore, finishing a task can give you a sense of closure—the feeling of personal accomplishment and self-satisfaction that comes from knowing that you "closed the deal." Placing a checkmark next to a completed task and seeing that it's one less thing you have to do can motivate you to continue working on the remaining tasks on your list.

Student Perspective

"To reduce distractions, work at a computer on campus rather than using one in your room or home."

—Advice to new college students from a first-year student

Student Perspective

"I'm very good at starting things but often have trouble keeping a sustained effort."

—First-year college student

◆ Summary and Conclusion

To manage time effectively, you need to

- **Analyze.** Break down time and become aware of how you spend it;
- **Itemize.** Identify the tasks you need to accomplish and their due dates; and
- **Prioritize.** Tackle your tasks in their order of importance.

Developing a comprehensive time-management plan involves long-, mid-, and short-range plans, such as

- Planning the total term (long-range);
- Planning your week (mid-range); and
- Planning your day (short-range).

A good time-management plan also has the following features:

- It sets aside time to take care of unexpected developments.
- It takes advantage of your natural peak periods and down times.
- It balances work and recreation.
- It gives you the flexibility to accommodate unforeseen opportunities.

The enemy of effective time management is procrastination, which often relies on the following myths:

- Better work occurs on the day or night before something is due.
- Advance studying wastes time because everything learned will be forgotten by test time.

Effective strategies for beating the procrastination habit include the following:

- Start with the work that is the most inviting or appealing.
- Divide a large task into manageable units.
- Organize work materials.
- Work in a location that minimizes distractions and temptations not to work.
- Intentionally arrange work tasks so that more enjoyable or stimulating tasks are the focus when you're vulnerable to procrastination.
- Maintain momentum, because it's often harder to restart a task than to finish one.

Mastering the skill of managing time is critical for success in college and in life beyond college. Time is one of the most powerful personal resources; the better use you make of it, the greater control you gain over your priorities and your life.

Learning More Through the World Wide Web

Internet-Based Resources for Further Information on Time Management

For additional information related to the ideas discussed in this chapter, we recommend the following Web sites:

Procrastination Elimination: **www.time-management-guide.com/procrastination.html**

Time-Management Strategies for All Students: **www.studygs.net/timman.htm**

Time-Management Strategies for Non-Traditional-Age Students:
www.essortment.com/lifestyle/timemanagement_sjmu.htm

5.1 Term at a Glance

Term _____,   Year _____

Review the syllabus (course outline) for all classes you're enrolled in this term, and complete the following information for each course.

Course ↓	Professor ↓	Exams ↓	Projects & Papers ↓	Other Assignments ↓	Attendance Policy ↓	Late & Makeup Assignment Policy ↓

Self-Assessment Questions

1. Is the overall workload what you expected? Are your surprised by the amount of work required in any particular course or courses?

2. At this point in the term, what do you see as your most challenging or demanding course or courses? Why?

3. Do you think you can handle the total workload required by the full set of courses you're enrolled in this term?

4. What adjustments or changes could you make to your personal schedule that would make it easier to accommodate your academic workload this term?

5.2 Taking a Personal Time Inventory

On the blank Week-at-a-Glance Grid that follows, map out your typical or average week for this term. Start by recording what you usually do on these days, including when you have class, when you work, and when you relax or recreate. You can use abbreviations (e.g., use J for job and R&R for rest and relaxation) or write tasks out in full if you have enough room in the box. List the abbreviations you created at the bottom of the page so that your instructor can follow them.

If you're a *full-time* student, find 25 *hours* in your week that you could devote to homework (HW). These 25 hours could be found between classes, during the day, in the evenings, or on the weekends. If you can find 25 hours per week for homework, in addition to your class schedule, you'll have a 40-hour workweek for coursework, which research has shown to result in good grades and success in college.

If you're a *part-time* student, find 2 *hours* you could devote to homework *for every hour* that you're in class (e.g., if you're in class 9 hours per week, find 18 hours of homework time).

Week-at-a-Glance Grid

	Sunday	Monday	Tuesday	Wednesday	Thursday	Friday	Saturday
7:00 a.m.							
8:00 a.m.							
9:00 a.m.							
10:00 a.m.							
11:00 a.m.							
12:00 p.m.							
1:00 p.m.							
2:00 p.m.							
3:00 p.m.							
4:00 p.m.							
5:00 p.m.							
6:00 p.m.							
7:00 p.m.							
8:00 p.m.							
9:00 p.m.							
10:00 p.m.							
11:00 p.m.							

1. Go to the following Web site: www.ulc.psu.edu/studyskills/time_management.html#monitoring_your_time

2. Complete the time management exercise at this site. The exercise asks you to estimate the hours per day or week that you spend doing various activities (e.g., sleeping, employment, and commuting). As you enter the amount of time you engage in these activities, the total number of remaining hours available in the week for academic work will be automatically computed.

3. After completing your entries, look at your week-at-a-glance grid and answer the following questions, or provide your best estimate.

Self-Assessment Questions

1. How many hours per week do you have available for academic work?

2. Do you have 2 hours available for academic work outside of class for each hour you spend in class?

3. What time wasters do you detect that might be easily eliminated or reduced to create more time for academic work outside of class?

Procrastination: The Vicious Cycle

Delilah has a major paper due at the end of the term. It's now past midterm, and she still hasn't started to work on her paper. She tells herself, "I should have started sooner."

However, Delilah continues to postpone starting her work on the paper and begins to feel anxious and guilty about it. To relieve her growing anxiety and guilt, she starts doing other tasks instead, such as cleaning her room and returning e-mails. This makes Delilah feel a little better because these tasks keep her busy, take her mind off the term paper, and give her the feeling that at least she's getting something accomplished. Time continues to pass, and the deadline for the paper is growing dangerously close. Delilah now finds herself in the position of having lots of work to do and little time in which to do it.

Source: Burka & Lenora (1983).

Reflection and Discussion Questions

1. What do you predict Delilah will do at this point?

2. Why did you make this prediction?

3. What grade do you think Delilah will receive on her paper?

4. What do you think Delilah will do on the next term paper she's assigned?

5. Other than starting sooner, what recommendations would you have for Delilah (and other procrastinators like her) to break this cycle of procrastination and prevent it from happening repeatedly?

Strategic Learning, Studying, and Test Taking

Deep-Learning Strategies

ACTIVATE YOUR THINKING | **Journal Entry**

What do you think is the key difference between learning and memorizing?

_____

_____

_____

_____

LEARNING GOAL

To develop a set of effective strategies that will enable you to learn deeply and remember longer.

◆ Stages in the Learning and Memory Process

Learning deeply, and remembering what you've learned, is a process that involves three stages:

1. **Sensory input (perception).** Taking information into the brain;
2. **Memory formation (storage).** Saving that information in the brain;
3. **Memory recall (retrieval).** Bringing information back to mind when you need it.

You can consider these stages of the learning and memory process to be similar to the way information is processed by a computer: (a) information is typed onto the screen (perceptual input), (b) the information is saved in a file (memory storage), and (c) the saved information is recalled and used when it's needed (memory retrieval).

These three stages in the learning–memory process are summarized visually in **Figure 6.1**.

This three-stage process can be used to create a systematic set of strategies for effectively using the two major routes through which you acquire information and knowledge in college:

• Taking notes as you listen to lectures, and
• Reading textbooks.

From "Thriving in College and Beyond" by Cuseo, Fecas, Thompson. © Kendall Hunt Publishing.

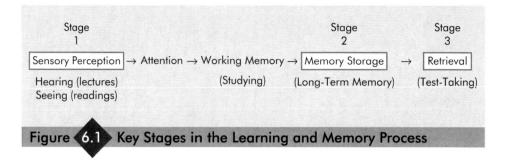

Stage 1			Stage 2		Stage 3
Sensory Perception	→ Attention → Working Memory →		Memory Storage	→	Retrieval
Hearing (lectures) Seeing (readings)		(Studying)	(Long-Term Memory)		(Test-Taking)

Figure **6.1** Key Stages in the Learning and Memory Process

◆ Effective Lecture-Listening and Note-Taking Strategies

The importance of effective listening skills in the college classroom is highlighted by a study of more than 400 first-year students who were given a listening test at the start of their first term in college. At the end of their first year, 49 percent of those students who scored low on the listening test were on academic probation, compared to only 4.4 percent of students who scored high on the listening test. On the other hand, 68.5 percent of students who scored high on the listening test were eligible for the honors program at the end of their first year, compared to only 4.17 percent of those students who had low listening test scores (Conaway, 1982).

Pause for Reflection

Do you think writing notes in class helps or hinders your ability to pay attention and learn from your instructors' lectures?

Why?

Studies show that information delivered during lectures is the number one source of test questions (and answers) on college exams (Brown, 1988; Kuhn, 1988). When lecture information appears on a test and hasn't been recorded in students' notes, it has only a 5 percent chance of being recalled (Kiewra, Hart, Scoular, Stephen, Sterup, & Tyler, 2000). When you write down information presented in lectures, rather than just listen to it, you're more likely to remember that information. For example, students who write notes during lectures achieve higher course grades than students who just listen to lectures (Kiewra, 1985), and students with a more complete set of notes are more likely to demonstrate higher levels of overall academic achievement (Johnstone, & Su, 1994; Kiewra & Fletcher, 1984).

Contrary to popular belief that writing while listening interferes with the ability to listen, students report that taking notes actually increases their attention and concentration in class (Hartley, 1998; Hartley & Marshall, 1974). Studies also show that when students write down information that's presented to them, rather than just listening to it, they're more likely to remember the most important aspects of that information when tested later (Bligh, 2000; Kiewra et al., 1991). For instance, one study discovered that successful students with grade point averages (GPAs) of 2.53 or higher record more information in their notes and retain a larger percentage of the most important information than do students with GPAs of less than 2.53 (Einstein, Morris, & Smith, 1985). These findings are not surprising when you consider that *hearing* lecture information, *writing* it, and *seeing* it while you write it lay down three different memory traces or tracks in the brain that combine to improve memory for that information.

Furthermore, students with a good set of notes have a written record of that information, which can be reread and studied later.

This research suggests that you should view each lecture as if it were a test-review session during which your instructor is giving out test answers and you're given the opportunity to write all those answers in your notes. Come to class with the attitude that your instructors are dispensing answers to test questions as they speak; your purpose for being there is to pick out and pick up these answers.

> ### Remember
> If important points your professors make in class make it into your notes, they can become points learned, and these learned points will turn into earned points on your exams (and higher grades in your courses).

The next sections give strategies for getting the most out of lectures at three stages in the learning process: before lectures, during lectures, and after lectures.

Prelecture Strategies: What You Can Do Before Hearing Lectures

1. Check your syllabus to see where you are in the course and determine how the upcoming class fits into the total course picture.

By checking your syllabus before individual class sessions, you will strengthen your learning because you will see how each part (individual class session) relates to the whole (the entire course). This also capitalizes on the human brain's natural tendency to seek larger patterns and the "big picture." Rather than seeing things in separate parts, the brain is naturally inclined to perceive parts as interconnected and forming a meaningful whole (Caine & Caine, 1991). It looks for meaningful patterns and connections rather than isolated bits and pieces of information (Nummela & Rosengren, 1986). In **Figure 6.2**, notice how your brain naturally ties together and fills in the missing information to perceive a meaningful whole pattern.

You perceive a white triangle in the middle of this figure. However, if you use three fingers to cover up the three corners of the white triangle that fall outside the other (background) triangle, the white triangle suddenly disappears. What your brain does is take these corners as starting points and fills in the rest of the information on its own to create a complete or whole pattern that has meaning to you. (Notice also how you perceive the background triangle as a complete triangle, even though parts of its left and right sides are missing.)

Figure 6.2 ▶ Triangle Illusion

2. Get to class early so that you can look over your notes from the previous class session and from any reading assignment that relates to the day's lecture topic.

Research indicates that when students preview information related to an upcoming lecture topic it improves their ability to take more accurate and complete lecture notes (Ladas, 1980). Thus, a good strategy to help you learn from lectures is to review your notes from the previous class session and read textbook information related to an upcoming lecture topic—before hearing the lecture. This strategy will help you better understand and take more detailed notes on the lecture. Reviewing previously learned information activates your previous knowledge, enabling you to build a mental bridge from one class session to the next and connect new information to what you already know, which is the key to deep learning (Piaget, 1978; Vygotsky, 1978). Acquiring knowledge isn't a matter of simply pouring information into the brain as if it were an empty jar. It's a matter of attaching or connecting new ideas to ideas that are already stored in the brain. When you learn deeply, you make a biological connection between nerve cells in the brain (Alkon, 1992), as illustrated in **Figure 6.3**.

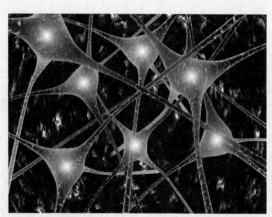

© Jurgen Ziewe, 2010. Under license from Shutterstock, Inc.

> When something is learned, it's stored in the brain as a link in an interconnected network of brain cells. Thus, deep learning involves making connections between what you're trying to learn and what you already know.

Figure **6.3** Network of Brain Cells

3. Adopt a seating location that maximizes your focus of attention and minimizes sources of distraction.

Student Perspective

"I tend to sit at the very front of my classrooms. It helps me focus and take notes better. It also eliminates distractions."

–First-year college student

Studies show that students who sit in the front and center of class tend to earn higher exam scores (Rennels & Chaudhair, 1988). These results are found even when students are assigned seats by their instructor, so it's not just a matter of more motivated and studious students tending to sit in the front of the classroom; instead, the academic performance of students sitting front and center is likely higher because a learning advantage is provided by this seating location. Front-and-center seating probably aids academic performance by improving vision of the board and hearing of the instructor's words—as well as allowing better eye contact with the instructor, which increases students' attention and heightens their sense of personal responsibility in the classroom. There's another advantage to sitting up front: It increases your comfort level about speaking in class because if you ask a question or contribute a comment you will not have numerous classmates sitting in front of you who turn around to look at you when you speak.

When you enter the classroom, get in the habit of heading for a seat in the front and center of class. In large classes, it is particularly important that you get "up close and personal" with your instructors. This not only will improve your attention, note taking, and participation in class but also should improve your instructors' ability to remember who you are and how well you performed in class, which will work to your advantage when you ask for letters of recommendation.

4. Be aware of the people who sit near you.

Intentionally sit near classmates who will not distract you or interfere with the quality of your note taking. Attention comes in degrees or amounts; you can give all of it or part of it to whatever task you're performing. Trying to grasp complex information in class is a task that demands your undivided attention.

> **! Remember**
>
> When you enter a class, you have a choice about where you're going to sit. Choose wisely by selecting a location that will maximize your attentiveness to the instructor and the aggressiveness of your note taking.

5. Adopt a seating posture that screams attention.

Sitting upright and leaning forward are more likely to increase your attention because these signals of bodily alertness will reach your brain and increase mental alertness. If your body is in an alert and ready position, your mind tends to pick up these bodily cues and follow your body's lead by also becoming alert and ready (to learn). Just as baseball players assume a ready position in the field before a pitch is delivered to put their body in position to catch batted balls, learners who assume a ready position in the classroom put themselves in a better position to catch ideas batted around in the classroom. Studies show that when humans are ready and expecting to capture an idea greater amounts of the brain chemical C-kinase are released at the connection points between brain cells, which increases the likelihood that a learning connection is formed between them (Howard, 2000).

There's another advantage to being attentive in class: You send a clear message to your instructor that you're a conscientious and courteous student. This can influence your instructor's perception and evaluation of your academic performance, which can earn you the benefit of the doubt at the end of the term if you're on the border between a higher and a lower course grade.

Student Perspective

"[In high school] the teacher knows your name. But in college they don't know your name; they might see your face, but it means nothing to them unless you make yourself known."

–First-year college student

Student Perspective

"I like to sit up front so I am not distracted by others and I don't have to look around people's heads to see the chalkboard."

–First-year college student

Listening and Note-Taking Strategies: What You Can Do During Lectures

1. Take your own notes in class.

Don't rely on someone else to take notes for you. Taking your own notes in your own words ensures they make sense and have personal meaning to you. You can collaborate with classmates to compare one another's notes for completeness and accuracy or to get notes if you happen to miss class. However, do not routinely rely on others to take notes for you. Studies show that students who record and review their own notes earn higher scores on memory tests for that information than do students who review the notes of others (Fisher, Harris, & Harris, 1973). These findings point to the importance of taking and studying your own notes because they will be most meaningful to you.

Students who take notes during lectures have been found to achieve higher class grades than those who just listen.

2. Focus your attention on important information.

Attention is the critical first step to successful learning and memory. Since the human attention span is limited, it's impossible to attend to and make note of every piece of given information. Thus, you need to use your attention *selectively* to focus on and choose the most important information. Here are some strategies for attending to and recording the most important information delivered by professors in the college classroom:

- Pay attention to information your instructors put in writing—on the board, on a slide, or in a handout. If your instructor takes the time and energy to write it out, that's usually a good clue the information is important and you're likely to see it again—on an exam.
- Pay attention to information presented during the first and last few minutes of class. Instructors are more likely to provide valuable reminders, reviews, and previews at the start and end of class.
- Use your instructor's verbal and nonverbal cues to detect important information. Don't just to tune in when the instructor is writing something down and tune out at other times. It's been found that students record almost 90 percent of information that is written on the board (Locke, 1977) but less than 50 percent of important ideas that professors state but don't write on the board (Johnstone & Su, 1994). Don't fall into the reflex-like routine of just writing something in your notes when you see your instructor writing on the board. You also have to listen actively to record important ideas in your notes that you hear your instructor saying. In **Box 6.1**, you'll find strategies for detecting important information that professors deliver orally during lectures.

3. Take organized notes.

Keep taking notes in the same paragraph if the instructor is continuing on the same point or idea. When the instructor shifts to a new idea, skip a few lines and shift to a new paragraph. Be alert to phrases that your instructor may use to signal a shift to a new or different idea (e.g., "Let's turn to . . ." or "In addition to . . ."). Use these phrases as cues for taking notes in paragraph form. By using paragraphs, you improve the organizational quality of your notes, which will improve your comprehension and retention of them. Leave an extra space between successive paragraphs (ideas) to give yourself room to add information that you may have missed or to translate the professor's words into your own words, making them more meaningful to you.

Take Action!

Detecting When Instructors Are Delivering Important Information During Class Lectures

6.1

1. Verbal cues
- Phrases signal important information (e.g., "The point here is . . ." or "What's most significant about this is . . .").
- Information is repeated or rephrased in a different way (e.g., "In other words, . . .").
- Stated information is followed with a question to check understanding (e.g., "Is that clear?" "Do you follow that?" "Does that make sense?" or "Are you with me?").

2. Vocal (tone of voice) cues
- Information is delivered in a louder tone or at a higher pitch than usual, which may indicate excitement or emphasis.
- Information is delivered at a slower rate or with more pauses than usual, which may be your instructor's way of giving you more time to write down these important ideas.

3. Nonverbal cues
- Information is delivered by the instructor with more than the usual
  - a. facial expressiveness (e.g., raised or furrowed eyebrows);
  - b. body movement (e.g., more gesturing and animation); or
  - c. eye contact (e.g., looking more directly and intently at the faces of students to see whether they are following or understanding what's being said).
- The instructor moves closer to the students (e.g., moving away from the podium or blackboard).
- The instructor's body is oriented directly toward the class (i.e., both shoulders directly or squarely face the class).

Another strategy for taking organized notes, the called the Cornell Note-Taking System, is summarized in **Box 6.2**.

4. If you don't immediately understand what your instructor is saying, don't stop taking notes.

Keep taking notes, even if you are temporarily confused, because this will at least leave you with a record of the information that you can review later—when you have more time to think about it and grasp it. If you still don't understand it after taking time to review it, check it out in your textbook, with your instructor, or with a classmate.

> **! Remember**
>
> Your primary goal during lectures is to get important information into your brain long enough to note it mentally and then physically by recording it in your notes. Making sense of that information often has to come later, when you have time to reflect on the notes you took in class.

Postlecture Strategies: What You Can Do After Lectures

1. As soon as class ends, quickly check your notes for missing information or incomplete thoughts.

Since the information is likely to be fresh in your mind immediately after class, a quick check of your notes at this time will allow you take advantage of your short-term memory. By reviewing and reflecting on it, you can help move the information into long-term memory before forgetting takes place. This quick review can be done alone or, better yet, with a motivated classmate.

Pause for Reflection

What do you tend to do immediately after a class session ends?

Why?

If you both have gaps in your notes, check them out with your instructor before he or she leaves the classroom. Even though it may be weeks before you will be tested on the material, the quicker you address missed points and clear up sources of confusion, the better, because you'll be able to use your knowledge to help you understand and learn upcoming material. Catching confusion early in the game also enables you to avoid the last-minute, mad rush of students seeking help from the instructor just before test time. You want to reserve the critical time just before exams for studying a set of notes that you know are complete and accurate, rather than rushing around and trying to find missing information and getting fast-food help on concepts that were presented weeks ago.

2. Before the next class session meets, reflect on and review your notes to make sense of them.

Your professors will often lecture on information that you may have little prior knowledge about, so it is unrealistic to expect that you will understand everything that's being said the first time you hear it. Instead, you'll need to set aside time for making notes or taking notes on your own notes (i.e., rewriting them in your own words so that they make sense to you).

During this reflect-and-rewrite process, we recommend that you take notes on your notes by:

- Translating technical information into your own words to make it more meaningful to you; and
- Reorganizing your notes to get ideas related to the same point in the same place.

Studies show that when students organize lecture information into meaningful categories they show greater recall on a delayed memory test for that information than do students who simply review their notes (Howe, 1970).

Take Action!

The Cornell Note-Taking System

6.2

1. On the page on which you're taking notes, draw a horizontal line about 2 inches from the bottom edge of the paper.
2. If there's no vertical line on the left side of the page, draw one line about 2½ inches from the left edge of the paper (as shown in the scaled-down illustration here).

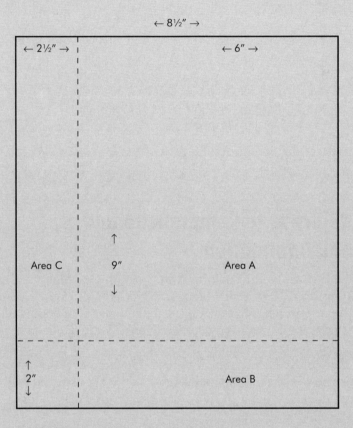

$\leftarrow 8\frac{1}{2}'' \rightarrow$

$\leftarrow 2\frac{1}{2}'' \rightarrow$ $\leftarrow 6'' \rightarrow$

Area C   ↑ 9″ ↓   Area A

↑ 2″ ↓   Area B

3. When your instructor is lecturing, use the large space to right of the vertical line (area A) to record your notes.
4. After a lecture, use the space at the bottom of the page (area B) to summarize the main points you recorded on that page.
5. Use the column of space on the left side of the page (area C) to write questions that are answered in the notes on the right.
6. Quiz yourself by looking at the questions listed in the left margin while covering the answers to them found in the class notes on the right.

Note: You can use this note-taking and note-review method on your own, or you could team up with two or more students and do it collaboratively.

! Remember

Look at note taking as a two-stage process: Stage 1 is aggressively taking notes in class (active involvement), and stage 2 occurs later—when you think about those notes more deeply (personal reflection).

Personal Story

My first year in college was mainly spent trying to manipulate my schedule to find some free time. I took all of my classes in a row without a break to save some time at the end of the day for relaxation and hanging out with friends before I went to work. Seldom did I look over my notes and read the material that I was assigned on the day I took the lecture notes and received the assignment. Thus, on the day before the test I was in a panic trying to cram the lecture notes into my head for the upcoming test. Needless to say, I did not perform well on many of these tests. Finally, I had a professor who told me that if I spent time each day after a couple of my classes catching up on reading and rewriting my notes I would retain the material longer, increase my grades, and decrease my stress at test time. I employed this system, and it worked wonderfully.

—*Aaron Thompson*

◆ Reading Strategically to Comprehend and Retain Textbook Information

Second only to lecture notes is information from reading assignments as a source of test questions on college exams (Brown, 1988). You're likely to find exam questions that your professors haven't talked about directly, or even mentioned, in class but that were drawn from your assigned reading. College professors often expect you to relate or connect what they are lecturing about in class with material that you've been assigned to read. Furthermore, they often deliver class lectures with the assumption that you have done the assigned reading, so if you haven't done it, you're likely to have more difficulty following what your instructor is talking about in class.

! Remember

Do the assigned reading and do it according to the schedule your instructor has established. It will help you better understand class lectures, improve the quality of your participation in class, and raise your overall grade in the course.

What follows is a series of strategies for effective reading at three stages in the learning process: before reading, while reading, and after reading. When completing your reading assignments, use effective reading strategies that are based on sound principles of human learning and memory, such as those listed here.

Prereading Strategies: What You Can Do Before Reading

1. Before jumping into your assigned reading, look at how it fits into the overall organizational structure of the book and course.

You can do this efficiently by taking a quick look at the book's table of contents to see where the chapter you're about to read is placed in the overall sequence of chapters, particularly in relation to chapters that immediately precede and follow the assigned chapter. This will give you a sense of how the particular part you're focusing on connects with the bigger picture. Research shows that if learners have advance knowledge of how the information they're about to learn is organized—if they see how the parts relate to the whole *before* they attempt to start learning the specifics—they're better able to comprehend and retain the material (Ausubel, 1978; Kintsch, 1994). Thus, the first step toward improving reading comprehension and retention of a textbook chapter is to see how its parts relate to the whole—before you begin to examine the chapter part by part.

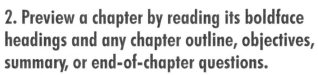

Pause for Reflection

Rate yourself in terms of how frequently you use these note-taking strategies according to the following scale:

4 = always, 3 = sometimes, 2 = rarely, 1 = never

1. I take notes aggressively in class.   4 3 2 1

2. I sit near the front of the room during class.   4 3 2 1

3. I sit upright and lean forward while in class.   4 3 2 1

4. I take notes on what my instructors say, not just what they write on the board.   4 3 2 1

5. I pay special attention to information presented at the start and end of class.   4 3 2 1

6. I take notes in paragraph form.   4 3 2 1

7. I review my notes immediately after class to check that they are complete and accurate.   4 3 2 1

2. Preview a chapter by reading its boldface headings and any chapter outline, objectives, summary, or end-of-chapter questions.

Get in the habit of previewing what's in a chapter to gain an overall sense of its organization before jumping right into the content. If you dive into details too quickly, you lose sight of how the smaller details relate to the larger picture. The brain's natural tendency is to perceive and comprehend whole patterns rather than isolated bits of information. Start by seeing how the parts of the chapter are integrated into the whole. This will enable you to better connect the separate pieces of information you encounter while you read, much like seeing the whole picture of a completed jigsaw puzzle helps you connect its separate pieces while assembling the puzzle.

Pause for Reflection

When you open a textbook to read a chapter, how do you start the reading process? That is, what's the first thing you do?

3. Take a moment to think about what you already know that relates to the material in the chapter.

By thinking about knowledge you possess about the topic you're about to read, you activate the areas of your brain where that knowledge is stored, thereby preparing it to make meaningful connections with the material you're about to read.

Strategies to Use While Reading
Read Selectively to Find Important Information

Rather than jumping into reading and randomly highlighting, effective reading begins with a plan or goal for identifying what should be noted and remembered. Here are three strategies to use while reading to help you determine what information should be noted and retained.

1. **Use boldface or dark-print headings and subheadings as cues for identifying important information.** These headings organize the chapter's major points; thus, you can use them as "traffic" signs that direct you to the most important information in the chapter. Better yet, turn the headings into questions and then read to find answers to these questions. This question-and-answer strategy will ensure that you read actively and with a purpose. (You can do this when you preview the chapter by placing a question mark after each heading contained in the chapter.) Creating and answering questions while you read also keeps you motivated; the questions help stimulate your curiosity, and finding answers as you read rewards you for reading (Walter, Knudsbig, & Smith, 2003). Lastly, this strategy is an effective way to prepare for tests because you are practicing exactly what you'll be expected to do on exams—answer questions. You can quickly write the heading questions on separate index cards and use them as flash cards to review for exams. Use the question on the flash card to flashback and attempt to recall the information from the text that answers the question.

2. **Pay special attention to words that are *italicized*, <u>underlined</u>, or appear in boldface print.** These usually represent building-block terms whose meanings must be understood before you can grasp the meanings of higher-level ideas and more general concepts covered in the reading. Don't simply highlight these words because their special appearance suggests they are important. Read these terms carefully and be sure you understand their meaning before you continue reading.

3. **Pay special attention to the first and last sentences in each paragraph.** These sentences contain an important introduction and conclusion to the ideas covered in that passage. When reading sequential or cumulative material that requires comprehension of what was previously covered to understand what will be covered next, it's a good idea to reread the first and last sentences of each paragraph before you move on to the next paragraph.

4. **Reread the chapter after you've heard your instructor lecture on the material contained in the chapter.** You can use your lecture notes as a guide to help you focus on what information in the chapter your instructor feels is most important. If you adopt this strategy, your reading before lectures will help you understand the lecture and take better class notes, and your reading after lectures will help you locate and learn the most important information contained in your textbook.

Remember

Your goal when reading is not merely to cover the assigned pages but to uncover the most important information and ideas contained in those pages.

Take Written Notes on What You're Reading

Just as you write notes in response to your instructor's lectures in class, take notes in response to the author's words in the text. For example, write short answers to the boldface heading questions in the text itself by using its side, top, and bottom margins or in a reading journal organized by chapters or units. Writing requires more active thinking than highlighting because you're creating your own words rather than passively highlighting words written by someone else. Don't get into the habit of using your textbook as a coloring book in which the artistic process of highlighting what you're reading with spectacular kaleidoscopic colors distracts you from the more important process of learning actively and thinking deeply.

> "I would advise you to read with a pen in your hand, and enter in a little book of short hints of what you find that is curious, or that might be useful; for this will be the best method of imprinting such particulars in your memory, where they will be ready."
>
> –Benjamin Franklin, eighteenth-century inventor, newspaper writer, and cosigner of the Declaration of Independence

Pause Periodically to Summarize and Paraphrase What You're Reading in Your Own Words

If you can express what someone else has written in words that make sense to you, this means that you understand what you're reading and can relate it to what you already know—which is a telltale sign of deep learning (Demmert & Towner, 2003). A good time to pause and paraphrase is when you encounter a boldface heading that indicates you're about to be introduced to a new concept. This may be the ideal place to stop and summarize what you read in the section you just completed.

!

Remember

Effective reading isn't a passive or mechanical process in which you just follow printed words on a page. Instead, it's a reflective process in which you actively search for and find meaning in the words you read.

Use the Visual Aids Included in Your Textbook

Don't fall into the trap of thinking that visual aids can or should be skipped because they're merely add-ons that are secondary to the written words of the text. Visual aids, such as charts, graphs, diagrams, and concept maps, are powerful learning and memory tools for a couple of reasons:

1. They enable you to "see" the information in addition to reading (hearing) it.
2. They organize separate pieces of information into an integrated picture.

Furthermore, visual aids allow you to periodically experience a mode of information input other than repeatedly reading words. This occasional change of pace brings variety to the reading process, which can recharge your attention and motivation to read.

Pause for Reflection

When reading a textbook, do you usually have the following tools on hand?

Highlighter:	yes	no
Pen or pencil:	yes	no
Notebook:	yes	no
Class notes:	yes	no
Dictionary:	yes	no
Glossary:	yes	no

Postreading Strategies: What Should Be Done After Reading

End a Reading Session With a Short Review of the Information You've Noted or Highlighted

Most forgetting that takes place after you receive and process information occurs immediately after you stop focusing on the information and turn your attention to another task (Underwood, 1983). (See **Figure 6.4.**) Taking a few minutes at the end of your reading time to review the most important information locks that information into your memory before you turn your attention to something else and forget it.

The graph in Figure 6.4 represents recall of information at different intervals after it was originally learned. As you can see, most forgetting of information occurs right after learning (e.g., after 20 minutes, the participants in the study forgot more than 60 percent of it). This suggests that reviewing information from reading or a lecture immediately after it's been acquired is an effective strategy for intercepting the forgetting curve and improving memory.

Seek Outside Help From Informed Sources

If you find you can't understand a concept explained in your text, even after rereading and repeatedly reflecting on it, try the following strategies:

1. **Look at how another textbook explains it.** Not all textbooks are created equally; some do a better job of explaining certain concepts than others. Check to see whether your library has other texts in the same subject as your course, or check your campus bookstore for textbooks in the same subject area as the course you're taking. A different text may be able to

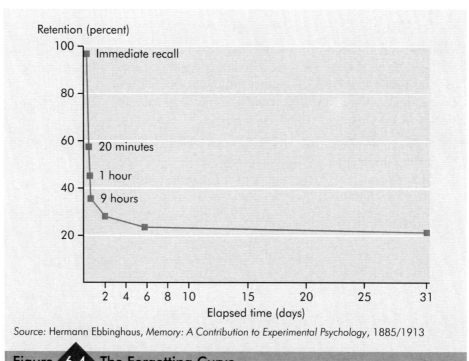

Source: Hermann Ebbinghaus, *Memory: A Contribution to Experimental Psychology*, 1885/1913

Figure 6.4   The Forgetting Curve

explain a hard-to-understand concept much better than the textbook you purchased for the course.

2. **Seek help from your instructor.** If you read carefully and made every effort to understand a particular concept but still can't grasp it, your instructor should be willing to assist you. If your instructor is unavailable or unwilling to assist you, seek help from the professionals and peer tutors in the Learning Center or Academic Support Center on campus.

Another technique for organizing and remembering strategies for improving reading comprehension and retention is the SQ3R method. See **Box 6.3** for a summary of steps involved in this reading method.

Take Action!

6.3

The SQ3R Method

SQ3R is an acronym of the five steps you can take to increase textbook-reading comprehension and retention, particularly when reading highly technical or complex material. The sequence in this method is as follows:

1. Survey
2. Question
3. Read
4. Recite
5. Review

S = **S**urvey: *Get a preview and overview of what you're about to read.*

1. Read the title to activate your thoughts about the subject and prepare your mind to receive information related to it.
2. Read the introduction, chapter objectives, and chapter summary to become familiar with the author's purpose, goals, and most important points.
3. Note the boldface headings and subheadings to get a sense of the chapter's organization before you begin to read. It will help you understand or create a mental structure for the information to come.
4. Notice any graphics, such as charts, maps, and diagrams. They provide valuable visual support and reinforcement for the material you're reading, so don't ignore them.

5. Pay special attention to reading aids (e.g., italics and boldface font) that you can use to identify, understand, and remember key concepts.

Q = **Q**uestion: *Stay active and curious.*
As you read, use the boldface headings to formulate questions you think will be answered in that particular section. When your mind is actively searching for answers to questions, it becomes more engaged in the learning process. As you continue to read, add any questions that you have about the reading.

R = **R**ead: *Find the answer to the question or questions.*
Read one section at a time, with your questions in mind, and search for answers to these questions. Also, keep an eye out for new questions that need to be asked.

R = **R**ecite: *Rehearse your answers.*
After you read each section, recall the questions you asked and see whether you can answer them from memory. If not, look at the questions again and practice your answers to them until you can recall them without looking. Don't move onto the next section until you're able to answer all questions in the section you've just completed.

R = **R**eview: *Look back and get a second view of the whole picture.*
Once you've finished the chapter, review all the questions you've created for different parts or sections. See whether you can still answer them all without looking. If not, go back and refresh your memory.

◆ Study Strategies for Learning Deeply and Remembering Longer

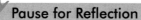

Pause for Reflection

Rate yourself in terms of how frequently you use these reading strategies according to the following scale:

4 = always, 3 = sometimes, 2 = rarely, 1 = never

1. I read the chapter outlines and summaries before I start reading the chapter content.　　4　3　2　1

2. I preview a chapter's boldface headings and subheadings before I begin to read the chapter.　　4　3　2　1

3. I adjust my reading speed to the type of subject I am reading.　　4　3　2　1

4. I look up the meaning of unfamiliar words and unknown terms that I come across before I continue reading.　　4　3　2　1

5. I take written notes on information I read.　　4　3　2　1

6. I use the visual aids included in my textbooks.　　4　3　2　1

7. I finish my reading sessions with a review of important information that I noted or highlighted.　　4　3　2　1

Learning gets information into your brain; the next step is to save that information in your brain (memory storage) and bring it back to mind at test time (memory retrieval). Described here is a series of effective study strategies for acquiring knowledge (learning) and keeping that knowledge in your brain (memory).

The Importance of Undivided Attention

Attention comes in a fixed amount. You only have so much of it available to you at any point in time, and you can give all or part of it to whatever task you're working on. If study time is spent on multiple tasks that provide sources of external stimulation (e.g., listening to music, watching TV, or text-messaging friends), the total attention time available for studying is subtracted and divided among the other tasks. In other words, studying doesn't receive your undivided attention.

Studies show that when people multitask they don't pay equal attention to all tasks at the same time. Instead, they divide their attention by shifting it back and forth between tasks (Howard, 2000), and their performance on the task that demands the most concentration or deepest thinking is the one that suffers the most (Crawford & Strapp, 1994). Furthermore, research shows that multitasking can increase boredom with tasks that involve concentration. One study found that with even a low level of distraction, such as a TV turned on a low volume in the next room, students were more likely to describe the mental task they were concentrating on as "boring" (Damrad-Frye & Laird, 1989).

When performing tasks that cannot be done automatically (mindlessly), including complex mental tasks, other tasks and sources of external stimulation interfere with the quiet, internal reflection needed for permanent connections to form between brain cells (Jensen, 1998)—which is what has to happen biologically for deep, long-lasting learning to take place.

! | **Remember**

Without attention first, there can be no retention later.

Meaningful Association

Relating what you're trying to learn to something you already know is a powerful learning strategy because learning is all about making connections in the brain. People tend to perceive meaningful patterns in information because knowledge is stored in the form of a connected network of brain cells (Coward, 1990).

The brain's natural tendency to seek meaningful, whole patterns applies to words, as well as images. The following passage once appeared (anonymously) on the Internet. See whether you can read it and grasp its meaning.

Aoccdrnig to rscheearch at Cmabridge Uinverstisy, it deos't mattaer in what order the ltteers in a word are, the only iprmoetnt thing is that the frist and lsat ltteer be at the rghit pclae. The rset can be a total mses and you can still raed it wouthit a porbelm. This is bcusae the human mind deos not raed ervey lteter by istlef, but the word as a wlohe. Amzanig huh?

Notice how easily you found the meaning of the misspelled words by naturally transforming them into correctly spelled words—which you knew because they were stored in your brain. Thus, whenever you learn something, you do so by connecting what you're trying to understand to what you already know.

Learning by making meaningful connections is referred to as deep learning (Entwistle & Ramsden, 1983). It involves moving beyond shallow memorization to deeper levels of understanding. This is a major a shift from the old view that learning occurs by passively absorbing information like a sponge, for example, by receiving it from the teacher or text and studying it in the same, prepackaged form as you received it. Instead, you want to adopt an approach to learning that involves actively transforming the information you receive into a form that's meaningful to you (Entwistle & Marton, 1984; Feldman & Paulsen, 1994). This enables you to move beyond surface-level memorization of information to deeper learning and acquisition of knowledge.

Before you start to repeatedly pound what you're learning into your head like a hammer hitting a nail, first look for a hook to hang it on by relating it to something you already know that's stored in your brain. It may take a little while to discover the right hook, but once you've found it, the information will store in your brain quickly and remain there a long time. For example, consider a meaningful way to learn and remember how to correctly spell one of the most frequently misspelled words in the English language: "separate" (not "seperate"). By remembering that "to par" means to divide, as in the words *par*ts or *par*tition, it makes sense that the word "separate" should be spelled se*par*ate because its meaning is "to divide into parts."

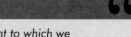

"The extent to which we remember a new experience has more to do with how it relates to existing memories than with how many times or how recently we have experienced it."

–Morton Hunt, *The Universe Within: A New Science Explores the Human Mind*

Remember

The more meaningful you make what you're learning, the deeper you learn it and the longer you remember it.

Meaning in Academic Terms

Each academic field has specialized vocabulary that can sound like a foreign language to someone who has no experience with the subject area. Before you start to brutally beat these terms into your brain through sheer repetition, try to find some meaning in them. You can make a term more meaningful to you by looking up its word root in the dictionary or by identifying its prefix or suffix, which may give away the term's meaning. For instance, suppose you were studying the autonomic nervous system in biology, which is the part of the

---

Personal Story

Some time ago, I had to give up running because of damage to my right hip, so I decided to start riding a stationary bike instead. My wife found an inexpensive, used stationary bike at a garage sale. It was an old and somewhat rusty bike that made a repeated noise that sounded like "ee-zoh" as the wheel spun. One evening I was riding it and, after about 10 minutes, I noticed that I was hearing the words "zero," "rosy," and "Rio" off and on in my head. My brain was taking a meaningless sound ("ee-zoh"), which it apparently grew bored of hearing as the wheels spun, and transforming that sound into words that provided it with variety and meaning. Perhaps this was a classic case of how the human brain naturally prefers to seek meaning rather than mindless repetition.

—Joe Cuseo

Pause for Reflection

Can you think of information you're learning in a course this term that you could form a meaningful association to remember?

What is the information you're attempting to learn?

What is the meaningful association you could use to help you remember it?

nervous system that operates without your conscious awareness or voluntary control (e.g., your heart beating and lungs breathing). The meaning of the phrase is given away by the prefix "auto," which means self-controlling—as in the word "automatic" (e.g., automatic transmission).

If the term's root, prefix, or suffix doesn't give away its meaning, then see whether you can make it more meaningful to you in some other way. For instance, suppose you looked up the root of the term "artery" and nothing about the origins of this term suggested its meaning or purpose. You could then create your own meaning for this term by taking its first letter (a), and have it stand for "*a*way"—to help you remember that arteries carry blood away from the heart. Thus, you've taken a biological term and made it personally meaningful (and memorable).

Compare and Contrast

When you're studying something new, get in the habit of asking yourself the following questions:

1. Is this idea similar or comparable to something that I've already learned? (Compare)
2. How does this idea differ from what I already know? (Contrast)

Research indicates that this simple strategy is one of the most powerful ways to promote learning of academic information (Marzano, Pickering, & Pollock, 2001). The power of the compare-and-contrast strategy probably stems from asking the question, "How is this similar to and different from concepts that I already know?" By working to answer this question, you make learning more personally meaningful because you are relating what you're trying to learn to what you already know.

Integration and Organization

Pull together or integrate information from your class notes and assigned reading related to the same major concept or category. For example, get this information in the same place by recording it on the same index card under the same category heading. Index cards are a good tool for such purposes; you can use

each card as a miniature file cabinet for a separate category of information. The category heading on each card functions like the hub of a wheel, around which individual pieces of related information are attached like spokes. Integrating information related to the same topic in the same place and studying it at the same time helps divide the total material you need to learn into more identifiable and manageable parts. In contrast, when ideas pertaining to the same point or concept are spread all over the place, they're more likely to take that form in your mind—leaving them mentally disconnected and leaving you confused (as well as feeling stressed and overwhelmed).

Pause for Reflection

Are you more likely to study in advance of exams or cram just before exams?

Why?

Divide and Conquer

Effective learning depends not only on how you learn (your study method); it also depends on *when* you learn (your study timing). Although cramming just before exams is better than not studying, it is far less effective than studying that's spread out across time. Rather than cramming all your studying into one long session, use the distributed practice method, which spreads study time over several shorter sessions. Research consistently shows that short, periodic practice sessions are more effective than a single marathon session.

Distributing your study time over several shorter sessions improves your learning and memory by:

- Reducing loss of attention due to fatigue or boredom; and
- Reducing mental interference by giving the brain some down-time to cool down and lock in information that it's received without being interrupted by the need to deal with additional information (Murname & Shiffrin, 1991).

Spreading out your studying into shorter sessions improves your memory by reducing loss of attention due to fatigue.

If the brain's downtime is interfered with by the arrival of additional information, it gets overloaded and its capacity for handling information becomes impaired. This is what cramming does—it overloads the brain with lots of information in a limited period. In contrast, distributed study does just the opposite—it uses shorter sessions with downtime between sessions, thereby giving the brain the time and opportunity to save (retain) the information that it's processing (studying).

Another major advantage of distributed study is that it's less stressful and more motivating than cramming. Shorter sessions can be an incentive to study because you know that you're not going to be doing it for a long stretch of time or lose any sleep over it. It's easier to maintain your interest and motivation for any task that's done for a shorter rather than a longer period. Furthermore, you should feel more relaxed because if you run into difficulty understanding anything you know there's still time to get help with it before you're tested and graded on it.

The Part-to-Whole Study Method

The part-to-whole method of studying is a natural extension of the distributed practice just discussed. With the part-to-whole method, you break the material you need to study into separate parts and study those parts in separate sessions in advance of the exam. You then use your last study session just

Student Perspective

"When I have to re-tain knowledge, I do not procrastinate; I can usually slowly remember everything. The knowledge is in [my] long-term memory, so I usually have no problems retaining it."

–First-year college student

Student Perspective

"Do not cram. If you start to prepare for a test about 3–5 days before, then you will only need to do a quick review the night before."

–Advice to new college students from an experienced student (Walsh, 2005)

before the exam to review (restudy) all the parts that you previously studied in separate sessions. Thus, your last study session is a review session, rather than a study session, because you're not trying to learn information for the first time.

Don't buy into the myth that studying in advance is a waste of time because you'll forget it all by test time. This is the myth that procrastinators use to put off studying until the last moment, when they cram for their exams. Do not underestimate the power of breaking material to be learned into smaller parts and studying those parts some time before a major exam. Even if you cannot recall what you previously studied, when you start reviewing it you'll find that you will relearn it much faster than when you studied it the first time. This proves that studying in advance is not pointless, because it takes less time to relearn the material. The memory of it remains in your brain from the time you studied it earlier (Kintsch, 1994).

Reviewing

For sequential or cumulative subjects that build on understanding of previously covered material to learn new concepts (e.g., math), it's especially important to begin each study session with a quick review of what you learned in your previous study session.

Research shows that students of all ability levels learn material in college courses more effectively when it's studied in small units and when progression to the next unit takes place only after the previous unit has been mastered or understood (Pascarella & Terenzini, 1991, 2005). This strategy has two advantages: (a) it reinforces your memory for what you previously learned and (b) it builds on what you already know to help you learn new material. This is particularly important in cumulative subjects that require memory for problem-solving procedures or steps, such as math and science. By repeatedly practicing these procedures, they become more automatic and you're able to retrieve them quicker (e.g., on a timed test) and use them efficiently without having to expend a lot of mental effort and energy (Newell & Rosenbloom, 1981). This frees your working memory for more important tasks, such as critical thinking and creative problem solving (Schneider & Chein, 2003).

Variety in the Study Process

The following strategies can be used to infuse variety and a change of pace into your study routine, which can increase your concentration and motivation.

1. Periodically vary the type of academic work you do while studying.

Changing the nature of your work activities or the type of mental tasks you're performing while studying increases your level of alertness and concentration by reducing habituation—a psychological term referring to the attention loss that occurs after repeated engagement in the same type of mental task (McGuiness & Pribram, 1980). To combat attention loss due to habituation, occasionally vary the type of study task you're performing. For instance, shift periodically among tasks that involve reading, writing, studying (e.g., rehearsing or reciting), and practicing skills (e.g., solving problems).

2. Study different subjects in different places.

Studying in different locations provides different environmental contexts for learning, which reduces the amount of interference that normally builds up when all information is studied in the same place (Anderson & Bower, 1974). Thus, in addition to spreading out your studying at different times, it's a good idea to spread it out in different places. The great public speakers in ancient Greek and Rome used this method of changing places to remember long speeches by walking through different rooms while rehearsing their speech, learning each major part of their speech in a different room (Higbee, 1998).

Changing the nature of the learning task and the learning environment provides changes of pace that infuse variety into the learning process, which improves attention and concentration. Although it's useful to have a set time and place to study for getting you into a regular work routine, this doesn't mean that learning occurs best by habitually performing all types of academic tasks in the same place. Instead, research suggests that you should periodically change the learning tasks you perform and the environment in which you perform them to maximize attention and minimize interference (Druckman & Bjork, 1991).

! Remember

Change of pace and place while studying can stimulate your attention to, and your interest in, what you're studying.

3. Mix long study sessions with short study breaks that involve physical activity (e.g., a short jog or brisk walk).

Study breaks that include physical activity not only refresh the mind by giving it a rest from studying but also stimulate the mind by increasing blood flow to your brain, which will help you retain what you've already studied and regain concentration for what you'll study next.

4. Use all of your senses.

When studying, try to use as many sensory channels as possible. Research shows that information perceived through multiple sensory modalities or channels is remembered better (Bjork, 1994; Schacter, 1992) because it forms more interconnections in long-term memory areas of the brain (Zull, 2002). When a memory is formed in the brain, different sensory aspects of it are stored in different areas. For example, when your brain receives visual, auditory (hearing), and motor (movement) stimulation that accompany with what you're learning, each of these associations is stored in a different part of the brain. See **Figure 6.5** for a map of the surface of the human brain; you can see how different parts of the brain are specialized to receive input from different sensory modalities. When you use all of these sensory modalities while learning, multiple memory traces of what you're studying are recorded in different parts of your brain, which leads to deeper learning and stronger memory (Education Commission of the States, 1996).

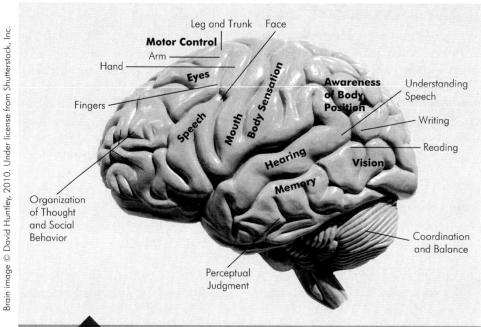

Brain image © David Huntley, 2010. Under license from Shutterstock, Inc.

Figure 6.5 A Map of the Functions Performed by the Outer Surface of the Human Brain

5. Learn visually.

The human brain consists of two hemispheres (half rounds): the left and the right hemispheres (see **Figure 6.6**).

Each hemisphere of the brain specializes in a different type of learning. In most people, the left hemisphere specializes in verbal learning, dealing primarily with words. In contrast, the right hemisphere specializes in visual–spatial learning, dealing primarily with images and objects that occupy physical space. If you use both hemispheres while studying, you lay down two different memory traces in your brain: one in left hemisphere, where words are stored, and one in the right hemisphere, where images are stored. This process of laying down a double memory trace (verbal and visual) is referred to as dual coding (Paivio, 1990). When this happens, memory for what you're learning is substantially strengthened, primarily because two memory traces are better than one.

To capitalize on the advantage of dual coding, use any visual aids that are available to you. Use the visual aids provided in your textbook and by your instructor, or create your own by drawing pictures, symbols, and concept maps, such as flowcharts or branching tree diagrams. See **Figure 6.7** for a concept map that could be used to help you remember the parts and functions of the human nervous system.

Pause for Reflection

Would you say that you're more of a visual learner or verbal learner?

How do you think most people would answer this question?

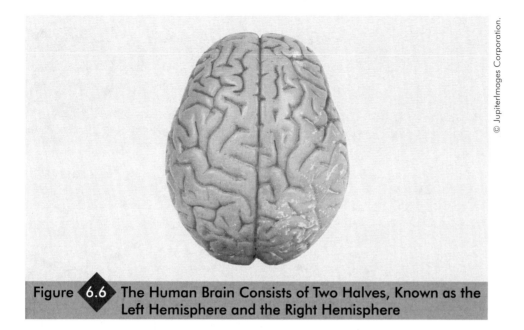

© JupiterImages Corporation.

Figure **6.6** **The Human Brain Consists of Two Halves, Known as the Left Hemisphere and the Right Hemisphere**

! Remember

Drawing and other forms of visual illustration are not just artistic exercises; they also can be powerful learning tools (i.e., you can draw to learn). Drawing keeps you actively involved with the material you're trying to learn. By representing the material in visual form, you're able to dual-code the information you're studying, thus doubling its number of memory traces in your brain. As the old saying goes, "A picture is worth a thousand words."

Student Perspective

"I have to *hear* it, *see* it, *write* it, and *talk* about it."

—First-year college student responding to the question: "How do you learn best?"

6. Learn by moving or using motor learning (a.k.a. muscle memory).

In addition to hearing and seeing, movement is a sensory channel. When you move, your brain receives kinesthetic stimulation—the sensations generated by your muscles when your body moves. Research shows that memory traces for movement are commonly stored in an area of your brain that plays a major role for all types of learning (Middleton & Strick, 1994). Thus, associating movement with what you're learning can improve your ability to retain it because you record an additional muscle memory trace of it to another area of your brain.

You can use movement to help you learn and retain academic information by using your body to act out what you're studying or to symbolize it with your hands (Kagan & Kagan, 1998). For example, if you're trying to remember five points about something (e.g., five consequences of the Civil War), when you're studying these points, count them on your fingers as you try to recall each of them. Also, remember that talking involves muscle movement of your lips and tongue. Thus, by speaking aloud when you're studying, either to a friend or to yourself, your memory of what you're studying may be improved by adding kinesthetic stimulation to your brain (in addition to the auditory or sound stimulation your brain receives from hearing what you're saying).

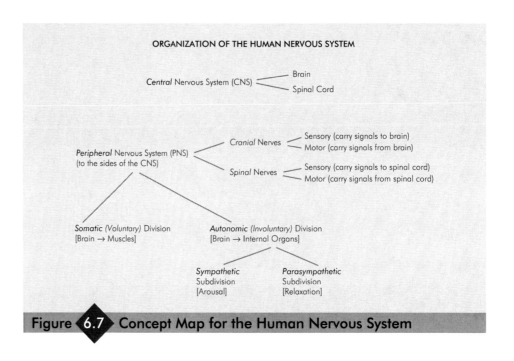

ORGANIZATION OF THE HUMAN NERVOUS SYSTEM

Figure 6.7 Concept Map for the Human Nervous System

7. Learn with emotion.

Information reaches the brain through your senses and can be stored in the brain as a memory trace. The same is true of emotions. Numerous connections occur between brain cells in the emotional and memory centers (Zull, 1998). For instance, when you're experiencing emotional excitement about what you are learning, adrenaline is released and is carried through the bloodstream to your brain. Once adrenaline reaches the brain, it increases blood flow and glucose production, which can stimulate learning and strengthen memory (LeDoux, 1998; Rosenfield, 1988). If you have an emotionally intense experience, such a substantial amount of adrenaline is released in your body that it can lead to immediate, long-term storage of that memory; you'll remember the experience for the rest of your life. For instance, most people remember exactly what they were doing at the time they experienced such emotionally intense events as the September 11 terrorist attack on the United States, their first kiss, or their favorite team winning a world championship.

What does this emotion–memory link have to do with helping you remember academic information that you're studying? Research indicates that emotional intensity, excitement, and enthusiasm affect memory of academic information just as they affect memory for life events and personal experiences. If you get psyched up about what you're learning, you have a much better chance of learning and remembering it. Even telling yourself that it's important to remember what you're learning can increase your memory of it (Howard, 2000; Minninger, 1984).

Pause for Reflection

Think of a course you're taking this term in which you're learning related pieces of information that could be joined together to form a concept map. In the space that follows, make a rough sketch of this map that includes the information you need to remember.

> **Personal Story**
>
> I was talking about memory in class one day and mentioned that when I temporarily forget how to spell a word its correct spelling comes back to me once I start to write it. One of my students raised her hand and said the same thing happens to her when she forgets a phone number—it comes back to her when she starts dialing it. In both of these cases, motor memory brings information back to mind that was temporarily forgotten, which points to the power of movement for promoting learning and memory.
>
> —Joe Cuseo

!

> **Remember**
>
> You will learn most effectively when you actively involve all your senses (including bodily movement) and when you learn with passion and enthusiasm. In other words, learning grows deeper and lasts longer when you put your whole self into it—your heart, your mind, and your body.

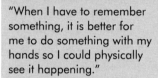

Student Perspective

"When I have to remember something, it is better for me to do something with my hands so I could physically see it happening."

–First-year college student

8. Learn with others.

One way to put the power of group learning into practice is by forming study groups. Research indicates that college students who work regularly in small groups of four to six become more actively involved in the learning process and learn more (Light, 2001).

To maximize the power of study groups, each member should study individually before studying in a group and should come prepared with specific information or answers to share with teammates, as well as questions or points of confusion that the team can attempt to help answer or clarify.

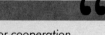

"We are born for cooperation, as are the feet, the hands, the eyelids, and the upper and lower jaws."

–Marcus Aurelius, Roman emperor

Self-Monitoring Learning

Successful learners reflect and check on themselves to see whether they really understand what they're attempting to learn. They monitor their comprehension as they go along by asking themselves questions such as "Am I following this?" "Do I really understand it?" and "Do I know it for sure?"

How do you know if you really know it? Probably the best answer to this question is "I find meaning in it—that is, I can relate to it personally or put it in terms that make sense to me" (Ramsden, 2003). When you really understand a concept, you learn it at a deeper level than by merely memorizing it. You're also more likely to remember that concept because the deeper its roots, the more durable its memory trace that enables you to retain it long term (Kintsch, 1970).

Discussed here are some strategies for checking whether you truly understand what you're trying to learn. They help you answer the question, "How do I know if I really know it?" These strategies can be used as indicators or checkpoints for determining whether you're just memorizing information or you're learning deeply and acquiring knowledge.

- **Can you restate or translate what you're learning into your own words?** When you can paraphrase what you're learning, you're able to complete the following sentence: "In other words, . . ." If you can complete that sentence in your own words, this is a good indication that you've moved beyond memorization to comprehension because you've trans-

Student Perspectives

"I would suggest students get to know [each] other and get together in groups to study or at least review class material. I find it is easier to ask your friends or classmates with whom you are comfortable 'dumb' questions."

–Advice to first-year students from a college sophomore (Walsh, 2005)

"Most things used to be external to me—of out a lecture or textbook. It makes learning a lot more interesting and memorable when you can bring your experiences into it. It makes you want to learn."

–Reentry (adult) first-year student (Wilkie & Thompson, 1993)

> *"When you know a thing, to recognize that you know it; and when you do not, to know that you do not know; that is knowledge."*
>
> –Confucius, influential Chinese thinker and educator

Student Perspective

"I learn best through teaching. When I learn something and teach it to someone else, I find that it really sticks with me a lot better."

–College sophomore

formed what you're learning into words that are meaningful to you. Thus, you learn deeply not by simply stating what your instructor or textbook states but by restating the information in words that are your own.

- **Can you explain what you're learning to someone who is unfamiliar with it?** If you can explain to a friend what you've learned, this is a good sign that you've moved beyond memorization to comprehension because you are able to translate it into less technical language that someone hearing it for the first time can understand. Often, you won't realize how well you know or don't know something until you have to explain it to someone who's never heard it before (just ask any teacher). Simply put, if you can't explain it to someone else, you don't really understand it yourself. Studies show that students gain deeper levels of understanding for what they're learning when they're asked to explain it to someone else (Chi, de Leeuw, Chiu, & LaVancher, 1994). If you cannot find someone else to explain it to, then explain it aloud as if you were talking to an imaginary friend.

- **Can you think of an example of what you've learned?** If you can come up with an instance of what you're learning that is your own example—not one given by your instructor or textbook—this is a good sign that you truly comprehend it. It shows you're able to take a general, abstract concept and apply it to a specific, real-life experience (Bligh, 2000). Furthermore, a personal example is a powerful memory tool. Studies show that when people retrieve a concept from memory they first recall an example of it, which then serves a memory-retrieval cue to trigger their memory of other details about the concept, such as its definition and relationship to other concepts (Norman, 1982; Park, 1984).

Personal Story

When I was in my senior year of college, I had to take a theory course by independent study because the course would not be offered again until after I planned to graduate. Another senior found himself in the same situation. The instructor allowed both of us to take this course together and agreed to meet with us every 2 weeks. My fellow classmate and I studied independently for the first 2 weeks. I prepared for the biweekly meetings by reading thoroughly, yet I had little understanding of what I had read. After our first meeting, I left with a strong desire to drop the course but decided to stick with it. Over the next 2 weeks, I spent many sleepless nights trying to prepare for our next meeting and was feeling pretty low about not being the brightest student in my class of two. During the next meeting with the instructor, I found out that the other student was also having difficulty. Not only did I notice, so did the instructor. After that meeting, the instructor gave us study questions and asked us to read separately and then get together to discuss the questions. During the next 2 weeks, my classmate and I met several times to discuss what we were learning (or attempting to learn). By being able to communicate with each other about the issues we were studying, we both ended up gaining greater understanding. Our instructor was delighted to see that he was able to suggest a learning strategy that worked for both of us.

—Aaron Thompson

- **Can you represent or describe what you've learned in terms of an analogy or metaphor that compares it to something that has similar meaning or that works in a similar way?** Analogies and metaphors are basically ways of learning something new by understanding it in terms of its similarity to something you already understand. For instance, the computer can be used as a metaphor for the human brain to get a better understanding of learning and memory as a three-stage process in which information is (a) perceived or received (through lectures and readings), (b) stored or saved (through studying), and (c) retrieved (recalled at test time). If you can use an analogy or metaphor to represent what you're learning, you're grasping it at a deep level because you're able to build a mental bridge that connects it to what you already know (Cameron, 2003).

- **Can you apply what you're learning to solve a new problem that you haven't previously seen?** The ability to use your knowledge shows deep learning (Erickson & Strommer, 2005). Learning specialists refer to this mental process as decontextualization—taking what you learned in one context (situation) and applying it to another (Bransford, Brown, & Cocking, 1999). For instance, you know that you've learned a mathematical concept when you can use that concept to solve math problems that are different from the ones initially used by your instructor or textbook to help you learn it. This is why your math instructors rarely include on exams the exact problems solved in class or in your textbook. They're not trying to trick you at test time; they're trying to test your comprehension to determine whether you've learned the concept or principle deeply or just memorized it superficially.

Pause for Reflection

Rate yourself in terms of how frequently you use these study strategies according to the following scale:

4 = always, 3 = sometimes, 2 = rarely, 1 = never

1. I block out all distracting sources of outside stimulation when I study.   4 3 2 1

2. I try to find meaning in technical terms by looking at their prefix or suffix or by looking up their word root in the dictionary.   4 3 2 1

3. I compare and contrast what I'm currently studying with what I've already learned.   4 3 2 1

4. I organize the information I'm studying into categories or classes.   4 3 2 1

5. I integrate or pull together information from my class notes and readings that relate to the same concept or general category.   4 3 2 1

6. I distribute or spread out my study time over several short sessions in advance of the exam, and I use my last study session before the test to review the information I previously studied.   4 3 2 1

7. I participate in study groups with my classmates.   4 3 2 1

Summary and Conclusion

Information delivered during lectures is most likely to form questions and answers on college tests. At exam time, students who did not record lectures in notes have a slim chance of recalling the information presented. Thus, effective note taking is critical to successful academic performance in college.

Information from reading assignments is the next most common source of test questions on college exams. Professors often won't discuss these assignments in detail in class and sometimes don't even bring up the information from this reading. Thus, doing the assigned reading, and doing it in a way that's most effective for promoting comprehension and retention, plays an important role in your academic success.

The most effective strategies for promoting effective classroom listening, textbook reading, and higher-level thinking are those that reflect three of the college-success principles discussed in Chapter 2: (a) active involvement,

"Each problem that I solved became a rule which served afterwards to solve other problems."

—Rene Descartes, seventeenth-century French philosopher and mathematician

(b) interpersonal interaction and collaboration, and (c) personal reflection and self-awareness.

Active involvement is critical for learning from lectures (e.g., actively taking notes while listening to lectures) and learning from reading (e.g., actively taking notes while reading). While active involvement is necessary for learning because it engages your attention and thus enables information to reach your brain, personal reflection is necessary for deep learning because it promotes consolidation, retaining information in your brain by locking it into long-term memory. Reflection also encourages deep learning by promoting self-awareness. By periodically pausing to reflect on whether you are truly attending to and understanding the words you're hearing in lectures and the words you're seeing while reading, you become a more self-aware learner and a more effective learner.

Lastly, learning from note taking, reading, and higher-level thinking can all be magnified if they're done collaboratively. You can collaborate with peers to take better notes in class, to identify what's most important in your assigned reading, and to ask questions of one another that promote higher-level thinking.

Learning More on Your Own Through the World Wide Web

Internet-Based Resources for Further Information on Liberal Arts Education

For additional information related to the ideas discussed in this chapter, we recommend the following Web sites:

www.Dartmouth.edu/~acskills/success/index.html

www.utexas.edu/student/utlc

www.muskingum.edu/~cal/database/general/

www.pima.edu/library/online-distance/study-guides/StudySkills.shtml

Learning Math and Overcoming Math Anxiety:

www.mathacademy.com/pr/minitext/anxiety

www.onlinemathlearning.com/math-mnemonics.html

6.1 Self-Assessment of Note-Taking and Reading Habits

Look back at the ratings you gave yourself for effective note-taking (**p. 114**), reading (**p. 122**), and studying (**p. 128**) strategies. Add up your total score for these three sets of learning strategies (the maximum score for each set is 28):

Note Taking = _____

Reading = _____

Studying = _____

Total Learning Strategy Score = _____

Self-Assessment Questions

1. In which learning strategy area did you score lowest?

2. Do you think that the strategy area in which you scored lowest has anything to do with your lowest course grade at this point in the term?

3. Of the seven strategies listed within the area in which you scored lowest, which ones could you immediately put into practice to improve your lowest course grade this term?

4. What is the likelihood that you will put the preceding strategies into practice this term?

6.2 Consultation with a Learning Center or Academic Development Specialist

Make an appointment to visit your Learning Center or Academic Support Center on campus to discuss the results of your note-taking, reading, and studying self-assessment in Exercise 6.1 (or any other learning self-assessment you may have taken). Ask for recommendations about how you can improve your learning habits in your lowest-score area. Following your visit, answer the following questions.

Learning Resource Center Reflection

1. Date of appointment _____

2. Who did you meet with in the Learning Center? _____

3. Was your appointment useful (e.g., did you gain any insights or acquire any new learning or test-taking strategies)?

4. What steps were recommended to you for improving your academic performance?

5. How likely is it that you will take the steps mentioned in the previous question: (a) definitely, (b) probably, (c) possibly, or (d) unlikely? Why?

6. Do you plan to visit the Learning Center again? If yes, why? If no, why not?

Too Fast, Too Frustrating: A Note-Taking Nightmare

Joanna Scribe is a first-year student who is majoring in journalism, and she's enrolled in an introductory course that is required for her major (Introduction to Mass Media). Her instructor for this course lectures at a rapid rate and uses vocabulary words that go right over her head. Since she cannot get all the instructor's words down on paper and cannot understand half the words she does manage to write down, she becomes frustrated and stops taking notes. She wants to do well in this course because it's the first course in her major, but she's afraid she will fail it because her class notes are so pitiful.

Reflection and Discussion Questions

1. Can you relate to this case personally, or do know any students who are in the same boat as Joanna?

2. What would you recommend that Joanna do at this point?

3. Why did you make the preceding recommendation?

Successful Essay Writing

How to Effectively Attack Critical Composition

Separated from the act of thinking and creating, writing becomes merely a skill that can be learned through grammar drills and through the production of pointless essays that students do not want to write and that teachers do not want to read. This is the view of writing possessed by many first-year students when they show up at our gates to begin their college careers. It is the challenge of faculty across the discipline to show them other ways of imagining writing.

—John C. Bean *Engaging Ideas*

Only by wrestling with the conditions of the problem at first hand, seeking and finding his own way out, does [the student] think.

—John Dewey *Democracy and Education*

Few students make smooth transitions from writing in high school or community college to writing in the university setting. But most students find out through a harsh process of trial and error that university instructors are not looking for merely *better* writing, but a *different* kind of writing. Since this is the case, you will not succeed in college by writing slightly better high school essays. Instead you will have to direct your skills and intelligence to your new expectations.

The inclusion of critical thought and the way in which that thought is communicated to the audience are the primary differences between high school and college writing. College writing assignments force students to explore an idea by delving into its complexities and then clearly theorizing what makes that idea operate. Critical thought is an important component of college writing.

This chapter is not intended to be an all-encompassing guide to every writing assignment you will encounter in college. You will be asked to write many different types of papers throughout college. Sometimes you will be asked to respond to a reading or write a journal containing your thoughts about an issue. There may be occasions when your instructor only wants a summary of the information provided in the course. It is likely that you are familiar with these types of writing from high school or community college. As a result, these forms of composition are not the main focus of this chapter. Instead, this section aims to examine the main purpose of the hardest form of collegiate writing: critical composition.

From *"The University Mind: Essential Skills for Academic Success"* Second Edition by Regents of the University of California.
Copyright © 2005 by Kendall Hunt Publishing Company. Used with permission.

◆ New Expectations

Upon entering college, you will be expected to think on par with the professional researchers who teach your classes. Professors construct whole classes around problems that have no definitive answer. Consequently, in sharing these difficult problems with you, they expect you to contribute to the discussion of these issues. You are not expected to "solve" the problem, but you must at least understand its complexities while addressing its ambiguities. It is this form of critical composition that is new and puzzling to new college students.

◆ The Assignment

It is absolutely crucial that you understand the boundaries and requirements of the assignment. If your assignment has any terms or key phrases, make sure that you have a clear understanding of what they mean. If any information is unclear or poorly worded, ask a teaching assistant or professor for clarification.

In addition, make sure you have a clear understanding of the verbs used in the prompt. For instance, you won't be able to write a great essay that asks you to "analyze" if you don't know that to analyze means "to examine methodically by separating into parts and studying their interrelations."

The majority of assignments posed in college are problem-based. More specifically, the prompt will ask a question or pose a problem that needs to be solved using critical thought. As previously defined, critical thinking is "a rational response to questions that cannot be answered definitely and for which all the relevant information may not be available."[1] Since college courses are designed to tackle these persistent questions, college writing has the same goal: to devise a resolution to the discordance or lack of information presented. In providing solutions to these problems, you will inevitably establish the key feature in critical composition: the argument.

◆ The Argument

In college, an argument is central to the development of an idea that answers a critical question. The argument is the perfect backdrop for discussing unanswerable questions because it instigates questions, inspires new thoughts, and demands supportive evidence. An argument concerns itself with coherently presenting three elements:[2]

- a *claim* or *thesis* that initiates the reader's interest, encouraging him/her to say, "That's interesting. Tell me more."
- *objective evidence* and *reasons* for your thesis, making it plausible, reasonable, and even persuasive.
- consideration of the *limits* and *objections* to your claim. Any and all interesting claims can be reasonably challenged. Readers seek the answers to questions like "But what about . . . ?" and "Have you considered . . . ?" or even the daunting "Why?" to be contained within the argument itself.

College writing is about joining an ongoing academic discussion about a certain topic. Both you and your instructors are trying to answer the critical questions that form the basis for your course. Thus, by writing a paper you are essentially talking back to your professor about the issues raised in class. You do not want to mirror the professor's points, nor do you want to make incredibly exaggerated claims. Instead, you want to state and defend your unique point of view on the issue using the evidence at hand. While your claim in this discussion is based on opinion and judgments, you are expected to argue and defend it thoroughly against counterarguments.

Even though your argument does reflect your individual judgment on this particular issue, do not think that your essay's claim is undeniable because it is merely a matter of opinion. To believe that all opinions are equal is a fundamental mistake of dualism or multiplicity. While it is true that all of us are entitled to our own opinions, it is a fallacy to believe that all opinions are equally plausible. This is the point of argumentation: to determine the validity of an opinion based upon its claim, its evidence, and its ability to withstand objections. Since all knowledge is incomplete (on some level), the exploration of knowledge through research and argumentation is an important way to join the academic discussion by formulating reasonable answers to critical questions.

◆ Thinking on Paper

This chapter will constantly mention rewriting and revising large portions of your paper. Basically, it is in your best interest to compose more than one draft of a composition. The actual act of writing causes further discovery, modification, and development of ideas. The first draft of an essay is usually awkwardly muddled because the process of writing is the process of thinking through a topic. The early drafts of any essay should allow the author to clarify his/her own understanding of a topic. Only after these drafts are completed should the writer worry about making the essay clear and coherent to the reader. These late drafts should "create 'reader-based' prose, which aims to meet readers' needs for effective organization, adequate development, and clarity."[3] While there is no specific number, a good essay should go through numerous drafts (official and unofficial) before the author believes that he/she understands the topic thoroughly, has contributed a meaningful piece of knowledge, and has crafted a clear message containing that knowledge. The final product should be substantially different from your first draft because you have spent considerable time developing your ideas and clarifying your methods of communication. According to John C. Bean, professor of English at Seattle University, "a C essay is an A essay turned in too soon."[4]

When writing, you critically think and synthesize solutions and analyses in a thorough manner. Therefore, why not use these solutions and analyses to further enhance a second draft of your paper? It requires more effort; yet, it will result in a far higher-quality paper.

◆ Thesis as Theory

Your thesis will determine the direction and content of your argument. A thesis is a proposition that is maintained by an argument. A good thesis should pose a question and try to answer it or address and articulate a complex idea. Yet, a thesis does not have to be a solution. It can merely expand the analysis or perspective on a particular issue.

In a lot of ways, a thesis is theoretical in nature. A theory is a general or abstract principle intended to explain an unsolved problem. Similarly, a thesis is theoretical in that it attempts to solve a critical question, but can never do so completely. Theories address both the abstract and the concrete by answering a general question without directly referring to evidence, but having been founded by the evidence. Likewise, thesis statements must do the same. Both a thesis and theory go beyond answering "what?" and seek to answer "how?" or "why?" Both are subject to speculation, skepticism, and revision. And both are the only means we have to address questions that cannot be answered completely.

More often than not, your thesis is the most important sentence in your paper. It sums up the most important point you want to make as a result of your reading, thinking, research, and writing. A good thesis has several key characteristics. It should:

- say something significant about what you have studied, something that helps you and your readers understand it better;
- state an idea that is not obvious, something that your reader didn't already know;
- make at least a mildly contestable assertion that you might not agree with just by reading it;
- claim something that can plausibly be supported in the allotted page limit, not a book; and
- intrinsically answers "how" and "why" the claim operates.

Take a look at the following thesis:

Lewis Carroll's Alice's Adventures in Wonderland *subjects the reader to a silly world governed by nonsense.*

So what? The reader probably already knows this. This statement isn't significant concerning the text nor does it help the reader understand it better. Additionally, this thesis does not aim to answer any critical questions about the text; it is merely an observation. It is not contributing to the conversation. Now, look at the following thesis:

Lewis Carroll's illogical world of Wonderland in Alice's Adventures in Wonderland *and* Through the Looking Glass *and* What Alice Found There *introduces several characters that constantly repeat the same nonsensical actions in order to meet the expectations of their respective roles.*

This thesis is an improvement. At least it is now introducing a potentially new idea to the discussion. However, the reader is still unconvinced as to why this is important. This thesis thoroughly addresses the "what?" without bothering to address the "how?" or "why?" Why should the reader care about the repetitive actions of Carroll's characters? What larger function do they play? If a thesis were to answer these larger, critical questions, it would serve your essay better than these previous examples.

In Alice's Adventures in Wonderland *and* Through the Looking Glass *and* What Alice Found There, *Lewis Carroll satirizes the restrictive, repetitive, and nonsensical societal roles of his age through the restrictive, repetitive, and nonsensical roles of the characters in Wonderland.*

Now here is an interesting thesis that proposes *why* Carroll wrote his books and *how* Wonderland operates. It attempts to answer the critical questions: "What was Carroll's purpose in constructing Wonderland" and "How does he accomplish this purpose?" This claim isn't obvious within the text and is both contestable and interesting. It contributes to the larger discussion at hand by mentioning a potentially new thought not only about the content of a topic, but its functional value as well.

You should recognize, however, that you will only rarely be able to make a good claim like this *before* you write your first draft. Much more often, you *discover* good points during or at the end of the process of drafting. The development of your thesis could easily go through the stages of the examples outlined above. Writing is a way of thinking through a problem, of discovering what you want to say. So, do not feel that you should begin to write only when you have a fully articulated point in mind. Instead, write to discover and then to refine. Feel free to begin writing your first draft with a "draft thesis" that can be revised along with the rest of your essay.

The Composing Processes of Expert Academic Writers

According to Bean, author of *Engaging Ideas: The Professor's Guide to Integrating Writing, Critical Thinking, and Active Learning in the Classroom*, expert academic writers rarely

> write a thesis statement and outline before embarking on extensive exploration, conversation, correspondence with colleagues, and even, on some occasions, writing one or more drafts. A thesis statement often marks a moment of discovery and clarification—an "aha!" experience ("So this is my point! Here is my argument in a nutshell!")—not a formulaic planning device at the very start of the process.[5]

Instead, Bean suggests that expert academic writers approach composition from a problem-driven perspective, represented in the steps below.

1. *Starting point: perception of a problem.* Expert writers feel an uncertainty, doubt a theory, note a piece of unexplained data, puzzle over an observation, confront a view that seems mistaken, or otherwise articulate a question or problem.
2. *Exploration.* The expert writer gathers data through library or laboratory and field research and through probing of memory; explores ideas in a journal or research log, in the margins of texts, or on note cards or the backs of envelopes; analyzes, compares, puzzles, talks with others, writes to self; focuses intensely on problem. The expert writer often explores ideas by rapid drafting of potential pieces of the essay or by making notes, doodles, or tentative outlines.
3. *Incubation.* The writer takes time off from the problem, does other things, and lets ideas cook in the subconscious. These first three states are all recursive—as writers alternate between exploration and incubation, their perception of the problem may change.
4. *Writing the first draft.* Expert writers try to get ideas down on paper in preliminary form. Some writers make an informal outline prior to writing; others discover direction as they write, often pursuing different branches of ideas without worrying about coherence. To avoid writer's block, expert writers lower expectations. They do not try to make first drafts perfect as they go.

5. *Reformulation or revision.* Having gone once through the territory, expert writers take another look at the problem and think it through again. Many writers report dismantling their first drafts and starting afresh, often discovering their true thesis at the conclusion of their first draft. At this point, writers often make new outlines; they begin considering audience; they clarify their rhetorical purpose; they try to make the essay work for readers. Several drafts are often necessary as writer-based prose is gradually converted to reader-based prose.

6. *Editing.* At this point, craftsmanship takes over from initial creativity. Writers worry about unity, coherence, paragraphing, sentence structure. Finally, writers begin to polish by correcting spelling and punctuation. Often, the recursive nature of the process is again felt as a writer, working on sentence structure, discovers new meanings or new intentions that require the rethinking of minor or even major parts of the essay.[6]

Bean's model exemplifies how professors write and, consequently, how they expect you to write. As this model points out, the first step in synthesizing a thesis is approaching a critical question. After researching this question and critically analyzing evidence concerning this issue, you will probably discover an idea that seems promising. Yet, due to the complicated nature of knowledge, your thought process cannot end after preliminary research. Be persistent in your pursuit of knowledge. Talk to a peer, professor, or teaching assistant and attempt to explain what you want to write about. Keep working with this idea and start writing or outlining its possibilities. Write a draft to see whether you can plausibly support your argument with an argument. The act of writing is inextricably linked to the act of critical thinking. Through the process of critically writing, you will refine the idea and potentially change it substantially. Don't worry, this is a good thing. Learning is an act of change, moving from not knowing to knowing.

Often, after you've written out your entire argument, you may find that your thoughts and analysis have led your claim in a slightly different direction. If this is the case, you have discovered a more refined statement of your argument. Take the time to include these developed thoughts into another revision of your argument and your thesis. *Don't be afraid to change your thesis.* The discovery of new ideas is the intended goal of writing.

◆ The Consequences of Avoiding a Thesis

Bean's book *Engaging Ideas* also discusses what he calls "three cognitively immature essay structures" that result when writers are unable to produce a thesis-governed essay.[7]

Poor Writing Style	*Characterized by . . .*	*Problems*
"And Then" Writing, or Chronological Structure: In "and then" writing the essay is a chronological narrative in which the writer tells what happens between time point A and time point B without focus, selection, pacing or tension. Students tend to produce "and then" structures whenever they resort inappropriately to chronological organization.	A typical example is writing a summary instead of an argument when asked to review an article or producing a straight chronological narrative instead of a casual analysis when asked to write about an interpretive problem in history. The same tendency is exhibited in research papers when the writer presents data in chronological order rather than using the data to support points or when the writer recounts the story of his or her particular research process rather than arranging material to meet the needs of the reader.	If your reader wanted to know the chronology of a story, they could just read the book itself. You can anticipate your professor asking: "Why should I read your essay on *Hamlet* when it's just a plot summary of the play. I could just read *Hamlet* instead." Your job as a writer is to analyze, interpret, and make conclusions about interesting ideas in any given topic. Your job is not to parrot the material back to your instructor.
"All About" Writing, or Encyclopedic Order: The "all about" tries to say a little bit of everything about a topic. When well written, such papers may seem organized hierarchically because the writer usually groups data by category. But the categories do not function as reasons in support of a thesis.	An "all about" paper will resemble your fifth-grade social studies report on North Dakota. The "all about" paper promises to be encyclopedic and uninteresting. Instead of stringing details in chronological order, this essay actually organizes information, but ultimately lacks a new idea.	Once again, your job as a college writer is not to reproduce evidence or rewrite the encyclopedia. An interesting essay proposes an argument that is driven by the exploration of an unanswered question. The "all about" style is organized, but answers nothing.
"Data Dump" Writing, or Random Organization: While the previous two styles have discernable organizational plans, "data dump" writing, by contrast, has no clear structure. It reveals a student overwhelmed with information and uncertain what to do with it.	Commonly encountered in research papers, "data dump" writing patches together quotes, statistics, and other raw information without a thesis or a coherent organizational plan. It takes all the data the writer gathered about topic X and dumps it, as it were, on the reader's desk.	Even if a topic is difficult, your professor will not be impressed by your ability to gather all relevant information on a topic. Your writing assignments should not include the mere accumulation of information. Your reader wants to learn a new and interesting claim derived from this information.

Without a problem-based thesis, an essay lacks an argumentative core, a theme that holds its parts together, and, most importantly, critical thought. A closer inspection of these "cognitively immature essay structures" reveals a common theme: the fixation on retelling facts. An essay not governed by a thesis will neglect the critical questions of "how?" or "why?" Be sure that your entire essay is devoted to resolving a critical problem.

◆ Writing as Communication

In college, writing is a medium intended to show what you know. While you may have a great understanding of a topic, your ability to communicate that knowledge to someone else might be limited.

This ability to communicate information clearly is extremely important. Universities are research-driven institutions, valuing the sharing of new knowledge and understanding as much as the pursuit of it. Professors expect you to critically think through, analyze, and discuss a particular topic. Yet, it doesn't end there. How you communicate information is just as important as what you have to say.

◆ Evidence

Your problem-based thesis should always be governed by analysis of evidence. Since a thesis theorizes a resolution to a critical question, you must inspect both the problem at hand and all the available evidence surrounding that problem. Some writers like to make a claim and then determine if it can be reasonably supported with relevant data, later revising the thesis through the analysis of evidence. Others prefer to first analyze the information at hand and then proceed to formulate their claims. Either way, your discussion of a critical problem must involve the analysis and evaluation of all the available evidence.

Evidence could be in the form of facts, quotations, references, numbers, or events that are relevant to your assignment and, more specifically, your claim.

Gathering Relevant Data[8]

- Go through your readings/notes first and mark *everything* you think is relevant to answering the problem.
- To get a better sense of this material, go through a second time, skimming over and reviewing what you have gathered.
- Review the material a third time, noting passages/data that seem *most* central to your problem. Specifically, look for repetitious keywords and concepts to see what connections you can make.
- Categorize those passages/data according to how they support different points. Which ones support one idea, which ones support a differing concept? Even take the time to find data that might support opposing points. This contrasting information allows you to critically balance one idea against another.
- As a result of this brainstorming, write down the central concepts that emerge.
- Find supporting ideas to these central concepts and note the kinds of relationships they share to the central concepts (i.e., cause and effect, comparison, contrast, consequence, example, etc.). Devote time to establishing these relationships, reordering lists of the central concepts, and finding categories and subcategories.
- Then formulate a working logic outline around topics suggested by your central concepts and categories of evidence.

Hopefully, this method of sorting through data will provide you with a broad base of information to work with. Afterwards, critically analyze the components of the evidence, their relationship to one another, and their relationship to the underlying issue of the course.

Be careful not to overlook evidence that contradicts your claim. Ideally, the evidence should *speak* to you and control where your argument goes. In other words, your evidence will direct the content of your paper, not vice versa.

Logical Argument Outline: Following the direction of the Thesis

Your paper must follow a logical process that uses evidence to support the claims proposed. This means that, either before you start to write a final draft or during the editing/revising process, your argument must be assessed for logical continuity. While the thesis of an essay will propose its purpose, subsequent supporting paragraphs or topics should be stages that follow the logical direction of the thesis. If you change your thesis as the result of refinement after writing your first draft, then the logical argument of your paper has evolved and made your initial thesis obsolete. In either circumstance, each subsequent topic mentioned must follow stages of the argument as it evolves throughout the course of the paper.

Often, students will use their supporting paragraphs as lists of evidence supporting the claim. In order to create a strong argument, evidence supporting your claim must guide the reader through a thought process, not a laundry list of examples.

Let's say that you are trying to make the claim that watching professional wrestling increases violence among children. Take a look at the difference in which the same evidence supporting a thesis can be either listed or organized as stages of a logical argument.

Facts/Evidence

- child violence has increased recently
- children imitate professional wrestlers when acting violent
- children are watching more professional wrestling recently
  Using these facts alone, you can only construct a weak argument.

"Laundry List" Support Outline

Claim: professional wrestling increases violence among children

Support #1: fact: child violence has increased recently
Support #2: fact: children are watching more professional wrestling recently
Support #3: fact: children imitate professional wrestlers when acting violent

While it seems that the laundry list support outline follows a logical pattern, it is not specifically stated. The author of this outline has rearranged the sequence of the evidence in order to create a correlation between increased child violence and increased viewing of professional wrestling. Yet, this logic is flawed because correlation does not prove causation. In addition, the entire argument rests solely on the *arrangement* of evidence *without drawing conclusions or making analyses* about the relationships between the facts and the claim. By including analysis and logic in addition to facts, you can construct an actual claim about the topic at hand.

Stages of Logical Argument Outline

Claim: professional wrestling *causes* an increase in violence among children

Stage #1: fact: children are watching more professional wrestling recently

Stage #2: fact: child violence has increased recently

Stage #3: fact: the facts in Stage #1 & #2 are correlated; it's possible that TV influences behavior

Stage #4: fact: if TV influences behavior, then there should be a similarity between TV content and child behavior

Stage #5: fact: the content of professional wrestling is violent

Stage #6: fact: children imitate professional wrestlers when acting violent

Stage #7: fact: therefore, watching violent TV may result in imitating violent behavior

The second outline realized the logic of the claim. The claim stated that an increase in violence among children is the result of watching professional wrestling (a causal relationship). Therefore, the support must prove how one causes a change in the other (not through correlation). Notice that half of the stages in the logical argument outline utilize the relationships between the facts (i.e., Stages #3, 4, 5, & 7) to provide support for the claim through logical steps. The same amount of evidence is used in both outlines. Yet, the logical argument outline follows a thought process, not a simplistic listing.

Even when the logic connecting the evidence seems obvious to you, be sure to specifically organize the structure of the support around the stages of an argument, not the facts themselves. Each stage doesn't have to be a separate paragraph, but they must be present in a sequence of supportive statements. By making sure this logical thought process is evident to your reader, you will increase his/her ability to understand the ideas you are communicating.

Please also note that each person goes about writing a paper differently. Some people like to thoroughly organize every last detail before they type one word. Others just start writing and reorganize and edit later. Regardless of how you create your first draft, you should be able to make a logical argument outline either before or after your first draft.

Exploring Limits and Objections

A truly sound solution will have thought out its boundaries, consequences, and possible other solutions. Be skeptical of your best ideas, no matter how long they took to form. Some of the best arguments are those that take into account and disprove counterarguments in the process. By including objections in your paper, you are getting one step ahead of the reader.

◆ Redefining Revision

Revising does not refer to simply editing for grammatical or spelling errors. Revision is a process that evaluates ideas, organization, coherence, unity, and intent. "Many writers dismantle their first drafts and start afresh, often discovering their true thesis at the conclusion of their initial draft."[9] Revising is a time to make new outlines, begin considering the audience's expectations, and clarify the essay's purpose. Several drafts are often necessary to ensure that an essay is communicating clearly to the reader.

Revising should constitute at least half of the time spent on each paper you compose. Not only will you not get it perfect the first time around, but your thinking will reach a higher level simply through the act of writing. This refinement should be included in the final draft.

Timeline for Thorough Essay Construction and Revision

Two weeks before your essay is due, you need a systematic strategy to critically think, write, and revise your paper. While everyone approaches essay writing differently, this 14-day countdown method incorporates some essential elements for the critical writing process.

14 Days Before: Review the prompt and analyze the key terms being asked. Ponder the purpose of the course and ask what are the critical questions driving this topic of study? Begin to accumulate all available data from lectures on the essay topic. Set up a time or an appointment with a peer, tutor, or instructor four days before the essay is due.

13 Days Before: Still compile data and begin research if necessary. If you have multiple prompts to choose from, you should pick one now. Start making connections between pieces of information. Begin to formulate ideas and concepts that appear through repetition.

12 Days Before: Write the first draft of your thesis statement. It will be a rough draft, but it will also focus your paper's intent and scope. After writing it, ask yourself: How well does this thesis establish an interesting idea that *contributes* to the discussion without mimicking the professor's lectures? Begin to gather data to support this rough claim.

11 Days Before: Write your first-logic outline using the supporting evidence you have gathered. Be sure to follow the guidelines mentioned in this chapter. Always have your prompt in front of you when writing.

10 Days Before: Write the first third of all the supporting paragraphs that follow your thesis (e.g., if you plan to have three total supporting paragraphs, write one; if six total, write two, etc.). Don't worry about your introduction just yet. Since your paper will undergo substantial revision, it is premature to construct your introduction.

9 Days Before: Write the second third of all the supporting paragraphs that follow your thesis. Compare your supporting paragraphs with your thesis. Are they communicating the exact same message? If they do, then that's great. If not, then you have a significant opportunity to make your essay better.

8 Days Before: Write the final third of all the supporting paragraphs that follow your thesis. Again, compare them to the message of the thesis. Have any new understandings arisen? Do not be afraid to make changes; you have plenty of time to revise the ideas of your essay.

7 Days Before: Now write your introduction and conclusions, keeping in mind that they are still likely to change. Revisit your thesis and determine how well your professor would value its claim.

6 Days Before: Take a break from the essay. You've finished your first draft nearly a week in advance. Take time to incubate the ideas subconsciously and think about other schoolwork.

5 Days Before: Evaluate your entire essay. Is it coherent? Does every sentence contribute to the overall understanding of the thesis statement?

Have you considered all the objections and limitations of your argument? Are all of your points supported by logical use of evidence? Will your organization hold up to your instructor's scrutiny? Begin to make revisions of the essay based upon your answers to these questions. Construct another logic outline from your existing paper.

4 Days Before: Continue to make revisions. Evaluate your essay's "readability." Can a reader other than yourself understand your message and each sentence? Are you skipping steps that *you* understand, but someone else might miss? Are your sentences clearly phrased? This is a good time to have a peer, tutor, or instructor proofread your paper.

3 Days Before: Make revisions based upon the feedback you receive from your meeting. You still have time to make significant revisions if necessary. You need to start finalizing your thesis and support, as well as introductory and concluding paragraphs.

2 Days Before: Proofread for grammar, spelling, and clarity issues. Make sure you cite your sources properly.

1 Day Before: Print your paper out manually and proofread one last time. Read the entire paper out loud to hear how well you have written and force yourself to verbally catch any errors. Ask a friend or roommate to read it over for safety's sake. After you have finished making these last revisions, print out your final draft.

Due Date: Make sure your paper looks professional. Don't be late to class. Turn in your paper on time.

Do not assume what *you* see is what your reader will be able to comprehend. You are biased toward your own work. Often, when we synthesize our own information, the mistakes become transparent to us. Try to set aside your paper before revising it in hopes of forgetting your thought process when you were writing it. This amnesia is a blessing: it will enable you to revise more accurately and refresh your writing.

Here are some specifics to check for:[10]

- Double-check that you spelled out for the reader how it is specifically that the data count as evidence for your claim.
- An effective *introduction* will satisfy the important role of giving a brief statement about the question or problem that you are answering or solving. You can do this by suggesting something that is puzzling, not entirely understood, perhaps overlooked, not noticed, or undervalued. The intention is to make the reader feel that you have answered a question that is worth asking, that you have seen something that helps make sense out of a reading.
- An effective *conclusion* will begin by stating or restating the thesis, or its evolved form. You can end your composition by suggesting the significance of your conclusion in terms of its consequences, by stating further questions that your paper raises, or possibly including a quotation from the text that brings your paper to a graceful close.
- Using your first-draft outline, or by creating one from a draft, make sure you can find your argument in logical stages throughout your paper. By the time you are finished, a stranger should be able to make a logical argument outline using your composition. In order to do this, check the presence of your logical steps in each section's introduction and conclusion.

- Consider rewriting your introduction (or hold off writing it until the final stages). Your thesis has gone through an evolution during the stages of logical argumentation. Be sure that you start your essay with a claim similar to one you end with. If the evolved thesis is superior, why not use it?
- Sometimes all you need to make your paper stand out from the rest is a little creativity or originality. Don't overdo it, but add a little flavor to your style.
- Find and utilize the academic resources made available to you. There are classmates, peers, office hours, and tutoring sessions that can help you refine your paper.
- As always, check your entire paper for spelling, grammar, syntax, and diction that is appropriate. One of the best ways to check for errors is to read your paper out loud in an audible voice. This might seem silly, but voicing your paper will force you to read every letter of your words that your eyes might automatically skip over.
- Write clear, active sentences (see example below).

Revising Your Sentences

Many students have been trained over the years to appreciate "stuffy" academic writing that excessively uses prepositional phrases while lacking clear action. A good number of professors speak and write in poorly structured sentences that *sound* abstract, knowledgeable, and deep. In turn, students aim to mimic this overly "academic" style because it makes them sound smart and it takes up considerable space on the page. Follow these steps to revise your sentences for clarity.

Example Sentence

The nominalization of verbs and hiding of subjects in overly academic writing often results in the mystification of the reader.

1. **Find the action**
   Keep in mind, the action of the sentence might not be a verb. You will probably find it nominalized, that is, turned into a noun.
   - revision: main verb = mystify (hidden in nominalized "mystification")
2. **Ask "Who or what is actually performing this action?"**
   This question will determine the *true* subject of your sentence.
   - revision: overly academic writing is what mystifies
3. **Turn the action into a simple active verb. Place the subject in front of your new main verb**
   This steps forms the construction of plain, active writing: [subject] [verb].
   - revision: [subject] [verb] = Overly academic writing mystifies . . .
4. **Eliminate any unnecessary stringing of prepositional phrases**
   One prepositional phrase is fine, two in a row sometimes unavoidable, but three in a row should raise a red flag.
   - revision: eliminated "in overly academic writing" by making it the subject; eliminated "of verbs . . . of subject"

Revised Sentence

Overly academic writing often mystifies readers by nominalizing verbs and hiding subjects.

Short, active sentences are the clearest way to communicate your ideas and engage your reader. Do not be turned off by the shorter length of this "plain" style. Any professor would prefer that you turn in a clear paper under the page limit than a confusing, long paper. Additionally, your readers (and graders) will appreciate your efforts to communicate clearly and concisely.

Knowing Your Audience

Each instructor will hold a different expectation concerning your writing. Visit your professors or teaching assistants to team their own personal preferences on writing for a particular paper. You can also ask them during office hours what *they think* a good paper should include.

Humanities versus Social Science: A Difference in Style

Be wary of the significant difference in writing styles between the humanities (Literature, Philosophy, etc.) and the social sciences (Sociology, Political Science, etc.). Using the same style for these different departments will get you into trouble.

One distinction we might make between a humanities and social science paper is that a social science paper focuses on the message (the content, the material), while a humanities paper focuses on the medium (the text, images, codes, style, tone, etc.). A humanities paper tries to unravel and analyze the way content is transmitted; a Social Science paper is typically more interested in that content itself.

A humanities paper might be more complex in its composition, but a social science paper has different regulations. Especially in Social Science classes, be sure to define terms that discuss the relative nature of experience and language (e.g., in the sentence: "It wasn't a normal club." What is meant by "normal"?). Also, use concrete examples and provide unedited evidence (e.g., "He was richly dressed" versus "He was wearing a wool suit, with leather shoes, and a top hat.").

◆ Avoiding Plagiarism

Attribution and citation of materials you used to develop your thoughts is mandatory for academic honesty at the university. Citation is not strictly reserved for quotations within your text. Even if you summarized, paraphrased, or drew upon the ideas of a source, it needs to be cited properly. There is no shame in admitting that other sources contributed to your understanding of a particular topic. Knowledge is a constantly evolving work in progress. Everyone gets ideas from everyone else. Many instructors will be pleased with the fact that you performed such thorough research. Don't forget, professors cite hundreds of sources in their publications because they think it's fair to give credit where due. If you are not sure if a source needs to be cited, ask an instructor or, just to be safe, cite it anyway. Avoid plagiarism and the consequences that follow (such as failing, probation, or expulsion) by citing all your sources properly.

Improving Your Writing

The best way to improve your writing is to carefully listen to the feedback you receive from instructors. Undergraduates have a nasty habit of immediately flipping to the last page of their returned essay to see their grade. Far too many students take this grade as the only method of feedback, telling themselves to simply do better next time. Yet, receiving a grade and knowing *why* you received that grade are two very different kinds of feedback. Most good instructors will write comments at the end and throughout your paper, pointing out weaknesses and making suggestions for improvement. The next time you receive a graded paper, read the comments from front to back *before* you look at the grade, to understand your instructor's thought process on what makes a good paper. In addition, seek additional one-on-one feedback with your professor or teaching assistant. During office hours or an appointment, approach your instructor by stating, "I am trying to improve the quality of my writing. I would like to talk to you about your comments on my most recent paper and how you think I could improve for the next one." There is no better way of improving than receiving personalized feedback about your writing straight from the instructor. In addition to the faculty, make use of the other writing resources on your campus. Most colleges have a writing help center, tutoring, and composition classes that are all intended to help you better your writing. You are not expected to figure out the complexities of academic writing all by yourself. But, it is up to you to want to improve and seek help from the resources available to you.

Conclusions

One of the main goals of an undergraduate education is to learn how to express complex ideas clearly. By writing thesis-governed essays, you will ensure that you are communicating critical thought to your readers. Remember, since the use of critical thinking skills is the primary difference between high school and college, it is explicitly expected of you to address complex problems and theorize possible solutions. These solutions must be carefully weighted and measured to formulate the best argument possible. Additionally, never underestimate the importance of *how* you express your thoughts on paper. An essay is not successful simply by the inclusion of critical thoughts and innovative ideas alone. A successful essay will always keep the reader in mind by clearly communicating those thoughts and ideas.

Suggested Readings

The Elements of Style (Strunk & White)
Writing with Style (Trimble)
Revising Prose (Lanham)
Clear and Simple as the Truth (Thomas & Turner)
MLA Handbook for Writers of Research Papers (Gibaldi)
The Bedford Researcher (Palmquist)
How to Write a Scientific Paper (Day)
A Guide to Writing Sociology Papers (Roy et al.)
Engaging Ideas (Bean)

◆ Notes

1. Joanne G. Kurfiss, *Critical Thinking: Theory, Research, and Possibilities* (Texas: Association for the Study of Higher Education, 1988), 7–8.
2. Three elements paraphrased from Joseph M. Williams and McEnerney, *Writing in College: A Short Guide to College Writing*, September 1, 1995. http://writing-program.uchicago.edu/resources/collegewriting/high_school_v_college.htm (April 12, 2004).
3. John C. Bean, "How Writing Is Related to Critical Thinking," in *Engaging Ideas* (San Francisco: Jossey-Bass, 1996), 29.
4. Bean, 29.
5. Bean, 30.
6. Bean, 30–31.
7. Chart paraphrased from Bean, 20–24.
8. Paraphrased from Williams and McEnerney, 1995.
9. Bean, 31.
10. Most suggestions paraphrased from Williams and McEnerney, 1995.

◆ Journal Questions

What is the purpose of writing essays? What does it show about you as a student?

Why should you be concerned with "joining the discussion"?

What are some critical components of a thesis? What distinguishes a good thesis from a bad thesis?

What are the consequences of non-thesis-governed essays?

Why is revision so important in college writing?

List some helpful tools for revising your college essay.

Critical Thinking: An Incredibly Short Introduction

8

Ian J. Dove
Department of Philosophy
University of Nevada, Las Vegas

The introductory chapter mentioned that critical thinking is a major University Undergraduate Learning Outcomes, as well as a skill expected of college graduates. Being able to think critically is central to what it means to be both smart and educated. As you move through your undergraduate degree, you will have a chance to learn and to practice how to think critically. One of the first steps in critical thinking is thinking about the steps or elements involved in thinking critically. In this chapter we introduce you to those elements.

◆ 1. Introduction

Perhaps you believe that tuition is too expensive, or that flying cars will be the norm in ten years, or that hyper-intelligent ants will soon lead an insect rebellion against humans. On the one hand, great, good for you. On the other, if you wanted to make one of your beliefs the thesis of some paper, presentation, or discussion in one of your college courses, then critical thinking could help. There are many competing definitions of *critical thinking*. For the purposes of this chapter, we'll define critical thinking as the methods and procedures used to produce, analyze, and evaluate reasoning.

◆ 2. Reasoning

For our purposes, reasoning comes in two forms: arguments and explanations. The difference is subtle, but important. An argument supports a claim with evidence, premises, or reasons. An explanation clarifies a claim with definitions, causes, or principles. One way to distinguish between an argument and explanation regards the status of the claim in question. If the claim is controversial (in the sense that there is lively debate regarding its truth), then an argument will help to establish the claim (as true or as false). If, on the other hand, the claim is uncontroversial (in the sense that its truth value is not up for debate), then an explanation will help elucidate the claim. Sometimes, reasoning is both argument and explanation, i.e., sometimes by supporting a claim one thereby explains the claim.

To see this in action, consider the following list of claims. Ask yourself whether or not you think the truth of these is established or not.

a) To stay healthy, you should drink water (or some other liquid) every day.
b) Great white sharks can live in fresh water.
c) Las Vegas should increase the fines for wasting water.

Of the three claims, (a) seems the least controversial. But, there are ways in which this claim could be clarified. For example, it is vague in regard to the amount of water. Hence, an explanation could both clarify *why* you should drink water, as well as *why* you should drink at least some specified amount of water.

There is, apparently, some controversy surrounding the truth of claim (b). However, one could easily find an argument from (perhaps scientific) authority that great white sharks need salt water to survive. For example, from the Discovery Channel's website, you could read about how sharks that live in fresh water need a way to keep their internal salinity intact while swimming in fresh water.[1] Some sharks have this ability, others do not. Great whites, it seems, do not. Hence, they cannot survive in freshwater for very long.

Regarding claim (c), one would expect there to be some controversy as to its acceptability. Hence, it would need an argument to establish it (or to undermine it). Here's an attempt to support it: (1) The fines for wasting water in Las Vegas are so low that they don't deter anyone from wasting water. (2) Las Vegas, which is in the midst of an extreme drought, needs to have its citizens conserve water. Therefore, (c) Las Vegas should increase the fines on wasting water.

To summarize, you will need to distinguish between two kinds of reasoning in your college career. Arguments are used to support, justify, and establish claims that are controversial. Explanations are used to clarify, elucidate, and illuminate claims that are unclear, poorly understood, or confused. Sometimes you will do both.

◆ 3. Arguments

As was noted above, arguments justify claims. To justify (or establish or support) a claim, you usually have to do two things. First, you need to cite evidence for the claim. Second, you need to rebut evidence against the claim. Consider the following passage. While you read it, try to identify, first, the claim that is being supported. Then, identify the evidence cited in support of that claim. Finally, identify the rebuttal to evidence against the claim.

d) There is quite a debate about what to do regarding the use of fertilizer on golf courses in Henderson. The problem is that so much of it is washing off of the golf courses and into the drains, washes, and creeks that feed Lake Mead—our main source of drinking water. I propose that Henderson pass strict environmental protection laws that would

---

[1] http://dsc.discovery.com/tv-shows/shark-week/bios/freshwater-sharks.htm (accessed June 5, 2013)

fine golf courses for runoff, and for which all proceeds from the fines be used to clean up the runoff. Since it is unlikely that we will find another source of drinking water, we must protect the main source we have. Moreover, the use of fines would target the specific entities responsible for the pollution, rather than passing along an unnecessary cost to average citizens. Finally, although this could be an extreme expense for some golf courses, the laws could be written so that golf courses that take preventative measures (e.g., by having unfertilized green space between the course and drains, by using less harsh fertilizers, or that prevent runoff in other ways), would be given incentives. In this way, Henderson can help to make safe drinking water a real part of everyone's future.

What is the main claim being supported? There are a couple of possibilities. In general, we hope that authors will give their main claims (or theses) explicitly. There are occasions where it might be acceptable to leave the thesis tacit, but generally, one should state one's conclusions explicitly. If the author (or speaker) is being explicit, then the conclusion/claim will be one of the sentences given. In this case, the claim being supported is, "Henderson [should] pass strict environmental protection laws that would fine golf courses for runoff, and for which all proceeds from the fines be used to clean up the runoff." In practice it can be difficult to identify the main thesis of the writing of others. You can use a *because-test* to see whether a sentence is a conclusion. Simply take the sentence, place it before the word "because," then put some of the other sentences after "because." See whether the resulting (though possibly very weird) sentence seems to be what the author intended. In this case, we take the sentence I suggested, put it before "because," then put some of the other sentences from the passage after "because" to see what results.

e) Henderson [should] pass strict environmental protection laws that would fine golf courses for runoff, and for which all proceeds from the fines be used to clean up the runoff **BECAUSE** it is unlikely that we will find another source of drinking water, we must protect the main source we have. Moreover, the use of fines would target the specific entities responsible for the pollution, rather than passing along an unnecessary cost to average citizens. Finally, although this could be an extreme expense for some golf courses, the laws could be written so that golf courses that take preventative measures, (e.g., by having unfertilized green space between the course and drains by using less harsh fertilizers, or that prevent runoff in other ways), would be given incentives.

This does seem to be exactly what the author intended. Moreover, this method has allowed us to see the other parts of the argument as well. That is, at least some of the stuff that happens after "because" gives evidence in favor of the conclusion. And, some of the stuff after "because" undermines reasons against the conclusion.

To be clear, it looks like there is one line of support for the conclusion that offers positive reasons in favor of Henderson adopting stronger environmental protections. And, there are two lines of reasoning that rebut possible objections to Henderson adopting stronger environmental protections. Here is one of the positive lines of reason.

f) Since it is unlikely that we will find another source of drinking water, we must protect the main source we have. AND [Lake Mead is our main source of drinking water.] And [Runoff from golf courses is getting into Lake Mead.] So, Henderson should . . .

The two sentences in brackets are paraphrased from other parts of the passage. Here is another line of positive reason.

g) Moreover, the use of fines would target the specific entities responsible for the pollution, rather than passing along an unnecessary cost to average citizens. [It is better to charge those responsible for damage, rather than passing along the cost to everyone.] So, Henderson should . . .

In this case, the bracketed sentence isn't in the original passage. You can add things to your analysis of arguments as long as it serves to make the author's intentions clearer or stronger. The author seems to have something like the bracketed sentence in mind. The reasoning in (g) rebuts the idea that everyone should pitch in for the cleanup. This does not mean that the rebuttal is perfect. For example, one can imagine a golf course owner arguing that because golf courses bring revenue to Henderson, all residents benefit and should therefore help to pay the costs. But, that is a question of evaluation, which we'll turn to shortly. There is a final rebuttal.

h) Finally, although this could be an extreme expense for some golf courses, the laws could be written so that golf courses that take preventative measures (e.g., by having unfertilized green space between the course and drains, by using less harsh fertilizers, or that prevent runoff in other ways), would be given incentives. [The fines, then, would mostly harm those responsible for runoff, while those who ameliorate the runoff would receive benefit.] So, Henderson should . . .

Again, the bracketed sentence isn't explicit in the passage, but it does serve to clarify and strengthen the author's reasoning.

What we've been doing is called *analysis*. For arguments, there are really two things to do. First, determine whether there is an argument at all. If there isn't, then there is no need to further analyze *the argument*, as there isn't one. Second, identify the components of the argument. This means distinguishing the reasons from the conclusion and the two kinds of reasons. Once you've done these things, then you're ready to assess the argument's strength.

To evaluate an argument, there are three things to consider. First, are the reasons acceptable? Second (if the reasons are acceptable), how well do they support the conclusion? And, finally, how well does the argument answer objections. We'll start with the first question.

In general, it would be best to use only true statements as reasons. But, the world is an imperfect place, etc., so we go with what we can. Here is something called the *meh[2]-scale*. The more to the right side of the *meh-scale* your reasons, the better they are at affirmatively answering the first question.

Falsity	Very Unlikely	Unlikely	Meh	Likely	Very Likely	Truth
(Bad)			50/50			(Good)

---

[2] If you are unfamiliar with "meh," it is roughly synonymous with "whatever."

Let's use the *meh-scale* with the reasons in (f). Here are the reasons from (f): (f1) Since it is unlikely that we will find another source of drinking water, we must protect the main source we have. (f2) [Lake Mead is our main source of drinking water.] (f3) [Runoff from golf courses is getting into Lake Mead.]

I am not an expert on water issues in Nevada. This means that the truth of (f1), (f2), and (f3) are not part of my background knowledge. This means that I need to do some research before I can decide where these things fit on the *meh-scale*. But, a quick Internet search leads me to think that (f1) is pretty likely.[3] The same article that made me think that (f1) is pretty likely, also leads me to think that (f2) is true (which is stronger than just likely). From the book, *Environment*, I judge (f3) to be very likely.[4] This means that in regard to the first question, the reasons from (f) seem pretty good.

The second question is conditional. Suppose that the reasons were good. Would the truth of the reasons make the truth of the conclusion any more likely? If so, how much? In the case of (f), it seems that even if the reasons are true, they don't guarantee that the conclusion, i.e., Henderson should enact stricter environmental protections and fines, etc. Indeed, what is missing is that there might be better ways of protecting Lake Mead. Or, the passage doesn't tell us how bad the problem of golf course runoff is for the lake. Before accepting the conclusion on the basis of these reasons, I would like to know what the other problems are facing Lake Mead. I'd like to know whether the fines would be sufficient to cover the cost of cleanup, etc. So, in terms of the second question, the reasons in (f) are less good. The conditional support that reasons, if true, give to their conclusions also comes on a scale. In this case, the strongest support would be guarantee and the weakest would be contradiction. Here's the scale.

Contradicts	Opposes	None	Weak	Strong	Guarantees
←					→
(Terrible!)			(Bad)		(Good)

Again, it is better if your support is on the right side of the scale. If someone's argument has support on the left side, that would call his/her rationality into question.

The third question regards what some folks call our *dialectical obligations*. For any argument, there are infinitely many objections that can be raised against it. If you were to answer all possible objections, your arguments would be infinitely long. So, as a rule of thumb, you should answer the strongest or best objections to your arguments. When you are evaluating someone else's arguments, you should first ask whether the rebuttals offered are good, and then whether there are other good/important objections that the author should have considered. For the present argument, let's look at the reasons (i.e., rebuttals) in (g). Here they are. (g1) The use of fines would target the specific entities responsible for the pollution rather than passing along an unnecessary cost to average citizens. (g2) [It is better to charge those responsible for damage rather than passing along the cost to everyone.] What is the objection to which the author is responding? One interpretation is that the author thinks that the citizens of Henderson might propose in the light of the problem is to collectively pay for the cleanup—say through donations or taxes or what have

---

[3] http://www.lasvegassun.com/news/topics/water/#axzz2VNQYaFWi (accessed June 5, 2013)

[4] *Environment*, by Raven, Berg, and Hassenzahl, John Wiley and Sons, p. 179 (2012).

you. Are the reasons in (g) sufficient to rebut this claim? They do seem to give good reason to think that the golf courses should pay. So, on this measure, the rebuttal is good.

What about other possible objections? This is often very difficult. The problem is that one really needs to have specific knowledge of a topic in order to know what the possible objections are. In cases where you simply lack the expertise to know what the objections are, you have (at least) two choices. One, choose a different topic. Or two, do some research. In this case, as I noted, I'm not an expert on water issues in Nevada. But, there are some *commonsense* issues I think should occur to most people. First, is golf course runoff a big problem for Lake Mead? As a question, it isn't an objection. But, we can turn it in to one. Objection: Golf course runoff from Henderson golf courses isn't a big problem for Lake Mead. Notice that if this objection is true, then the conclusion for the original argument is weakened. Second, how much does it cost to cleanup golf course runoff. Again, as a question, it isn't an objection. But the objection is easy to state. Objection: It doesn't cost much to clean up golf course runoff. Again, if this objection is true, then the conclusion is weakened. Since the passage doesn't address these questions/objections, the argument is weakened. Overall, then, even though the reasons seemed likely be true, they didn't support the claim very strongly, nor did the rebuttals answer all the good objections. So, the argument is judged to be bad. Try to analyze the practice problems at the end of the chapter using the same steps.

◆ 4. Explanations

Explanations explain. Well, that's probably not helpful. Explanations are usually answers to why-questions. These answers attempt to make a claim more understandable by tracing its causal history, showing it as a particular example of a general rule, unifying it with other claims that are well understood, or otherwise clarifying or elucidating the claim. Although not a perfect indicator of the difference between these two kinds of reasoning, a rule of thumb is that the conclusion of an argument is something that is in dispute—otherwise, why argue about it—while the thing being explained is not in dispute. Consider:

i)   The space shuttle Challenger exploded during takeoff.

Claim (i) is not in dispute. You may not have known that it was true, but you could easily find out. Hence, you don't need an argument for (i).

As you don't need an argument in support of (i), one question you may have is, "Why did the space shuttle Challenger explode during take off?" The explanation is that a rubber o-ring failed, which allowed liquid oxygen to ignite.[5] You might ask for a further explanation regarding why the o-ring failed. The explanation is that the o-rings become brittle when cold, the o-rings were sealing liquid oxygen tanks, and the temperature in Florida was unseasonably cold at the time of the launch. In explanations, the claim being explained is called the *explanandum*, which is Latin for, the thing being explained. The stuff that does the explaining is called the *explanans*. We can use this distinction to analyze the two explanations we encountered above. Our analysis simply identifies the elements explicitly. It might make you analysis better if you make the explanandum an explicit *why-question*.

[5] http://history.nasa.gov/rogersrep/genindex.htm (accessed April 3, 2012)

Explanation One

Explanandum: Why did the space shuttle Challenger explode during takeoff?

Explanans: Because an o-ring sealing a liquid oxygen tank failed, which allowed liquid oxygen to ignite.

Explanation Two

Explanandum: Why did the o-ring fail?

Explanans: Because the o-rings sealing the liquid oxygen tanks become brittle when cold, and the temperature was cold (for Florida).

There is a very interesting story regarding why NASA didn't heed the warnings that the o-rings might become brittle in cold weather; but I leave that story for you to discover on your own. Your assessment of the quality of the explanations regards how well you think the *explanans* answers the why-question that is the *explanandum*. The better you understand the answer, the better the explanation.

◆ 5. Fallacies

Some reasons that seem good aren't. When enough people use these apparently good but really awful structures, logicians give them a name. These are fallacies. There are so many named fallacies that there are entire textbooks devoted just to cataloging all of the varieties.[6] In this short introduction, I will give you just a few examples. I recommend that you familiarize yourself with as many fallacies as you want. You can avoid them simply by arguing from acceptable premises using valid or strong inferences. The first fallacy we'll consider is a form of circular reasoning. It's called *begging the question*. Begging the question occurs when you use as a premise the thing you are trying to support. Here's a silly example.

j)   My wife is so great because, well, she's just so awesome.

Here I've merely substituted a near synonym in the conclusion—"so awesome"—for the claim in the premise—"so great." For a slightly more philosophically interesting example, consider an argument regarding the justification of induction. Induction is the process of generalizing from specific instances.

k)   We can be sure that induction is generally useful because it has proved so in the past.

Notice that the justification offered in the premises is precisely what is at issue in the conclusion. Another way of stating (k): Induction works because induction works.[7] It looks as if induction is the reason for thinking induction works. But, if induction is what is at issue to begin with, merely appealing to induction cannot work as a justification.

---

[6] Walton, D. (2008). *Informal Logic,* Cambridge University Press.

[7] A more detailed version of this is known as Hume's Riddle of Induction.

Another common fallacy occurs when one accepts or rejects the conclusion of an argument; not because of its content, but because of the character of the person who put it forward.[8] This is called an *Ad Hominem fallacy*.[9]

l)   Little Jeffery didn't eat those cookies because he is such a good little boy.
m) Dr. Evil said that the university won't raise tuition, but, since he is such a jerk, that means that they will raise tuition.

In (l) one depends on the good character to justify the conclusion; in (m) the moral failings justify the conclusion. In each case, the argument for the conclusion is weak, because it doesn't depend on reasonable criteria.[10]

You may be wondering about what happens in some legal cases where the character of a person is either called into question to undermine his/her testimony, or is offered in support of his/her testimony. In general, relying on character is a weak form of evidence. But, in some cases, a person's character is the only justification or refutation of the veracity of claims. Consider the following two arguments in some imagined legal proceeding.

n)   Mr. X, a known liar, thief, embezzler, and murderer, testified in favor of your alibi. There is no other evidence in favor of your alibi. Therefore, your alibi stands.
o)   There is a time stamped photograph from the coffee shop that verifies your alibi. Therefore, your alibi stands.

Though I'm not an expert in jurisprudence, I know which argument I would hope to have if I were facing trial.

In general, your arguments should stand on their own merits. They needn't be festooned with the characters with whom they may be associated. Instead, if the grounds are acceptable and the inferences strong, the arguments are good, regardless of who offers them.

There are many fallacies associated with appeals to emotion, pity, intimidation, and other nonrational sources of persuasion. For example, there are many commercials that appeal to the fears parents have regarding the safety of their children. The commercials argue that you should buy this or that product because the world is so scary. In one example, the world is depicted as having all these scary elements associated with driving. Therefore, you should buy this product—for which no evidence is offered to distinguish it from other similar products. If there were these distinguishing elements, then the argument would be rational. Yet, since there is only the fear of the scary world on offer, the argument is fallacious.

◆ 6. Biases

If you've followed along so far, it's possible that you are a good critical thinker. But, even if you are trying to support your controversial claims and explain your poorly understood ones, it is possible for some common biases to get in

---

[8] This is also an error of criticism. If you think that an argument is bad simply because of the person who offered it, you are guilty of an *ad hominem* attack.

[9] *Ad Hominem* is Latin for "against the man."

[10] This is related to a common ploy in which a critique will relate a position to someone of general dislike (or like). We jokingly call it the *Ad Hitlerium* fallacy. It occurs when someone relies on the fact that Adolf Hitler held a belief similar to the one on offer. This is supposed to justify the rejection of the conclusion. But, just because Hitler liked dogs isn't reason for you to hate dogs, is it?

the way. I'm simply going to list the biases with a brief explanation. The lists of cognitive (and social and . . .) biases seems to get bigger every day. My advice is that you familiarize yourself with the most common biases. If you recognize such traits in yourself, well, admitting you have a problem is the first step in the cure. But, more importantly, knowing what kinds of biases *tend* to affect our thinking can help you to analyze which ones to guard against.

1. Confirmation Bias: People tend to accept (uncritically) data that confirm or support their already existing beliefs and hypotheses. (Also known as *Selective Perception.*)
2. *Semmelweis*[11] Reflex: People tend to reject data that do not fit with common practices. (This is a kind of confirmation bias.)
3. Negativity Bias: Some people tend to find negative evidence and experiences more convincing than positive evidence and experiences. (This seems to contradict both 1 and 2 above. But, insofar as these biases are a kind of *irrationality*, it is possible for one person to have all three.)
4. Probability Neglect: People tend to neglect or exaggerate (uncritically) statistical and probabilistic information.
5. Base Rate Fallacy: People tend to underestimate the importance that the base rate (the proportion of a population that has some characteristic, i.e., its prevalence in the population) has in determining the conditional probability of that characteristic. (I said I was just going to list these with brief explanations, but this one is technical and important.)

Suppose that some test for steroids is very accurate, let's say that it is 95% accurate (or that it gives a false negative 5% of the time). Let us further suppose that some Major League Baseball player, call him "Sammy," tests positive for steroids using this test. How likely is it that Sammy used steroids given that he tested positive? Let's call this the question of guilt. Many folks are very tempted by the answer that it is highly likely that Sammy is guilty because he tested positive. However, it turns out that it matters how common steroid usage is among the population tested to determine the actual probability that Sammy used steroids given that he tested positive. If the prevalence of steroid use is high—let's say that at least 30% of all MLB players use steroids—then the likelihood that Sammy used steroids given that he tested positive would be about 89%. If the prevalence of steroid use were much lower, say about 4% of all MLB players used steroids, then the likelihood that Sammy used steroids given that he tested positive would fall below 50% to just 47.5%. Base rates matter.

There are many lists of cognitive biases. There are too many individual biases for you to worry about memorizing all of them. But, you need to be aware that these biases can undermine an otherwise rational case.

◆ 7. Conclusion and Something about Attitudes

Although some critical thinking texts emphasize cognitive or attitudinal elements, such things are both difficult to adopt as well as being hard to measure. Instead, I want to discuss several instrumental attitudes or approaches you

---

[11] Semmelweis is the doctor who discovered that it is important for doctors to wash their hands before treating patients. The idea was so radical at the time that most other doctors simply refused to believe that it was true. The problem was that there wasn't a good mechanism to explain why washing your hands would be beneficial, because there theory of germs hadn't yet been invented.

should take in your college career. First, you should approach your studies with instrumental fallibility. This means that you will proceed as if it is always possible that you are wrong, mistaken, or otherwise in error. Of course, this doesn't mean that you have in fact made an error. Rather, as an approach, it allows you to accept that for almost every claim you will need to make in college, it is better to offer reasons in support of it than to merely assert it.

Relatedly, you should become open-minded. This means that you should be aware that opinions, principles, and claims that are different from yours might be true. Hence, you need to be able to rebut the opinions, principles, and claims of others.

You should also adopt an attitude of charity regarding your interpretations of the work of other folks. This means that whenever you depend upon an interpretation, you should make sure that it presents the work of others in a way that gives it the best chance of being accurate or acceptable to the original author.[12]

A related notion is the principle of fidelity. It suggests that whenever you interpret the work of others, you should not stray from the meaning intended in what the original author actually wrote. You should remain faithful to the text. As you can imagine, it is possible for the principles of charity and fidelity to conflict. In such cases, let your charity be accurate and your fidelity be explicit.

You always have both a positive burden of proof—you need to defend your claims—and an obligation to consider objections. In giving explanations, you are obliged to use *explanans* that are credible to your audience. When in doubt about whether to offer another argument or a more detailed explanation, it is better to err on the side of too much argument or explanation than of too little.

Finally, in all things, aim for clarity. You will be writing papers, essays, exam answers, lab reports, mock memos, and who knows what else. No one will ever complain that your writing is too clear. Indeed, if you aren't sure who your audience is, write to an intelligent, but uniformed person. This is a person who is unaware of the particular lectures you've attended, who hasn't read the books and papers assigned for the class, or who hasn't participated in the late night discussions where you've solidified your views. But, this person isn't a moron. So, explain whatever technical terminology or jargon such a person would need in order to understand the topic. Then, write so that such a person would understand your arguments and explanations. Good luck.

◆ 8. Practice Problems

a) In the 1970s when I was a kid growing up in New Jersey, I noticed that a surprising number of quarters that came in to my possession were painted red. Offer three different possible explanations for this phenomenon. (Of course, you could use the Internet to find the actual explanation, but try to come up with three different but plausible explanations for why there were so many quarters painted red in the 1970s in New Jersey). For each explanation you offer, make sure that the *explanans*—the thing doing the explaining—really does explain the

---

[12] My principle of charity is different from many other textbook presentations. For example, Simon Blackburn suggests that this principle urges you to make your interpretations have the best chance of being true. (Blackburn 1994: 62). Others urge that you not attribute any error to the original author in your interpretation. In general, I agree that you shouldn't attribute idiocy without warrant. But, if warranted, attribute away.

explanandum.

b) Many students are upset about the increase in tuition (not just at UNLV, but across the country). See if you can construct an argument against raising the tuition at UNLV. Make your target the administration at UNLV. Also, be sure to consider possible objections that your target audience is likely to raise against your argument.

c) Some good explanations trace the causal history of the thing they explain—even when that causal history is unpleasant. Explain why UNLV raised its tuition last year. In this case you should aim to offer the actual explanation. Does this causal history seem morally justifiable? Explain why or why not.

d) It is currently illegal for U.S. citizens to sell their kidneys. However, there is a shortage of kidneys in the U.S. Moreover, when folks have tried to subvert the law, the organs were going to be sold for quite a bit of money (one ebay auction was rumored to have reached $6 million before ebay pulled the plug). Construct an argument for or against the sale of kidneys. Be sure to consider possible objections.

For each of the following, decide whether the claim is in need of argumentative support or explanation or both. Explain your answer.

a) American lions went extinct in what is now North America at about the same time that the first human settlers appeared.

b) The first settlers of what is now North America crossed the Pacific Ocean in boats.

c) The age limit for first-time drivers should be raised to 18 years.

d) More teenagers die in car accidents per capita in the United States than in Europe.

For each of the following passages: (1) decide if there is reasoning, if there is, state whether it is an explanation or an argument; (2) analyze the reasoning into its component parts; and (3) evaluate the reasoning's quality. If the passage doesn't contain reasoning, just write, "No reasoning." Remember that part of the evaluation of arguments regards whether the stated argument adequately rebuts good objections.

a) The cheetah is a large cat that lives mostly in Africa. Cheetahs usually have two cubs that are born to coincide with the migrations of prey animals. Cheetahs are endangered.

b) Although there are competing theories regarding why the megafauna went extinct at around the same time that man first settled in what is now North America, it is likely that early human settlers had something to do with that extinction. First, consider the correlation in time. The first settlers arrived sometime around 14,000 years before the present. The megafauna went extinct within 1,000 years of this arrival date. Second, it has been well established by both archeological evidence and early art that the first settlers hunted megafauna. As only megafauna went extinct at this time, it is unlikely that there was an obvious geological or climate-related cause. So, the case is pretty compelling: humans helped to cause the extinction of North American megafauna.

c) Because of the internal stylistic inconsistencies of the play, *All's Well That Ends Well*, it is likely that Shakespeare had a co-author on that play. As none of the other plays have similar internal stylistic inconsistencies, it is unlikely that those can be attributed to Shakespeare alone.

d) Although a surprising percentage of humans are lactose intolerant, many of those afflicted are able to eat yogurt. The reason is that the bacteria that convert milk into yogurt convert the some of the lactose into a more digestible form of sugar.

e) We urge the Southern Nevada Water Authority to seek new sources of water for Las Vegas. Although conservation would greatly help our water crisis, we believe that the population is unlikely to follow through on any voluntary conservation efforts.

f) The coroner's report indicated that the victim was bitten by a large canine. We ruled out wolves. And, there are no jackals in America, so we didn't need to consider them. Hence, the canine that bit the victim was probably a coyote.

g) In about 9% of the cases of untreated syphilis, the patient develops the degenerative disorder known as paresis. Uncle Everett's syphilis was untreated. Still, he won't develop paresis.

h) There are only a small number of species of sharks that are capable of killing a human. Among the most well known are great white sharks, tiger sharks, and bull sharks. Of these, both tiger sharks and bull sharks are capable of surviving in fresh water. There are no known cases of great white sharks swimming in fresh water. Several of the attacks in 1916 took place in fresh water or brackish water. Hence, it is unlikely that it was a great white shark. This leaves only the tiger shark and the bull shark as likely suspects. Tiger sharks are distinctive when compared to either great white sharks or bull sharks. And, there were several eyewitnesses to these attacks. None claimed to see any of the distinguishing features of a tiger shark. Hence, the culprit is probably a bull shark.

i) Generals of the biblical armies rode on chariots; their apparatus traveled on carts. But 2,000 years later, by the sixth century A.D., wheels virtually disappeared as a means of transportation from Morocco to Afghanistan. They were replaced by camels (Richard W. Bulliet, *The Camel and the Wheel*, 1975). Bulliet cites several reasons for this counterintuitive switch. The Roman roads had begun to deteriorate, and camels were not bound to them. Craftsmanship in harnesses and wagons had suffered a sharp decline. But, most important, camels (as pack animals) were more efficient than carts pulled by draft animals (even by camels). (Gould 1984: 158)[13]

For each of the following, decide which, if any, cognitive biases should be ruled out before accepting the claim.

a) Jenny cites three studies that support her conclusion that austerity measures work.

b) In her dissertation defense, Jenny notes that there are two papers relevant to her thesis: one is consistent with her conclusion, and one contradicts her conclusion. Her dissertation committee recommends rejecting her dissertation upon hearing this.

c) The Promotion and Tenure Committee at Idaho State University is

---
[13] Gould, S. J. (1984). "Kingdoms Without Wheels," in *Hen's Teeth and Horse's Toes*, Norton, pp. 158–165.

considering an associate professor's application to become a full professor. In his dossier, Professor Chewbacca lists his most recent book, *Bigfoot: A Field Researcher's Guide*, as evidence that he is a scholar with an international reputation. The Promotion and Tenure Committee denied his promotion because of the subject matter of the book.

d) As part of the usual screening for donating blood, Jimmy gets an AIDS test. To his horror, he gets a letter from the Red Cross four weeks later, informing him that the test was positive. Jimmy spends the rest of the day pondering how he will live the rest of his life as an AIDS patient.

e) As Jimmy and Jenny are driving to California, Jenny says that she wants to take surfing lessons. Jimmy, incredulous, says that he'll never get into the water because of the sharks.

Information Literacy and the UNLV Libraries

9

Anne E. Zald
University Libraries
University of Nevada, Las Vegas

◆ The Information Age

We are living in the Information Age, during which not only can information be easily created, stored, and shared, but dependence upon information has become the driving characteristic of the global economy. During the Industrial Age, which extended from the mid-18th through the 20th centuries, the economy was characterized by the growth and spread of manufacturing, particularly large-scale, technologically driven production of goods. Many of our parents and grandparents worked in factories that produced all kinds of goods ranging from airplanes to Zambonis, or in businesses that supported the manufacture, distribution, and sale of industrial goods. The following statements give us an idea of the impact of living in the Information Age, and how our lives will be different from those of our parents and grandparents:

> *"By 2020 the available body of information will double every 73 days."*[1]

> *"20% of knowledge generated within a company is obsolete in less than one year."*[2]

> *"By the time a student studying engineering graduates, half of his/her knowledge is already obsolete."*[3]

> *"60% of new jobs in the 21st century will require skills only 20% of the current workforce has."*[4]

These statements illustrate that in the Information Age, the only constant is the constantly increasing pace of change. The Bureau of Labor Statistics reported that people born between 1957 and 1964 changed jobs an average

---

[1] Breivik, Patricia Senn. *Student Learning in the Information Age.* Phoenix: American Council on Education/Oryx Press, 1998.

[2] Rikin, Jeremy. *The Age of Access: The New Culture of Hypercapitalism.* New York: J.P. Tarcher/Putnam, 2000.

[3] Tapscott, Dan. *Growing Up Digital: The Rise of the Net Generation.* New York: McGraw Hill, 1998.

[4] U.S. Department of Education. *Before It's Too Late: A Report to the Nation from the National Commission on Mathematics and Science Teaching for the 21st Century.* Washington, D.C.: Government Printing Office, 2000. http://www2.ed.gov/inits/Math/glenn/report.pdf

of 11 times between the ages of 18 and 44.[5] That's a new job every 2.3 years (on average). Contrast that with the job tenure of older persons. A study conducted in 1983 showed that nearly one-third of workers aged 45 and older had been with the same employer for over twenty years.[6] There could be any number of reasons for changing jobs, but there is a strong likelihood that many job changes involve applying knowledge and skills in different contexts and "learning on the job." Basing your academic success strictly on memorization and rote learning of the content of your major will not be sufficient for your long-term success. In addition to mastering the content of your major area of study, you also need to master a variety of intellectual skills that you can use both during and after college. These lifelong learning skills are articulated in the University Undergraduate Learning Outcomes (UULOs), which were described in Chapter 1. Your ability to communicate effectively, both in writing and orally, your ability to think critically, your ability to work with people of diverse skills and cultural backgrounds, your ability to find and use information to learn new things, and then to use that knowledge to make decisions or solve problems will be what you use most consistently after you graduate from college. The content knowledge of your major may well be helpful to you when getting your first job, or if you plan to pursue graduate education. However, when you start looking for your next job, or your next career, your ability to think critically, to access and evaluate information, and to continue to learn will be what carries you forward. In other words, information literacy is vitally important.

◆ Information Literacy

The University Library, and the staff who work there, take an active interest in your academic success. The mission of the Library is stated as follows:

> . . . the Libraries contribute to and support self-sufficient learners who can discover, access, and use information effectively for academic success, research, and lifelong learning.[7]

These words, "self-sufficient learners who can *discover, access, and use information effectively*" follow directly from the definition of *information literacy* developed by the American Library Association in 1989.

> To be information literate, a person must be able to recognize when information is needed and has the ability to locate, evaluate, and use effectively the needed information.[8]

---

[5] U. S. Bureau of Labor Statistics. "Number of Jobs Held, Labor Market Activity, and Earnings Growth among the Youngest Baby Boomers: Results from a Longitudinal Survey." *News Release,* September 10, 2010. http://www.bls.gov/news.release/nlsoy.toc.htm Web. 12 March 2012.

[6] Sehgal, Ellen. 1984. "Occupational Mobility and Job Tenure in 1983." *Monthly Labor Review,* 107.10 (1984): 18–23.

[7] UNLV Libraries Strategic Plan 2009—2011. http://library.nevada.edu/about/strategic_plan09-11.pdf. Web. 12 March 2012.

[8] American Library Association. Presidential Committee on Information Literacy: Final Report, 1989. http://www.ala.org/acrl/publications/whitepapers/presidential. Web. 12 March 2012.

Another element of information literacy is the importance of using information within legal and ethical limits. Just because information is easy to copy, paste, and pass off as your work, doesn't mean that it is legal, ethical, or smart to do that. Integrity, as discussed in Chapter 4, applies to all aspects of your academic and personal pursuits.

Information literacy is all well and good, but maybe you are wondering whether this is relevant to you in the age of Google. You are probably a savvy Google searcher, and you have probably been able to do your school and personal projects using Google, which is easy and fast.

◆ Google and Libraries

Google has been astonishingly successful at providing easy access to information on the Internet. We've reached the point where "*Google* it" means to search the Web for information. But, the power of Google can make it easy to forget, or ignore, that Google does not provide access to everything on the Internet.

Let's repeat that so you can be sure you read it correctly: *Google does not provide access to everything on the Internet.* Despite the power, ease and reach of Google, there remains a vast and growing reservoir of information available in what is called the "Deep" Web that Google does not include in its search results. The following statistics illustrate this claim.

> Google represents only 63% of the total indexed content of the Surface Web.[9]
>
> The Surface Web contains an estimated 2.5 billion documents, growing at a rate of 7.5 million documents per day.[10]
>
> Public information on the Deep Web is currently 400 to 550 times larger than the commonly defined World Wide Web.[10]
>
> More than half of the deep Web content resides in topic-specific databases.[10]
>
> And
>
> The Deep Web . . . has been rapidly expanding, with 3–7 times increases [sic] between 2000–2004.[11]

The "Surface" Web consists of those web pages that you can get to with a Web address (also known as a URL) and that search engines like Google are able to include in their search results using "spider" technology. Spider software functions by traveling the Surface Web from one hyperlink to another, indexing the content on a page, then moving on to the next linked page to repeat the process. What you search when using Google is the index of websites created through the "crawling" process. The "Deep" Web consists largely of databases that have some kind of search interface through which users enter keywords and

---

[9] Bright Planet. Deep Web FAQs. http://www.brightplanet.com Web. 14 March 2012.

[10] Bergman, Michael K. "White Paper: The Deep Web: Surfacing Hidden Value." *Journal of Electronic Publishing*, 7.1: 2001. doi:http://dx.doi.org/10.3998/3336451.0007.104. Web. 12 March 2012.

[11] Table 3 Summary of Survey Findings. He, Bin, Mitesh Patel, Zhen Zhang, and Kevin Chen-Chuan Chang. "Accessing the Deep Web." *Communications of the ACM*, 50.5 (2007): 100.

retrieve materials. Spider software cannot interact with a database search interface, and therefore remains "ignorant" of the content of databases. Many of the databases that constitute the "Deep" Web contain public information, meaning that they can be searched without fee once the database and its search screen is located. However, there are significant Deep Web resources, including those that provide scholarly information, that are not available free of charge. The UNLV Libraries subscribe to approximately 200 databases of scholarly content that can be searched by UNLV students, faculty, and staff. To ensure that you use a variety of information resources for your academic work, with particular attention paid to the scholarly sources that your professors require, you will have to add searching library databases to your habits.

◆ Libraries Organize Information

Think about a typical day in your life. How much information do you receive, sort, share, or delete? How many devices or portals do you use on a regular basis? Smartphones, computers, radio, Facebook, podcasts, television, blogs, Twitter, instant messaging (the list is nearly endless). You are constantly choosing what to pay attention to and what just won't fit into your life. The way you do that is based on a deep knowledge of your own life, family and friends, interests, how all those people interact in your life, and which of those bits of information you judge to be of value for whatever you need to do, whenever you may need to do it.

How do you organize all the details of your life so that you can get to them when you need them? Are you able to remember every detail, or do you have a method of organizing your stuff so that you can find details when you need them? Maybe you organize course materials separately from job-related things, or your club activities. Ring binders with dividers or pocket folders can help you keep the syllabus, assignments, and paper handouts from each course together. Maybe everything is on your laptop in digital folders, or on your phone, organized by App. The organization you impose on your "stuff," on the information of your life, is one that makes sense to you.

The Library has also developed systems for organizing information. Maybe they don't make sense to you just yet, but trust me, they are there. The Library is collecting and organizing information on all the topics that are studied and researched at UNLV, so the organizational schemes have to accommodate the broad extent of human knowledge. Google uses mathematical algorithms[12] to present your search results so that what you want appears on the first page of your 1.8 million matches, seemingly by magic. Libraries contain materials in a variety of physical and digital formats that are stored in different locations and organized using multiple schemas. Library staff are working constantly to improve the web pages and search tools that help you identify library materials, regardless of the organizational scheme or their physical location.

One way that the Library organizes material is in separate branch libraries and physical areas within the library building. Branch libraries house materials on a particular subject. Books are shelved separately from journals in all UNLV Libraries. Media materials and rare books are each kept in separate departments within the Lied Library. Here are some of the unique library locations that focus on materials in specific formats or topics.

---

[12] Google. Technology Overview. http://www.google.com/about/company/tech.html. 12 March 2012.

There are five libraries on the UNLV campus that all UNLV students, faculty, and staff may use:

- Lied Library is the "main" library, holding materials in the humanities, fine arts, social sciences, business, sciences, and engineering, and the topical and format collections described below.
- The Curriculum Materials Library houses materials that support the education of new teachers, as well as continuing education for current teachers. A children's literature collection is also housed there.
- The Architecture Studies Library has books, journals, media, and other materials to support programs in architecture, landscape architecture, interior design, construction, and urban planning.
- The Music Library houses books, musical recordings and scores, and videos about music and music performance; journals about music are in the Lied Library.
- The Law Library is located in the William S. Boyd School of Law and holds books, journals, and other materials related to statutory, regulatory, and case law.

Within the Lied Library are several topical and format collections that you may use as you pursue your studies.

Lied Automated Storage and Retrieval (LASR)

Located on the first floor of Lied Library, LASR is a storage area where older or less frequently used items are kept in order to make room on the shelves for newer material. Use the request button in the library catalog to have item(s) retrieved for your use in approximately 10 minutes.

Media and Computer Services (MCS)

Located on the ground floor of Lied Library, MCS collects media in all subject areas and in a variety of formats to support the university curriculum. This collection includes such items as videocassettes, DVDs, audiocassettes, and streaming videos for use in the library and classroom. Along with this collection, multimedia computers and laptop checkout services are available to the campus community.

The Media Lab

Also on the ground floor of Lied Library (in the northwest corner), the Media Lab features specialized hardware and software for all current UNLV students, staff, and faculty to use for multimedia projects and presentations. Equipment available allows you to capture and edit audio and video on the computer, dub VHS video to DVD, convert cassette tapes or LP records to MP3 or CD, scan large-format documents up to 11" x 17", and perform other multimedia tasks.

Special Collections

Located on the third floor of the Lied Library, they contain the unique, rare, and specialized research material that documents the history, culture; and physical environment of the city of Las Vegas, the Southern Nevada region, the gaming industry, and the University of Nevada, Las Vegas.

The Center for Gaming Research

Located in Special Collections, they provide support for scholarly inquiry into all aspects of gambling, including the business of gaming, its economic and social impacts, and its historical and cultural manifestations.

The Oral History Research Center (OHRC)

Also located in Special Collections, OHRC conducts and collects audio taped interviews, sometimes supplemented by video segments, of persons selected for their ability to provide firsthand observations on a variety of historical topics in Las Vegas and Southern Nevada.

◆ Evaluating Information

A crucial information literacy skill is evaluating information to be sure that it is appropriate for whatever task, decision, or project you have at hand. Some information on the Internet is created to entertain you; other information is designed to sell you products; still other pages want to persuade you to adopt their opinions or beliefs. The Internet is an open marketplace of commerce and ideas, which makes it very exciting, useful and convenient; but there are fewer quality controls imposed on information before it is distributed on the Internet. Many journalists and publishers who distribute information over the Internet retain those quality controls and editorial processes.[13]

The *CRAAP* Test

To be information literate it is crucial that you continuously evaluate information. CRAAP is a mnemonic to help you remember a set of questions to ask about any potential information before you determine whether or not you want to use it. The more you are able to answer YES to these questions, the better "score" the information source gets on the CRAAP Test, the better the information is for your project.

C   Currency—The timeliness of the information
   • Can you find the date the information was posted or updated?
   • How important is it to have current information for your question?
   • For some questions, such as personal health, scientific research, or financial investments, having current information is crucial.
R   Relevance—The importance of the information for your question
   • Does this relate to your topic?
   • Does it help you answer your research question?
   • Does it provide background, "flavor," or evidentiary information?
   • Can it help you find other information related to your question or topic?
   • Is the information at the appropriate level for your audience?
A   Authority—The source of the information
   • Are you able to determine who published or posted this information?
   • Is the author or organization qualified to speak on this subject?
   • Can you determine the author's credentials or affiliation?

---

[13] See the Code of Ethics provided online by the Society of Professional Journalists for an example at: http://www.spj.org/ethicscode.asp

- Is there contact information such as a publisher or email address?

A   Accuracy—The correctness and reliability of the information
- Are the facts listed corroborated by other sources?
- Does the author acknowledge other perspectives or differing opinions?
- Are arguments supported with evidence?
- Can the information be verified in some way?

P   Purpose—The reason for the information
- Is the author free from a conflict of interest that would bias what she or he has to say? (i.e., they work for the drug company that produces the drug they are reporting on, they have stock in the product they are testing, etc.)
- Are the motives of the author or sponsoring organization clearly stated? (Is it an opinion piece? Political message? Product advertisement?)
- Does the information seem to be free from bias?

◆ Academic, Scholarly, and Peer-Reviewed Publications

Navigating the increasingly blurred lines of information produced in the media-sphere is a challenge for everyone, but college students are also expected to use scholarly publications for assignments. Your professors will require you to find and integrate materials that are written by and for scholars in the academic disciplines. Your professor may describe these materials using a number of terms including "scholarly," "academic," or "peer-reviewed." The terms "scholarly" or "academic" may be loosely defined as books, articles, websites, or other materials that are credible and reliable, from reputable publishers or organizations, and intended for an academic audience. Peer review is a very specific label that describes an editorial process that distinguishes scholarly publications from newspapers, magazines, books, blogs, and any number of other types of information sources that are often categorized as "popular."

Before digging into the definition of "peer review" it is important to emphasize that popular information sources aren't necessarily *bad* information sources. Popular sources, including newspapers and magazines, serve a different purpose than scholarly or peer-reviewed sources, and can make important contributions to your academic work. Popular sources often provide factual and contextual information that is crucial to your ability to understand scholarly information sources. Popular sources often point you to the names of researchers or organizations, or the existence of data, books, and other materials that you can track down. Popular and peer-reviewed publications complement each other and you will need to use them both.

Now we can return to our description of peer review. As implied by the phrase, peer review is a process whereby work is reviewed by a peer, or a group of peers, prior to publication. In the academic context those peers are other experts in the subject area of the author and the work being reviewed (biologists review the work of biologists; economists review the work of economists). When experts review material for publication they question everything included in the work, and hold it to the most rigorous standards, not only of accuracy and credibility but also for asking a question important to the field, using appropriate methods to study the question, supporting all claims or conclusions in the work with evidence (typically gathered by doing original research, often being reported in the article itself), and making a unique contribution to knowledge in the field. These experts can approve a work for publication, they can suggest revisions to the work before it can be published (which are then sent to the original author), or they can refuse to publish the work. Many of your professors are publishing peer-reviewed articles or other scholarly works (books, websites, etc.), and in doing so are building their own, and UNLV's, scholarly reputation.

When looking at something you find on the computer, how can you tell whether or not it is peer-reviewed? Sadly, peer-reviewed articles are rarely labeled clearly as having been through the peer-review process before publication. However, there are some distinct characteristics that you can look for to decide whether a particular article is likely to have been peer-reviewed. The box below lists those characteristics and uses them to compare scholarly and popular materials.

Scholarly/Peer-Reviewed Journal	*Characteristics to Consider*	*Popular Magazines and Sources*
Usually a researcher, scholar, or academic (i.e., professor) who is an expert in the subject area. The author's university, research center, or academic credential (Ph.D., Masters) is provided	Who Is the Author?	Typically reporters or freelance writers who may or may not have expertise in the subject matter. Author's affiliation or education credential is generally not provided.
Academic faculty, professionals, researchers, and students.	Who Is the Audience?	General public. People who work in a particular industry or trade.
Use of jargon/specialized vocabulary related to subject area. Typically longer (5+ pages).	Language and Length	Simple, everyday language; layman's terms. Typically shorter (1–5 pages).
Quarterly, semi-annually, annually	Frequency of Publication	Daily, weekly, monthly
Articles may follow a predictable structure: abstract, introduction, literature review, methods, results, analysis/discussion, conclusion, and references. May contain tables, graphs, and charts. Limited or no advertisements.	Appearance/ Organization	Slick, attractive appearance. Often tells a story as a narrative. Often contains lots of pictures or advertisements.
Content typically reviewed by several experts or editorial board in the subject area (peer review) to ensure accuracy and research quality.	Information Checking	Content selected by editors employed by the magazine or trade publication.
Yes. Lists the sources where quotes and information were taken from. Can be verified.	References/ Bibliography	Probably not. May refer to other sources (people, organizations, publications), but they are difficult to verify.
American Journal of Sociology *Child Abuse & Neglect* *Journal of Abnormal Psychology* *American Economic Review* *Labor History*	Examples	**Popular Magazines:** *Time, Ebony, People, Sports Illustrated, Psychology Today, Smithsonian, History Today, The Economist, Scientific American* **Trade Magazines:** *Architectural Lighting, Frozen Food Age, Beverage World* **Newspapers:** *New York Times, USA Today, Las Vegas Review Journal*

◆ Reading the Different Types of Research in Scholarly Publications

Research practices differ significantly between scholars working in the humanities, social sciences, and the sciences. These differences in research practices are reflected in the content, format, and style of scholarly publications in the different disciplines.

In the humanities (English, foreign languages, history, philosophy) the predominant mode of research is the analysis of primary sources, supplemented with secondary materials (for definitions, see the section below on **Primary and Secondary Sources**). Analysis and interpretation are presented in the scholarly publications of these fields. In the sciences, social sciences, and the applied fields of business and hospitality, empirical research is the dominant mode, during which researchers formulate a question and then conduct observations or gather evidence (data) that they will use to answer that question. In Interdisciplinary Studies and fields that are inherently interdisciplinary, such as Women's Studies and Ethnic Studies, scholars may use either empirical or interpretive research modes. In all of these fields, whether in the humanities, business, the social sciences or the sciences, analysis of evidence is critical to scholarship, but the nature of the evidence differs significantly. In the humanities, evidence tends to be textual in nature; in the social sciences and sciences the evidence tends to be statistical. Of course, characterizing research in these terms is a gross generalization. Examples of scholarly work in the humanities or social sciences that fall into the mode dominant in another field are common.

Scholarly articles presenting the results of empirical (or experimental) research, particularly in the sciences, social sciences, business, and hospitality are typically organized in labeled sections. You can use the organizational scheme of research articles to improve your reading comprehension. Humanities research articles can also be organized in sections, but the labels used are much more varied and are not characterized here.

Your reading strategies for scholarly articles should be different from those you use for reading fiction. In fiction, plot and characters change from beginning to end of the work, and therefore reading the entire work in sequence is very important. In scholarly articles this is not the case. The function of each section of the article can help you better understand both the purpose and the findings of the research. It may help you to read the sections out of order, or to skip more technical sections (such as methods) until later in your academic career when you have a stronger basis for understanding them.

Title—article titles can describe the article content.

Authors—scholarly articles provide the institutional affiliation(s) of the authors, so readers can contact them.

Abstract—a concise summary of the article, providing a preview of the article's purpose, methods of inquiry, results, and conclusions. Placed at the start of the article, the abstract helps readers decide whether the entire article is relevant to their own work.

Introduction/Literature Review—establishes the questions to be studied in the article, and how they are related to previous research published in the discipline. Citations to prior research are included and can be numerous.

Methods/Methodology—the techniques used to study the questions identified in the introduction. The methods section of an article is often technical and detailed, so that other researchers can reproduce the research and verify the results.

Results/Findings—The results of the research and what was learned that is new knowledge in answer to the questions stated in the introduction. Charts, graphs, and other illustrations of data or evidence are often included.

Discussion/Conclusion—this section provides a summary of the research and its implications for the discipline, society, or future research.

Bibliography—a list of citations used by the author(s) in their research. This is a standard feature of scholarly work in all disciplines, and can be used by the reader to locate additional material on the topic.

Many types of information are used by scholars in business, hospitality, social sciences, and humanities disciplines in addition to journal articles, including books, government publications, newspapers, magazines, opinion polls, and the multiple kinds of Web-specific information, e.g., web pages, wikis, blogs, Twitter feeds, and other social media. An important way to evaluate the usefulness of these various types of information is to consider whether they are primary or secondary sources about your research topic.

◆ Primary and Secondary Sources

Primary sources are produced by the activity being studied, or those that provide a firsthand, original account of events. Secondary sources discuss information that was originally presented elsewhere and that provide an analysis or interpretation of events or ideas. Secondary sources are useful starting points to learn about a topic, but to verify the information and evaluate how it has been interpreted, it is important to look for primary sources.

Different kinds of materials will be considered primary and secondary in the different disciplines. The chart provides examples of primary and secondary sources for several disciplines:

Discipline	Examples of Primary Sources	Examples of Secondary Sources
Anthropology	Notes of field observations Oral histories Interview recordings or transcripts	Journal articles reporting research Books Reference works—encyclopedias, dictionaries, etc.
Biology or Chemistry	Research article published in a peer-reviewed journal (The research article is the first report of an experimental study.) Data sets Lab notes	Magazine or newspaper articles reporting scientific discoveries Literature review, systematic review, or meta-analysis; often published as an article in a peer-reviewed journal; provides analysis of research findings and gaps in a subject area.

Discipline	Examples of Primary Sources	Examples of Secondary Sources
History	Letters (e.g., written by a soldier during the Civil War or Abraham Lincoln) Diaries (individuals recording events of their personal lives and the times they lived in) Letters and diaries published as books Newspapers or government publications produced at the time of the events	Journal articles Books Reference books—encyclopedias, biographical dictionaries, etc. Magazine articles about historical topics
Literature	Literary works of the author (published) Manuscripts of literary works (unpublished) Letters and diaries of the author or their associates Letters and diaries published as books	Journal articles Literary criticism, whether published as articles or books Reviews of literary works, (e.g. novels, plays, etc.) Reference works (e.g., plot summaries, compilations of criticism, dictionaries, etc.)
Political Science	Data sets (e.g., voting results, exit polls, opinion polls, survey data) Government publications Declassified government documents Legislation and documents produced during the legislative process Statements of government officials—some compiled as books (e.g., *Public Papers of the President*) Newspapers and magazines published at the time of events	Journal articles Books Reference books
Psychology	Research article published in a peer-reviewed journal (The research article is the first report of an experimental study.) Data sets Lab notes	Literature review—often published as an article in a peer-reviewed journal, provides analysis of research findings and gaps in a subject area Articles in newspapers or magazines about psychological topics for a popular audience Books
Philosophy	Texts of specific philosophers' writings Letters and diaries of philosophers	Books or articles about the philosophical ideas of one or more philosophers
Sociology	Research article published in a peer-reviewed journal Large data sets (e.g., census data, survey responses) Letters and diaries of sociologists	Literature review—often published as an article in a peer-reviewed journal, provides analysis of research findings and gaps in a subject area Articles in newspapers or magazines about sociological topics for a popular audience Books about sociological topics Reference books

◆ The Information Cycle

Popular and scholarly, primary and secondary, books, journals, magazines, newspapers, websites, social media, radio, TV, podcasts, blogs: all these different types of information are overwhelming! All these different types of information can seem to be "out there" in a great jumble, but there are patterns to how information is produced and distributed. Familiarity with those patterns can help you figure out the context for, and improve your understanding of, any specific information source that you find. The Information Cycle is one way to describe these patterns. As with any generalization, there are always exceptions to the patterns described by the Information Cycle. When you notice things that don't seem to fit into this pattern, see if you can figure out why. If not, ask a librarian!

View the seven minute video entitled, "Information Cycle," which is linked to this web page under the Information Cycle tab (http://guides.library.unlv.edu/COLA100). The video describes information produced in response to an event; specifically, the shootings at Columbine High School in 1999. Although the event used in this video is tragic, and perhaps occurred when you were too young for it to register in your memory, events like this generate a tremendous amount of news reporting, public debate, and analysis which is conveyed in a variety of types of information sources. The chart below simplifies the concepts presented in the video, summarizing the types of information sources produced in the days, weeks, months, and years following an event, as well as the informational value each type of source can contribute to your knowledge.

Day of Event	Day(s) After	Week(s) After	Month(s) After	Year(s) After
Twitter Social media Internet news sites Broadcast media (radio, television)	Newspapers (print) Blogs	Popular magazines	Academic/ scholarly journals	Books Government publications Reference books
Contributes . . .	Contributes . . .	Contributes . . .	Contributes . . .	Contributes . . .
Facts = Who, What, Where, When Immediate impressions or reactions	Facts Interviews Opinion (editorials, letters to the editor, blogs)	Summarize facts, relate the event to other events or phenomena	Research Analysis Typically not event-specific but relate the event to themes, trends, or issues	Synthesis Context Overview, bibliography of sources on the topic

Some information types such as news (whether distributed in print, broadcast, or on the Internet) will continue to produce information about an event throughout the cycle. Think about how news coverage of an event changes over the days, weeks, and months that follow. For what kinds of projects would it be important to use reports published as soon after the event as possible? What are the limitations of reports published shortly after an event? Do different news outlets emphasize different aspects of the event? Notice that it takes time for scholarly articles and books to be published (peer review does slow things down!), and therefore you are unlikely to find scholarly articles about recent events. What strategies can you use to bring scholarly analysis from journal articles into your study of a recent event? For example, have there been articles published about similar events or activities that happened elsewhere? Does the event relate to a broader topic that may have been studied by researchers? When you conduct a search and pull up a list of material about your topic, start the process of evaluating sources by determining for each item what type of information source it is, and considering what weight you will give to that source in your work.

◆ Where to Start Looking for Information Sources

This chapter has explained different types of information that you need to use for your course assignments, and warned you that Google doesn't help you find scholarly information that is available in databases that are only meant for those who pay subscription fees or that must be accessed through a specific portal. Where should you start your search for information when you have a course assignment? UNLV Librarians have created custom web pages for different subject areas to direct you to the best starting places to look for primary and secondary sources, and popular and scholarly materials. Each subject guide also provides contact information for the librarian who specializes in that subject.

Here is a list of just a few Web-based subject guides pertinent to selected academic programs at UNLV:

Anthropology	http://guides.library.unlv.edu/anthropology
Business and Economics	http://guides.library.unlv.edu/business
History	http://guides.library.unlv.edu/history
Hospitality	http://guides.library.unlv.edu/hospitality
Interdisciplinary Studies	http://guides.library.unlv.edu/interdisciplinary
Literature	http://guides.library.unlv.edu/literature
Philosophy	http://guides.library.unlv.edu/philosophy
Political Science	http://guides.library.unlv.edu/politicalscience
Psychology	http://guides.library.unlv.edu/psychology
Sociology	http://guides.library.unlv.edu/sociology
Women's Studies	http://guides.library.unlv.edu/womens_studies

Information Search Process

Research into college students' process of conducting research in the Information Age suggests that it is more difficult now to do research than it was in the pre-Internet era.[14] The proliferation of technology, tools, sources, and choices are at the root of this seeming contradiction. Don't freak out. Research is manageable if you think of it as a process with several stages. You may not always go through the stages directly from beginning to end, but knowing that these stages exist may help you to plan your work. As you work through a research project, it is common to experience a range of emotions.[15] You may experience confusion or anxiety at the beginning of a research project but you will gain confidence as you learn more about your topic, so don't give up!

The chart, "Model of the Information Search Process,"[16] summarizes the stages of research, the activities conducted at each stage, and the emotions that may accompany those activities. The description of each stage of the search process is described below the chart, and is drawn from Carol Kuhlthau's book, *Guided Inquiry: Learning in the 21st Century.*

---

[14] Head, Alison J. and Michael B. Eisenberg. *Finding Context: What Today's College Students Say about Conducting Research in the Digital Age.* Seattle, WA: The Information School, University of Washington, 2009. Page 2. http://projectinfolit.org/pdfs/PIL_ProgressReport_2_2009.pdf

[15] Kuhlthau, Carol C., Leslie K. Maniotes, and Ann K. Caspari. 2007. *Guided Inquiry: Learning in the 21st Century.* Westport, CT: Libraries Unlimited.

[16] Kuhlthau, Carol C. 2004. *Seeking Meaning: A Process Approach to Library and Information Services.* Westport, CT: Libraries Unlimited. Page 82.

**Model of the
Information Search
Process**

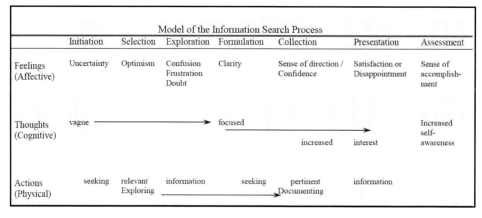

Model of the Information Search Process

	Initiation	Selection	Exploration	Formulation	Collection	Presentation	Assessment
Feelings (Affective)	Uncertainty	Optimism	Confusion Frustration Doubt	Clarity	Sense of direction / Confidence	Satisfaction or Disappointment	Sense of accomplish-ment
Thoughts (Cognitive)	vague ――――――――→			focused	increased	interest	Increased self-awareness
Actions (Physical)	seeking	relevant Exploring	information	seeking	pertinent Documenting	information	

Initiation—getting started on a research project, especially in your first years of college, is typically because of a course requirement. At this time the topic is broad, your ideas about the topic may be vague, and you may be experiencing uncertainty or anxiety.

Selection—selecting the topic for your research can be exciting if you work on a topic that interests you. At this point the topic remains fairly broad and poorly defined. Your tasks at this stage are exploring information resources that provide topical overviews and background, so you learn more about the broad topic and select an area or question within it. As shown on the chart, optimism and uncertainty may be your emotions at this stage.

Exploration—exploring the general topic in order to refine your focus is the next stage. As you gather and read sources about the topic, they may contradict each other and your own preconceptions. This can be confusing and frustrating. You may want to change your topic. Since most topics you research will include this confusing stage, try to work through this stage, perhaps by clearly distinguishing your ideas and the range of views represented among the information sources you have located. Organizing and categorizing the ideas may help you decide which direction to pursue.

Formulation—at this stage you have to start formulating the focus for your research. This will influence your further efforts to gather information on your topic. Factors to consider as you choose your focus can be personal interest, assignment requirements, or feasibility of the topic, due either to the amount of available material or the time you have to complete the project. Confusion or anxiety should decrease at this stage as you clarify the topic and scope of the task.

Collection—the focus of your research will influence the information you gather at this stage of the information search process. Up to now you have reviewed broad treatments of the topic, or a variety of perspectives on the topic. With a refined focus you now emphasize seeking sources that define, extend, and support that focus. With a clearer sense of direction at this stage your confidence may grow.

Presentation—at this stage you formulate the information gathered for a presentation, whether written, oral, or in another format. This is a satisfying and exciting aspect of the research process, although you may have some negative emotions as you recognize that you haven't been able to meet your own expectations for the project.

Assessment—any disappointments with the project can be used to assess the project and what you have learned about the information seeking process. As you reflect on the content and the process of the project, determine what went wrong or what you might do differently in the future. Self-awareness of your abilities and your own learning are an important element of lifelong learning.

◆ Plagiarism: What Is It?

Plagiarism is taking someone else's idea, language, or creative work and passing it off as your own. High-profile instances of plagiarism have resulted in serious consequences for the offender. The short video entitled "Consequences of Plagiarism" on the COLA 100/100E web page[17] describes several real-world instances of plagiarism and the negative impact on the income, employment, and professional reputations of the plagiarists.

Plagiarism is a common form of academic dishonesty. Examples of intentional plagiarism are obvious and include turning in a paper written by a friend or purchased online. This kind of intentional plagiarism is also obvious to a professor when the paper is turned in. The same technology that makes it easy to copy/paste or purchase papers online is also available to detect plagiarism. Remember, your professors are pretty smart people.

More difficult to understand is that plagiarism can also be unintentional, but students can still be held responsible for it as a violation of academic integrity. For example, not indicating that you have paraphrased or quoted ideas from someone else's work is plagiarism, as is turning in the same paper for two different classes.[18]

One reason that plagiarism is a common form of academic dishonesty is the complexity of the reading, writing, and thinking tasks that are required of you in college. Avoiding plagiarism will require you to become adept with several skills that help you express your own ideas while crediting the work of others who have contributed to your knowledge. These skills are paraphrasing, summarizing, and citing sources.

◆ Practice Activities to Prevent Accidental Plagiarism

The Purdue Online Writing Lab (OWL) is a wonderful resource to develop your skills with all aspects of writing. Guidelines for knowing what is common knowledge are provided to help you decide whether or not to cite something,[19] along with activities you can use to practice your paraphrasing and summarizing skills.

The web page accompanying this textbook provides links to the Purdue OWL and additional resources about writing, plagiarism, and how to avoid plagiarism (http://guides.library.unlv.edu/integrity). See especially the boxes

---

[17] http://guides.library.unlv.edu/COLA100. See the tab for "Academic Integrity & Plagiarism."

[18] Yes, it is, even though it is your own work! See the Academic Misconduct Policy, section II.C. "Turning in the same work in more than one class (or when repeating a class), unless permission is received in advance from the instructor." You really should review the Academic Misconduct Policy at: http://studentconduct.unlv.edu/misconduct/policy.html.

[19] Purdue Online Writing Lab, "Is It Plagiarism Yet?", http://owl.english.purdue.edu/owl/resource/589/02/ (accessed March 12, 2012).

for "Purdue Online Writing Lab (OWL)" and "Principles of Paraphrasing Tutorial." If your instructor does not assign one or more of these activities, you are encouraged to complete tutorials that address skills you know you need to improve. Invest some time now to save a lot of time (and potentially a lot of heartache and hassle) later. These skills are *critical* and you will use them over and over again.

◆ Citing Sources Is a Conversation between Scholars over Time

Why do we have to cite our sources? At this point in your academic career you know a pragmatic answer to that question is, "To avoid committing plagiarism, which is a form of academic misconduct, which can result in serious punishment including, in the worst cases, expulsion from the University." Another more interesting reason to cite sources is that citing sources is vital to the creation and sharing of knowledge. Your professors spend their professional lives conducting research to create new knowledge. They are active participants in the extended conversation of research, which involves people across geographic space and through historic time. The creation of knowledge through research is incremental, and thus it is always related in some way to work that has been done before.

An example may help illustrate the idea of research as an incremental conversation over time. Before Neal Smatresk became president of UNLV, he was a professor of biology at the University of Texas, and published many articles reporting the results of his research experiments. In 1994 he published an article in the publication, *American Zoologist*, about certain types of fishes that breathe both in water and in the air, and the implications for the evolution of air-breathing animals (see the box below). The box includes citation information and a brief description of this article, known as an abstract.

RESPIRATORY CONTROL IN THE TRANSITION FROM WATER TO AIR-BREATHING IN VERTEBRATES

Author(s): SMATRESK, NJ (SMATRESK, NJ)

Source: AMERICAN ZOOLOGIST Volume: 34 Issue: 2 Pages: 264-279 Published: 1994

Times Cited: 19 (from Web of Science)

Cited References: 72 [view related records]   ▦ Citation Map

Abstract: Studies on extant bimodally breathing vertebrates offer us a chance to gain insight into the changes in respiratory control during the evolutionary transition from water to air breathing. In primitive Actinopterygian air-breathing fishes (Lepisosteus and Amia), gill ventilation is driven by an endogenously active central rhythm generator that is powerfully modulated by afferent input from internally and externally oriented branchial chemoreceptors, as it is in water-breathing Actinopterygians. The effects of internal or external chemoreceptor stimulation on water and air breathing vary substantially in these aquatic air breathers, suggesting that their roles are evolutionarily malleable. Air breathing in these bimodal breathers usually occurs as single breaths taken at irregular intervals and is an on-demand phenomenon activated primarily by afferent input from the branchial chemoreceptors. There is no evidence for central CO_2/pH sensitive chemoreceptors and air-breathing organ mechanoreceptors have little influence over branchial- or air-breathing patterns in Actinopterygian air breathers. In the Sarcopterygian lungfish Lepidosiren and Protopterus, ventilation of the highly reduced gills is relatively unresponsive to chemoreceptor or mechanoreceptor input. The branchial chemoreceptors of the anterior arches appear to monitor arterialized blood, while chemoreceptors in the posterior arches may monitor venous blood. Lungfish respond vigorously to hypercapnia, but it is not known whether these responses are mediated by central or peripheral chemoreceptors. A major difference between the Sarcopterygian and Actinopterygian bimodal breathers is that lungfish can inflate their lungs using rhythmic bouts of air breathing, and lung mechanoreceptors influence the onset and termination of these lung inflation cycles. The control of breathing in amphibians appears similar to that of lungfish. Branchial ventilation may persist as rhythmic buccal oscillations in most adults, and stimulation of peripheral chemoreceptors in the aortic arch or carotid labyrinths initiates short bouts of breathing. Ventilation is much more responsive to hypercapnia in adult amphibians than in Actinopterygian fishes because of central CO_2/pH sensitive chemoreceptors that act to convert periodic to more continuous breathing patterns when stimulated.

Accession Number: WOS:A1994NX12400010

Document Type: Article; Proceedings Paper

Language: English

KeyWords Plus: SPINAL-CORD PREPARATION; FISH AMIA-CALVA; LUNGFISH PROTOPTERUS; MECHANORECEPTOR ACTIVITY; LEPISOSTEUS-OCULATUS; AFRICAN LUNGFISH; CHANNEL CATFISH; SPOTTED GAR; VENTILATION; GILL

Reprint Address: SMATRESK, NJ (reprint author), UNIV TEXAS,DEPT BIOL,ARLINGTON,TX 76019, USA

Citation information from the Web of Science database, Thomson Reuters.

The information marked inside the box indicates that this article includes 72 cited references. That means that in the bibliography for this article Dr. Smatresk lists 72 works published by other authors that he used to inform his research.

Also marked in the box is the "Times Cited" notation, which indicates that since this article was published in 1994, there are 19 articles that reference the article by Dr. Smatresk. In other words, 19 authors who published their work between 1994 and March of 2012 (when the information in the box was copied) cited Dr. Smatresk's article, just as Dr. Smatresk acknowledged the 72 works that preceded his own.

Another way to visualize this chain of intellectual connections is provided by the citation map in the next box. The 1994 article by Dr. Smatresk is represented by the box in the center of the map. The overlapping boxes to the left each represent an article published before Smatresk's work in 1994, and cited by it. Each box to the right of the central box represents an article published after the Smatresk article in 1994, and that cite it.

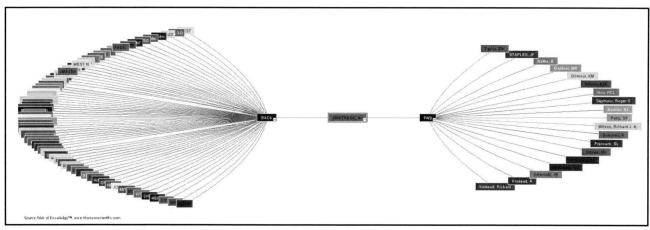

Citation map created in the Web of Knowledge database, Thomson Reuters, March 12, 2012.

A similar map could be created for each of the works represented by a box on this chart. Knowledge is a web that is constantly expanding. You could read one or more of the articles on the right-hand side of this map to see how the research about air- and water-breathing fishes has continued to develop. How have the questions that Dr. Smatresk discussed in this 1994 research formed the basis for additional discoveries? Are there questions that Dr. Smatresk did not answer in 1994 that have been addressed more completely since he published this paper?

Formatting Citations for Sources Using Style Manuals

The sad, sorry truth of the matter is that the actual work of citing sources is detail-oriented and tricky. No one particularly likes doing it, but it must be done. The fact that different disciplines ask you to format citations using different styles is just icing on the cake, so to speak. Why are there different citation styles? Well, that is one of the eternal mysteries of the universe, right up there with, "What prompted the Mona Lisa's smile?", and, "How did those big rock heads end up on Easter Island?". There is plenty of speculation, and several conspiracy theories, but not too many short answers. Typically your professors will tell you what style to use for projects in their courses, but a general rule of thumb is:

MLA Style Manual (MLA = Modern Language Association) often used by Humanities students and scholars, e.g., English, Foreign Languages, Philosophy.

APA Style Manual (APA = American Psychological Association) often used by Social Sciences students and scholars, e.g., Anthropology, Psychology, Political Science, Sociology.

Chicago Manual of Style (Chicago = University of Chicago Press) often used by faculty and students in History. *A Manual of Style for Writers of Research Papers, Theses, and Dissertations*, 7th edition by Kate Turabian is based upon *Chicago* Style and written with students in mind. Turabian requires some information (e.g., page numbers) that is considered optional in Chicago.

Remember that the most important function of a citation is to guide your reader to the source material. In order to do that successfully your citations must be complete. Consistently formatting the citations using a style guide is a great service to your readers.

◆ Practice Activity #1

Go to http://guides.library.unlv.edu/evalaute and work on **Activity: Popular or Scholarly Websites**. Four websites about the relationship between using cell phones and brain cancer are provided. For each website, use this worksheet to record your notes and conclusions as to whether the site is one that you would use for a course assignment. Use at least three different CRAAP criteria to justify your decision.

CRITERIA	*NOTES*
Currency	
Relevance	
Authority	
Accuracy	
Purpose	
I WOULD/WOULD NOT USE THIS WEBSITE FOR A COURSE ASSIGNMENT	WHY? Use at least three different CRAAP criteria to justify your decision.

◆ Practice Activity #2

Go to http://guides.library.unlv.edu/evaluate and work on **Activity: Popular or Scholarly Articles**. Examine each article linked there and use the worksheet below to record your decision as to whether the article is popular or scholarly. Use at least three different criteria from the "Popular or Scholarly Articles" chart also linked to this web page to justify your decision.

	Popular or Scholarly?	*Use at least three different criteria to justify your choice:*
Frey, William H. 1998. "The diversity myth." *American Demographics.* 20(6): 38–43.		
Frey, William H. 1996. "Immigration, domestic migration, and demographic Balkanization in America: New evidence for the 1990s." *Population and Development Review,* 22(4): 741–763.		
Mollica, Richard, & McDonald, Laura. 2002. "Refugees and mental health." *UN Chronicle,* 39(2): 29–30.		
Chung, Rita Chi-Ying, & Bemak, Fred. 2002. "Revisiting the California Southeast Asian mental health needs assessment data: An examination of refugee ethnic and gender differences." *Journal of Counseling and Development,* 80(1): 111–119.		
Young, Marta Y. 2001. "Moderators of stress in Salvadoran refugees: The role of social and personal resources." *The International Migration Review,* 35(3): 840–869.		
Lipman, Zada. 2002. "A dirty dilemma: The hazardous waste trade." *Harvard International Review,* 23(4): 67–71.		
EXTRA CREDIT: Frey, William H. 2003. "Metropolitan Magnets for International and Domestic Migrants." Washington DC: Brookings Institution Center on Urban & Metropolitan Policy. Brookings Census 2000 Series.		

Diversity and Global Awareness

10

Learning About and from Human Differences

ACTIVATE YOUR THINKING   **Journal Entry** **10.1**

Complete the following sentence:

When I hear the word "diversity," the first thoughts that come to my mind are . . .

_____

_____

_____

LEARNING GOAL

To help you appreciate the value of human differences and acquire skills for making the most of diversity in college and beyond.

◆ The Spectrum of Diversity

The word "diversity" derives from the Latin root *diversus*, meaning "various." Thus, human diversity refers to the variety of differences that exist among the people who comprise humanity (the human species). In this chapter, we use "diversity" to refer primarily to differences among the major groups of people who, collectively, comprise humankind or humanity. The relationship between diversity and humanity is represented visually in **Figure 10.1**.

The relationship between humanity and human diversity is similar to the relationship between sunlight and the spectrum of colors. Just as the sunlight passing through a prism is dispersed into all groups of colors that make up the visual spectrum, the human species that's spread across the planet is dispersed into all groups of people that make up the human spectrum (humanity).

As you can see in Figure 10.1, groups of people differ from one another in numerous ways, including physical features, religious beliefs, mental and physical abilities, national origins, social backgrounds, gender, and sexual orientation.

Since diversity has been interpreted (and misinterpreted) in different ways by different people, we begin by defining some key terms related to diversity that should lead to a clearer understanding of its true meaning and value.

> "We are all brothers and sisters. Each face in the rainbow of color that populates our world is precious and special. Each adds to the rich treasure of humanity."
>
> –Morris Dees, civil rights leader and cofounder of the Southern Poverty Law Center

What Is Race?

A racial group (race) is a group of people who share some distinctive physical traits, such as skin color or facial characteristics. The U.S. Census Bureau (2000) identifies three races: White, Black, and Asian. However, as Anderson

From "Thriving in College and Beyond" by Cuseo, Fecas, Thompson. © Kendall Hunt Publishing.

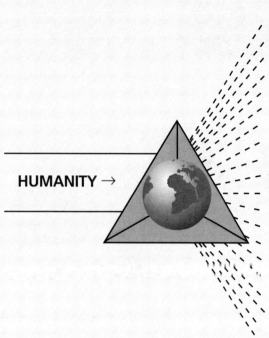

SPECTRUM
of
DIVERSITY

Gender (male-female)
Age (stage of life)
Race (e.g., White, Black, Asian)
Ethnicity (e.g., Native American, Hispanic, Irish, German)
Socioeconomic status (job status/income)
National *citizenship* (citizen of U.S. or another country)
Native (first-learned) *language*
National *origin* (nation of birth)
National *region* (e.g., raised in north/south)
Generation (historical period when people are born and live)
Political ideology (e.g., liberal/conservative)
Religious/spiritual beliefs (e.g., Christian/Buddhist/Muslim)
Family status (e.g., single-parent/two-parent family)
Marital status (single/married)
Parental status (with/without children)
Sexual orientation (heterosexual/homosexual/bisexual)
Physical ability/disability (e.g., able to hear/hearing impaired)
Mental ability/disability (e.g., mentally able/challenged)
Learning ability/disability (e.g., absence/presence of dyslexia)
Mental health/illness (e.g., absence/presence of depression)

HUMANITY →

– – – – – – = dimension of diversity

*This list represents some of the major dimensions of human diversity; it does not represent a complete list of all possible forms of human diversity. Also, disagreement exists about certain dimensions of diversity (e.g., whether certain groups should be considered races or ethnic groups).

Figure ◀10.1▶ **Humanity and Diversity**

Pause for Reflection

Look at the diversity spectrum in Figure 10.1 and look over the list of groups that make up the spectrum. Do you notice any groups that are missing from the list that should be added, either because they have distinctive backgrounds or because they have been targets of prejudice and discrimination?

and Fienberg (2000) caution, racial categories are social–political constructs (concepts) that are not scientifically based but socially determined. There continues to be disagreement among scholars about what groups of people constitute a human race or whether distinctive races exist (Wheelright, 2005). No genes differentiate one race from another. In other words, you couldn't do a blood test or any type of internal genetic test to determine a person's race. Humans have simply decided to categorize people into races on the basis of certain external differences in physical appearance, particularly the color of their outer layer of skin. The U.S. Census Bureau could just as easily have divided people into categories based on such physical characteristics as eye color (blue, brown, and green) or hair texture (straight, wavy, curly, and frizzy).

The differences in skin color that now occur among humans are likely due to biological adaptations that evolved over long periods among

Personal Experience My mother was from Alabama and was dark in skin color, with high cheek bones and long curly black hair. My father stood approximately 6 feet and had light brown straight hair. His skin color was that of a Western European with a slight suntan. If you did not know that my father was of African American descent, you would not have thought of him as Black. All of my life I have thought of myself as African American, and all of the people who are familiar with me thought of me as African American. I have lived half of a century with that as my racial description. Several years ago, after carefully looking through records available on births and deaths in my family history, I discovered that fewer than 50 percent of my ancestors were of African lineage. Biologically, I am no longer Black. Socially and emotionally, I still am. Clearly, race is more of a social concept than a biological fact.

—Aaron Thompson

groups of humans who lived in regions of the world with different climatic conditions. For instance, darker skin tones developed among humans who inhabited and reproduced in hotter regions nearer the equator (e.g., Africans), where darker skin enabled them to adapt and survive by providing their bodies with better protection from the potentially damaging effects of the sun (Bridgeman, 2003) and allowing their bodies to better use the vitamin D supplied by sunlight (Jablonski & Chaplin, 2002). In contrast, lighter skin tones developed over time among humans inhabiting colder climates that were farther from the equator (e.g., Scandinavia) to enable their bodies to absorb greater amounts of sunlight, which was in shorter supply in their region of the world.

While humans may display diversity in skin color or tone, the biological reality is that all members of the human species are remarkably similar. More than 98 percent of the genes that make up humans from different racial groups are the same (Bridgeman, 2003; Molnar, 1991). This large amount of genetic overlap among humans accounts for the many similarities that exist, regardless of what differences in color appear at the surface of skin. For example, all people have similar external features that give them a human appearance and clearly distinguish people from other animal species, all humans have internal organs that are similar in structure and function, and regardless of the color of their outer layer of skin, when it's cut, all humans bleed in the same color.

What Is Culture?

"Culture" may be defined as a distinctive pattern of beliefs and values learned by a group of people who share a social heritage and traditions. In short, culture is the whole way in which a group of people has learned to live (Peoples & Bailey, 1998); it includes style of speaking (language), fashion, food, art, music, values, and beliefs.

Cultural differences can exist within the same society (multicultural society), within a single nation (domestic diversity), or across different nations (international diversity).

Pause for Reflection

What race do you consider yourself to be? Would you say you identify strongly with your race, or are you rarely conscious of it?

I was proofreading this chapter while sitting in a coffee shop in the Chicago O'Hare airport. I looked up from my work for a second and saw what appeared to be a while girl about 18 years old. As I lowered by head to return to my work, I did a double-take to look at her again because something about her seemed different or unusual. When I looked at her more closely the second time, I noticed that although she had white skin, the features of her face and hair appeared to be those of an African American. After a couple of seconds of puzzlement, I figured it out: she was an albino African American. That satisfied me for the moment, but then I began to wonder: Would it still be accurate to say that she is Black even though her skin is white? Would her hair and facial features be sufficient for her to be considered or classified as Black? If yes, then what about someone who had a black skin tone but did not have the typical hair and facial features characteristic of Black people? Is skin color the defining feature of being African American, or are other features equally important? I was unable to answer these questions, but I found it amusing that these thoughts were taking place while I was working on a book dealing with diversity. Later, on the plane ride home, I thought again about that albino African American girl and realized that she was a perfect example of how classifying people into races is based not on objective, scientifically determined evidence but on subjective, socially constructed categories.

—Joe Cuseo

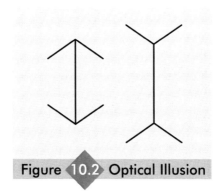

Figure 10.2 Optical Illusion

A major advantage of culture is that it helps bind its members together into a supportive, tight-knit community; however, it can blind them to other cultural perspectives. Since culture shapes the way people think, it can cause groups of people to view the world solely through their own cultural lens or frame of reference (Colombo, Cullen, & Lisle, 1995). Optical illusions are a good illustration of how cultural perspectives can blind people, or lead them to inaccurate perceptions. For instance, compare the lengths of the two lines in **Figure 10.2**.

If you perceive the line on the right to be longer than the line on the left, welcome to the club. Virtually all Americans and people from Western cultures perceive the line on the right to be longer. Actually, both lines are equal in length. (If you don't believe it, take out a ruler and check it out.) Interestingly, this perceptual error is not made by people from non-Western cultures who live in environments populated with circular structures rather than structures with linear patterns and angled corners, like Westerners use (Segall, Campbell, & Herskovits, 1966).

The key point underlying this optical illusion is that cultural experiences shape and sometimes distort perceptions of reality. People think they are seeing things objectively or as they really are, but they are often seeing things subjectively from their limited cultural vantage point. Being open to the viewpoints of diverse people who perceive the world from different cultural vantage points widens the range of perception and helps people overcome their cultural blind spots. As a result, people tend to perceive the world around them with greater clarity and accuracy.

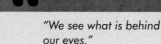

"We see what is behind our eyes."

–Chinese proverb

Remember

One person's reality is not everyone's reality; current perceptions of the outside world are shaped (and sometime distorted) by prior cultural experiences.

What Is an Ethnic Group?

An ethnic group (ethnicity) is a group of people who share the same culture. Thus, culture refers to what an ethnic group has in common and an ethnic group refers to people who share the same culture. Unlike a racial group, whose members share physical characteristics that they are born with and that have been passed on biologically, an ethnic group's shared characteristics have been passed on through socialization—that is, their common characteristics have been learned or acquired through shared social experiences.

Culture is a distinctive pattern of beliefs and values that develop among a group of people who share the same social heritage and traditions.

Major ethnic groups in the United States include the following:

- Native Americans (American Indians)
  - Cherokee, Navaho, Hopi, Alaskan natives, Blackfoot, etc.
- African Americans (Blacks)
  - People who have cultural roots in the continent of Africa, the Caribbean islands, etc.
- Hispanic Americans (Latinos)
  - People who have cultural roots in Mexico, Puerto Rico, Central America, South America, etc.
- Asian Americans
  - Cultural descendents from Japan, China, Korea, Vietnam, etc.
- European Americans (Whites)
  - Descendents from Scandinavia, England, Ireland, Germany, Italy, etc.

Currently, European Americans are the majority ethnic group in the United States because they account for more than 50 percent of the American population. Native Americans, African Americans, Hispanic Americans, and Asian Americans are considered to be ethnic minority groups because each of these groups represents less than 50 percent of the American population.

As with the concept of race, whether a particular group of people is defined as an ethnic group can be arbitrary, subjective, and interpreted differently by different groups of people. Currently, the only races recognized by the U.S. Census Bureau are White, Black, and Asian; Hispanic is not defined as a race but is classified as an ethnic group. However, among those who checked "some other race" in the 2000 Census, 97 percent were Hispanic. This fact has been viewed by Hispanic advocates as a desire for their ethnic group to be reclassified as a racial group (Cianciotto, 2005).

This disagreement illustrates how difficult it is to conveniently categorize groups of people into particular racial or ethnic groups. The United States will continue to struggle with this issue because the ethnic and racial diversity of its population is growing and members of different ethnic and racial groups are forming cross-ethnic and interracial families. Thus, it is becoming progressively more difficult to place people into distinct categories based on their race or ethnicity. For example, by 2050, the number of people who will identify themselves as being of two or more races is projected to more than triple, growing from 5.2 million to 16.2 million (U.S. Census Bureau, 2008).

Pause for Reflection

Which ethnic group or groups do you belong to or identify with?

What are the most common cultural values shared by your ethnic group or groups?

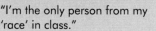

Student Perspective

"I'm the only person from my 'race' in class."

—Hispanic student commenting on why he felt uncomfortable in his Race, Ethnicity, & Gender class

> **Personal Experience**
>
> As the child of a Black man and a White woman, someone who was born in the racial melting pot of Hawaii, with a sister who's half Indonesian but who's usually mistaken for Mexican or Puerto Rican and a brother-in-law and niece of Chinese descent, with some blood relatives who resemble Margaret Thatcher and others who could pass for Bernie Mac, family get-togethers over Christmas take on the appearance of a UN General Assembly meeting. I've never had the option of restricting my loyalties on the basis of race, or measuring my worth on the basis of tribe.
>
> —Barack Obama (2006)

Pause for Reflection

List three human experiences that you think are universal—that is, they are experienced by all humans in all cultures:

1.

2.

3.

What Is Humanity?

It is important to realize that human variety and human similarity coexist and complement each other. Diversity is a "value that is shown in mutual respect and appreciation of similarities and differences" (Public Service Enterprise Group, 2009. Experiencing diversity not only enhances appreciation of the unique features of different cultures but also provides a larger perspective on the universal aspects of the human experience that are common to all humans, no matter what their particular cultural background may be. For example, despite racial and cultural differences, all people express the same emotions with the same facial expressions (see **Figure 10.3**).

Other human characteristics that anthropologists have found to be shared across all groups of people in every corner of the world include storytelling, poetry, adornment of the body, dance, music, decoration of artifacts, families, socialization of children by elders, a sense of right and wrong, supernatural beliefs, explanations of diseases and death, and mourning of the dead (Pinker, 1994). Although different ethnic groups may express these shared experiences in different ways, these universal experiences are common to all humans.

> **!** **Remember**
>
> Diversity represents variations on the common theme of humanity. Although people have different cultural backgrounds, they are still cultivated from the same soil—they are all grounded in the common experience of being human.

"We are all the same, and we are all unique."

–Georgia Dunston, African American biologist and research specialist in human genetics

Thus, different cultures associated with different ethnic groups may be viewed simply as variations on the same theme: being human. You may have heard the question, "We're all human, aren't we?" The answer to this important question is "yes and no." Yes, humans are all the same, but not in the same way.

A good metaphor for understanding this apparent contradiction is to visualize humanity as a quilt in which we are all joined by the common thread of humanity—by the common bond of being human. Yet the different patches that make up the quilt represent diversity—the distinctive or unique cultures

Humans all over the world display the same facial expressions when experiencing certain emotions. See if you can detect the emotions being expressed in the following faces. (To find the answers, turn your book upside down.)

Answers: The emotions shown. Top, left to right; anger, fear, and sadness. Bottom, left to right; disgust, happiness, and surprise.

All images © JupiterImages Corporation.

Figure 10.3

that comprise our common humanity. The quilt metaphor acknowledges the identity and beauty of all cultures. It differs from the old American melting pot metaphor, which viewed differences as something that should be melted down or eliminated, or the salad bowl metaphor, which suggested that America is a hodgepodge or mishmash of cultures thrown together without any common connection. In contrast, the quilt metaphor suggests that the cultures of different ethnic groups should be recognized and celebrated. Nevertheless, differences can be woven together to create a unified whole—as in the Latin expression *E pluribus unum* ("Out of many, one"), the motto of the United States, which you will find printed on all U.S. coins.

To appreciate diversity and its relationship to humanity is to capitalize on the power of differences (diversity) while still preserving collective strength through unity (humanity).

> "We have become not a melting pot but a beautiful mosaic."
> —Jimmy Carter, 39th president of the United States and winner of the Nobel Peace Prize

> **! Remember**
>
> By learning about diversity (differences), people simultaneously learn about their commonality (shared humanity).

Personal Experience   When I was 12 years old and living in New York City, I returned from school one Friday afternoon and my mother asked me if anything interesting happened at school that day. I mentioned to her that the teacher went around the room, asking students what we had eaten for dinner the night before. At that moment, my mother began to become a bit agitated and nervously asked me, "What did you tell the teacher?" I said, "I told her and the rest of the class that I had pasta last night because my family always eats pasta on Thursdays and Sundays." My mother exploded and fired back at me, "Why couldn't you tell her that we had steak or roast beef!" For a moment, I was stunned and couldn't figure out what I had done wrong or why I should have lied about eating pasta. Then it suddenly dawned on me: My mother was embarrassed about being an Italian American. She wanted me to hide our family's ethnic background and make it sound like we were very "American." A few moments later, it also became clear to me why her maiden name was changed from the Italian-sounding DeVigilio to the more American-sounding Vigilis, and why her first name was changed from Carmella to Mildred (and why my father's first name was also changed from Biaggio to Blase). Their generation wanted to minimize discrimination and maximize their assimilation (absorption) into American culture.

I never forgot this incident because it was such an emotionally intense experience. For the first time in my life, I became aware that my mother was ashamed of being a member of the same group to which every other member of my family belonged, including me. After her outburst, I felt a combined rush of astonishment and embarrassment. However, these feelings eventually faded and my mother's reaction ended up having the opposite effect on me. Instead of making me feel inferior or ashamed about being Italian American, her reaction that day caused me to become more aware of, and take more pride in, my Italian heritage.

As I grew older, I also grew to understand why my mother felt the way she did. She grew up in America's melting pot era—a time when different American ethnic groups were expected to melt down and melt away their ethnicity. They were not to celebrate diversity; they were to eliminate it.

—Joe Cuseo

Student Perspective

When you see me, do not look
    at me with disgrace.
Know that I am an African-
    American
Birthed by a woman of style
    and grace.
Be proud
    To stand by my side.
Hold your head high Like me.
Be proud.
    To say you know me.
Just as I stand by you, proud
    to be me.

—Poem by Brittany Beard, first-year student

What Is Individuality?

It's important to keep in mind that the individual differences within the same racial or ethnic group are greater than the average differences between two different groups. For example, although you live in a world that is conscious of differences among races, differences in physical attributes (e.g., height and weight) and behavior patterns (e.g., personality characteristics) among individuals within the same racial group are greater than the average differences among various racial groups (Caplan & Caplan, 1994).

As you proceed through this chapter, keep in mind the following distinctions among humanity, diversity, and individuality:

- **Diversity.** We are all members of *different groups* (e.g., different gender and ethnic groups).
- **Humanity.** We are all members of the *same group* (the human species).
- **Individuality.** Each of us is a *unique person* who is different from any person in any group to which we may belong.

"*Every human is, at the same time, like all other humans, like some humans, and like no other human.*"

–Clyde Kluckhohn, American anthropologist

◆ Major Forms or Types of Diversity

International Diversity

Moving beyond your particular country of citizenship, you are also a member of an international world that includes multiple nations. Global interdependence and international collaboration are needed to solve current international problems, such as global warming and terrorism. Communication and interaction across nations are now greater than at any other time in world history, largely because of rapid advances in electronic technology (Dryden & Vos, 1999; Smith, 1994). Economic boundaries between nations are also breaking down due to increasing international travel, international trading, and development of multinational corporations. Today's world really is a small world after all, and success in it requires an international perspective. By learning from and about different nations, you become more than a citizen of your own country; you become cosmopolitan—a citizen of the world.

Taking an international perspective allows you to appreciate the diversity of humankind. If it were possible to reduce the world's population to a village of precisely 100 people, with all existing human ratios remaining the same, the demographics of this world village would look something like this:

> 60 Asians, 14 Africans, 12 Europeans, 8 Latin Americans, 5 from the United States and Canada, and 1 from the South Pacific.
>   51 males, 49 females
>   82 non-Whites, 18 Whites
>   67 non-Christians, 33 Christians
>   80 living in substandard housing
>   67 unable to read
>   50 malnourished and 1 dying of starvation
>   33 without access to a safe water supply
>   39 who lack access to improved sanitation
>   24 without any electricity (and of the 76 who do have electricity, most would only use it for light at night)
>   7 with access to the Internet
>   1 with a college education
>   1 with HIV
>   2 near birth; 1 near death
>   5 who control 32 percent of the entire world's wealth; all 5 would be citizens of the United States
>   33 who receive and attempt to live on just 3 percent of the world village's income

Source: Family Care Foundation (2005).

Ethnic and Racial Diversity

America is rapidly becoming a more racially and ethnically diverse nation. In 2008, the minority population in the United States reached an all-time high of 34 percent of the total population. The population of ethnic minorities is now growing at a much faster rate than the White majority. This trend is expected to continue, and by the middle of the twenty-first century, the minority population will have grown from one-third of the U.S. population to more than one-half (54 percent), with more than 60 percent of the nation's children expected to be members of minority groups (U.S. Census Bureau, 2008).

By 2050, the U.S. population is projected to be more than 30 percent Hispanic (up from 15 percent in 2008), 15 percent Black (up from 13 percent), 9.6 percent Asian (up from 5.3 percent), and 2 percent Native Americans (up from 1.6 percent). The native Hawaiian and Pacific Islander population is expected to more than double between 2008 and 2050. In the same time frame, the percentage of Americans who are White will drop from 66 percent (2008) to 46 percent (2050). As a result of these population trends, ethnic and racial minorities will become the new majority because they will constitute the majority of Americans by the middle of the twenty-first century. (See **Figure 10.4**.)

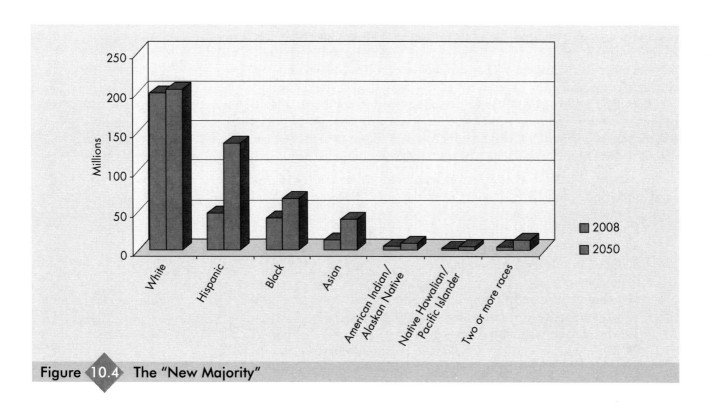

Figure 10.4   The "New Majority"

Generational Diversity

Humans are also diverse with respect to the generation in which they grew up. "Generation" refers to individuals born during the same historical period and may have developed similar attitudes, values, and habits based on the similar events that took place in the world during their formative years of development. Each generation experiences different historical events, so it's likely that generations will develop different attitudes and behaviors as a result.

Snapshot Summary 10.1 provides a brief summary of the major generations, the key historical events that occurred during the formative periods of the people in each generation, and the personal characteristics that have been associated with a particular generation (Lancaster & Stillman, 2002).

Snapshot Summary

10.1

Generational Diversity

- **The Traditional Generation, a.k.a. the Silent Generation** (born 1922–1945). This generation was influenced by events such as the Great Depression and World Wars I and II. Characteristics associated with this generation include loyalty, patriotism, respect for authority, and conservatism.
- **The Baby Boomer Generation** (born 1946–1964). This generation was influenced by events such as the Vietnam War, Watergate, and the human rights movement. Characteristics associated with this generation include idealism, personal fulfillment, and a concern for equal rights.
- **Generation X** (born 1965–1980). This generation was influenced by Sesame Street, the creation of MTV, AIDS, and soaring divorce rates that produced the first generation of latchkey children, who let themselves into their home after school (with their own key) because their parents, or their single parent, would be out working. Characteristics associated with this generation include self-reliance, resourcefulness, and being comfortable with change.

- **Generation Y, a.k.a. Millennials** (born 1981–2002). This generation was influenced by the September 11, 2001, terrorist attack on the United States, the shooting of students at Columbine High School, and the collapse of the Enron Corporation. Characteristics associated with this generation include a preference for working and playing in groups, being technologically savvy, and a willingness to provide volunteer service in their community (the civic generation). They are also the most ethnically diverse generation, which may explain why they are more open to diversity and see it as a positive experience.

"I don't even know what that means."

–Comment made by 38-year-old basketball coach after hearing one of his younger players say, "I'm trying to find my mojo and get my swag back."

Source: Lancaster & Stillman (2002).

◆ Diversity and the College Experience

There are more than 3,000 public and private colleges in the United States. They vary in size (small to large) and location (urban, suburban, and rural), as well as in their purpose or mission (research universities, comprehensive state universities, liberal arts colleges, and community colleges). This variety makes the American higher-education system the most diverse and accessible in the world. The diversity of educational opportunities in American colleges and universities reflects the freedom of opportunity in the United States as a democratic nation (American Council on Education, 2008).

Pause for Reflection

Look back at the characteristics associated with your generation. Which of these characteristics most accurately reflect your attitudes, values, or personality traits?

Which clearly do not?

America's system of higher education is also becoming more diverse with respect to the variety of people enrolled in it. College students in the United States are growing more diverse with respect to age; almost 40 percent of all undergraduate students in America are 25 years of age or older, compared to 28 percent in 1970 (U.S. Department of Education, 2002). The ethnic and racial diversity of students in American colleges and universities is also rapidly rising. In 1960, Whites made up almost 95 percent of the total college population; in 2005, that percentage had decreased to 69 percent. At the same time, the percentage of Asian, Hispanic, Black, and Native American students attending college increased (Chronicle of Higher Education, 2003).

Pause for Reflection

1. What diverse groups do you see represented on your campus?

2. Are there groups on your campus that you did not expect to see or to see in such large numbers?

3. Are there groups on your campus that you expected to see but do not see or see in smaller numbers than you expected?

◆ The Benefits of Experiencing Diversity

Diversity Promotes Self-Awareness

Learning from people with diverse backgrounds and experiences sharpens your self-knowledge and self-insight by allowing you to compare and contrast your life experiences with life experiences of others that differ sharply from your own. This comparative perspective gives you a reference point for viewing your own life, which places you in a better position to see more clearly how your unique cultural background has influenced the development of your personal beliefs, values, and lifestyle. By viewing your life in relation to the lives of others, you see more clearly what is distinctive about yourself and how you may be uniquely advantaged or disadvantaged.

When students around the country were interviewed about their diversity experiences in college, they reported that these experiences often helped them learn more about themselves and that their interactions with students from different races and ethnic groups produced unexpected or jarring self-insights (Light, 2001).

Student Perspective

"I remember that my self-image was being influenced by the media. I got the impression that women had to look a certain way. I dyed my hair, wore different clothes, more makeup . . . all because magazines, TV, [and] music videos 'said' that was beautiful. Luckily, when I was 15, I went to Brazil and saw a different, more natural beauty and came back to America more as myself. I let go of the hold the media image had on me."

–First-year college student

Remember

The more opportunities you create to learn from others who are different from yourself, the more opportunities you create to learn about yourself.

Diversity Enriches a College Education

Diversity magnifies the power of a college education because it helps liberate you from the tunnel vision of ethnocentricity (culture-centeredness) and egocentricity (self-centeredness), enabling you to get beyond yourself and your own culture to see yourself in relation to the world around you. Just as the various subjects you take in the college curriculum open your mind to multiple perspectives, so does your experience with people from varied backgrounds; it equips you with a wide-focus lens that allows you to take a multicultural perspective. A multicultural perspective helps

you become aware of cultural blind spots and avoid the dangers of group think—the tendency for tight groups of people to think so much alike that they overlook flaws in their thinking that can lead to poor choices and faulty decisions (Janis, 1982).

Diversity Strengthens Learning and Critical Thinking

Research consistently shows that people learn more from those who are different from them than from those who are similar to them (Pascarella, 2001; Pascarella & Terenzini, 2005). When your brain encounters something that is unfamiliar or different from what you're accustomed to, you must stretch beyond your mental comfort zone and work harder to understand it because doing so forces you to compare and contrast it to what you already know (Acredolo & O'Connor, 1991; Nagda, Gurin, & Johnson, 2005). This mental stretch requires the use of extra psychological effort and energy, which strengthens and deepens learning.

> "When all men think alike, no one thinks very much."
>
> —Walter Lippmann, distinguished journalist and originator of the term "stereotype"

© 2005 Ann Telnaes and Women's eNews. Used with the permission of the Cartoonist Group. All rights reserved.

A good example of how "group think" can lead to ethnocentric decisions that are ineffective (and unjust).

Diversity Promotes Creative Thinking

Experiences with diversity supply you with broader base of knowledge and wider range of thinking styles that better enable you to think outside your own cultural box or boundaries. In contrast, limiting your number of cultural vantage points is akin to limiting the variety of mental tools you can use to solve new problems, thereby limiting your creativity. When like-minded people only associate with other like-minded people, they're unlikely to think outside the box.

Drawing on different ideas from people with diverse backgrounds and bouncing your ideas off them is a great way to generate energy, synergy, and serendipity—unanticipated discoveries and creative solutions.

> "When the only tool you have is a hammer, you tend to see every problem as a nail."
>
> —Abraham Maslow, humanistic psychologist, best known for his self-actualization theory of achieving human potential

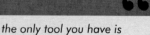

Diversity Enhances Career Preparation and Success

Learning about and from diversity has a practical benefit: It better prepares you for the world of work. Whatever career you choose to pursue, you are likely find yourself working with employers, employees, co-workers, customers, and clients from diverse cultural backgrounds. America's workforce is now more diverse than at any other time in the nation's history, and it will grow ever more diverse. For example, the percentage of America's working-age population that represents members of minority groups is expected to grow from 34 percent in 2008 to 55 percent in 2050 (U.S. Bureau of Labor Statistics, 2009).

In addition to increasing diversity in America, today's work world is characterized by a global economy. Greater economic interdependence among nations, more international trading (imports and exports), more multinational corporations, and almost-instantaneous worldwide communication increasingly occur—thanks to advances in the World Wide Web (Dryden & Vos, 1999; Smith, 1994). Because of these trends, employers of college graduates now seek job candidates with the following skills and attributes: sensitivity to human differences, the ability to understand and relate to people from different cultural backgrounds, international knowledge, and foreign language skills (Fixman, 1990; National Association of Colleges & Employers, 2003; Office of Research, 1994; Smith, 1997). In one national survey, policymakers, business leaders, and employers all agreed that college graduates should be more than just aware or tolerant of diversity; they should have experience with diversity (Education Commission of the States, 1995).

> "Empirical evidence shows that the actual effects on student development of emphasizing diversity and of student participation in diversity activities are overwhelmingly positive."
>
> –Alexander Astin, *What Matters in College* (1993)

> **!**
>
> **Remember**
>
> The wealth of diversity on college campuses today represents an unprecedented educational opportunity. You may never again be a member of a community that includes so many people from such a rich variety of backgrounds. Seize this opportunity! You're now in the right place at the right time to experience the people and programs that can infuse and enrich the quality of your college education with diversity.

Pause for Reflection

Have you ever been stereotyped, such as based on your appearance or group membership? If so, how did it make you feel and how did you react?

Have you ever unintentionally perceived or treated someone in terms of a group stereotype rather than as an individual? What assumptions did you make about that person? Was that person aware of, or affected by, your stereotyping?

◆ Stumbling Blocks and Barriers to Experiencing Diversity

Stereotypes

The word "stereotype" derives from a combination of two roots: *stereo* (to look at in a fixed way) and *type* (to categorize or group together, as in the word "typical"). Thus, stereotyping is viewing individuals of the same type (group) in the same (fixed) way.

In effect, stereotyping ignores or disregards a person's individuality; instead, all people who share a similar group characteristic (e.g., race or gender) are viewed as having the same personal characteristics—as in the expression, "You know what they are like; they're all the same." Stereotypes involve bias, which literally means "slant." A bias can be either positive or negative. Positive bias results in a favorable stereotype (e.g., "Italians are great lovers"); negative bias produces an unfavorable stereotype (e.g., "Italians are in the Mafia"). **Box 10.1** lists some common stereotypes.

Take Action!

Examples of Common Stereotypes

10.1

Muslims are terrorists.
Whites can't jump (or dance).
Blacks are lazy.
Asians are brilliant in math.
Irish are alcoholics.
Gay men are feminine; lesbian women are masculine.
Jews are cheap.
Hispanic men are abusive to women.
Men are strong.
Women are weak.

Personal Experience   When I was 6 years old, I was told by another 6-year-old from a different racial group that all people of my race could not swim. Since I could not swim at that time and she could, I assumed she was correct. I asked a boy, who happened to be of the same racial group as that little girl, if that statement were true; he responded: "Yes, it is true." Since I was from an area where few other African Americans were around to counteract this belief about Blacks, I bought into this stereotype until I finally took swimming lessons as an adult. I am now a lousy swimmer after many lessons because I did not even attempt to swim until I was an adult. The moral of this story is that group stereotypes can limit the confidence and potential of individuals who are members of the stereotyped group.

—Aaron Thompson

Prejudice

If virtually all members of a stereotyped group are judged or evaluated in a negative way, the result is prejudice. (The word "prejudice" literally means to "pre-judge.") Technically, prejudice may be either positive or negative; however, the term is most often associated with a negative prejudgment or stigmatizing—associating inferior or unfavorable traits with people who belong to the same group. Thus, prejudice may be defined as a negative judgment, attitude, or belief about another person or group of people, which is formed before the facts are known. Stereotyping and prejudice often go hand in hand because individuals who are placed in a negatively stereotyped group are commonly prejudged in a negative way.

Someone with a prejudice toward a group typically avoids contact with individuals from that group. This enables the prejudice to continue unchallenged because there is little chance for the prejudiced person to have positive experiences with a member of the stigmatized group that could contradict or disprove the prejudice. Thus, a vicious cycle is established in which the prejudiced person continues to avoid contact with individuals from the stigmatized group, which, in turn, continues to maintain and reinforce the prejudice.

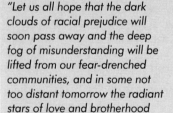

"Let us all hope that the dark clouds of racial prejudice will soon pass away and the deep fog of misunderstanding will be lifted from our fear-drenched communities, and in some not too distant tomorrow the radiant stars of love and brotherhood will shine over our great nation."

–Martin Luther King Jr., civil rights activist and clergyman

"'See that man over there?'
'Yes.'
'Well, I hate him.'
'But you don't know him.'
'That's why I hate him.'"

–Gordon Allport, *The Nature of Prejudice* (1954)

"A lot of us never asked questions in class before—it just wasn't done, especially by a woman or a girl, so we need to realize that and get into the habit of asking questions and challenging if we want to—regardless of the reactions of the profs and other students."

–Adult female college student (Wilkie & Thompson, 1993)

"The best way to beat prejudice is to show them. On a midterm, I got 40 points above the average. They all looked at me differently after that."

–Mexican American college student (Nemko, 1988)

Discrimination

Literally translated, the term "discrimination" means "division" or "separation." Whereas prejudice involves a belief or opinion, discrimination involves an action taken toward others. Technically, discrimination can be either negative or positive—for example, a discriminating eater may be careful about eating only healthy foods. However, the term is most often associated with a negative action that results in a prejudiced person treating another person, or group of people, in an unfair way. Thus, it could be said that discrimination is prejudice put into action. Hate crimes are examples of extreme discrimination because they are acts motivated solely by prejudice against members of a stigmatized group. Victims of hate crimes may have their personal property damaged or they may be physically assaulted, sometimes referred to as gay bashing if the victim is a homosexual. Other forms of discrimination are more subtle and may take place without people being fully aware that they are discriminating. For example, evidence shows that some White, male college professors tend to treat female students and students from ethnic or racial minority groups differently from the way they treat males and nonminority students. In particular, females and minority students in classes taught by White, male instructors tend to:

- Receive less eye contact from the instructor;
- Be called on less frequently in class;
- Be given less time to respond to questions asked by the instructor in class; and
- Have less contact with the instructor outside of class (Hall & Sandler, 1982, 1984; Sedlacek, 1987; Wright, 1987).

In most of these cases, the discriminatory treatment received by these female and minority students was subtle and not done consciously or deliberately by the instructors (Green, 1989). Nevertheless, these unintended actions are still discriminatory, and they may send a message to minority and female students that their ideas are not worth hearing or that they are not as capable as other students (Sadker & Sadker, 1994).

The following practices and strategies may be used to accept and appreciate individuals from other groups toward whom you may hold prejudices, stereotypes, or subtle biases that bubble beneath the surface of your conscious awareness.

1. Consciously avoid preoccupation with physical appearances.

Go deeper and get beneath the superficial surface of appearances to judge people not in terms of how they look but in terms of whom they are and how they act. Remember the old proverb "It's what's inside that counts." Judge others by the quality of their personal character, not by the familiarity of their physical characteristics.

Pause for Reflection

Prejudice and discrimination can be subtle and only begin to surface when the social or emotional distance among members of different groups grows closer. Rate your level of comfort with the following situations:

Someone from another racial group

1. going to your school;   high   moderate   low
2. working in your place of employment;   high   moderate   low
3. living on your street as a neighbor;   high   moderate   low
4. living with you as a roommate;   high   moderate   low
5. socializing with you as a personal friend;   high   moderate   low
6. being your most intimate friend or romantic partner; or   high   moderate   low
7. being your partner in marriage.   high   moderate   low

For any item you rated "low," what do you think was responsible for the low rating?

Snapshot Summary

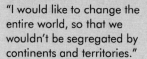

10.2

Stereotypes and Prejudiced Belief Systems About Group Inferiority

- **Ethnocentrism.** Considering one's own culture or ethnic group to be central or normal, and viewing different cultures as deficient or inferior. For example, people who are ethnocentric might claim that another culture is weird or abnormal for eating certain animals that they consider unethical to eat, even though they eat certain animals that the other culture would consider unethical to eat.

- **Racism.** Prejudice or discrimination based on skin color. For example, Cecil Rhodes (Englishman and empire builder of British South Africa), once claimed, "We [the British] are the finest race in the world and the more of the world we inhabit the better it is for the human race." Currently, racism is exemplified by the Ku Klux Klan, a domestic terrorist group that believes in the supremacy of the White race and considers all other races to be inferior.

"The Constitution of the United States knows no distinction between citizens on account of color."

–Frederick Douglass, abolitionist, author, advocate for equal rights for all people, and former slave

- **Classism.** Prejudice or discrimination based on social class, particularly toward people of low socioeconomic status. For example, a classicist might focus only on the contributions made by politicians and wealthy industrialists to America, ignoring the contributions of poor immigrants, farmers, slaves, and pioneer women.

- **Nationalism.** Excessive interest and belief in the strengths of one's own nation without acknowledging its mistakes or weaknesses, the needs of other nations, or the common interests of all nations. For example, blind patriotism blinds people to the shortcomings of their own nation, causing patriots to view any questioning or criticism of their nation as disloyalty or unpatriotic (as in the slogans "America: right or wrong" and "America: love it or leave it!")

- **Regionalism.** Prejudice or discrimination based on the geographical region of a nation in which an individual has been born and raised. For example, a Northerner might think that all Southerners are racists.

Student Perspective

"I would like to change the entire world, so that we wouldn't be segregated by continents and territories."

–College sophomore

- **Religious Bigotry.** Denying the fundamental human right of other people to hold religious beliefs or to hold religious beliefs that differ from one's own. For example, an atheist might force nonreligious (secular) beliefs on others, or a member of a religious group may believe that people who hold different religious beliefs are immoral or sinners.

Student Perspective

"Most religions dictate that theirs is the only way, and without believing in it, you cannot enter the mighty Kingdom of Heaven. Who are we to judge? It makes more sense for God to be the only one mighty enough to make that decision. If other people could understand and see [it] from this perspective, then many religious arguments could be avoided."

–First-year college student

- **Xenophobia.** Extreme fear or hatred of foreigners, outsiders, or strangers. For example, someone might believe that all immigrants should be kept out of the country because they will increase the crime rate.

- **Anti-Semitism.** Prejudice or discrimination toward Jews or people who practice the religion of Judaism. For example, someone could claim to hate Jews because they're the ones who "killed Christ."
- **Genocide.** Mass murdering of one group by another group. An example is the Holocaust during World War II, in which millions of Jews were murdered. Other examples include the murdering of Cambodians under the Khmer Rouge, the murdering of Bosnian Muslims in the former country of Yugoslavia, and the slaughter of the Tutsi minority by the Hutu majority in Rwanda.
- **Terrorism.** Intentional acts of violence against civilians that are motivated by political or religious prejudice. An example would be the September 11, 2001, attacks on the United States.
- **Ageism.** Prejudice or discrimination based on age, particularly prejudice toward the elderly. For example, an ageist might believe that all elderly people are bad drivers with bad memories.

- **Ableism.** Prejudice or discrimination toward people who are disabled or handicapped— physically, mentally, or emotionally. For example, someone shows ableism by avoiding interaction with handicapped people because of anxiety about not knowing what to say or how to act around them.
- **Sexism.** Prejudice or discrimination based on sex or gender. For example, a sexist might believe that no one should vote for a female running for president because she would be too emotional.
- **Heterosexism.** Belief that heterosexuality is the only acceptable sexual orientation. For example, using the slang "fag" or "queer" as an insult or put down or believing that gays should not have the same legal rights and opportunities as heterosexuals shows heterosexism.
- **Homophobia.** Extreme fear or hatred of homosexuals. For example, people who engage in gay bashing (acts of violence toward gays) or who create and contribute to antigay Web sites show homophobia.

Pause for Reflection

Have you ever held a prejudice against a particular group of people?

If you have, what was the group, and how do you think your prejudice developed?

Student Perspective

"I grew up in a very racist family. Even just a year ago, I could honestly say 'I hate Asians' with a straight face and mean it. My senior AP language teacher tried hard to teach me not to be judgmental. He got me to be open to others, so much so that my current boyfriend is half Chinese!"

–First-year college student

2. Perceive each person with whom you interact as having a unique personal identify.

Make a conscious effort to see each person with whom you interact not merely as a member of a same group but as a unique individual. Form your impressions of each person case by case rather than by using some rule of thumb.

This may seem like an obvious and easy thing to do, but research shows that humans have a natural tendency to perceive and conceive of individuals who are members of unfamiliar groups as being more alike (or all alike) than members of their own group (Taylor, Peplau, & Sears, 2006). Thus, you may have to consciously resist this tendency to overgeneralize and lump together individuals into homogenous groups; instead, make an intentional attempt to focus on treating each person you interact with as a unique human.

Remember

While it is valuable to learn about different cultures and the common characteristics shared by members of the same culture, differences exist among individuals who share the same culture. Don't assume that all individuals from the same cultural background share the same personal characteristics.

Interacting and Collaborating with Members of Diverse Groups

Once you overcome your biases and begin to perceive members of diverse groups as unique individuals, you are positioned to take the next step of interacting, collaborating, and forming friendships with them. Interpersonal contact between diverse people takes you beyond multicultural awareness and moves you up to a higher level of diversity appreciation that involves intercultural interaction. When you take this step to cross cultural boundaries, you transform diversity appreciation from a value or belief system into an observable action and way of living.

Your initial comfort level with interacting with people from diverse groups is likely to depend on how much experience you have had with diversity before college. If you have had little or no prior experience interacting with members of diverse groups, it may be more challenging for you to initiate interactions with diverse students on campus.

However, if you have had little previous experience with diversity, the good news is that you have the most to gain from interacting and collaborating with those of other ethnic or racial groups. Research consistently shows that when humans experience social interaction that differs radically from their prior experiences they gain the most in terms of learning and cognitive development (Acredolo & O'Connor, 1991; Piaget, 1985).

Meeting and Interacting with People from Diverse Backgrounds

1. Intentionally create opportunities for interaction and conversation with individuals from diverse groups.

Consciously resist the natural tendency to associate only with people who are similar to you. One way to do this is by intentionally placing yourself in situations where individuals from diverse groups are nearby and potential interaction can take place. Research indicates that meaningful interactions and friendships are more likely to form among people who are in physical proximity to one another (Latané, Liu, Nowak, Bonevento, & Zheng, 1995). Studies show that stereotyping and prejudice can be sharply reduced if contact between members of different racial or ethnic groups is frequent enough to allow time for the development of friendships (Pettigrew, 1998). You can create this condition in the college classroom by sitting near students from different ethnic or racial groups or by joining them if you are given the choice to select whom you will work with in class discussion groups and group projects.

2. Take advantage of the Internet to chat with students from diverse groups on your campus or with students in different countries.

Electronic communication can be a more convenient and more comfortable way to initially interact with members of diverse groups with whom you have had little prior experience. After you've communicated successfully *online*, you

"The common eye sees only the outside of things, and judges by that. But the seeing eye pierces through and reads the heart and the soul, finding there capacities which the outside didn't indicate or promise."

–Samuel Clemens, a.k.a. Mark Twain; writer, lecturer, and humorist

"Stop judging by mere appearances, and make a right judgment."

–Bible, John 7:24

"You can't judge a book by the cover."

–Title of the 1962 hit song by Elias Bates, a.k.a. Bo Diddley (Note: A bo diddley is a one-stringed African guitar)

Student Perspective

"I am very happy with the diversity here, but it also frightens me. I have never been in a situation where I have met people who are Jewish, Muslim, atheist, born-again, and many more."

–First-year college student (Erickson, Peters, & Strommer, 2006)

may then feel more comfortable about interacting with them *in person*. Online and in-person interaction with students from other cultures and nations can give you a better understanding of your own culture and country, as well as increase awareness of its customs and values that you may have taken for granted (Bok, 2006).

Pause for Reflection

Rate the amount or variety of diversity you have experienced in the following settings:

1. The high school you attended   high moderate low

2. The college or university you now attend   high moderate low

3. The neighborhood in which you grew up   high moderate low

4. Places where you have worked or been employed   high moderate low

Which setting had the most and which had the least diversity?

What do you think accounts for this difference?

3. Seek out the views and opinions of classmates from diverse backgrounds.

For example, during or after class discussions, ask students from different backgrounds if there was any point made or position taken in class that they would strongly question or challenge. Seeking out divergent (diverse) viewpoints has been found to be one of the best ways to develop critical thinking skills (Kurfiss, 1988).

4. Join or form discussion groups with students from diverse backgrounds.

You can gain exposure to diverse perspectives by joining or forming groups of students who differ from you in terms of such characteristics as gender, age, race, or ethnicity. You might begin by forming discussion groups composed of students who differ in one way but are similar in another way. For instance, form a learning team of students who have the same major as you do but who differ with respect to race, ethnicity, or age. This strategy gives the diverse members of your team some common ground for discussion (your major) and can raise your team's awareness that although you may be members of different groups you can, at the same time, be similar with respect to your educational goals and life plans.

Remember

Including diversity in your discussion groups not only provides social variety but also promotes the quality of the group's thinking by allowing its members to gain access to the diverse perspectives and life experiences of people from different backgrounds.

5. Form collaborative learning teams.

A learning team is more than a discussion group or a study group. It moves beyond discussion to collaborative learning—in other words, members of a learning team "co-labor" (work together) as part of a joint and mutually supportive effort to reach the same goal. Studies show that when individuals from different ethnic and racial groups work collaboratively toward the attainment of a common goal it reduces racial prejudice and promotes interracial friendships (Allport, 1954; Amir, 1976). These positive findings may be explained as follows: If individuals from diverse groups work on the same team, no one is a member of an "out" group (them); instead, all are members of the same "in" group (us; Pratto et al., 2000; Sidanius et al., 2000).

◆ Summary and Conclusion

Diversity refers to differences among groups of people who, together, comprise humanity. Experiencing diversity increases appreciation of the features unique to different cultures, and it gives a wider perspective on aspects of the human experience that are common to all people, regardless of their particular cultural background.

Culture is formed by the beliefs and values of a group with the same traditions and social heritage. It helps bind people into supportive, tight-knit communities. However, it can also lead people to view the world solely through their own cultural lens, known as ethnocentrism, which can blind them to other cultural perspectives. Ethnocentrism can contribute to stereotyping—viewing individual members of the same group in the same way and as having similar personal characteristics.

Evaluating members of a stereotyped group negatively results in prejudice—a negative prejudgment about another person or group of people, which is formed before the facts are known. Stereotyping and prejudice often go hand in hand because if the stereotype is negative, individual members of the stereotyped group are then prejudged negatively. Discrimination takes prejudice one step further by converting the negative prejudgment into action that results in unfair treatment of others. Thus, discrimination is prejudice put into action.

If stereotyping and prejudice are overcome, you are then positioned to experience diversity and reap its multiple benefits, which include sharpened self-awareness, social stimulation, broadened personal perspectives, deeper learning, higher-level thinking, and career success.

The increasing diversity of students on campus, combined with the wealth of diversity-related educational experiences found in the college curriculum and cocurriculum, presents you with an unprecedented opportunity to infuse diversity into your college experience. Seize this opportunity and capitalize on the power of diversity to increase the quality of your college education and your prospects for future success.

Internet-Based Resources for Further Information on Diversity

For additional information related to the ideas discussed in this chapter, we recommend the following Web sites:

www.tolerance.org

www.amnesty.org

Chapter 10 Exercises

10.1 Self-Awareness of Multigroup Identities

You can be members of multiple groups at the same time, and your membership in these overlapping groups can influence your personal development and self-identity. In the figure that follows, consider the shaded center circle to be yourself and the six nonshaded circles to be six groups you belong to that you think have influenced your personal development or personal identity.

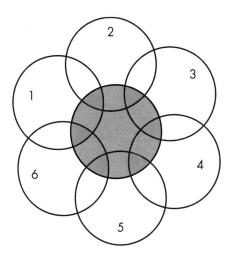

Fill in the nonshaded circles with the names of groups to which you belong that have had the most influence on your personal development. You can use the diversity spectrum that appears on the second page of this chapter to help you identify different groups. Do not feel you have to come up with six groups and fill all six circles. What is more important is to identify those groups that have had a significant influence on your personal development or identity.

Self-Assessment Questions

1. Which one of your groups has had the greatest influence on your personal identity, and why?

2. Have you ever felt limited or disadvantaged by being a member of any group or groups?

3. Have you ever felt that you experienced advantages or privileges because of your membership in any group or groups?

10.2 Intercultural Interview

Find a student, faculty member, or administrator on campus whose cultural background is different from yours, and ask if you could interview that person about his or her culture. Use the following questions in your interview:

1. How is "family" defined in your culture, and what are the traditional roles and responsibilities of different family members?

2. What are the traditional gender (male vs. female) roles associated with your culture? Are they changing?

3. What is your culture's approach to time (e.g., Is there an emphasis on punctuality? Is doing things quickly valued or frowned upon?)

4. What are your culture's staple foods or favorite foods?

5. What cultural traditions or rituals are highly valued and commonly practiced?

6. What special holidays are celebrated?

10.3 Hidden Bias Test

Go to www.tolerance.org/activity/test-yourself-hidden-bias and take one or more of the hidden bias tests on the Web site. These tests assess subtle bias with respect to gender, age, Native Americans, African Americans, Asian Americans, religious denominations, sexual orientations, disabilities, and body weight. You can assess whether you have a bias toward any of these groups.

Self-Assessment Questions

1. Did the results reveal any bias that you were unaware of?

2. Did you think the assessment results were accurate or valid?

3. What do you think best accounts for or explains your results?

4. If your parents and best friends took the test, how do you think their results would compare with yours?

Hate Crime: A Racially Motivated Murder

Jasper County, Texas, has a population of approximately 31,000 people. In this county, 80 percent of the people are White, 18 percent are Black, and 2 percent are of other races. The county's poverty rate is considerably higher than the national average, and its average household income is significantly lower. In 1998, the mayor, president of the Chamber of Commerce, and two councilmen were Black. From the outside, Jasper appeared to be a town with racial harmony, and its Black and White leaders were quick to state that there was racial harmony in Jasper.

However, on June 7, 1998, James Byrd Jr., a 49-year-old African American male, was walking home along a road one evening and was offered a ride by three White males. Rather than taking Byrd home, Lawrence Brewer (age 31), John King (age 23), and Shawn Berry (age 23), three individuals linked to White-supremacist groups, took Byrd to an isolated area and began beating him. They then dropped his pants to his ankles, painted his face black, chained Byrd to their truck, and dragged him for approximately 3 miles. The truck was driven in a zigzag fashion to inflict maximum pain on the victim. Byrd was decapitated after his body collided with a culvert in a ditch alongside the road. His skin, arms, genitalia, and other body parts were strewn along the road, while his torso was found dumped in front of a Black cemetery. Medical examiners testified that Byrd was alive for much of the dragging incident.

While in prison awaiting trial, Brewer wrote letters to King and other inmates. In one letter, Brewer wrote: "Well I did it and am no longer a virgin. It was a rush and I'm still licking my lips for more." Once the trials were completed, Brewer and King were sentenced to death. Both Brewer and King, whose bodies were covered with racist tattoos, had been on parole before the incident, and they had previously been cellmates. King had spent an extensive amount of time in prison, where he began to associate with White males in an environment which each race was pitted against the other.

As a result of the murder, Byrd's family created the James Byrd Foundation for Racial Healing in 1998. January 20, 1999, a wrought iron fence that separated Black and White graves for more than 150 years Jasper Cemetery was removed in a special unity service. Members of the racist Ku Klux Klan have since the gravesite of Byrd several times, leaving racist stickers and other marks that have angered the Jasper munity and Byrd's family.

Sources: Houston Chronicle (June 14, 1998); San Antonio Express News (September 17, 1999); L Weekly (February 3, 2003).

Reflection and Discussion Questions

1. What factors do you think were responsible for causing this incident to take place?

2. Could this incident have been prevented? If yes, how? If no, why not?

3. What do you think will be the long-term effects of this incident on the town?

4. How likely do you think it is that an incident like this could take place in your hometown or near your college campus?

...is event took place in your hometown, how would you and members of your family and community react?

'e
th
ent
in

On
rs in
visited
com-

ouisiana

Leadership and Service

11

A Foundation for Living a Life of Leadership and Service

◆ What Is Leadership?

Leadership is a complex and intricate phenomenon. Do a search for "Leadership" on the Internet and you will find many definitions, examples, and options for framing your definition of leadership. For example, a search may lead you to any one of the following definitions:

> "Leadership is a matter of how to be, not how to do. We spend most of our lives mastering how to do things, but in the end it is the quality and character of the individual that defines the performance of great leaders" (Hesselbein, 1999, introduction, p. xii).

> "Leadership requires orchestrating . . . conflicts among and within the interested parties . . ." (Heifetz, 1994, p. 22).

> "Effective Leadership addresses problems that require people to move from a familiar but inadequate equilibrium—through disequilibrium—to a more adequate equilibrium" (Daloz Parks, 2005, p. 9).

> "An act or instance of leading; guidance; direction" (Dictionary.com, 2007).

> "A leader takes people where they want to go. A great leader takes people where they don't necessarily want to go, but ought to be" Rosalynn Carter, US First Lady.

> "Leadership is a combination of strategy and character. If you must be without one, be without the strategy" General H. Norman Schwarzkopf.

> "Leadership is the art of mobilizing others to want to struggle for shared aspirations" (Kouzes & Posner, 1995, p. 30).

Leadership is not black and white. Your challenge, as you explore leadership, is to define what leadership means to you and characterize it in the framework of your values, experiences, and discussions spurred from this text.

There are many lenses from which you can view leadership, and throughout this chapter and others to follow, you will be introduced to several of these approaches. From the many different theories and new research on leadership to its different styles, this chapter will challenge you to analyze and apply your own style of leadership and the leadership of others with whom you interact.

While defining leadership and exploring different approaches to leadership, you will also need to consider the function service and civic engagement play in

From "Leadership and Service," 1/e by George McGovern et al. Copyright 2008. Kendall Hunt Publishing. Reprinted by permission.

your role as a leader. Additionally, the examination of your college or university environment for unique, hands-on experiences to test, study, and challenge your perceptions of leadership and service will be critical as you search for the role leadership and service will play in your life. This chapter will introduce you to all of these concepts and encourage you to participate in some of the challenges posed and experiences suggested, as well as to read some of the examples listed as you define leadership for yourself. The chapter will end with a discussion of civic responsibility and examine the role leaders have to give back to their community.

To begin our discussion of leadership, it is important to provide a definition to serve as a foundation for the remainder of the chapter. While we provide you with the following definition to use as a framework, we challenge you to develop one that reflects the importance of leadership to you as you continue through your search for the meaning of leadership throughout your life. **Leadership** is the process by which a leader facilitates change. It is the function of three elements: leaders, followers, and situation. Leadership occurs when all three of these elements interact and work together, while respecting the role each piece plays in the process. When the personality, position, and expertise of the leader(s) work in combination with the values, norms, and cohesiveness of followers and interact and respect the environment, history, and task of the situation, leadership occurs (Hughes, Ginnett, & Curphy, 2006). A **leader** is someone who is able to lead others to effect change. While leaders often improve conditions for others within society, not all leaders facilitate positive change. Adolf Hitler, for example, was the undisputed leader of Germany but few people today would argue that the changes he brought to Germany were positive. **Followers** are individuals who come together to support the vision of a leader(s) and use their personal strengths, knowledge, and skills to assist in reaching a common goal. **Situation** is defined as the environment in which a task is undertaken, in combination with knowledge and human interaction.

When these three elements act with a foundation of **ethics,** a system of moral values and principles that guides behavior, **ethical leadership** occurs (Prince, 2007). Having a foundation of ethics is critical, as our society has seen how unethical leaders can cause the demise of an organization, others, and

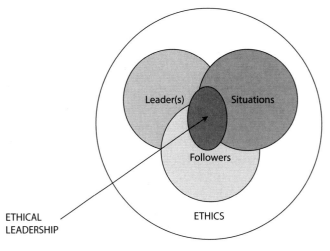

Source: Prince, 2007.

themselves. Think of some examples you have seen in recent news. Whether it is a politician or a business executive, unethical behavior has an impact on all levels of leadership, creating distrust and a lack of productivity.

While many texts and courses may focus on developing leaders, the focus of this chapter will concentrate on developing your understanding of the leadership process. Developing personal leadership skills, understanding active followership, and gaining an understanding of the situation will be the focus of this discussion on leadership.

◆ Why Explore Leadership During College?

College is likely the first time you are on your own. It can be an opportunity for you to explore who you are and allow you to shape who you would like to become as an individual, apart from a family or community. The college environment usually encourages students to take advantage of time, access, and opportunity to engage in leadership and service. Approach all of your college experiences with the hope of learning something new about yourself and the world around you. College and university campuses are the perfect environment to examine, practice, and critically think about leadership and service, as you are exposed to a wide range of people, ideas, and experiences, thereby increasing your understanding of the world and society.

Furthermore, the study of leadership and the practice of being a leader are a great match in the college setting. For this reason, make sure you link your academic study of leadership to your co-curricular involvement by applying what you learn in the classroom to your college leadership involvement: Don't leave that exploration in the classroom! Your ability to connect the intellectual with the practical will reinforce the concepts and theories you learn and strengthen your leadership skills during college and beyond.

Today, more people are entering the workforce with a college degree, so it is important to consider what will make you stand out after you complete your undergraduate degree and begin to explore your chosen field of study. Leadership and service experiences are one way to stand out. Employers are seeking well-rounded candidates to join the ranks of their organizations, and leadership and service involvement often fit this bill. You can gain a great deal of knowledge and skills from leadership and service experiences at the college level that can help you with your future career. Additionally, you will be more successful during the interview process if you are able to articulate your skills and abilities and connect them to practical experiences.

Among many transferable skills, leadership allows you to practice verbal and nonverbal communication, recognize and manage ethical issues, delegate responsibility, deal with multiple tasks, lead a team, resolve conflicts, motivate people into action, establish and attain goals, and work with people from diverse backgrounds.

College offers the opportunity for you not only to study leadership but also to observe and engage others practicing leadership as you define your personal leadership style and fine-tune your skills. College is one of the few times in your life when you can immerse yourself in organizations and programs that are time consuming. Take advantage of the multitude of programs and services offered on your campus. For many, college will be a time when you will have the most access to diverse lectures, movies, panel discussions, musicians, leadership workshops, and conferences.

For some students, the numerous opportunities to engage with the campus community can be overwhelming. Enjoy and explore this exciting environment. Developing leadership skills begins with involvement, so focus on learning and participating, not just obtaining a position. Some of the best leaders you'll meet do not hold a formal leadership position but lead through their actions. To explore the involvement possibilities, consider attending a student organization fair, visiting the Dean of Students' office, participating in a leadership conference, getting behind an issue that you are passionate about, attending a lecture sponsored by your multicultural student services office, or further exploring your passion in an area of campus life.

Student Organizations

Student organizations are often the most accessible route to leadership on a college campus. Student organizations allow you to manage a broad scope of issues related to leadership and service. Challenge yourself to think beyond leadership position goals and to consider what experiences would be most valuable to you as a person and your campus community. Possible types of student organizations on your campus include:

- Academic
- Cultural
- Educational
- Greek
- Honorary
- International
- Media
- Political
- Professional
- Recreational/athletic
- Religious
- Service
- Social
- Special interest
- Student governance

Leadership and Service Opportunities

Everyone has the capacity to lead. As you begin your exploration, adopt the idea that you are a leader, and recognize the skills you have and then decide where you want to go. Find programs, services, and departments on campus that promote interdisciplinary leadership development and service opportunities. These offices or organizations might also provide some of the following resources to you:

- Workshops
- Conferences
- Leadership libraries
- Volunteer opportunities/programs

Leadership Employment Opportunities

Your campus has many opportunities for employment, including work-study, internships, and paraprofessional opportunities. Campus employment provides you not only with extra income but also with the convenience of working on campus and flexible scheduling. On-campus employment may also afford you opportunities to network with faculty, staff, and other students and increase your knowledge of university resources. Moreover, your on-campus work experience will allow you to practice interpersonal skills, make greater contributions to the university community, and grow personally and professionally. Consider some of the following options:

- Resident advisors
- Peer academic advisors
- Orientation leaders/advisors
- Residential community coordinators
- Student affairs interns
- Student ambassadors
- Peer leaders/mentors

Although there are a multitude of reasons to engage with your campus community, you will be more successful if you have the drive to make a difference and are passionate about something. Passion will afford you the persistence to follow through with your initiative or involvement. Furthermore, it is important to consider "fit" as you make decisions to participate. For example, consider whether it would be more valuable for you to explore many offerings or narrow your involvement experiences to those that align with your academic discipline. Whatever your chosen involvement path, just remember that a collegiate environment is a unique laboratory that allows you to observe, study, and practice in a controlled environment. We encourage you to take leadership risks during college, as it is a place that celebrates and embraces educational growth. The lessons you learn can create a foundation for future growth and learning in leadership.

Leadership Philosophies and Styles

Now that you have a foundation of what leadership is, why college represents a dynamic arena to practice it, and some activities you can become involved with, let us explore some philosophies and styles that guide the current practice of leadership. While many philosophies of leadership exist, this chapter will focus on five. An in-depth look at each of these philosophies, in combination with your exploration into leadership styles, will aid you in the development of your personal philosophy of leadership. Over the next few pages, you will gain insight into the situational, transformational, authentic, social change, and servant-leadership philosophies of leadership. Look for elements with which you agree, question, disagree, or want to further explore. These insights can provide a great discussion.

The Situational Leadership Model

The situational leadership model was first introduced by Hersey and Blanchard as a way to analyze leader behaviors using two broad categories: initiating structure and consideration. These two categories have evolved over the years to become task structures and relationship behaviors. Task structures describe how the leader gives information about responsibilities, including what is to be accomplished, how, when, and who is to accomplish the task. Relationship behaviors involve how much the leader engages in communication and relationship building, including listening, encouraging, and giving support (Hersey, 1984; Hersey & Blanchard, 1995; Hughes, Ginnett, & Curphy, 2006).

The situational leadership model is a good way to look at leadership from the lens of being flexible. It communicates the importance of not acting toward all people in the same way. Hersey and Blanchard's situational leadership model describes how leadership varies based on the interactions of task and relationship behaviors. The interaction of these behaviors creates the following four quadrants on a graph (see below).

An important element of the model addresses how the success of behaviors is impacted by follower readiness, defined as the ability and willingness of followers to complete a task (Hersey, 1984; Hersey & Blanchard, 1995). As you can see from the graph, follower readiness plays an important role in the connection between the task and relationship behavior. The curved line added on the graph represents the leadership behavior that is most effective, depending on the level of follower readiness. To apply the model, leaders assess the readiness level of the followers. Draw a vertical line from the center of the readiness level up to the point where it intersects with the curved line in the graph. Where this intersection occurs is the quadrant that represents the best opportunity to produce the most successful results in leadership (Hersey, 1984; Hughes, Ginnett, & Curphy, 2006).

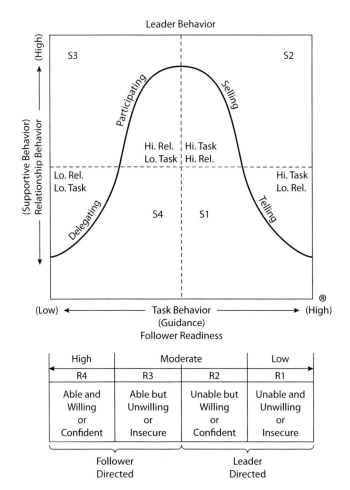

Source: Hughes, Ginnett, & Curphy, 2006.

The situational leadership model highlights the importance of your skills and abilities as a leader, while focusing on the importance of knowing your followers. As a leader, you will be able to apply many of these skills and abilities in a variety of situations, and this model is a good representation of how you can transfer skills from one area of leadership to other areas of your life.

Transformational Leadership Theory

The transformational leadership theory, made popular by political sociologist James MacGregor Burns (1978) links the roles and values of leaders and followers. Burns defined leaders as those who seek to understand the drive of followers to better reach the goals of both leaders and followers (Burns, 1978). Transformational leadership serves to change the status quo by appealing to followers' values and their sense of high purpose. They articulate problems in the current systems and create a compelling vision for what is possible (Hughes, Ginnett, & Curphy, 2006). Transformational leaders reframe issues, ignite enthusiasm for change within followers, and encourage and develop followers to become leaders in the change movement. Transformational leaders inspire followers to see the impact they can have on society.

Transformational leaders do the following (Hughes, Ginnett, & Curphy, 2006):

- Focus on building trust, admiration, loyalty, and respect among their followers
- Convey a strong vision and form emotional connections/bonds with followers to help followers meet their goals and needs
- Be willing to embrace controversy, make self-sacrifices, and remain strong and focused to reach their vision, despite criticism
- Possess a strong standard of moral and ethical conduct and can be counted on to do the right thing
- Communicate a direction that transforms the values and norms of the organization
- Maintain a consistent emphasis on individual and organizational learning

Followers who work with transformational leaders are motivated, are inspired, and are transformed by the relationship with their leaders. It is the goal of transformational leaders to impact each follower, and in the end, to ensure that followers become leaders. Transformational leaders seek to engage the whole person by focusing on followers' motives, strengths, and values to empower them to act. They use this passion within their followers to mobilize and change social systems while building up those around them.

Authentic Leadership Theory

Authentic leadership is described as a root concept (Avolio & Gardner, 2005) that underlies positive approaches to leadership, such as transformational, charismatic, and servant-leadership. The foundation of authentic leadership is developing authenticity and increasing self-awareness.

In the book *True North: Discover Your Authentic Leadership*, Bill George and Peter Sims (2007) wrote the following about authentic leaders:

> [T]hese leaders recognize that leadership is *not* about their success or about getting loyal subordinates to follow them. They know the key

to a successful organization is having empowered leaders at all levels, including those that have no direct reports.

Authentic leaders not only inspire those around them, they empower them to step up and lead. Thus, we offer the new definition of leadership: *The authentic leader brings people together around a shared purpose and empowers them to step up and lead authentically in order to create value for all stakeholders.*

Authentic leaders know themselves. They serve others through their leadership and are more interested in empowering people than gaining power for themselves. They learn from their and others' mistakes and successes to build a positive strength initiative within their organizations (Avolio & Luthans, 2005).

Authentic leaders know their strengths and weaknesses. They recognize their shortcomings and work to overcome them. They are consistent, self-disciplined, and committed to life-long learning. The key to becoming an authentic leader is to develop one's own style. A leader who imitates the leadership styles of others is not being authentic and will most likely not succeed. A leader's style must be congruent with his or her own personality and character; the style must also be consistent with who he or she is.

There are five essential qualities of being an authentic leader (George, 2003; George & Sims, 2007). Authentic leaders must:

- Understand their purpose
- Practice solid values
- Lead with heart
- Establish connected relationships
- Demonstrate self-discipline

Authentic leadership has received much more attention since the recent ethical failures of leaders in the demise of well-known corporations, such as Enron and WorldCom, and George (2003) argues it is the way to restore confidence among followers in such corporations. While the research in this area is still ongoing, there is much to be learned by studying and engaging in the practice of authentic leadership.

Social Change Model of Leadership Development

The social change model is based on the research of college students and the influence of peer groups. Alexander Astin (1993) discovered that peer influence and interaction impact leadership development among college students more than any other factor.

The social change model is designed to use student peer groups to enhance individual leadership development in students. The model strives to prepare leaders to effect positive change both in and out of traditional leadership roles. The social change model views the leader as a change agent who influences change through collective action with followers.

The following are the key assumptions and primary goals of the social change model (Higher Education Research Institute, 1996):

- Leadership is concerned with effecting change on behalf of others and society.
- Leadership is collaborative.

- Leadership is a process rather than a position.
- Leadership should be value-based.
- All students (not just those holding formal leadership positions) are potential leaders.
- Service is a powerful vehicle for developing student leadership skills.

The two primary goals of the model are to enhance student learning and to develop self-knowledge and leadership competence in order to facilitate positive social change.

The model examines leadership development through three levels: the individual, group process, and community/societal levels. Within those three levels are seven values: (1) consciousness of self, (2) congruence, (3) commitment, (4) collaboration, (5) common purpose, (6) controversy with civility, and (7) citizenship. These levels and values constantly interact to produce leadership.

All the levels of the social change model are concerned with impacting growth and change in the other levels of the model, thereby producing a dynamic interaction of values and people within leadership development (Higher Education Research Institute, 1996).

Servant-Leadership

The servant-leadership theory was developed by Robert K. Greenleaf, a retired AT&T executive. He developed the theory out of his growing concern for college students' attitudes. Servant-leadership is a practical philosophy that describes leaders who choose to serve first and then lead as a means of extending service to others. Servant-leaders may or may not hold formal leadership positions. They emerge from all parts of the organization, depending on the situation and need. Servant-leaders operate through collaboration, trust, foresight, listening, and the ethical use of power and empowerment (Greenleaf, 1995).

Greenleaf wrote *The Servant as Leader* in 1977; in it, he described servant-leadership:

> The servant-leader is servant first . . . It begins with the natural feeling that one wants to serve, to serve *first*. Then conscious choice brings one to aspire to lead. He or she is sharply different from the person who is *leader* first, perhaps because of the need to assuage an unusual power drive or to acquire material possessions. For such it will be a later choice to serve—after leadership is established. The leader-first and the servant-first are two extreme types. Between them there are shadings and blends that are part of the infinite variety of human nature.
>
> The difference manifests itself in the care taken by the servant-first to make sure that other people's highest priority needs are being served. The best test, and difficult to administer, is this: Do those served grow as persons? Do they, *while being served*, become healthier, wiser, freer, more autonomous, more likely themselves to become servants? And, what is the effect on the least privileged in society? Will they benefit or at least will they not be further deprived? (1977, pp. 13–14)

Larry Spears, former CEO of the Greenleaf Center, has identified ten critical principles of servant-leadership: (1) listening, (2) empathy, (3) healing of relationships, (4) awareness, (5) persuasion, (6) conceptualization, (7) foresight, (8) stewardship,

(9) commitment to the growth of people, and (10) building community (Baker, 2001).

Leadership Styles

In addition to the models and theories previously presented, it is important to have an understanding of the different types of leadership styles that can be demonstrated and utilized. Three of the most common styles of leadership are autocratic/authoritarian, democratic/participatory, and laissez-faire/delegative (Bass, 1990; Lewin, Lippit & White, 1939). Being able to recognize different leadership styles can assist you in becoming an active member in the leadership process, both as a leader and as a follower. As you learn to integrate, with equal importance, the roles of leader, follower, and situation, your knowledge of appropriate styles will be key to your success. Additionally, these styles may assist you in creating your personal definition of leadership. As you read the descriptions of the styles, think about a time when you or someone you have worked with has exhibited each of the following styles.

Autocratic/Authoritarian

An autocratic, or authoritarian, leader makes decisions without consulting followers. An autocratic leader maintains all control, giving no power to followers. The decision is made without any form of consultation and is often used when a determination needs to be made quickly or decisions need to be made that have little to no impact on others. Since the autocratic leader does not seek input from others, this style, if used frequently, can lead to low morale among followers and feelings of distrust.

Democratic/Participatory

The democratic leader is also referred to as the participatory leader. A democratic leader involves followers in decision making and focuses on group consensus. This style of leadership is effective in making people feel valued and appreciated. However, if there are multiple opinions, it can be time consuming and cumbersome. Decisions that need to be made quickly may not be best served by this leadership style. Decisions that require commitment and investment from people within a group may be best served with a democratic style.

Laissez-Faire/Delegative

The laissez-faire, or delegative, style of leadership minimizes the leader's involvement in decision making. A laissez-faire leader steps back to "let it be," allowing people to make their own decisions. This style of leadership works best when followers are skilled, capable, and motivated to make sound decisions. The laissez-faire style gives followers freedom to determine goals, make decisions, and resolve problems on their own. The leader provides feedback to followers but allows them to chart their own course.

This chapter references only three of the more common styles of leadership, but there are many other styles, and variations of styles, of leadership. Some of the others will be discussed later in other chapters.

◆ Applying What You Know About Leadership on Your Campus

During college, you will have many opportunities to observe and analyze leadership and service in action. Using the previous discussions on definitions, philosophies, and styles of leadership, it is now your responsibility to take action! As you observe and interact with individuals and constituent groups on your campus, it will be valuable for you to have an understanding of the organization and community culture. Take the time to study your college campus and understand how it operates. This is important because a leader's success often depends, to a great extent, on his or her understanding of an organization's culture. In evaluating your institution, the following questions will help guide you to a better understanding of the structure, operation, and culture of your campus community.

- How is leadership exhibited on your college campus?
- Who holds the power on campus and who influences decision-making processes?
- What is your institution's mission or strategic plan?
- How effective is your student governance structure?
- Which student organizations or student leaders have access to the administration?
- How do the administration, faculty, and staff consider the student voice?
- How do students communicate their interests and needs to the administration?
- What institutional policies and resources are available that empower students in the campus decision-making process?

After you have a foundational understanding of your campus, you will be able to better understand your leadership and service observations. Many faculty, staff, and students engage in leadership and service every day. The campus community engages in classroom teaching and leadership, service through campus committees, teamwork and collaboration with colleagues and peers, administrative responses to issues facing the campus community, role modeling of appropriate behavior, and good stewardship of money.

As you interact with your campus community you should critically examine and process all that is going on around you. As you observe people in the campus environment, ask yourself questions that will help you better understand what leadership skills, techniques, and attitudes you would like to replicate.

- Who is authentic in their interactions with others?
- Who excites you when you hear him or her speak?
- Who considers others?
- Who leads with integrity?
- Who is consistent in decision making and policy development?

When considering leadership roles on your college campus, remember that leaders may be defined as positional or nonpositional, depending on the situation. Positional leaders are given authority on a college campus. These leaders are able to control and command different aspects of the higher education system. Examples of positional leaders you will find on your campus are the governing board/board of trustees, college president, provost, vice president for student affairs, chair of the faculty senate, president of the student govern-

> **! Leadership Challenge**
>
> Identify one positional leader and one nonpositional leader on your campus. Compare and contrast their impact on the campus community. From your perspective, who has more power and influence? Do you know someone on campus who is a nonpositional leader who has more power and influence than someone who is a positional leader?

ment association, and college deans. Positional leaders often have power and authority derived from their formal roles. Successful positional leaders balance their power and authority with ethical actions and inclusive behaviors.

Nonpositional leaders are people at all levels of an organization who lead but lack authority or power derived from a formal position. They can also be individuals who do not aspire to positions of leadership. Nonpositional leaders often act as facilitators to help groups reach a common goal.

◆ Responsibilities of Leaders in Action

As a student interested in leadership, you have many responsibilities. As you represent yourself, consider if your words and actions align with your goals, values, and beliefs. As an organization leader, consider how your organization communicates its goals and priorities. Do members' actions and words align with organization values? In addition to asking these questions, elevate your intellect by surrounding yourself with people who have ideas that are different from yours and people who will intellectually engage and challenge your beliefs and values. Also, reading is a great way to expose yourself to different concepts and ideas. Make sure that you comprehend the material and know the source of what you are reading. Read not only what aligns with your beliefs but also that which conflicts. Challenge narrow-minded thinking and encourage yourself and others to examine situations and people from a broad, nonjudgmental basis.

When exploring and experiencing your college environment, it is important to remember that the current philosophies, styles, and theories of leadership are a critical component of your growth as an emerging leader, in conjunction with discovering your personal strengths and weaknesses. All leaders are a reflection of their previous experiences, leadership mentors, beliefs, values, and other important elements of self. Identifying what is most important to you will create a support network and will help you create change-powered leadership.

The next section of the chapter explores the responsibilities you have as a leader. These responsibilities include personal responsibility, responsibility to others, and the responsibility to give back to society. These responsibilities all combine to formulate **civic-based leadership,** which is using your skills, knowledge, and passion for leadership and service. The examination of this topic will continue throughout the chapter.

You have probably heard the phrase "With leadership comes much responsibility." This responsibility can be explored in many ways, and through the next section, you will examine ways successful leaders interact with their followers and will consider the situations in which they find themselves.

Spirituality and Understanding Yourself

Gaining an understanding of who you are and reflecting your core values and beliefs within your everyday actions are key to strong leadership. This idea of consciousness of self and congruence was also introduced in the social change model of leadership (Higher Education Research Institute, 1996). Hagberg (1994) charges leaders to participate in a soul leadership process by discovering passion, practicing vulnerability, experiencing solitude regularly, letting go of control, facing fear, and participating in the spiritual journey of continual change and deepening of self-understanding that takes you to your core. Embracing and sharing this self-awareness only makes the connections among leader, follower, and situation stronger. As these connections increase and the leader is honest with self and others about what drives him or her, leadership becomes more dynamic.

Critical Thinking

Leaders have a responsibility to critically evaluate their environments, their strengths and weaknesses, and all the situations they encounter. Leaders don't simply accept the status quo, or "the way it has always been"; rather, leaders challenge the process and think outside the box. When thinking about how actions can impact others, leaders think about the short- and long-term outcomes. They also consider the effects decisions may have on all stakeholders, not just the people close at hand. Critical thinking demands knowledge of the strengths and weaknesses you have, and it requires you to step outside of your own experiences to see what the experiences of others may look like.

Global Awareness

It is clear that the world is becoming smaller and smaller. That is, people from all parts of the world are interacting with one another more frequently than in the past. A responsible leader is one who embraces the differences that exist among people. Leaders must be aware of their own cultural selves as well as the cultural identities of all possible followers. What is a multicultural or global leader? A multicultural leader plays the same role in leadership that any good leader should. As a leader who is interacting with followers and/or a situation or environment that is different from your own, it is your responsibility to adapt your leadership style to incorporate your followers and environment. It is true that leadership is viewed differently across the world, so what works in one culture may not work in another culture or area of the world. Your commitment to understanding others will lead you to success.

Your Influence as a Leader

As a leader, you live in a fish bowl! This silly metaphor is a great way to picture your level of influence on the people around you. As a leader, you constantly have eyes on you, even if you are not formally in a position or a setting that defines you as a leader. People around you will notice your every move, both good and bad. You must constantly be aware of how congruent your behaviors and actions are with your values and beliefs. You are influencing your followers and your situation even when you do not know it. You have power and responsibility with this influence. Consider this influence as you examine your role as a leader and as you study leadership.

Professionalism and Presentation of Self

A professional is someone who engages in an activity with knowledge of the area and within ethical standards. Being a professional and leader requires you to think about your responsibilities to yourself and others with whom you interact. Think about the many environments and people you have seen act professionally and unprofessionally.

Additionally, how you present yourself, both in words and appearance, can have a large bearing on how you are perceived. As a leader, you need to be concerned with being approachable and well informed. Using correct grammar and paying attention to details in written and spoken presentations will send a message of professionalism to those around you. In addition to what you say, how you dress sends a message of professionalism. As a leader, you need to understand the expectations of your situation and followers, then meet those needs with your attire. Wearing a business suit to a student organization meeting may not be necessary, but wearing flannel pajama pants to the same meeting may also be inappropriate. Know your environment and respect it, so that the people within it will give you the respect you deserve.

Technology

Proper use of technology is a responsibility of all, but particularly of leaders. As a leader, you must stay abreast of new technology that will positively or negatively impact your followers or environment. Additionally, the use and misuse of technology should be at the forefront of your mind. For example, burning copies of copyrighted materials may be helpful for your organization and a great new discovery in technology, but it is clearly unprofessional, unethical, and illegal.

As a leader, it is important to think about the implications that the accessibility of information via technology will have on your followers. Much more information is available through technology and it can be obtained much more quickly, so educating yourself and others about safety and ethics regarding the information that is so readily accessible is key.

Whether it is Facebook, MySpace, or some other on-line community, as a leader, you must take responsibility for the image you portray both in person and through cyberspace. Pictures, comments, hobbies, events you attend, people you connect yourself with, and much more are all a reflection on your professionalism or lack thereof.

Make sure you do not misrepresent yourself, and consider that these sites are public domains where people can view information and form opinions about you without even knowing you.

Leaders Balance Responsibilities

As a leader, you will be charged with balancing the role of being practical, visionary, and strategic. How you balance competing tasks from day to day

Leadership Challenge

Visit an on-line community of someone you consider to be a leader. Write down a few things you learned about this person. What was negative? Positive?

with providing a strategic plan to being visionary is a delicate balance that leaders face daily. All three responsibilities are important. If you don't have a vision of where you are going, your followers will have a difficult time following you and sharing a purpose. If you don't have a blueprint that outlines the long-term goals and details of how adopting specific strategies and approaches will help you reach these goals, your vision will not be realized. And if you do not pay attention to the day-to-day needs of your organization and followers, including meeting agendas, payroll, and recognition, you will not be as successful in meeting your goals to reach your vision. Thus, how do you prioritize these responsibilities on a daily basis? It depends on the situation. If you constantly put off the big picture vision and strategic plan while focusing only on the practical needs, you'll never reach your potential. If you focus only on your vision, without setting goals, the vision will be too far away and out of reach. You must plan time to balance the needs of all three and include your followers in all areas of planning. Their investment in all aspects of the process only makes the process stronger.

There is no simple formula for effective leadership. Leadership is a dynamic and complex process by which you need to explore your own strengths, values, and beliefs and watch how they interact with the people and environments around you. Leaders constantly need to be aware of the world around them and learn to use their leadership experiences and studies of leadership to make the best decisions in given situations. Leaders must recognize that leadership is not about the leader, but about the impact a leader can have on others and society. Humility and focus on what changes can be made, as opposed to one's specific role in making those changes, make for a lasting imprint on society.

◆ Service and Civic-Based Leadership

A responsibility all leaders share is to give back to their communities. What is service? And how does it relate to leadership? **Service** is defined as work done by an individual or a group that benefits others. We are going to take service to the next level and challenge you to think about civic engagement when you think about leadership. "**Civic engagement** means working to make a difference in the civic life of our communities and developing the combination of knowledge, skills, values and motivation to make that difference. It means promoting the quality of life in a community, through both political and non-political processes" (Ehrlich, 2000, preface, p. vi). When leaders commit to giving back to society, civic engagement goes a step beyond service and opens the doors into many additional learning and growth opportunities for all involved.

Simply participating in service projects does not open up the possibilities to explore how service relates to leadership and how a leader can use skills, values, and knowledge to serve as a change agent in society. As you participate in service and challenge others to join you, it is critical that you frame the service experience for yourself and others. This process is often referred to as service-learning. The Campus Compact National Center for Community Colleges defines service-learning as

> A teaching method which combines community service with
> academic instruction as it focuses on critical, reflective thinking and
> civic responsibility. Service-learning programs involve students in

organized community service that addresses local needs, while developing their academic skills, sense of civic responsibility and commitment to the community. (Kendall and Associates, 1990, p. 10)

Service Learning
Donald A. Watt, Contributing Author

The formal structure of a college professor lecturing a group of students has been a standard of education for centuries. In the early twentieth century, however, new educational methodologies were attempted. For example, in several Appalachian schools, cooperative or experiential education was initiated, where employment was an integral aspect of the educational experience. As experiments with new ideas were tried, new programs developed. One of the most successful experiments was service learning. According to the National Service-Learning Clearinghouse, the term *service learning* was first used during the 1966–1967 academic year in eastern Tennessee.[1] Since that time, it has evolved into a nationwide movement.

Service learning is the process whereby learning outcomes are designed into outreach programs of service. Thus, it differs from traditional service projects in that it has a dual purpose. The service performed is also designed as an opportunity for student growth and learning. Due to the nature of the program, students participate in various stages of planning, although often the service is pre-selected by the instructor or advisor. Participation in the planning process and reflection is integral to leadership development among the students.

Mandatory aspects of service learning include the following. (1) The project must address a real need within the community. (2) Planning must include a student analysis of the problem, including steps that might be taken to change the situation or alleviate the problem. (3) Students must work through any special aspects as to how interaction should take place. The best service learning takes place through a partnership developed between the students and those served. (4) If the service project occurs within a curricular setting, skills being developed should relate to the learning outcomes of the class. For co-curricular groups, the skills should relate to the mission of the organization. (5) After completion, all aspects of the project should be assessed. Planning, the activity, the impact on those served, and the impact on those doing the service should all be examined. Reflection by each participant on what has been learned is a key component of the assessment activity.

True service learning should be structured so that the students use critical thinking, ideas, and skills learned from the class or the organization and communication skills, in addition to planning and assessment techniques. When done properly, service learning results in positive learning experiences and a stronger sense of community. Leadership skills are at the heart of service learning. Examining the situation, planning tasks to affect the situation, adapting when initial plans do not seem to be working, communicating with others, and assessing outcomes are all important aspects of successful leadership. Thus, service learning can be an important component of leadership education.

[1.] See http://www.servicelearning.org/what_is_service-learning/history/index.php.

As a leader, you have a role in making service to your community meaningful, not only for yourself but also for those around you. Your campus will most likely have many structures set up to connect you with service opportunities, but you can always create experiences for yourself that will fit your personal needs. First, select an area of service that reflects a commitment or passion that you hold. The higher the level of commitment you have for an issue, the more passion you will take and exude to others around you. Additionally, prior to going into the field, research the history of the cause or issue at hand, understand the population served, read about any legislation or community efforts to address the issue, and hold pre-service meetings with others who will attend with you. Share with others the information you have found and encourage a lively discussion about what role your peers can play in addressing the issue during their service and after.

Why should you use service-learning as a leader? Service-learning promotes learning through active participation, provides an opportunity to use skills and knowledge in real-life situations, fosters a sense of caring for others, and improves critical thinking skills (Reiff, 2006). During the service experience, don't just be a participant—be an active learner by observing and questioning things you see. Consider the relationships between your followers, and think about the role you may continue to play in the understanding of this service. After participating in service-related activities, create opportunities for dialogue between participants. This reflection time about their experiences allows them to take the service experience beyond the act and into action that will follow. Encourage your peers to think about ways they can become more involved and serve as change agents in society. Just as important as the service experience itself is that service be authentic. Authentic and successful service-learning is positive, meaningful, and real to the participants. It encourages cooperative rather than competitive experiences, thereby promoting teamwork and citizenship; assists students in identifying the most important issues within a real-world situation through critical thinking; and promotes deeper learning, stressing that there are no "right answers" (Reiff, 2006).

When service-learning or civic engagement and leadership are combined, you have civic-based leadership—the kind of leadership that serves as a change agent in society. Civic-based leadership is the kind of leadership you should be exploring in college and challenging others to explore with you. Engaging in these types of opportunities will strengthen your knowledge, relationships with others, and leadership skills while positively impacting society and others you encourage to join you.

◆ Conclusion

This chapter is meant to be a foundation for your exploration of leadership and service in the college environment—don't stop here! The examination of leadership and service should be a life-long learning process. As you continue to reevaluate your leadership philosophy, expose yourself to diverse individuals and ideas, question your current systems of thinking, and challenge yourself to move beyond the status quo. Get involved with something that supports your passion, take your role to the next level, and be an agent of change for the betterment of society. With your knowledge about leadership and service, you now have power! Use your power to influence positive change on your campus or another community of which you are a member. Create support networks that will propel you and your vision to success and that will make a difference in the lives of others.

◆ Key Terms

Civic-Based Leadership—The combination of leadership and civic engagement with a commitment to serve as a change agent in society.

Civic Engagement—Working to make a difference in the civic life of the community and developing the combination of knowledge, skills, values, and motivation to make a difference.

Ethical Leadership—Leadership guided by a system of moral values and principles that guides behavior.

Ethics—A system of moral values and principles that guide behavior.

Followers—Individuals who come together to support the vision of a leader(s) and use their personal strengths, knowledge, and skills to assist in reaching a common goal.

Leader—Someone who is able to lead others, known as followers, to effect change.

Leadership—The process by which a leader facilitates change. It is the function of three elements: leaders, followers, and the situation. Leadership occurs when all three of these elements interact and work together, while respecting the role each piece plays in the process.

Service—Work done by a group or an individual that benefits others.

Situation—The environment in which a task is undertaken, in combination with knowledge and human interaction.

◆ Suggested Readings

Arbinger Institute, Inc. 2002. *Leadership and Self-Deception: Getting Out of the Box*. San Francisco: Berrett-Koehler.

Collins, J. 2001. *Good to Great: Why Some Companies Make the Leap and Others Don't*. New York: HarperCollins.

George, B. & Sims, P. 2007. *True North: Discover Your Authentic Leadership*. San Francisco: Jossey-Bass.

Chapter Eleven Review Questions

1. Leadership is presented in this chapter as an interaction between individuals at many levels. Cite three examples of leadership that you have observed on your campus. Identify the interaction between individuals for each example cited.

_____

_____

_____

2. Why is it important to include ethics when discussing leadership?

_____

_____

_____

3. What is unique about a college or university campus that makes it the perfect environment to examine, practice, and critically think about leadership and service?

_____

_____

_____

4. Discuss two leadership theories or styles and which aspects most connect with your current philosophy of leadership. Additionally, explain why it is important that leaders have an understanding of self and their personal philosophy.

_____

_____

_____

5. What are the personal and societal benefits of participation in service? What impact does service have on leadership?

_____

_____

_____

Chapter Eleven Self-Test

1. _____ behavior has an impact on all levels of leadership, creating distrust and a lack of productivity.

2. _____ is the process by which a leader facilitates change.

3. _____ are individuals who come together to support the vision of a leader.

4. _____, _____, and _____ are three types of student organizations on a typical college campus.

5. Transformational leadership theory was made popular by political sociologist James McGregor _____.

6. _____ leaders make decisions without consulting followers.

7. The democratic leader is also referred to as the _____ leader.

8. A _____ leader steps back to "let it be," allowing people to make their own decisions.

9. _____ demands knowledge of the strengths and weaknesses you have.

10. A _____ is someone who engages in an activity with knowledge of the area and within ethical standards.

The Greater Good

Ethics and Leadership

◆ How Individual Beliefs Shape Society

In the history of seafaring, the tale of Edward Collins, the founder of the Collins Line, is one of both success and tragedy. More important, it is a lesson in the moral conduct of one's life.

Throughout the 1840s, Collins claimed America had an interest in the transatlantic passenger trade. After accepting a hefty government subsidy, he built four 282-feet, 2,860-ton steamers that were considered the finest of their time. However, they possessed one fatal flaw: At a time when his British rivals were building iron-hulled liners—which had proven to be more resistant to weather and collision—Collins had forged his vessels out of wood. By the launch of his fleet in April 1849, the line's namesake was wholly convinced that his were the finest ships afloat protected by the divine hand of God himself.

On September 25, 1854, in the midst of a thick, ominous North Atlantic fog, the Collins liner *Artic* collided with the iron-hulled French steamer *Vesta*. Only forty-five passengers and crew survived, and among those drowned were Collins' wife and two of his children. A year later, the Collins liner *Pacific* struck an iceberg and sank without any survivors. Within a few months of the latter disaster, the Collins Line—the foremost American transatlantic passenger carrier of its time—ceased to exist (Wall, 1977, p. 124).

Collins' story is a cogent reminder that actions resulting from one's beliefs invariably affect others. The basic question is whether Edward Collins had the right to hold to his convictions in lieu of prevailing evidence to the contrary, which made him culpable for the deaths of his passengers. Social interaction is inevitable. No judgment or action, no matter how miniscule, is made in a vacuum. Our decisions and what we believe have an effect on others. To quote philosopher William Clifford, "No simplicity of mind, no obscurity of station, can escape the universal duty of questioning all that we believe" (Clifford, 1984, p. 150). When one is occupying a leadership role, one's value judgments are vital. However, they demand a standard because our beliefs and actions influence the long-term progress of humanity.

The very foundation of philosophy was stated by Socrates nearly three millennia ago in his *Apology:* "[T]he unexamined life is not worth living" (Segal, 1986, p. 22). In human existence, it is not enough to believe in something, for most of what we conceive to be true is based on the experiences of our lives. A philosophical exploration of what constitutes virtuous or willful conduct is **ethics,** the discipline whose goal is to differentiate genuine knowledge from mere opinion through objective reasoning. It requires a full commitment to discerning the intrinsic good, something desirable for its own sake, and the instrumen-

From "Leadership and Service," 1/e by George McGovern et al. Copyright 2008. Kendall Hunt Publishing. Reprinted by permission.

The USM steamship Baltic was one of the oldest and most dependable ships of the Collins Line. It was sold at auction with the remainder of the fleet in 1859.

Library of Congress.

tal good, a means to something else that is desired, for the benefit of self and of others. If philosophy is concerned with perceptions of the world, ethics are concerned with the actions wrought from it. Ethics provide a standard to aspire to, goals to pursue; in striving toward their full realization, we become more conscientious human beings.

◆ Ethical Concepts and Moral Consequences

The primary responsibility of a leader is to exemplify **morality** and, thus, inspire others to follow likewise, yet the definition of an intrinsic good for a single individual is difficult enough, never mind in a communal setting. In a media-driven age of instant analysis and interpretation of issues and events, careful reflection requires time that many consider better spent on other, more pressing matters related to daily life. Furthermore, such a self-examination sometimes involves questions—many of them—questions to which there are no easy answers. The best place to begin is often with an examination of the basic philosophies and concepts of ethics and their criticisms. The following is a brief introduction to these concepts.

The first of these abstract concepts is **relativism,** the view that there are no moral values or standards applicable to *all* peoples, cultures, and societies. Within such a context, moral practices can be *actually* right in one society yet be *actually* wrong when forced onto another. However, by appealing to the detrimental consequences of moral intervention, there are objective value judgments being made that have universal applications. To assume otherwise is to define what is right as merely socially acceptable, rather than what is objectively valuable and defensible. Under such standards, cultures could neither pass judgment on one another as inferior or superior nor gauge moral progress or call into doubt the questionable practices of others. Such openness and toleration would demand a strict policy of nonintervention even in cases of human atrocity, yet any ethical standard that valued human dignity would obviously demand otherwise.

The second of these abstract concepts is **utilitarianism,** the view that the utility for society is *the* intrinsic good. Because every society evolves in its unique manner, the determination of social good cannot be guided by a "one-size-fits-all" moral code; therefore, the principle of utilitarianism must be applied according to each circumstance. What if, however, the rules were specifically designed by a small group of people, as in an oligarchy, bent on social control? Or what of a dictatorship in which the mere whims of a single individual determine what is best for the society as a whole? And what role do the polar opposite concepts of justice and revenge play in the making of such edicts? Is the utilitarian paradigm best represented in the establishment or the implementation of the moral imperative?

The third of these abstract concepts is **egoism,** the view that human nature is so constructed that a person cannot help but act out of self-interest. When one acts out of generosity, it causes one to feel self-satisfaction; therefore, even when acting out of kindness one is always selfish. Furthermore, society is better off when each person pursues his or her own interests exclusively, for altruism is degrading to human beings, as it makes one the servant of the other and submerges individual initiative through dependency. Though the primary argument of egoism is that human beings are incapable of acting out of nothing more than selfishness, one cannot deny that multitudes of people throughout human history have answered calls to human responsibility and duty. Through personal gestures from donating to neighborhood food drives or attending local benefit dinners to participating in national events, such as Live Aid, or volunteering for military ser-vice, people have responded to human need on a level that transcends mere self-interest. Paradoxically, how would an egoist explain a "death wish," a conflict between self-interest and the pursuit of pleasure in which one's compulsive behavior acts against self-interest? Thus, egoism provides what some would consider a false dichotomy, in that it proposes there are but two options in life—self-concern and altruism—while assuming there is an incompatibility between the two.

The fourth of these abstract concepts is **hedonism,** the view that all pleasures are intrinsically good and that all intrinsic goods involve pleasure. In a manner similar to egoism, because pleasure is the root of human happiness, good is equal to the pleasure it carries. However, the human race has been enriched by the reflection on the entire spectrum of emotion. One of the best examples is artistic expression, in which the wide expanse of feeling and intellect melds to produce works that move us in a manner not rooted in pleasure alone. From the paintings of Vincent Van Gogh to those of Edvard Munch, from the writings of Edgar Allan Poe to those of Virginia Woolf, from the music of classical composer Hugo Wolf to that of alternative rocker Kurt Cobain, the articulation of emotional pain has led to breathtaking and haunting works of art. To judge what is intrinsically good based solely on what is pleasurable is to ignore experiences that sometimes provide inspiration and insight, which produce the great works of art, personal growth, and reflection that feed our souls.

The fifth of these abstract concepts is **natural law,** the view that what occurs in nature is an intrinsic good and, therefore, provides the universal standard to which all social and moral systems must be consistent. In turn, all human-made law that is not uniform with nature is illegitimate and, thus, immoral. The most apparent problem with this view is that it has the potential to thwart human progress by demanding a strict adherence to natural processes. If all new discoveries must be consistent with nature, it would deny the development of medicines and technology, for they are the products of humanity's manipulation of nature. Furthermore, not everyone interprets what is "natural" in the same manner. Due to this difference, often justified by the commandments of a "supreme being," by what manner can a universally applied "natural" law be determined and applied?

The sixth of these abstract concepts is the **categorical imperative,** the view that one should always act on that maxim that can be defined as universal. In making such a determination, one must have comprehendible reasons that can be easily stated and understood. The problem with the categorical imperative is that it reduces complex moral principles to inflexible rules. Once these laws are institutionalized, morality becomes a mere game of abstractions, rather than a practice based on a living and flexible ethical code. Another problem arises when there are conflicting duties that require unique considerations outside of a staid code of law. Finally, this paradigm assumes that all human beings are wholly rational and that all logical assumptions lead to the same universal conclusion, when rarely this is the case.

The seventh, and final, of the abstract concepts to be explored in this chapter is **existentialism,** the view that there is no ethereal structure involved with human existence; therefore, it is up to each individual to assemble a reality based on personal perception. This structure is a fluid amalgam of ideas regarding intrinsic goods that changes and reshapes itself over time. In tandem, it also demands complete personal responsibility for one's actions and their consequences, yet the immediate problem is that there is no universal law that is applicable, because all moral perceptions are arbitrary. Under such a paradigm, neither an individual nor a society can hold others accountable for immoral behavior. Furthermore, in order to secure a code of conduct for an ordered society, others must cede their individual moral sense or code to that of the group or a ruling individual, even if they perceive it to be a false one. Though it is clear that all moral philosophies are the product of human perception and thus are flawed, what is important is that the application of personal moral principles be consistent.

◆ Duty to the State versus Duty to Self

Perhaps the foundational question of public leadership is whether a citizen's foremost duty is to the community or to one's own conscience. In modern society, it is self-evident that no one exists as an island, for all necessary goods and services of contemporary life are intertwined in such a way that one break in this dependent chain will cause chaos. Without recognition of innate human individuality, however, humanity's existence is little more than a cog in a much larger machine—vital for its operation yet replaceable at a moment's notice when perceived as broken. But the machine is rendered inoperable once any part has ceased to perform its function properly; therefore, any effective maintenance requires attention paid both to the machine as a whole and to each mechanism.

The quandary, then, becomes which is of greater value for the survival of a community or, for that matter, a nation. Every machine is accompanied by a set of instructions that tells the user how to operate it properly. Laws accomplish this function within a society and are based on both the goals of its citizens and what the society perceives to be its standards of conduct. Are we obligated to obey an unjust law? By what authority does one defy such social edicts, and to what degree are we morally beholden to the social consequences of our actions?

There is much precedent to support the adage that the needs of the community outweigh the needs of the individual. The English political philosopher Thomas Hobbes argued in his book *Leviathan* that, in order to promote stability, citizens enter into a social contract in which they trade a portion of their liberty for a degree of safety. In doing so, they pledge their loyalty to a political authority and the laws it mandates (Hobbes, 1996, pp. 122, 143, 153, 231). Within the US Constitution, this notion is codified in Article VI § 1, which states that this governing charter represents "the supreme law of the land." Furthermore, the US Supreme Court's unanimous ruling in the case *Jones v. Van Zandt* (1847) mandates that an American citizen is bound to uphold the Constitution and the laws that have proceeded from it, even if those edicts conflict with their conscience.

However, a nation is comprised of individual citizens, distinct from one another in goals, beliefs, and worldview. Within this context, how can *any* governmental authority compel all people to adhere to a common objective? Should not the leader of a nation allow the individual to flourish and thrive as ambitions and conscience dictate? The French political philosopher Jean-Jacques Rousseau put forward in his social contract theory that any government that did not guarantee the liberty of the individual was illegitimate (Rousseau, 1973, p. 5). Furthermore, the US Constitution, in its Ninth and Tenth Amendments, guarantees that the rights and privileges left unclaimed by the federal government are to be given back to the citizens. This was made clear in the case of *Grannis v. Ordean* (1914), in which the US Supreme Court ruled that the Constitution's amendments—the Fifth and Fourteenth, specifically—assure every individual American citizen of "[t]he fundamental requisite of due process"—in other words, not even the federal government can run roughshod over the rights of individual citizens.

Though a leader may philosophically favor one side of this argument over the other, he or she must tread the fine line between these two diametrically opposed paradigms. Unfortunately, there is neither a magic formula nor a moral equation that when readily applied would accomplish this goal. It is up to the individual to find such equilibrium and, using his or her own moral code as a guide, to navigate these often treacherous waters. A leader must not be deterred by the fact that not all under his or her charge will agree with the course of action chosen; however, if such a course is the product of moral reflection and contemplation of outcomes, it is wholly defensible.

◆ What Is Right Versus What Is Popular

When he made the decision not to fight a war with France over the X-Y-Z Affair, President John Adams sacrificed both his extraordinary political career and his historical reputation. Following the president's public disclosure of the incident involving a French minister demanding tribute from a delegation of American representatives, members from both the Federalist Party, led by Alexander Hamilton, and the Democratic-Republican Party, led by Vice President Thomas Jefferson, called for immediate military action. Adams resisted such cries, convinced that such a conflagration would lead to certain defeat for the young nation. As a result, both parties castigated President Adams during his bid for reelection in 1800, a defeat that was wrought primarily by the fact that even his own party abandoned him (Smith, 1962, pp. 1038–47, 1059–63).

Within a few months of his inauguration the following year, newly elected President Thomas Jefferson initiated a military conflict with pirates stationed at Tripoli who were sponsored by the French government. The hostilities proved disastrous, in that it cost the United States what few naval vessels it had constructed for its fledgling fleet (Randall, 1993, pp. 560–63). John Adams may have been on the wrong side of popular opinion, but many today would argue that he was not on the wrong side of history.

The essential element of any republic is that public policy is determined by the support of the majority of its citizens. When any bill is first proposed in Congress, the public becomes engaged in an honest discussion relating to its morality, administration, and pertinent repercussions. Following a prolonged debate, the public registers their assessment through either written or verbal correspondence that instructs their elected representatives as to the appropriate course of action. In the end, a law will rise or fall on the will of the populace, yet this process begs an important question: Is a mere numerical majority the indispensable element of democratic leadership? What safeguards are there for a vocal minority who challenges such group decisions by a social or political majority? Most important, is the majority *always* right? Eminent political scientist Kenneth J. Arrow spent the bulk of his five-decade career studying this problem and ultimately concluded that, given the choice between supporting policies that supported their community and supporting those that benefited their own selfish interests, without fail the public would choose the latter (Arrow, 1983, p. 49). These implications are staggering, for, given that it is the majority of engaged citizens who determine public policy, if the benefit to self matters more than community, what are the implications for the latter's long-term survival?

In the wake of the Panic of 1893, President Grover Cleveland took a brazen stand that cost him both the presidency and his historical reputation. Within three months of taking office for the second of his nonconsecutive terms, Cleveland was faced with a national economic meltdown brought on by a dangerous mixture of the uncontrolled government purchasing of silver and a highly protectionist tariff, both enacted in 1890. To keep the country from sliding into a long-term depression, the president called the Congress into special session and demanded the repeal of the Sherman Silver Purchase and the McKinley Tariff

Most historians believe that President John Adams sacrificed his political career when he decided to ignore popular opinion and refused to go to war with France, but they also believe that history has proven his decision correct.

Library of Congress.

! **Leadership Challenge**

Reflect on a time in your life in which you were encouraged by peer pressure to do something that you would not typically do. Did you follow the crowd or follow your own path? If you followed the crowd, why did you do so? If not, why didn't you?

acts—even threatening to refuse its adjournment until it had accomplished what he wanted done. Against the mainstream of his political party, President Cleveland championed the return to the gold standard as the means by which the national currency could be stabilized. In 1896, during his bid for a third term, the Democrats abandoned the incumbent president of their party in favor of Nebraska congressman William Jennings Bryan, who energized convention delegates with his blistering attack against Cleveland and the steps he had taken to repair the nation's failing economy. Ironically, the policies enacted by President Cleveland during that crucial time laid the foundation for his successor, William McKinley's, successful first term (Brodsky, 2000, pp. 305–9).

Grover Cleveland acted on what he viewed as the best interests of his country, but in doing so he forfeited his future political career. The president of Princeton University and future president of the United States, Woodrow Wilson, acknowledged the caliber of leadership Cleveland had provided for the nation when he made the following statement:

> In the midst of the shifting scene Mr. Cleveland personally came to be seen as the only fixed point. He alone stood firm and gave definite utterance to principles intelligible to all. (Wilson, 1903, p. 220)

Within the hindsight of history, and a thorough examination of his record by a generation who have no direct memory of him, Cleveland is now regarded as one of the American nation's finest chief executives (DeGregorio, 1984, p. 329).

In the arena of leadership and service, one must be ever mindful of the timbre of discussion and debate and perpetually ask the following question: Are the options presented either ethical or expedient? Policy that results from rumination on the outcomes and their moral viability are dependent on how they provide the greatest good to the greatest number. President Cleveland demonstrated this adage when he charted a national course wholly unpopular with the members of his own political party and the majority of American citizens. Too often, the option that gains the desired outcome in a timely manner is also that which causes the greatest long-term carnage. Furthermore, a leader's moral authority is undercut when decisions are made for the sake of immediate public acclaim, for in its wake paths are taken and allies are gained that, under normal circumstances, would have been reprehensible. The intrinsic good for the greatest number, for both enemy and ally, is often lost for the sake of popular appeal and expediency.

During World War II, the United States entered the fray to bring down the Nazi regime of Adolf Hitler, a government that had implemented a policy of mass ethnic genocide, which summarily ended the lives of millions of Jews, Slavs, Gypsies, and others, yet in that cause the United States made binding political agreements with the Soviet Union under its premier, Josef Stalin, who was responsible for the execution of over 30 million of his own people (Hart, 1970, pp. 310–12, 523). In the postwar era, the United States offered aid to the devastated countries of Europe, but only if they promised not to adopt political systems that were similar to our perceived enemies (Hamby, 1995, pp. 396–98, 510). Soon after, the United States participated in covert missions under the authority of the Central Intelligence Agency throughout the Middle East, Central America, and South America that assassinated popularly elected leaders who supported socialism and then installed puppet capitalist governments favorable to American economic interests (Woodward, 1987, pp. 362, 389). Finally, after President Harry S Truman announced his policy of Communist containment within his 1949 inaugural address, Soviet Premier Stalin, seeking to repair the Soviet Union's shattered relations with its former ally, called for two-party talks, which were completely rejected by the Truman administration (McCoy, 1984, pp. 191–93).

Events such as these beg for further discussion with regard to their ethical viability. First, why did the United States forge a wartime political alliance with a tyrannical Communist regime against an equally tyrannical National Socialist regime, especially when both were involved in mass genocide? Why were human lives within the Soviet Union more expendable than those within Nazi Germany? Where is the morality in offering necessary humanitarian aid in return for loyalty? How can such relief be truly "altruistic" if it comes with a political price tag? What is ethical about a "democratic" government that thwarts another country's popular will by exterminating democratically elected leaders and installing governments loyal to its own interests, rather than that of a supposedly sovereign nation's own people? Finally, where is the morality in choosing confrontation over peace, especially toward a nation with which a peaceful alliance already exists?

Had any one of the above questions been pondered with the aim of producing an ethical outcome, the course of American history in the post–World War II era would have been radically different. The pertinent query regarding American policies toward the Soviet Union during this period should be focused on the premise of the necessity of such a military and political alliance. Could the Nazi regime, the mutual enemy of both the United States and the Soviet Union, have been defeated without the fusion of their military efforts? Did conditional humanitarian aid ultimately produce reliable allies in the fight against communism? Was American intervention into the political affairs of other sovereign nations and the murder of their leaders morally defensible? Was communism the pervasive threat that the American government contended it was? All of these queries do much to prove that contemporary political leadership is not based on ethical reflection but on the Machiavellian paradigm that the ends justify the means. Furthermore, few, if any, contemporary leaders are willing to follow in the footsteps of John Adams and Grover Cleveland and sacrifice their own political careers for the sake of doing what is best for the long-term good of the nation, especially if it means saying, "The public be damned."

◆ The Choices We Make

When it comes to choices in life, we are conceived and born without one, and we die only after making a plethora of them. When it is critical to make choices, we either jump at the opportunity to get them over with quickly or postpone them to the last possible minute. In the necessity to optimize them, we routinely miss the best prospect to enjoy their benefits. We make choices because ultimately nobody else can make them for us, yet not every choice has to be the right one. Humans are prone to error, but such mistakes are often the means by which we experience personal growth, learn, and progress. Ultimately, our responsibility is to keep our own personal destiny, as well as the destiny of those we lead, from entering the realm of tragedy.

The 1850s were a perilous time in American politics, for it was an era in which the interests of "self" superseded those of "nation." Elected president of the United States in 1852, Franklin Pierce sought to enact policies of expansion in trade and territory, coupled with the strident reform of both the military and the civil service; during the fourteen months between his inauguration in March 1853 and May 1854, he achieved much of it, yet Pierce's accomplishments will be forever shadowed by one controversial act: his signature on the Kansas-Nebraska Act.

President Pierce never wanted the Kansas-Nebraska Act to become law, primarily because he was opposed to the "popular sovereignty" clause, which effectively repealed the 1820 Missouri Compromise. The president's position was that, if the compromise was to be eliminated, it should be through a decision of the US Supreme Court, rather than a legislative act, for it would lend it an air of legitimacy. Though he actively sought to thwart the bill's passage, going so far as to draft the "popular sovereignty" clause in a way that made this law unamendable by Congress, his efforts came to naught in May 1854, when both houses of Congress overwhelmingly passed it. Pierce was then faced with a dilemma: Should he veto the act and risk the secession of the South—and with it inevitable civil war—or should he enact it into law, hold the Union together, but effectively end his political career? As history records, the president did the latter and, as a result, the nation degenerated into violent chaos and he gained an ignoble place within American history (Nichols, 1931, pp. 333–38).

When one occupies a position of leadership, situations arise that do not always present an obvious ethical and moral path. The solution to such matters often requires deep inner reflection and a contemplation of every option that will produce an ethical outcome—coupled with the knowledge that throughout human history many decisions based on sound ethical and moral choices, in the end, produced discordant and devastating consequences. Thus, the soundest test of any personal and societal code of ethics occurs when one is faced with a decision in which every outcome will inevitably produce harm.

In the waning months of World War II, following the surrender of Germany, President Harry S. Truman was faced with the ultimate dilemma: whether to drop the atomic bomb. With the surrender of Germany a few months before, the commander-in-chief had at his disposal a vast and effective military force that could successfully effect a land invasion of Japan, yet such an incursion of the Japanese mainland would be long and costly. There was also a further and more deadly option open to the president. On assuming the presidency with the death of his predecessor, Franklin Delano Roosevelt, President Truman was made aware of a powerful weapon, which had been developed by the fusion of atoms, that had the capability of leveling highly populated metropolitan centers (Hart, 1970, pp. 691–98). On weighing the options carefully, President Truman came to the conclusion that, though hundreds of thousands of lives would be lost in its use, it would force a timely end to the war and, as such, save millions of both American and Japanese lives (Truman, 1955, p. 419).

Though at first glance President Truman's choice to use the atomic bomb on Japanese civilian targets may seem inconceivable in any ethical assessment,

President Harry S. Truman's decision to use the atomic bomb was one of the most difficult in human history. He was faced with a decision in which every outcome would inevitably produce incredible human suffering.

Library of Congress.

in real terms it achieved the desired goal—the end of war and with it the further slaughter of human life. What this serious moment in history demonstrates is that, for a leader, sometimes difficult choices, right or wrong, crucial or ephemeral, are inescapable.

On the surface, the mere existence of such dilemmas seems to undermine the purpose of ethical decision making, for the goal of a moral code of conduct is to lead and serve all justly. In facing off against an enemy, such as the genocidal regime of Germany under Nazism or a tribal civil war between the African nations of Rwanda and Burundi, what path can a leader take that will not allow the nation he or she represents to become the embodiment of what the nation is fighting against? During World War II, Mahatma Gandhi was posed this question with regard to an enemy such as Adolf Hitler; recognizing the dilemma within the query itself, he replied that one must be willing to accept many defeats until, in the end, good would triumph over evil (Fischer, 1954, p. 215). If, in seeking a moral end to conflict, for expediency's sake a leader must engage in actions that are morally questionable, is that leader not the moral equivalent of his or her enemy? And, as such, where is the moral validation of actions if a nation must become the moral and ethical mirror image of what it is struggling to defeat?

◆ Complacency Versus Activism

A consistent code of ethics is an impossible course to maintain unless it is demonstrated in the everyday conduct of one's life. To proclaim a life philosophy as your own, and then to act in conflict with it, is little more than intellectual self-gratification. This planet can be ruthless to those who possess a confident sense of self, and even more so to those who do not; thus, we are devastated when our highly esteemed leaders are found to be nothing more than mere mortals. Though the path of leadership and service to others is rarely glorious, it is vital for one very important reason: Progressions throughout human history have been wrought not by people who have submitted to the system for the sake of order but by those who have acted on their ethical and moral beliefs and refused to back down until their issue was seriously addressed.

One such application has been the fight against the governmental restriction of a guaranteed right, such as the liberty of speech and expression. The fundamental question to be posed here is whether in a truly free society there are subjects that are too obscene or dangerous to be discussed in a public forum. One who actively challenged the preconceptions of social hypocrisy on this issue was comedian Lenny Bruce. Using a cutting-edge combination of outrageousness and "blue" language, Bruce's social commentary confronted established social definitions of untouchable concepts of decency, obscenity, faith, and class. Throughout the last six years of his life, he was a favorite target of moralists on both sides who used the law to stifle expression—a struggle that cost him his life. Bruce's crusade against arbitrary definitions of the Constitution's First Amendment opened the door for such controversial commentators, critics, and satirists as Bill Maher, Rush Limbaugh, Al Franken, George Carlin, Richard Pryor, Chris Rock, and Richard Belzer, who not only engage, entertain and sometimes make audiences laugh but also force the public to ponder the dysfunction of society (Collins & Skover, 2002).

Another abstract idea that challenged popular preconceptions was the definition of peace, championed by singer/songwriter John Lennon and embodied by his composition "Imagine." After attaining international superstardom as one-fourth of the Beatles, Lennon later used his immense fame to put forward complex intellectual treatises, set to popular music, on themes such as the meaning of peace, the mistreatment of human beings within social institutions, and the outcomes of violence and discrimination. The most salient question posed by Lennon was simple: Is "peace" merely the lack of violence between enemies or the result of people freeing themselves from the elements that cause friction within human society? He asked his audience to ponder a utopian world, stripped of all intellectual complexity, in which race, religion, class, and gender issues did not exist. Though he was assassinated by a disgruntled fan on December 8, 1980, over a quarter-century later his music and his message endure (Coleman, 1984, pp. 441–65).

On a deeper examination of history, there are a myriad of events and people who, through their spirited actions, fought for causes greater than themselves and enriched the awareness of the human condition. In the case of discrimination and segregation based on the color of skin, one needs only to study the extraordinary lives of Dr. Martin Luther King, Jr., and the Reverend Ralph Abernathy and the popular civil rights movement they commanded for well over three decades. In tandem, seeking a goal of gender equality were courageous women such as Alice Paul, Betty Friedan, Eleanor Smeal, and Gloria Steinem. Within the pages of her 1962 book *Silent Spring*, none were more influential in warning the world against the impending danger caused by pollution than Dr. Rachel Carson, who implored us to take a further look at how our arrogance was destroying our fragile planet. Then there are the stories of those who championed the plight of the less fortunate, not only in their own countries but around the globe—men and women such as Senator George McGovern, Mother Teresa, Florence Nightingale, and musician Harry Chapin. And there are a myriad of other issues and the champions who were willing to sacrifice for them—so numerous, in fact, that to give them the credit they so richly deserve would be impractical within the parameters of this tome.

The salient point here is that, if one leads by example, the code of ethics by which they live will be readily apparent. One has to lead and serve by action, not by mere assertion.

◆ Conclusion: A Pebble in a Pond

In 1871, future president James Garfield stated, "I would rather believe something and suffer for it, than to slide along into success without opinions" (Peskin, 1978). Garfield won the presidency in 1880 by the slimmest popular majority in American history—fewer than 9,500 votes out of 9 million ballots cast—primarily because he was a highly vocal and controversial political reformer at a time of dominance by political machines (DeGregorio, 1984, p. 300). During his brief term in office, Garfield challenged the stalwarts of his own party and toppled the boss of New York's Tammany Hall political machine, Senator Roscoe Conkling. He was shot in the back by a disgruntled office seeker four months into his term on July 2, 1881, and died in agony two months later (DeGregorio, 1984, pp. 302–3). As a tribute to Garfield's leadership, his successor, Chester Arthur, a former machine politician, signed into law a sweeping reform bill that both destroyed the endemic "spoils" system of patronage and established the modern civil service (Karabell, 2004, pp. 104–7). As a result, the standard by which all public servants are held to is an ongoing testament to President Garfield and the moral principles by which he lived his life.

When one takes a pebble and tosses it into a pond, what results is a small wave that spreads outward until it reaches the bank. In the same manner, every life touches others. Throughout the cycles of our lives, tragedy and comedy pass in front of us in clearly recognizable patterns that provide ample opportunities for growth and tears, based on the choices we make. Because we do not live in isolation, every choice we make profoundly affects the actions of other people, and it is because of this that the choices we make take on a greater importance than any of us could ever imagine. In human existence, there is no choice but to choose; however, through a clear understanding of which is moral, the benefit to the world might someday be immeasurable.

This chapter has attempted to explain the importance of ethics in leadership and service to humanity by examining the actions of leaders who have acted on their moral convictions. As such, it has led this author to conclude that there are specific tenets by which those in positions of leadership and service can conduct themselves:

- Be cognizant of the difference between what is best for both the group *and* each individual within it and, with soundness of judgment, seek options that maintain a balance between group and individual needs.
- Act in the pursuit of opportunities that achieve long-term good for the greatest number, even if it means the sacrifice of short-term popularity.
- Be ever aware of the benefits of maintaining ethical and moral consistency and never sacrifice it or be tempted by the lure of expediency.
- Recognize that choices are the inevitable by-product of leadership and must not be avoided—and do not be fearful of changing direction when new evidence or circumstances dictate such a change.
- If under normal circumstances the goal of ethical leadership is to consistently act for the greatest good for the largest number, then it follows that, in the face of a dilemma, one must assure the least harm to the smallest number or those who have no voice.
- It is not enough to verbalize foundational principles or ideas; they must be consistently demonstrated through action, for only a public display of those core personal values provides a cogent example for others to follow.

The true significance of ethics and moral principles, especially in the realm of leadership, are the lessons they teach both to us and to future generations, for in the most vital sense our world is but a pond and our lives the pebbles waiting for a place within it. Should we decide to take advantage of this moment in history, perhaps generations to come will demonstrate their gratitude by following in our footsteps.

◆ Key Terms*

Categorical Imperative—An absolute, unconditional requirement that exerts its authority in all circumstances, both required and justified as an end in itself.

Egoism—The worldview that it is necessary and sufficient for an action to be morally right if it maximizes one's self-interest.

Ethics—A branch of philosophy that studies the moral perceptions of a person or group, employing the analysis of concepts and perceptions of right and wrong, good and evil, and responsibility.

Existentialism—The worldview that individual human beings create the meanings and essence of their own lives.

Hedonism—The worldview that seeking pleasure is the most important pursuit of humanity.

Morality—A code of conduct held to be authoritative in matters of right and wrong, whether by society, philosophy, religion, or individual conscience.

Natural Law—The worldview that the existence of a law whose content is set by nature has validity everywhere.

Relativism—The worldview that no universal standard exists by which to assess an ethical proposition's truth.

Utilitarianism—The worldview that the moral worth of an action is solely determined by its contribution to overall utility.

◆ Suggested Readings

Aristotle. 2004. *Nicomachean Ethics.* Trans. J. A. K. Thomson. New York: Penguin.

Hobbes, T. 1996. *Leviathan.* Ed. R. Tuck. New York: Cambridge University Press.

Kant, I. 1993. *Grounding for the Metaphysics of Morals.* Trans. J. W. Ellington. Indianapolis: Hackett.

Maguire, D. C. & Fargnoli, A. N. 1991. *On Moral Grounds: The Art/Science of Ethics.* New York: Crossroad.

Marino, G. (ed.) 2004. *Basic Writings of Existentialism.* New York: Modern Library.

Oord, T. Jay. 2007. *The Altruism Reader: Selections from Writings on Love, Religion, and Science.* Philadelphia: Templeton Foundation Press.

Rosen, F. 2003. *Classical Utilitarianism from Hume to Mill.* London: Routledge Books.

Tännsjö, T. 1998. *Hedonistic Utilitarianism.* Edinburgh: Edinburgh University Press.

Wong, D. B. 1984. *Moral Relativity.* Berkeley: University of California Press.

* The definitions have been paraphrased from the *New Oxford Dictionary,* Wikipedia, and the *Stanford Encyclopedia of Philosophy.*

Chapter Twelve Review Questions

1. Do ethics require that a leader must pursue policies that reinforce the intrinsic good of his or her charge even if those policies are unpopular?

   _____

   _____

   _____

2. Do ethics require a rational basis for religious beliefs, especially of those in leadership positions?

   _____

   _____

   _____

3. To whom does a person owe his or her greatest allegiance: the state in which he or she lives or him- or her-self?

   _____

   _____

   _____

4. Is it appropriate for a leader to utilize unethical means to achieve an ethical end?

   _____

   _____

   _____

5. If you could select only one of the basic philosophies of ethics on which to base your life and work, which would you choose and why?

   _____

   _____

   _____

Chapter Twelve Self-Test

1. The story of the Collins Line is a reminder that actions resulting from one's beliefs invariably_____.

2. According to _____, "The unexamined life is not worth living."

3. _____ is the view that there are no moral values or standards applicable to all peoples or societies.

4. _____ is the view that all pleasures are intrinsically good.

5. English philosopher _____ argued that, in order to promote stability, citizens entered into a social contract.

6. Political scientist Kenneth Arrow concluded that, given a choice between what is best for the community and self-interest, the public would choose _____.

7. The true test of a code of ethics occurs when all outcomes will inevitably produce _____.

8. _____ is the belief that one can't help but act out of self-interest.

9. If you accept the concept of _____, you believe that it is up to each individual to assemble a reality based on perception.

10. In the case *Jones v. Van Zandt,* the Supreme Court unanimously ruled that American citizens are bound to uphold the Constitution and the laws that have proceeded from it, even if those edicts conflict with their_____.

Educational Planning and Decision Making

13

Making Wise Choices About Your College Courses and College Major

ACTIVATE YOUR THINKING **Journal Entry** **13.1**

LEARNING GOAL

To develop strategies for exploring different academic fields and for choosing an educational path that will enable you to achieve your personal and occupational goals.

Are you decided or undecided about a college major?

_____

_____

_____

If you are undecided, what subjects might be possibilities?

_____

_____

_____

If you are decided, what is your choice and why did you choose this major?

_____

_____

_____

How sure are you about that choice? (Circle one.)

- Absolutely sure

- Fairly sure

- Not too sure

- Likely to change

From *"Thriving in College and Beyond"* by Cuseo, Fecas, Thompson. © Kendall Hunt Publishing.

◆ To Be or Not to Be Decided About a College Major: What the Research Shows

Whether you have or have not decided on a major, here are some research findings related to student decisions about college majors that may be worth keeping in mind:

- Less than 10 percent of new college students feel they know a great deal about the field that they intend to major in.
- As students proceed through the first year of college, they grow more uncertain about the major they chose when they began college.
- More than two-thirds of new students change their mind about their major during the first year of college.
- Only one in three college seniors eventually major in the same field that they chose during their first year of college (Cuseo, 2005).

These findings point to the conclusion that the vast majority of students entering college are truly undecided about a college major. Most students do not make definite and final decisions about their major *before* starting their college experience; instead, they make these decisions *during* the college experience. Being uncertain about a major is nothing to be embarrassed about. The terms "undecided" and "undeclared" don't mean that you have somehow failed or are lost. As a new student, you may be undecided for various good reasons. For instance, you may be undecided simply because you have interests in various subjects. This is a healthy form of indecision because it shows that you have a range of interests and a high level of motivation to learn about different subjects. You may also be undecided simply because you are a careful, reflective thinker whose decision-making style is to gather more information before making any long-term commitments.

In one study of students who were undecided about a major when they started college, 43 percent had several ideas in mind but were not yet ready to commit to one of them (Gordon & Steele, 2003). These students were not clueless; instead, they had some ideas but still wanted to explore them and keep their options open, which is an effective way to go about making decisions.

As a first-year student, it's only natural to be at least somewhat uncertain about your educational goals because you have not yet experienced the variety of subjects and academic programs that make up the college curriculum. You may encounter fields of study in college that you never knew existed. One purpose of general education is to help new students develop the critical thinking skills needed to make wise choices and well-informed decisions, such as their choice of college major. The liberal arts curriculum is also designed to introduce you to various academic subjects, and as you progress through this curriculum, you may discover subjects that captivate you and capture your interest. Some of these subjects may represent fields of study that you never experienced before, and all of them represent possible choices for a college major.

In addition to finding new fields of possible interest, as you gain experience with the college curriculum, you are likely to gain more self-knowledge about your academic strengths and weaknesses. This is important knowledge to take into consideration when choosing a major, because you want to select a field that builds on your academic abilities and talents.

> **"**
> *"All who wander are not lost."*
>
> –J. R. R. Tolkien, *Lord of the Rings*

Student Perspective

"The best words of wisdom that I could give new freshmen [are] not to feel like you need to know what you want to major in right away. They should really use their first two years to explore all of the different classes available. They may find a hidden interest in something they never would have considered. I know this from personal experience."

–Advice to new students from a college sophomore (Walsh, 2005)

It's true that people can take too long and procrastinate on reaching decisions; however, it's also true that they can make decisions too quickly that result in premature choices made without sufficient reflection and careful consideration of all options. Judging from the large number of students who end up changing their minds about a college major, it's probably safe to say that more students make the mistake of reaching a decision about a major too quickly rather than procrastinating about it indefnitely. This may be because students hear the same question repeatedly, even before they step a foot on a college campus: "What are you going to major in when you go to college?" You probably also saw this question on your college applications, and you are likely to hear it again during your first term in college. The beginning of your college experience is when you'll meet many new people, and one of the first questions you're likely to hear from them soon after they meet you will be "What's your major?" Family members are also likely to ask you the same question, particularly if they're helping to pay the high cost of a college education, because they want some assurance that their investment will pay off and they feel more assured if they know you have a clear idea about what you're doing in college (your major) and what you'll do after college (your career).

Despite pressure you may be receiving from others to make an early decision, we encourage you not to make it an official and final commitment to a major until you gain more self-knowledge and more knowledge of your options. Even if you think you're sure about your choice of major, before you make a commitment to it, take a course or two in the major to test it out and confirm whether or not your choice is compatible with your personal interests, talents, and values.

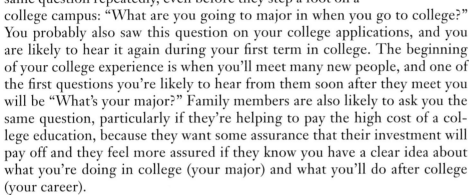

Pause for Reflection

If you have chosen a major or are considering a particular major, what or who led you to choose or consider this option?

Student Perspective

"I see so many people switch [their] major like 4 or 5 times; they end up having to take loads of summer school just to catch up because they invest time and money in classes for a major that they end up not majoring in anyway."

–College sophomore (Walsh, 2005)

◆ When Should You Reach a Firm Decision About a College Major?

It's OK to start off not knowing what your major will be and to give yourself some time and college experience before reaching a decision. You can take courses that will count toward your degree and stay on track for graduation, even if you haven't decided or declared your college major.

Similarly, if you've entered college with a major in mind, there's still time to change your mind without falling behind. If you realize that your first choice of a major wasn't a good choice, don't think that you're locked into your original plan and you're only options are to stick with it throughout college or drop out of college. Changing your original educational plans is not necessarily a bad thing. It may mean that you have discovered another field that's more interesting to you or that's more compatible with your personal interests and talents.

The only downside to changing your educational plan is that if you make that change late in your college experience it can result in more time to graduation (and more tuition) because you may need to complete additional courses for your newly chosen field. The key to preventing this scenario from happening later is to be proactive now by engaging in long-range educational planning.

> "When you get to a fork in the road, take it."
>
> –Yogi Berra, Hall of Fame baseball player

> **!** **Remember**
>
> As a rule, you should reach a fairly firm decision about your major during your second (sophomore) year in college. However, to reach a good decision within this time frame, the process of exploring and planning should begin now—during your first term in college.

◆ The Importance of Long-Range Educational Planning

College will allow you many choices about what courses to enroll in and what field to specialize in. By looking ahead and developing a tentative plan for your courses beyond the first term of college, you will position yourself to view your college experience as a full-length movie and get a sneak preview of the total picture. In contrast, scheduling your classes one term at a time just before each registration period (when everyone else is making a mad rush to get their advisor's signature for the following term's classes) forces you to view your academic experience as a series of short, separate snapshots that lack connection or direction.

Long-range educational planning also enables you to take a proactive approach to your future. Being proactive means you are taking early, preventative action that anticipates events before they sneak up on you, forcing you to react to events in your life without time to plan your best strategy. As the old saying goes, "If you fail to plan, you plan to fail." Through advanced planning, you can actively take charge of your academic future and make it happen *for* you, rather than waiting and passively letting it happen *to* you.

> "When you have to make a choice and don't make it, that is in itself a choice."
>
> –William James, philosopher and one of the founders of American psychology

Factors to Consider When Choosing Your Major or Field of Study

Gaining self-awareness is the critical first step in making decisions about a college major, or any other important decision. You must know yourself before you can know what choice is best for you. While this may seem obvious, self-awareness and self-discovery are often overlooked aspects of the decision-making process. In particular, you need awareness of your

- Interests—what you like doing;
- Abilities—what you're good at doing; and
- Values—what you feel good about doing.

Furthermore, research indicates that students are more likely to continue in college and graduate when they choose majors that reflect their personal interests (Leuwerke et al., 2004).

> "Education is our passport to the future, for tomorrow belongs to the people who prepare for it today."
>
> –Malcolm X, African American Muslim minister, public speaker, and human rights activist

> **!** **Remember**
>
> Any long-range plan you develop is not set in stone; it can change depending on changes in your academic interests and future plans. The purpose of long-range planning is not to lock you into a particular plan but to free you from shortsightedness, procrastination, or denial about choosing to control your future.

Multiple Intelligences: Identifying Personal Abilities and Talents

One element of the self that you should be aware of when choosing a major is your mental strengths, abilities, or talents. Intelligence was once considered to be one general trait that could be detected and measured by an intelligence quotient (IQ) test. Now, the singular word "intelligence" has been replaced by the plural word "intelligences" to reflect that humans can display intelligence or mental ability in many forms other than their paper-and-pencil performance on an IQ test.

Pause for Reflection

Consider the following statement: "Choosing a major is a life-changing decision because it will determine what you do for the rest of your life."

Would you agree or disagree with this statement?

Why?

Listed in **Box 13.1** are forms of intelligence identified by Howard Gardner (1983, 1993) from studies of gifted and talented individuals, experts in different lines of work, and various other sources. As you read through the types of intelligence, place a checkmark next to the type that you think represents your strongest ability or talent. (You can possess more than one type.) Keep your type or types of intelligence in mind when you're choosing a college major. Ideally, you want to select a major that taps into and builds on your strongest skills or talents. Choosing a major that's compatible with your abilities should enable you to master the concepts and skills required by your major more rapidly and deeply. Furthermore, if you follow your academic talents, you're likely to succeed or excel in what you do, which will bolster your 'academic self-confidence and motivation.

Pause for Reflection

You answered self-awareness questions related to each of these three elements of "self." Review your answers to these questions. Do you notice anything about your entries that suggests there might be certain majors or field of study that match your interests, abilities, and values?

Learning Styles: Identifying Your Learning Preferences

Your learning style is another important personal characteristic you should be aware of when choosing your major. Learning styles refer to individual differences in learning preferences—that is, ways in which individuals prefer to perceive information (receive or take it in) and process information (deal with it after taking it in). Individuals may differ in terms of whether they prefer to take in information by reading about it, listening to it, seeing an image or diagram of it, or physically touching and manipulating it. Individuals may also vary in terms of whether they like to receive information in a structured and orderly format or in an unstructured form that allows them the freedom to explore, play with, and restructure it in their own way. Once information has been received, individuals may also differ in terms of how they prefer to process or deal with it

---

Personal Story   In my family, whenever there's something that needs to be assembled or set up (e.g., a ping-pong table or new electronic equipment), I've noticed that my wife, my son, and myself have different learning styles in terms of how we go about doing it. I like to read the manual's instructions carefully and completely before I even attempt to touch anything. My son prefers to look at the pictures or diagrams in the manual and uses them as models to find parts; then he begins to assemble those parts. My wife seems to prefer not to look at the manual. Instead, she likes to figure things out as she goes along by grabbing different parts from the box and trying to assemble those parts that look like they should fit together—piecing them together as if she were completing a jigsaw puzzle.

—Joe Cuseo

Student Perspective

"I try to do more to please myself, and making good grades and doing well in school helps my ego. It gives me confidence, and I like that feeling."

–First-year college student (Franklin, 2002)

mentally. Some might like to think about it on their own; others may prefer to discuss it with someone else, make an outline of it, or draw a picture of it.

You can take specially designed tests to assess your particular learning style and how it compares with others. If you're interested in taking one, the Learning Center or Career Development Center are the two most likely sites on campus where you will be able to do so.

Probably the most frequently used learning styles test is the Myers-Briggs Type Indicator (MBTI; Myers, 1976; Myers & McCaulley, 1985), which is based on the personality theory of psychologist Carl Jung. The tests consists of four pairs of opposing traits and assesses how people vary on a scale (low to high) for each of these four sets of traits. The four sets of opposing traits are illustrated in **Figure 13.1**.

As you read the following four pairs of opposite traits, place a mark along the line where you think you fall with respect to each set of traits. For example, place a mark in the middle of the line if you think you are midway between these opposing traits, or place a mark at the far left or far right if you think you lean strongly toward the trait listed on either end.

Take Action!

Multiple Forms of Intelligence

- **Linguistic Intelligence.** Ability to communicate through words or language (e.g., verbal skills in the areas of speaking, writing, listening, or reading)
- **Logical–Mathematical Intelligence.** Ability to reason logically and succeed in tasks that involve mathematical problem solving (e.g., the skill for making logical arguments and following logical reasoning or the ability to think effectively with numbers and make quantitative calculations)
- **Spatial Intelligence.** Ability to visualize relationships among objects arranged in different spatial positions and ability to perceive or create visual images (e.g., forming mental images of three-dimensional objects; detecting detail in objects or drawings; artistic talent for drawing, painting, sculpting, and graphic design; or skills related to sense of direction and navigation)
- **Musical Intelligence.** Ability to appreciate or create rhythmical and melodic sounds (e.g., playing, writing, or arranging music)
- **Interpersonal (Social) Intelligence.** Ability to relate to others; to accurately identify others' needs, feelings, or emotional states

of mind; and to effectively express emotions and feelings to others (e.g., interpersonal communication skills or the ability to accurately "read" the feelings of others or to meet their emotional needs)

- **Intrapersonal (Self) Intelligence.** Ability to self-reflect, become aware of, and understand 'your own thoughts, feelings, and behavior (e.g., capacity for personal reflection, emotional self-awareness, and self-insight into personal strengths and weaknesses)
- **Bodily–Kinesthetic (Psychomotor) Intelligence.** Ability to use 'your own body skillfully and to acquire knowledge through bodily sensations or movements (e.g., skill at tasks involving physical coordination, the ability to work well with hands, mechanical skills, talent for building models and assembling things, or skills related to technology)
- **Naturalist Intelligence.** Ability to carefully observe and appreciate features of the natural environment (e.g., keen awareness of nature or natural surroundings or the ability to understand causes or results of events occurring in the natural world)

13.1

Source: Gardner (1993).

Extraversion	Introversion
Prefer to focus on "outer" world of persons, actions, or objects	Prefer to focus on "inner" world of thoughts and ideas
Sensing	*Intuition*
Prefer interacting with the world directly through concrete, sensory experiences	Prefer dealing with symbolic meanings and imagining possibilities
Thinking	*Feeling*
Prefer to rely on logic and rational thinking when making decisions	Prefer to rely on human needs and feelings when making decisions
Judging	*Perceiving*
Prefer to plan for and control events	Prefer flexibility and spontaneity

Figure 13.1 Traits and Learning Styles Measured by the Myers-Briggs Type Indicator (MBTI)

It's been found that college students who score high on the introversion scale of the MBTI are less likely to become bored than extroverts while engaging mental tasks that involve repetition and little external stimulation (Vodanovich, Wallace, & Kass, 2005). Students who score differently on the MBTI also have different learning preferences when it comes to writing and the type of writing assignments (Jensen & Ti Tiberio, cited in Bean, 2001). See **Figure 13.2** for the details on the findings.

These results clearly indicate that students have different learning styles, which, in turn, influence the type of writing assignments they feel most comfortable performing. This may be important to keep in mind when choosing your major because different academic fields emphasize different styles of writing. Some fields place heavy emphasis on writing that is structured and tightly focused (e.g., science and business), while other fields encourage writing with personal style, flair, or creativity (e.g., English and art). How your writing style meshes with the style emphasized by an aca-

Pause for Reflection

Which type or types of intelligence listed in **Box 13.1** represent you strongest area or areas?

Which majors or fields of study do you think may be the best match for your natural talents?

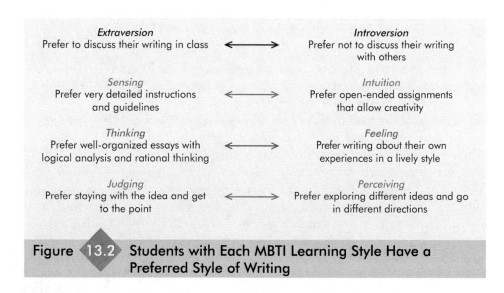

Figure 13.2 Students with Each MBTI Learning Style Have a Preferred Style of Writing

Pause for Reflection

For each of the following four sets of opposing traits, make a note about where you fall—middle, far left, or far right.

	Far Left	Middle	Far Right
Extraversion–Introversion			
Sensing–Intuition			
Thinking–Feeling			
Judging–Perceiving			

What majors or fields of study do you think are most compatible with your personality traits?

demic field may be an important factor to consider when making decisions about your college major.

Another popular learning styles test is the Learning Styles Inventory (Dunn, Dunn, & Price, 1990), which was originally developed by David Kolb, a professor of philosophy (Kolb, 1976, 1985). It is based on how individuals differ with respect to the following two elements of the learning process:

How Information Is *Perceived* (Taken in)

Concrete Experience
Learning through direct involvement or personal experience

Reflective Observation
Learning by watching or observing

How Information Is *Processed* (Dealt with after it has been taken in)

Abstract Conceptualization
Learning by thinking about things and drawing logical conclusions

Active Experimentation
Learning by taking chances and trying things out

When these two dimensions are crisscrossed to form intersecting lines, four sectors (areas) are created, each of which represents a different learning style, as illustrated in **Figure 13.3**. As you look at the four areas (styles) in the figure, circle the style that you think reflects your most preferred way of learning.

Research indicates that students majoring in different fields tend to display differences in these four learning styles (Svinicki & Dixon, 1987). For instance, "assimilators" are more often found majoring in mathematics and natural sciences (e.g., chemistry and physics), probably because these subjects stress reflection and abstract thinking. In contrast, academic fields where "accommodators" tend to be more commonly found are business, accounting, and law, perhaps because these fields involve taking practical action and making concrete decisions. "Divergers" are more often attracted to majors in the fine arts (e.g., music, art, and drama), humanities (e.g.,

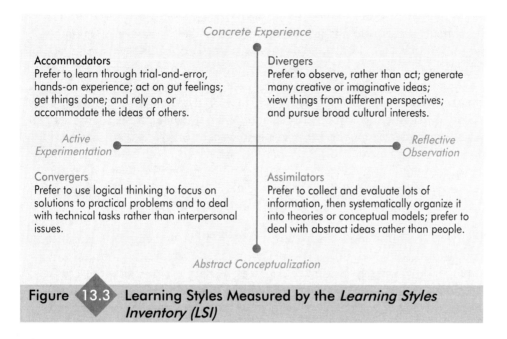

Figure 13.3 Learning Styles Measured by the *Learning Styles Inventory (LSI)*

history and literature), or social sciences (e.g., psychology and political science), possibly because these fields emphasize appreciating multiple viewpoints and perspectives. In contrast, "convergers" are more often found in fields such as engineering, medicine, and nursing, probably because these fields focus on finding solutions to practical and technical problems (Kolb, 1976). This same clustering of fields is found when faculty are asked to classify academic fields in terms of what learning styles they emphasize (Biglan, 1973; Carnegie Commission on Higher Education, cited in Svinicki & Dixon, 1987).

Since students have different learning styles and academic fields emphasize different styles of learning, it's important to consider how your learning style meshes with the style of learning emphasized by the field you're considering as a major. If the match seems to be close or compatible, then the marriage between you and that major could be one that leads to a satisfying and successful learning experience.

We recommend taking a trip to the Learning Center or Career Development Center on your campus to take a learning styles test, or you could try the learning styles assessment that accompanies this text (see the inside of the front cover for details). Even if the test doesn't help you choose a major, it will at least help you become more aware of your particular learning style. This alone could contribute to your academic success, because studies show that when college students gain greater self-aware of their learning styles they improve their academic performance (Claxton & Murrell, 1988).

To sum up, the most important factor to consider when reaching decisions about a major is whether it is compatible with four characteristics of the self: your (a) learning style, (b) your abilities, (c) your personal interests, and (d) your values (see **Figure 13.4**). These four pillars provide the foundation for effective decisions about a college major.

Pause for Reflection

Which one of the four learning style appears to most closely match your learning style? (Check one of the following boxes.)

☐ Accommodator

☐ Diverger

☐ Converger

☐ Assimilator

What majors or fields of study do you think would be a good match for your learning style?

Personal Story   I first noticed that students in different academic fields may have different learning styles when I was teaching a psychology course that was required for students majoring in nursing and social work. I noticed that some students in class seemed to lose interest (and patience) when we got involved in lengthy class discussions about controversial issues or theories, while others seemed to love it. On the other hand, whenever I lectured or delivered information for an extended period, some students seemed to lose interest (and attention), while others seemed to get "into it" and took great notes. After one class period that involved quite a bit of class discussion, I began thinking about which students seemed most involved in the discussion and which seemed to drift off or lose interest. I suddenly realized that the students who did most of the talking and seemed most enthused during the class discussion were the students majoring in social work. On the other hand, most of the students who appeared disinterested or a bit frustrated were the nursing majors.

When I began to think about why this happened, it dawned on me that the nursing students were accustomed to gathering factual information and learning practical skills in their major courses and were expecting to use that learning style in my psychology course. The nursing majors felt more comfortable with structured class sessions in which they received lots of factual, practical information from the professor. On the other hand, the social work majors were more comfortable with unstructured class discussions because courses in their major often emphasized debating social issues and hearing viewpoints or perspectives.

As I left class that day, I asked myself: Did the nursing students and social work students select or gravitate toward their major because the type of learning emphasized in the field tended to match their preferred style of learning?

—Joe Cuseo

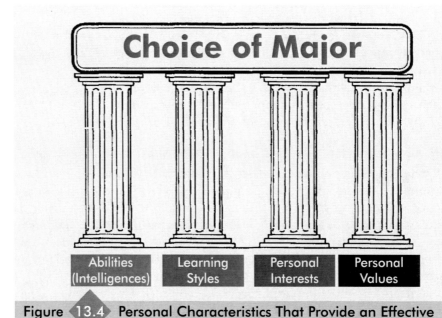

Figure 13.4   Personal Characteristics That Provide an Effective Foundation for Choice of a College Major

Strategies for Discovering a Major Compatible with Your Interests, Talents, and Values

If you're undecided about a major, there's no need to feel anxious or guilty. You're at an early stage in your college experience. Although you've decided to postpone your decision about a major, this doesn't mean you're a clueless procrastinator as long as you have a plan for exploring and narrowing down your options. Just be sure that you don't put all thoughts about your major on the back burner and simply drift along until you have no choice but to make a choice. Start exploring and developing a game plan now that will lead you to a wise decision about your major.

Similarly, if you've already chosen a major, this doesn't mean that you'll never have to give any more thought to that decision or that you can just shift into cruise control and motor along a mindless ride in the major you've selected. Instead, you should continue the exploration process by carefully testing your first choice, making sure it's a choice that is compatible with your abilities, interests, and values. In other words, take the approach that it's your *current* choice; whether it becomes your firm and *final* choice will depend on how well you perform, and how interested you are, in the first courses you take in the field.

To explore and identify majors that are compatible with your personal strengths and interests, use the following strategies.

> "Minds differ still more than faces."
>
> –Voltaire, eighteenth-century French author and philosopher

Pause for Reflection

In addition to taking formal tests to assess your learning style, you can gain awareness of your learning styles through some simple introspection or self-examination. Take a moment to complete the following sentences that are designed to stimulate personal reflection on your learning style:

I learn best if ...

I learn most from ...

I enjoy learning when ...

1. Use past experience to help you choose a major.

Think about the subjects that you experienced during high school and your early time in college. As the old saying goes, "Nothing succeeds like success itself." If you have done well and continue to do well in a certain field of study, this may indicate that your natural abilities and learning style correspond well with the academic skills required by that particular field. This could translate into future success and satisfaction in the field if you decide to pursue it as a college major.

You can enter information about your academic performance with high school courses at a Web site (www.mymajors.com), which will analyze it and provide you with college majors that may be a good match for you (based on your academic experiences in high school).

2. Use your elective courses to test your interests and abilities in subjects that you might consider as a major.

As its name implies, "elective" courses are those that you elect or choose to take. In college, electives come in two forms: free electives and restricted electives. Free electives are courses that you may elect (choose) to enroll in; they count toward your college degree but are not required for general education or your major. Restricted electives are courses that you must take, but you choose them from a restricted list of possible courses that have been specified by your college as fulfilling a requirement in general education or your major. For example, your campus may have a general education requirement in social or behavioral sciences that requires you to take two courses in this field, but you're allowed to choose those two courses from a menu of options in the field, such as anthropology, economics, political science, psychology, or sociology. If you're considering one of these subjects as a possible major, you can take an introductory course in this subject and test your interest in it while simultaneously fulfilling a general education requirement needed for graduation. This strategy will allow you to use general education as the main highway for travel toward your final destination (a college degree) and give you the opportunity to explore potential majors along the way.

You can also use your free electives to select courses in fields that you are considering as possible majors. By using some of your free and restricted electives in this way, you can test your interest and ability in these fields; if you find one that is a good match, you may have found yourself a major.

Naturally, you don't have to use all your electives for the purpose of exploring majors. As many as one-third your courses in college may be electives. This leaves you with a great deal of freedom to shape your college experience in a way that best meets your personal needs and future interests. For suggestions on how to make the best use of your free electives, see **Box 13.2**.

3. Be sure you know the courses that are required for the major you're considering.

In college, it's expected that students may know the requirements for the major they've chosen. These requirements vary considerably from one major to another. Review your college catalog carefully to determine what courses are required for the major you're considering. If you have trouble tracking down the requirements in your college catalog, don't become frustrated. These catalogs are often written in a technical manner that can sometimes be hard to interpret. If you need help identifying and understanding the requirements for a major that you are considering, don't be embarrassed about seeking assistance from a professional in your school's Academic Advisement Center.

4. Keep in mind that college majors often require courses in fields outside of the major, which are designed to support the major.

For instance, psychology majors are often required to take at least one course in biology, and business majors are often required to take calculus. If you are interested in majoring in particular subject area, be sure you are fully aware of such outside requirements and are comfortable with them.

Once you've accurately identified all courses required for the major you're considering, ask yourself the following two questions:

1. Do the course titles and descriptions appeal to my interests and values?
2. Do I have the abilities or skills needed to do well in these courses?

5. Look over an introductory textbook in the field you're considering as a major.

Find an introductory book in a major that you're considering, review its table of contents, and ask yourself whether the topics are compatible with your academic interests and talents. Also, read a few pages of the text to get some sense of the writing style used in the field and how comfortable you are with it. You

13.2

Take Action!

Top 10 Suggestions for Making the Most of Your College Electives

At most colleges and universities, approximately one of every three or four courses will be a free elective—your choice of the many courses that are listed in your college catalog. Your elective courses give you academic freedom and personal control of your college coursework. You can exercise this freedom strategically by selecting electives in a way that enables you to make the most of your college experience and college degree. Listed below are 10 suggestions for making strategic use of your college electives. As you read them, identify two suggestions that would be of most interest or use to you.

You can use your electives for the following purposes:

1. **Complete a minor or build an area of concentration.** Your electives can complement and strengthen your major or allow you to pursue a field of interest other than your major.
2. **Help you choose a career path.** Just as you can use electives to test your interest in a college major, you can use them to test your interest in a career. For instance, you could enroll in
   - career planning or career development courses; and
   - courses that involve internships or service learning experiences in a field that you're considering as a possible career (e.g., health, education, or business).
3. **Strengthen your skills in areas that may appeal to future employers.** For example, courses in foreign language, leadership development, and argumentation or debate develop skills that are attractive to future employers and may improve your employment prospects.
4. **Develop practical life skills that you can use now or in the near future.** You could take courses in managing personal finances, marriage and family, or child development to help you manage your money and your future family.
5. **Seek balance in your life and develop yourself as a whole person.** You can use your electives strategically to cover all key dimensions of self-development. For instance, you could

take courses that promote your emotional development (e.g., stress management), social development (e.g., interpersonal relationships), mental development (e.g., critical thinking), physical development (e.g., nutrition, self-defense), and spiritual development (e.g., world religions or death and dying).

> **Remember**
>
> Choose courses that contribute not only to your major and career but also to your quality of life.

6. **Make connections across different academic disciplines (subject areas).** Courses designed specifically to integrate two or more academic disciplines are referred to as interdisciplinary courses. For example, psychobiology is an interdisciplinary course that combines or integrates the fields of psychology (focusing on the mind) and biology (focusing on the body) and thus helps you see how the mind influences the body, and vice versa. Making connections across subjects and seeing how they can be combined to create a more complete understanding of a subject or issue can be a stimulating mental experience. Furthermore, the presence of interdisciplinary courses on your college transcript may be attractive to future employers because responsibilities and issues in the work world are not neatly packaged into separate majors; they require the ability to combine skills acquired from different fields of study.
7. **Help you develop broader perspectives on life and the world in which we live.** You can take courses that progressively widen your perspectives. For example, you could select courses that provide you with a societal perspective (e.g., sociology), a national perspective (e.g., political science), an international perspective (e.g., cultural geography), and a global perspective (e.g., ecology). These broadening perspectives widen your scope of knowledge and deepen your understanding of the world.
8. **Appreciate different cultural viewpoints and improve your ability to communicate with people from diverse cultural backgrounds.** You could take courses related to differences across nations (international diversity), such

as international relations, and you could take courses related to ethnic and racial differences in America (domestic diversity).

9. **Stretch beyond your familiar or customary learning style to experience different ways of learning or develop new skills.** Your college curriculum is likely to include courses that were never previously available to you and that focus on skills you've never had the opportunity to test or develop. These courses can stretch your mind and allow you to explore new ideas and acquire new perspectives.

10. **Learn something about which you were always curious or simply wanted to know more about.** For instance, if you've always been curious about how members of the other sex think and feel, you could take a course on the psychology of men and women. Or if you've always been fascinated by movies and how they are made, you might elect to take a course in filmmaking or cinematography.

> **! Remember**
>
> Your elective course in college will give you the opportunity to shape and create an academic experience that is uniquely your own. Seize this opportunity, and exercise your freedom responsibly and reflectively. Don't make your elective choices randomly, or solely on the basis of scheduling convenience (e.g., choosing courses to create a schedule with no early morning or late afternoon classes). Instead, make strategic choices of courses that will contribute most to your educational, personal, and professional development.

should find introductory textbooks for all courses in your college bookstore, in the college library, or with a faculty member in that field.

6. Talk with students majoring in the field you are considering and ask them about their experiences.

Try to speak with several students in the field so that you get a balanced perspective that goes beyond the opinion of one individual. A good way to find students in the major you're considering is to visit student clubs on campus related to the major (e.g., psychology club or history club). You could also check the class schedule to see when and where classes in you major are meeting and then go the classroom where these classes meet and speak with students about the major, either before class begins or after class lets out. The following questions may be good ones to ask students in a major that you're considering:

Pause for Reflection

What were the two primary strategies you selected from the list in **Box 13.2**?

Write a short explanation about why you chose each of these strategies.

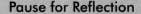

- What first attracted you to this major?
- What would you say are the advantages and disadvantages of majoring in this field?
- Knowing what you know now, would you choose the same major again?

Also, ask students about the quality of teaching and advising in the department. Studies show that different departments within the same college or university can vary greatly in terms of the quality of teaching, as well as their educational philosophy and attitude toward students (Pascarella & Terenzini, 1991).

7. Sit in on some classes in the field you are considering as a major.

If the class you want to visit is large, you probably could just slip into the back row and listen. However, if the class is small, you should ask the instructor's permission. When visiting a class, focus on the content or ideas being covered in class rather than the instructor's personality or teaching style. (Keep in mind that you're trying to decide whether you will major in the subject, not in the teacher.)

Speaking with students majoring in the discipline you are considering is a good way to get a balanced perspective.

© Jaimie Duplass, 2010. Under license from Shutterstock, Inc.

8. Discuss the major you're considering with an academic advisor.

It's probably best to speak with an academic advisor who advises students in various majors rather than to someone who advises only students in their particular academic department or field. You want to be sure to discuss the major with an advisor who is neutral and will give you unbiased feedback about the pros and cons of majoring in that field.

9. Speak with faculty members in the department that you're considering as a major.

Consider asking the following questions:

- What academic skills or qualities are needed for a student to be successful in your field?
- What are the greatest challenges faced by students majoring in your field?
- What do students seem to like most and least about majoring in your field?
- What can students do with a major in your field after college graduation?
- What types of graduate programs or professional schools would a student in your major be well prepared to enter?

10. Visit your Career Development Center.

See whether information is available on college graduates who've majored in the field you're considering and what they've gone on to do with that major after graduation. This will give you an idea about the type of careers the major can lead to or what graduate and professional school programs students often enter after completing a major in the field that you're considering.

11. Surf the Web site of the professional organization associated with the field that you're considering as a major.

For example, if you're thinking about becoming anthropology major, check out the Web site of the American Anthropological Association. If you're considering history as a major, look at the Web site of the American Historical Association. The Web site of a professional organization often contains useful information for students who are considering that field as a major. For example, the Web site of the American Philosophical Association contains information about nonacademic careers for philosophy majors, and the American Sociological Association's Web site identifies various careers that sociology majors are qualified to pursue after college graduation. To locate the professional Web site of the field that you might want to explore as a possible major, ask a faculty member in that field or complete a search on the Web by simply entering the name of the field followed by the word "association."

12. Be sure you know what academic standards must be met for you to be accepted for entry into a major.

Because of their popularity, certain college majors may be impacted or over-subscribed, which means that more students are interested in majoring in these fields than there are openings for them. For instance, preprofessional majors that lead directly to a particular career are often the ones that often become oversubscribed (e.g., accounting, education, engineering, premed, nursing, or physical therapy). On some campuses, these majors are called restricted majors, meaning that departments control their enrollment by limiting the number of students they let into the major. For example, departments may restrict entry to their major by admitting only students who have achieved an overall GPA of 3.0 or higher in certain introductory courses required by the majors, or they may take all students who apply for the major, rank them by their GPA, and then count down until they have filled their maximum number of available spaces (Strommer, 1993).

13. Be sure you know whether the major you're considering is impacted or oversubscribed and whether it requires certain academic standards to be met before you can be admitted.

As you complete courses and receive grades, check to see whether you are meeting these standards. If you find yourself failing to meet these standards, you may need to increase the amount of time and effort you devote to your studies and seek assistance from your campus Learning Center. If you're working at your maximum level of effort and are regularly using the learning assistance services available on your campus but are still not meeting the academic standards of your intended major, consult with an academic advisor to help you identify an alternative field that may be closely related to the restricted major you were hoping to enter.

14. Consider the possibility of a college minor in a field that complements your major.

A college minor usually requires about half the number of credits (units) required for a major. Most campuses allow you the option of completing a minor with your major. Check with your academic advisor or the course catalog if your school offers a minor that interests you, find out what courses are required to complete it.

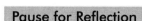

Pause for Reflection

Do you think that the major you're considering is likely to be oversubscribed (i.e., there are more students wanting to major in the field than there are openings in the courses)?

If you have strong interests in two different fields, a minor will allow you to major in one of these fields while minoring in the other. Thus, you can pursue two fields that interest you without having to sacrifice one for the other. Furthermore, a minor can be completed at the same time as most college majors without delaying your time to graduation. (In contrast, a double major will typically lengthen your time to graduation because you must complete the separate requirements of two different majors.) You can also pursue a second field of study alongside your major without increasing your time to graduation by completing a cognate area—a specialization that requires fewer courses to complete than a minor (e.g., four to five courses instead of seven to eight courses). A concentration area may have even fewer requirements (only two to three courses).

Taking a cluster of courses in a field outside your major can be an effective way to strengthen your résumé and increase your employment prospects because it demonstrates your versatility and allows you to gain experience in areas that may be missing or underemphasized in your major. For example, students majoring in the fine arts (e.g., music or theater) or humanities (e.g., English or history) may take courses in the fields of mathematics (e.g., statistics), technology (e.g., computer science), and business (e.g., economics)—all of which are not emphasized by their major.

◆ Summary and Conclusion

Here is a snapshot of the points that were made in this chapter:

* Changing your educational goal is not necessarily a bad thing; it may represent your discovery of another field that's more interesting to you or that's more compatible with your personal interests and talents.

- Several myths exist about the relationship between college majors and career that need to be dispelled:

  - **Myth 1.** When you choose your major, you're choosing your career.
  - **Myth 2.** After a bachelor's degree, any further education must be in the same field as your college major.
  - **Myth 3.** You should major business because most college graduates work in business settings.
  - **Myth 4.** If you major in a liberal arts field, the only career available is teaching.
  - **Myth 5.** Specialized skills are more important for career success than general skills.

- You should be aware of two important elements when choosing your major: your form or forms of multiple intelligence (your mental strengths or talents) and your learning style (your preferred way of learning).
- Strategically select your courses in a way that contributes most to your educational, personal, and professional development. Choose your elective courses with one or more of the following purposes in mind:

  - Choose a major or confirm whether your first choice is a good one.
  - Acquire a minor or build a concentration that will complement your major.
  - Broaden your perspectives on the world around you.
  - Become a more balanced or complete person.
  - Handle the practical life tasks that face you now and in the future.
  - Strengthen your career development and employment prospects after graduation.

Higher education supplies you with a higher degree of freedom of choice and a greater opportunity to determine your own academic course of action. Employ it and enjoy it—use your freedom strategically to make the most of your college experience and college degree.

Learning More Through the World Wide Web

Internet-Based Resources for Further Information on Educational Planning and Decision Making

For additional information related to the ideas discussed in this chapter, we recommend the following Web sites:

Identifying and Choosing College Majors:

www.mymajors.com

www.princetonreview.com/majors.aspx

Careers for Liberal Arts Majors:

www.eace.org/networks/liberalarts.html

13.1 Planning for a College Major

1. Go to your college catalog and use its index to locate pages containing information related to the major you have chosen or are considering. If you are undecided, select a field that you might consider as a possibility. To help you identify possible majors, you can use your catalog or go online and complete the short interview at the www.mymajors.com Web site. (Your learning-style assessment results from Figure 13.1 may also help you identify possibilities.)

   The point of this exercise is not to force you to commit to a major now but to familiarize you with the process of developing a plan, thereby putting you in a position to apply this knowledge when you reach a final decision about the major you intend to pursue. Even if you don't yet know what your final destination may be with respect to a college major, creating this educational plan will keep you moving in the right direction.

2. Once you've selected a major for this assignment, look at you college catalog and identify the courses that are required for the major you have selected. Use the form that follows to list the number and title of each course required by the major.

   You'll find that you must take certain courses for the major; these are often called core requirements. For instance, at most colleges, all business majors must take microeconomics. You will likely discover that you can choose other required courses from a menu or list of options (e.g., "choose any three courses from the following list of six courses"). Such courses are often called restricted electives in the major. When you find restricted electives in the major you've selected, read the course descriptions and choose those courses from the list that appeal most to you. Simply list the numbers and titles of these courses on the planning form. (You don't need to write down all choices listed in the catalog.)

   College catalogs can sometimes be tricky to navigate or interpret, so if you run into any difficulty, don't panic. Seek help from an academic advisor. Your campus may also have a degree audit program available, which allows you to track major requirements electronically. If so, take advantage of it.

College Major Planning Form

Major Selected: _____

Core Requirements in the Major
(Courses in your major that you must take)

Course #	Course Title	Course #	Course Title

Restricted Electives in the Major
(Courses required for your major that you choose to take from a specified list)

Course #	Course Title	Course #	Course Title

Self-Assessment Questions

1. Looking over the courses required for the major you've selected, would you still be interested in majoring in this field?

2. Were there courses required by the major that you were surprised to see or that you did not expect would be required?

3. Are there questions that you still have about this major?

13.2 Developing a Comprehensive Graduation Plan

A comprehensive, long-range graduation plan includes all three types of courses you need to complete a college degree:

1. General education requirements

2. Major requirements

3. Free electives

You planned for your required general education courses and required courses in your major. The third set of courses you'll take in college that count toward your degree consists of courses are called free electives—courses that are not required for general education or your major but that you freely choose from any of the courses listed in your college catalog. By combining your general education courses, major courses, and free-elective courses, you can create a comprehensive, long-range graduation plan.

- Use the "long-range graduation planning form" on pp. 279–280 to develop this complete educational plan. Use the slots to pencil in the general education courses you're planning to take to fulfill your general education requirements, your major requirements, and your free electives. (For ideas on choosing your free electives, see Box 13.2 on pp. 269–270.) Since this may be a tentative plan, it 's probably best to use a pencil when completing it in case you need to make modifications to it.

Notes

1. If you have not decided on a major, a good strategy might be to concentrate on taking liberal arts courses to fulfill your general education requirements during your first year of college. This will open more slots in your course schedule during your sophomore year. By that time, you may have a better idea of what you want to major in, and you can fill these open slots with courses required by your major. This may be a particularly effective strategy if you choose to major in a field that has many lower-division (first year and sophomore) requirements that must be completed before you can take upper-division (junior and senior) courses in the major. (These lower-division requirements are often referred to as premajor requirements.)

2. Keep in mind that the course number indicates the year in the college experience that the course is usually taken. Courses numbered in the 100s (or below) are typically taken in the first year of college, 200-numbered courses in the sophomore year, 300-numbered courses in the junior year, and 400-numbered courses in the senior year. Also, be sure to check whether the course you're planning to take has any prerequisites—courses that need to be completed before you can enroll in the course you're planning to take. For example, if you are planning to take a course in literature, it is likely that you cannot enroll in it until you have completed at least one prerequisite course in writing or English composition.

3. To complete a college degree in 4 years, you should complete about 30 credits each academic year.

Remember

Unlike high school, summer school in college isn't something you do to make up for courses that were failed, or should have been taken during the "regular" school year (fall and spring terms). Instead, it's an additional term that you can use to make further progress toward your college degree and reduce the total time it takes to complete your degree. Adopt the attitude that summer term is a regular part of the college academic year, and make strategic use of it to keep you on a four-year timeline to graduation.

4. Check with an academic advisor to see whether your college has developed a projected plan of scheduled courses, which indicates the academic term when courses listed in the catalog are scheduled to be offered (e.g., fall, spring, or summer) for the next 2 to 3 years. If such a long-range plan of scheduled courses is

available, take advantage of it because it will enable you to develop a personal educational plan that includes not only what courses you will take, but also when you will take them. This can be an important advantage because some courses you may need for graduation will not be offered every term. We strongly encourage you to inquire about and acquire any long-range plan of scheduled courses that may be available, and use it when developing your long-range graduation plan.

5. Don't forget to include out-of-class learning experiences as part of your educational plan, such as volunteer service, internships, and study abroad.

Your long-range graduation plan is not something set in stone that can never be modified. Like clay, its shape can be molded and changed into a different form as you gain more experience with the college curriculum. Nevertheless, your creation of this initial plan will be useful because it will provide you with a blueprint to work from. Once you have created slots specifically for your general education requirements, your major courses, and your electives, you have accounted for all the categories of courses you will need to complete to graduate. Thus, if changes need to be made to your plan, they can be easily accommodated by simply substituting different courses into the slots you've already created for these three categories.

Remember

The purpose of this long-range planning assignment is not to lock you into a rigid plan but to give you a telescope for viewing your educational future and a map for reaching your educational goals.

Graduation Planning Form

STUDENT: ID NO:

MAJOR: MINOR:

TERM:		TERM:		TERM:		TERM:	
Course	Units	Course	Units	Course	Units	Course	Units
TOTAL		TOTAL		TOTAL		TOTAL	

TERM:		TERM:		TERM:		TERM:	
Course	Units	Course	Units	Course	Units	Course	Units
TOTAL		TOTAL		TOTAL		TOTAL	

TERM:		TERM:		TERM:		TERM:	
Course	Units	Course	Units	Course	Units	Course	Units
TOTAL		TOTAL		TOTAL		TOTAL	

TERM:		TERM:		TERM:		TERM:	
Course	Units	Course	Units	Course	Units	Course	Units
TOTAL		TOTAL		TOTAL		TOTAL	

		COCURRICULAR EXPERIENCES	SERVICE LEARNING AND INTERNSHIP EXPERIENCES
Advisor's Signature	Date:		
Student's Signature	Date:		
Notes:			

Self-Assessment Questions

1. Do you think this was a useful assignment? Why or why not?

2. Do you see any way in which this assignment could be improved or strengthened?

3. Did completing this long-range graduation plan influence your educational plans in any way?

Whose Choice Is It Anyway?

Ursula, a first-year student, was in tears when she showed up at the Career Center. She had just returned from a weekend visit home, where she informed her parents that she was planning to major in art or theater. When Ursula's father heard about her plans, he exploded and insisted that she major in something "practical," like business or accounting, so that she could earn a living after she graduates. Ursula replied that she had no interest in these majors, nor did she feel she had the skills needed to complete the level of math required by them, which included calculus. Her father shot back that he had no intention of "paying 4 years of college tuition for her to end up as an unemployed artist or actress!" He went on to say that if she wanted to major in art or theater she'd "have to figure out a way to pay for college herself."

Reflection and Discussion Questions

1. What options (if any) do you think Ursula has now?

2. If Ursula were your friend, what would you recommend she do?

3. Do you see any way or ways in which Ursula might pursue a major that she's interested in and, at the same time, ease her father's worries that she will end up jobless after college graduation?

Career Exploration, Planning, and Preparation

14

ACTIVATE YOUR THINKING | Journal Entry 14.1

Before you start to dig into this chapter, take a moment to answer the following questions:

1. Have you decided on a career, or are you leaning strongly toward one?

_____

_____

2. If yes, why have you chosen this career? (Was your decision influenced by anybody or anything?)

_____

_____

_____

3. If no, are there any careers you're considering as possibilities?

_____

_____

_____

LEARNING GOAL

To acquire strategies that can be used now and throughout the remaining years of your college experience for effective career exploration, preparation, and development.

The Importance of Career Planning

College graduates in the twenty-first century are likely to continue working until age 75 (Herman, 2000). Once you enter the workforce full time, you'll spend most of the remaining waking hours of your life working. The only other single activity that you'll spend more time doing in your lifetime is sleeping. When you consider that such a sizable portion of your life is spent working and that your career can strongly influence your sense of personal identify and self-esteem, it becomes apparent that career choice is a critical process that should begin early in your college experience.

From "Thriving in College and Beyond" by Cuseo, Fecas, Thompson. © Kendall Hunt Publishing.

! Remember

When you're doing career planning, you're also doing life planning because you are planning how you will spend most of the waking hours of your future.

Even if you've decided on a career that you were dreaming about since you were a preschooler, the process of career exploration and planning is not complete because you still need to decide on what specialization within that career you'll pursue. For example, if you're interested in pursuing a career in law, you'll need to eventually decide what branch of law you wish to practice (e.g., criminal law, corporate law, or family law). You'll also need to decide what employment sector or type of industry you would like to work in, such as nonprofit, for-profit, education, or government. Thus, no matter how certain or uncertain you are about your career path, you'll need to begin exploring career options and start taking your first steps toward formulating a career development plan.

◆ Strategies for Career Exploration and Preparation

Reaching an effective decision about a career involves the same four steps you used in the goal-setting process:

1. **Awareness of yourself.** Your personal abilities, interests, needs, and values;
2. **Awareness of your options.** The variety of career fields available to you;
3. **Awareness of what best "fits" you.** The careers that best match your personal abilities, interests, needs, and values;
4. **Awareness of the process.** How to prepare for and gain entry into the career of your choice.

Step 1. Self-Awareness

The more you know about yourself, the better your choices and decisions will be. Self-awareness is a particularly important step to take when making career decisions because the career you choose says a lot about who you are and what you want from life. Your personal identity and life goals should not be based on or built around your career choice; it should be the other way around.

! Remember

Your personal attributes and goals should be considered first because they provide the foundation on which you build your career choice and future life.

One way to gain greater self-awareness of your career interests is by taking psychological tests or assessments. These assessments allow you to see how your interests in certain career fields compare with those of other students and professionals who've experienced career satisfaction and success. These comparative perspectives can give you important reference points for assessing whether your level of interest in a career is high, average, or low relative to other students and working professionals. Your Career Development Center is the place on campus where you can find these career-interest tests, as well as other instruments that allow you to assess your career-related abilities and values.

When making choices about a career, you may have to consider one other important aspect of yourself: your personal needs. A need may be described as something stronger than an interest. When you satisfy a personal need, you are doing something that makes your life more satisfying or fulfilling. Psychologists have identified several important human needs that vary in strength or intensity from person to person. Listed in **Box 14.1** are personal needs that are especially important to consider when making a career choice.

Your career choice should make you look forward to going to work each day.

© Stephen Coburn, 2010. Under license from Shutterstock, Inc.

Take Action!

14.1

Personal Needs to Consider When Making Career Choices

As you read the needs listed here, make a note after each one, indicating how strong the need is for you (high, moderate, or low).

1. **Autonomy.** Need to work independently without close supervision or control. Individuals high in this need may experience greater satisfaction working in careers that allow them to be their own boss, make their own decisions, and control their own work schedule. Individuals low in this need may experience greater satisfaction working in careers that are more structured and involve working with a supervisor who provides direction, assistance, and frequent feedback.

2. **Affiliation.** Need for social interaction, a sense of belonging, and the opportunity to collaborate with others. Individuals high in this need may experience greater satisfaction working in careers that involve frequent interpersonal interaction and teamwork with colleagues or co-workers. Individuals

Student Perspective

"To me, an important characteristic of a career is being able to meet new, smart, interesting people."

–First-year student

low in this need may be more satisfied working alone or in competition with others.

3. **Achievement.** Need to experience challenge and a sense of personal accomplishment. Individuals high in this need may be more satisfied working in careers that push them to solve problems, generate creative ideas, and continually learn new information or master new skills. Individuals low in this need may be more satisfied with careers that don't continually test their abilities and don't repeatedly challenge them to stretch their skills with new tasks and different responsibilities.

Student Perspective

"I want to be able to enjoy my job and be challenged by it at the same time. I hope that my job will not be monotonous and that I will have the opportunity to learn new things often."

–First-year student

4. **Recognition.** Need for high rank, status, and respect from others. Individuals high in this need may crave careers that are prestigious in the eyes of friends, family, or society. Individuals with a low need for recognition would feel comfortable working in a career that they find personally fulfilling, without being concerned

about how impressive or enviable their career appears to others.

5. **Sensory Stimulation.** Need to experience variety, change, and risk. Individuals high in this need may be more satisfied working in careers that involve frequent changes of pace and place (e.g., travel), unpredictable events (e.g., work tasks that vary considerably), and moderate stress (e.g., working under pressure of competition or deadlines). Individuals with a low need for sensory stimulation may feel more comfortable working in careers that involve regular routines, predictable situations, and minimal amounts of risk or stress.

Student Perspective

"For me, a good career is very unpredictable and interest-fulfilling. I would love to do something that allows me to be spontaneous."

–First-year student

"Don't expect a recluse to be motivated to sell, a creative thinker to be motivated to be a good proofreader day in and day out, or a sow's ear to be happy in the role of a silk purse."

–Pierce Howard, *The Owner's Manual for the Brain* (2000)

Personal Story

While enrolled in my third year of college with half of my degree completed, I had an eye-opening experience. I wish this experience had happened in my first year, but better late than never. Although I had chosen a career during my first year of college, my decision-making process was not systematic and didn't involve critical thinking. I chose a major based on what sounded prestigious and would pay me the most money. Although these are not necessarily bad factors, my failure to use a systematic and reflective process to evaluate these factors was bad. In my junior year of college I asked one of my professors why he decided to get his PhD and become a professor. He simply answered, "I wanted autonomy." This was an epiphany for me. He explained that when he looked at his life he determined that he needed a career that offered independence, so he began looking at career options that would offer that. After that explanation, "autonomy" became my favorite word, and this story became a guiding force in my life. After going through a critical self-awareness process, I determined that autonomy was exactly what I desired and a professor is what I became.

—*Aaron Thompson*

Pause for Reflection

Which of the five needs in **Box 14.1** did you indicate as being strong personal needs?

What career or careers do you think would best match your strongest needs?

Taken altogether, four aspects of yourself should be considered when exploring careers: your personal abilities, interests, values, and needs. As illustrated in **Figure 14.1**, these four pillars provide a solid foundation for effective career choices and decisions. You want to choose a career that you're good at, interested in, and passionate about and that fulfills your personal needs.

Lastly, since a career choice is a long-range decision that involves life beyond college, self-awareness should involve not only reflection on who you are now but also self-projection—reflecting on how you see yourself in the future. When you engage in the process of self-projection, you begin to see a connection between where you are now and where you want or hope to be.

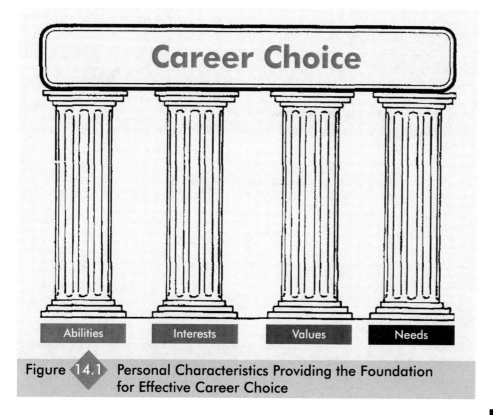

Career Choice

Abilities | Interests | Values | Needs

Figure 14.1   Personal Characteristics Providing the Foundation for Effective Career Choice

Ideally, your choice of a career should be one that leads to the best-case future scenario in which your typical day goes something like this: You wake up in the morning and hop out of bed enthusiastically—eagerly looking forward to what you'll be doing at work that day. When you're at work, time flies by, and before you know it, the day's over. When you return to bed that night and look back on your day, you feel good about what you did and how well you did it. For this ideal scenario to have any chance of becoming a reality, or even coming close to reality, you have to select a career path that is true to yourself—a path that leads you to a career that closely matches your abilities (what you do well), your interests (what you like to do), your values (what you feel good about doing), and your needs (what brings you satisfaction and fulfillment in life).

Step 2. Awareness of Your Options

To make effective decisions about your career path, you need to have accurate knowledge about the nature of different careers and the realities of the work world. The Career Development Center is the first place to go for this information and help with career exploration and planning. In addition to helping you explore your personal career interests and abilities, the Career Development Center is your campus resource for learning about the nature of different careers and for strategies on locating career-related work experiences.

Student Perspective

"I think that a good career has to be meaningful for a person. It should be enjoyable for the most part [and] it has to give a person a sense of fulfillment."

–First-year student

Pause for Reflection

Project yourself 10 years into the future and visualize your ideal career and life.

1. What are you spending most of your time doing during your typical workday?

2. Where and with whom are you working?

3. How many hours are you working per week?

4. Where are you living?

5. Are you married? Do you have children?

6. How does your work influence your home life?

If you were to ask people to name as many careers as they can, they wouldn't come close to naming the 900 career titles listed by the federal government in its Occupational Information Network. Many of these careers you may have never heard of, but some of them may represent good career options for you. You can learn about careers through nine major routes or avenues:

- Reading about careers them in books or online
- Becoming involved in cocurricular programs on campus related to career development
- Taking career development courses
- Interviewing people in different career fields
- Observing (shadowing) people at work in different careers
- Interning
- Participating in a co-op program
- Volunteering
- Working part time

Resources on Careers

Your Career Development Center and your College Library are campus resources where you can find a wealth of reading material on careers, either in print or online. Listed here are some of the most useful sources of written information on careers:

There are many resources for finding information on careers, many of which can be accessed on the Internet.

- *Dictionary of Occupational Titles* (www.occupationalinfo.org). This is the largest printed resource on careers; it contains concise definitions of more than 17,000 jobs. It also includes information on
- Work tasks that people in the career typically perform regularly;
- Types of knowledge, skills, and abilities that are required for different careers;
- Interests, values, and needs of individuals who find working in particular careers to be personally rewarding; and
- Background experiences of people working in different careers that qualified them for their positions.
- *Occupational Outlook Handbook* (www.bls.gov/oco). This is one of the most widely available and used resources on careers. It contains descriptions of approximately 250 positions, including information on the nature of work, work conditions, places of employment, training or education required for career entry and advancement, salaries, careers in related fields, and additional sources of information about particular careers (e.g., professional organizations and governmental agencies). A distinctive feature of this resource is that it contains information about the future employment outlook for different careers.
- *Encyclopedia of Careers and Vocational Guidance* (Chicago: Ferguson Press). As the name suggests, this is an encyclopedia of information on qualifications, salaries, and advancement opportunities for various careers.

- **Occupational Information Network (O*NET) Online (www.online. onetcenter.org).** This is America's most comprehensive source of online information about careers. It contains an up-to-date set of descriptions for almost 1,000 careers, plus lots of other information similar to what you would find in the *Dictionary of Occupational Titles*.

In addition to these general sources of information, your Career Development Center and College Library should have books and other published materials related to specific careers or occupations (e.g., careers for English majors).

You can also learn a lot about careers by simply reading advertisements for position openings in your local newspaper or online, such as at www.career-builder.com and college.monster.com. When reading position descriptions, make special note of the tasks, duties, or responsibilities they involve and ask yourself whether these positions are compatible with your personal profile of abilities, interests, needs, and values.

Career Planning and Development Programs

Periodically during the academic year, cocurricular programs devoted to career exploration and career preparation are likely to be offered on your campus. For example, the Career Development Center may sponsor career exploration or career planning workshops that you can attend for free. Also, the Career Development Center may organize a career fair on campus at which professionals working in different career fields are given booths on campus where you can visit with them and ask questions about their careers. Research indicates that career development workshops offered on campus are effective for helping students' plan for and decide on a career (Brown & Krane, 2000; Hildenbrand & Gore, 2005).

Career Development Courses

Many colleges offer career development courses for elective credit. These courses typically include self-assessment of your career interests, information about different careers, and strategies for career preparation. You should be doing career planning, so why not do it by taking a career development course that rewards you with college credit for doing it? Studies show that students who participate in career development courses experience significant benefits in terms of career choice and career development (Pascarella & Terenzini, 2005).

It might also be possible for you to take an independent-study course that will give you the opportunity to investigate issues in the career area you are considering. An independent study is a project that you work out with a faculty member, which usually involves writing a paper or detailed report. It allows you to receive academic credit for an in-depth study of a topic of your choice, without having to enroll with other students in a traditional course that has regularly scheduled classroom meetings. You could use this independent-study option to choose a project related to a career you've considered. To see whether this independent-study option is available at your campus, check the college catalog or consult with an academic advisor. You may be able to explore a career of interest to you in a writing or speech course if your instructor allows you to choose the topic that you'll write or speak about. If you're given this choice, use it to research a career that interests and make that the topic of your paper or presentation.

Information Interviews

One of the best and most overlooked ways to get accurate information about careers is to interview professionals who are working in career fields.

Pause for Reflection

If you were to observe or interview a working professional in a career that interests you, what position would that person hold?

Career development specialists refer to this strategy as information interviewing. Don't assume that working professionals would not be interested in taking time out of their day to speak with a student. Most are willing to be interviewed about their careers; they often enjoy it (Crosby, 2002).

Information interviews provide you inside information about what careers are like because you're getting that information directly from the horse's mouth. They also help you gain experience and confidence in interview situations, which may help you prepare for future job interviews. Furthermore, if you make a good impression during information interviews, the people you interview may suggest that you contact them again after graduation in case there are position openings. If there are openings, you might find yourself being the interviewee instead of the interviewer (and you might find yourself a job).

Because interviews are a valuable source of information about careers and provide possible contacts for future employment, we strongly recommend that you complete the information interview assignment included at the end of this chapter.

Career Observation (Shadowing)

In addition to learning about careers from reading and interviews, you can experience careers more directly by placing yourself in workplace situations or work environments that allow you to observe workers performing their daily duties. Two college-sponsored programs may be available on your campus that would allow you to observe working professionals:

- **Job Shadowing Programs.** These programs allow you to follow (shadow) and observe a professional during a typical workday.
- **Externship Programs.** This is basically an extended form of job shadowing, which lasts longer (e.g., 2–3 days).

Visit your Career Development Center to learn about what job shadowing or externship programs may be available on your college campus. If none are available in a career field that interests you, consider finding one on your own by using strategies similar to those we recommend for information interviews at the end of this chapter. The only difference is that instead of asking the person for an interview, you'd be asking whether you could observe that person at work. The same person who gave you an information interview might be willing to allow such observation. Keep in mind that just 1 or 2 days of observation will give you some firsthand information about a career but will not give you firsthand experience in that career.

Internships

In contrast to job shadowing or externships, whereby you observe someone at work, an internship program immerses you in the work itself and gives you the opportunity to perform career-related work duties. A distinguishing feature of internships is that you can receive academic credit and sometimes financial compensation for the work you do. An internship usually totals 120 to 150 work hours, which may be completed at the same time you're enrolled in a full schedule of classes when you're not taking classes (e.g., during summer term). An advantage of an internship is that it enables college students to avoid the classic catch-22 situation they often run into when interviewing for their first career position after graduation. The interview scenario usually goes something like this: The potential employer asks the college graduate, "What work experience have you had in this field?" The recent graduate replies, "I haven't had any work experience because I've been a full-time college student." This scenario can be avoided if you complete an internship during your college experience, which allows you to say, "Yes, I do have work experience in this field." We encourage you to participate in an internship while in college because it will enable you to beat the "no experience" rap after graduation and distinguish yourself from many other college graduates. Research shows that students who have internships while in college are more likely to develop career-relevant work skills and find employment immediately after college graduation (Pascarella & Terenzini, 2005).

Internships are typically available to college students during their junior or senior year; however, there may be internships available to first- and second-year students on your campus. You can also pursue internships on your own. Published guides describe various career-related internships, along with information on how to apply for them (e.g., *Peterson's Internships* and the *Vault Guide to Top Internships*). You could also search for internships on the Web (e.g., www.internships.com and www.vaultreports.com). Another good resource for possible information on internships is the local chamber of commerce in the town or city where your college is located or in your hometown.

Another option for gaining firsthand work experience is enrolling in courses that allow you to engage in hands-on learning related to your career interest. For instance, if you're interested in working with children, courses in child psychology or early childhood education may offer experiential learning opportunities in a preschool or daycare center on campus.

Cooperative Education (Co-op) Programs

A co-op is similar to an internship but involves work experience that lasts longer than one academic term and often requires students to stop their coursework temporarily to participate in the program. However, some co-op programs allow you to continue to take classes while working part time at a co-op position; these are sometimes referred to as parallel co-ops. Students are paid for participating in co-op programs but do not receive academic credit—just a notation on their college transcript (Smith, 2005).

Typically, co-ops are only available to juniors or seniors, but you can begin now to explore co-op programs by reviewing your college catalog and visiting your Career Development Center to see whether your school offers co-op programs in career areas that may interest you. If you find any, plan to get involved with one because it can provide you with authentic and extensive career-related work experience.

The value of co-ops and internships is strongly supported by research, which indicates that students who have these experiences during college:

- Are more likely to report that their college education was relevant to their career;
- Receive higher evaluations from employers who recruit them on campus;
- Have less difficulty finding an initial position after graduation;
- Are more satisfied with their first career position after college;
- Obtain more prestigious positions after graduation; and
- Report greater job satisfaction (Gardner, 1991; Knouse, Tanner, & Harris, 1999; Pascarella & Terenzini, 1991, 2005).

In one statewide survey that asked employers to rank various factors they considered important when hiring new college graduates, internship or cooperative education program received the highest ranking (Education Commission of the States, 1995). Furthermore, employers report that if full-time positions open up in their organization or company, they usually turn first to their own interns and co-op students (National Association of Colleges & Employers, 2003).

Volunteer Service

Engaging in volunteerism not only helps your community but also helps you by giving you the opportunity to explore different work environments and gain work experience in career fields that relate to your area of service. For example, volunteer service to different age groups (e.g., children, adolescents, or the elderly) and service in different environments (e.g., hospital, school, or laboratory) can provide you with firsthand work experience and simultane-

Personal Story

As an academic advisor, I was once working with two first-year students, Kim and Christopher. Kim was thinking about becoming a physical therapist, and Chris was thinking about becoming an elementary school teacher. I suggested to Kim that she visit the hospital nearby our college to see whether she could do volunteer work in the physical therapy unit. The hospital did need volunteers, so she volunteered in the physical therapy unit and loved it. That volunteer experience confirmed for her that physical therapy is what she should pursue as a career. She completed a degree in physical therapy and is now a professional physical therapist.

I suggested to Chris, the student who was thinking about becoming an elementary school teacher, that he visit some local schools to see whether they could use a volunteer teacher's aide. One of the schools did need his services, and Chris volunteered as a teacher's aide for about 10 weeks. At the halfway point during his volunteer experience, he came into my office to tell me that the kids were just about driving him crazy and that he no longer had any interest in becoming a teacher. He ended up majoring in communications.

Kim and Chris were the first two students I advised to get involved in volunteer work to test their career interests. Their volunteer experiences proved so valuable for helping both of them make a career decision that I now encourage all students I advise to get volunteer experience in the field they're considering as a future career.

—Joe Cuseo

ously give you a chance to test your interest in possibly pursuing future careers related to these age groups and work environments. (To get a sense of the range of service opportunities that may be available to you, go to www.usa. service.org.)

Volunteer service also enables you to network with professionals outside of college who may serve as excellent references and resources for letters of recommendation for you. Furthermore, if these professionals are impressed with your volunteer work, they may become interested in hiring you part time while you're still in college or full time when you graduate.

It may be possible to do volunteer work on campus by serving as an informal teaching assistant or research assistant to a faculty member. Such experiences are particularly valuable for students intending to go to graduate school. If you have a good relationship with any faculty members who are working in an academic field that interests you, consider asking them whether they would like some assistance (e.g., with their teaching or research responsibilities). Your volunteer work for a college professor could lead to making a presentation with your professor at a professional conference or may even result in your name being included as a coauthor on an article published by the professor.

Pause for Reflection

Have you done volunteer work? If you have, did you learn anything from your volunteer experiences that might help you decide which types of work best match your interests or talents?

Part-Time Work

Jobs that you hold during the academic year or during summer break should not be overlooked as potential sources of career information and as résumé-building experience. Part-time work can provide opportunities to learn or develop skills that may be relevant to your future career, such as organizational skills, communication skills, and ability to work effectively with co-workers from diverse backgrounds or culture.

Also, work in a part-time position may eventually turn into a full-time career. The following personal story illustrates how this can happen.

It might also be possible for you to obtain part-time work experience on campus through your school's work–study program. A work–study job allows you to work at your college in various work settings, such as the Financial Aid Office, college library, Public Relations Office, or Computer Services Center, and often allows you to build your employment schedule around your academic schedule. On-campus work can provide you with valuable career-exploration and résumé-building experiences, and the pro-

Personal Story

One student of mine, an English major, worked part time for an organization that provides special assistance to mentally handicapped children. After he completed his English degree, he was offered a full-time position in this organization, which he accepted. While working at his full-time position with handicapped children, he decided to go to graduate school part time and eventually completed a master's degree in special education, which qualified him for a promotion to a more advanced position in the organization, which he also accepted.

—Joe Cuseo

fessionals for whom you work can serve as excellent references for letters of recommendation to future employers. To see whether you are eligible for your school's work–study program, visit the Financial Aid Office on your campus.

Learning about careers through firsthand experience in actual work settings (e.g., shadowing, internships, volunteer services, and part-time work) is critical to successful career exploration and preparation. You can take a career-interest test, or you can test your career interest through actual work experiences. There is simply no substitute for direct, hands-on experience for gaining knowledge about careers. These firsthand experiences represent the ultimate career-reality test. They allow you direct access to information about what careers are like—as opposed to how they are portrayed on TV or in the movies, which often paint an inaccurate or unrealistic picture of careers, making them appear more exciting or glamorous than they are.

In summary, firsthand experiences in actual work settings equip you with five powerful career advantages that enable you to:

- Learn about what work is like in a particular field;
- Test your interest and skills for certain types of work;
- Strengthen your résumé by adding experiential learning to academic (classroom) learning;
- Acquire contacts for letters of recommendation; and
- Network with employers who may refer or hire you for a position after graduation.

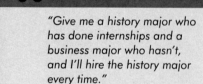

> "Give me a history major who has done internships and a business major who hasn't, and I'll hire the history major every time."
>
> –William Ardery, senior vice president, investor communications company

Furthermore, gaining firsthand work experience early in college not only promotes your job prospects after graduation but also makes you more a competitive candidate for internships and part-time positions that you may apply for during college.

Be sure to use your campus resources (e.g., the Career Development Center and Financial Aid Office), your local resources (e.g., Chamber of Commerce), and your personal contacts (e.g., family and friends) to locate and participate in work experiences that relate to your career interests. When you land an internship, work hard at it, learn as much as you can from it, and build relationships with as many people as possible at your internship site because these are the people who can provide you with future contacts, references, and referrals.

Pause for Reflection

1. Have you learned anything from your firsthand work experiences that may influence your future career plans?

2. If you could get firsthand work experience in any career field, what career would it be?

Step 3. Awareness of What Best Fits You

Effective decision making requires you to identify all important factors that should be considered when evaluating your options and to determine how much weight (influence) each of these factors should carry. As we emphasize throughout this chapter, the factor that should carry the greatest weight in career decision making is the match between your choice and your personal abilities, interests, needs, and values.

> ! **Remember**
> A good career decision should involve more than salary and should take into consideration how the career will affect all of your dimensions of self (social, emotional, physical, etc.) throughout all stages of your adult life: young adulthood, middle age, and late adulthood. It's almost inevitable that your career will affect your identity, the type of person you become, how you balance the demands of work and family, and how well you serve others beyond yourself. An effective career decision-making process requires you to make tough and thoughtful decisions about what matters most to you.

> *"Money is a good servant but a bad master."*
> –French proverb

> ! **Remember**
> A good career choice should be more than financially rewarding; it should be personally fulfilling.

Step 4. Awareness of the Process

Whether you're keeping your career options open or you think you've already decided on a particular career, you can start taking steps to prepare for career success by using the following strategies to prepare for successful career entry and advancement.

Self-Monitoring: Watching and Tracking Your Personal Skills and Positive Qualities

Don't forget that learning skills are also earning skills. The skills you're acquiring in college may appear to be just *academic* skills, but they're also *career* skills. For instance, when you're in the process of completing academic tasks such as taking tests and writing papers, you're using various career-relevant skills (e.g., analyzing, organizing, communicating, and problem solving).

Many students think that a college diploma is an automatic passport to a good job and career success (Ellin, 1993; Sullivan, 1993). However, for most employers of college graduates, what matters most is not only the credential but also the skills and personal strengths an applicant brings to the position (Education Commission of the States, 1995). You can start building these skills and strengths by self-monitoring (i.e., watching yourself and keeping track of the skills you're using and developing during your college experience). Skills are mental habits, and like all other habits that are repeatedly practiced, their development can be so gradual that you may not even notice how much growth is taking place—perhaps somewhat like watching grass grow. Thus, career development specialists recommend that you consciously track your skills to remain aware of them and to put you in a position to "sell" them to potential employers (Lock, 2000).

One strategy you can use to track your developing skills is to keep a career-development journal in which you note academic tasks and assignments you've completed, along with the skills you used to complete them.

> **Pause for Reflection**
> Answer the following questions about a career that you're considering or have chosen:
> 1. Why are you considering this career? (What led or caused you to become interested in it?)
> 2. Would you say that your interest in this career is motivated primarily by intrinsic factors—that is, factors "inside" of you, such as your personal abilities, interests, needs, and values? Or, would you say that your interest in the career is influenced more heavily by extrinsic factors—that is, factors "outside" of you, such as starting salary, pleasing parents, meeting family expectations, or meeting an expected role for your gender (male role or female role)?
> 3. If money were not an issue and you could earn a comfortable living in any career, would you choose the same career?

> *"If you want to earn more, learn more."*
> –Tom Hopkins, internationally acclaimed trainer of business and sales professionals

Be sure to record skills in your journal that you've developed in nonacademic situations, such as those skills used while performing part-time jobs, personal hobbies, cocurricular activities, or volunteer services. Since skills are actions, it's best to record them as action verbs in your career-development journal.

The key to discovering career-relevant skills and qualities is to get in the habit of stepping back from your academic and out-of-class experiences to reflect on what skills and qualities these experiences entailed and then get them down in writing before they slip your mind. You're likely to find that many personal skills you develop in college will be the same ones that employers will seek in the workforce. **Box 14.2** contains some important career-success skills that you're likely to develop during your college experience.

In addition to tracking your developing skills, track your positive traits or personal qualities. While it's best to record your skills as action verbs because they represent actions that you can perform for anyone who hires you, it may be best to track your attributes as adjectives because they describe who you are and what personal qualities you can bring to the job. **Box 14.3** gives a sample of personal traits and qualities that are relevant to success in multiple careers.

Remember

Keeping track of your developing skills and your positive qualities is as important to your successful entry into a future career as completing courses and compiling credits.

Take Action!

Personal Skills Relevant to Successful Career Performance

The following behaviors represent a sample of useful skills that are relevant to success in various careers (Bolles, 1998). As you read these skills, underline or highlight any of them that you have performed, either inside or outside of school.

advising	assembling	calculating	coaching	coordinating
creating	delegating	designing	evaluating	explaining
initiating	measuring	mediating	motivating	negotiating
operating	planning	producing	proving	researching
resolving	sorting	summarizing	supervising	synthesizing

> **Personal Story**
>
> After class one day, I had a conversation with a student (Max) about his personal interests. He said he was considering a career in the music industry and was working part time as a disc jockey at a night club. I asked him what it took to be a good disc jockey, and in less than 5 minutes of conversation, we discovered many more skills were involved in doing his job than either of us had realized. He was responsible for organizing 3 to 4 hours of music each night he worked; he had to read the reactions of his audience (customers) and adapt or adjust his selections to their musical tastes; he had to arrange his selections in a sequence that periodically varied the tempo (speed) of the music he played throughout the night; and he had to continually research and update his music collection to track the latest trends in hits and popular artists. Max also said that he had to overcome his fear of public speaking to deliver announcements that were a required part of his job.
>
> Although we were just having a short, friendly conversation after class about his part-time job, Max wound up reflecting on and identifying multiple skills he was using on the job. We both agreed that it would be a good idea to get these skills down in writing so that he could use them as selling points for future jobs in the music industry or in any industry.
>
> —Joe Cuseo

Self-Marketing: Packaging and Presenting Your Personal Strengths and Achievements

To convert your college experience into immediate employment, it might be useful to view yourself (a college graduate) as a product and employers as

Take Action!

Personal Traits and Qualities Relevant to Successful Career Performance   14.3

The following are some skills that are relevant to success in various careers. As you read these traits, underline or highlight any of them that you feel you possess or will soon possess.

conscientious	considerate	courteous	curious	dependable
determined	energetic	enthusiastic	ethical	flexible
imaginative	industrious	loyal	observant	open minded
outgoing	patient	persuasive	positive	precise
prepared	productive	prudent	punctual	reflective
sincere	tactful	team player	thorough	thoughtful

Pause for Reflection

Look back at the personal skills and traits listed in **Boxes 14.2** and **14.3** that you noted you possess or will soon possess.

1. Do you see your personal skills and traits as being relevant to the career or careers you're considering?

2. Do you see these skills and traits being as relevant, or more relevant, to any career or careers that you haven't yet considered?

intentional customers who may be interested in making a purchase (of your skills and attributes). As a first-year student, it could be said that you're in the early stages of the product-development process. Begin the process now so that by the time you graduate your finished product (you) will be one that employers notice and become interested in purchasing.

An effective self-marketing plan is one that gives employers a clear idea of what you can bring to the table and do for them. This should increase the number of job offers you receive and increase your chances of finding a position that best matches your interests, talents, and values.

You can effectively advertise or market your personal skills, qualities, and achievements to future employers through the following channels.

College Transcript

A college transcript is a listing of all courses you enrolled in and the grades you received in those courses. Two pieces of information included on your college transcript can influence employers' hiring decisions or admissions committee decisions about your acceptance to a 4-year college, graduate, or professional school: (a) the grades you earned in your courses and (b) the types of courses you completed.

Simply stated, the better your grades in college, the better your employment prospects after college. Research on college graduates indicates that the higher their grades, the higher:

- The prestige of their first job;
- Their total earnings; and
- Their job mobility.

This relationship between college grades and career success exists for students at all types of colleges and universities, regardless of the reputation or prestige of the institution they attend (Pascarella & Terenzini, 1991, 2005).

Cocurricular Experiences

Participation in student clubs, campus organizations, and other types of cocurricular activities can be a valuable source of experiential learning that can complement classroom-based learning and contribute to your career preparation and development. A sizable body of research supports the value of cocurricular experiences for career success (Astin, 1993; Kuh, 1993; Pascarella & Terenzini, 1991, 2005). Strongly consider getting involved cocurricular life on your campus, especially involvement with cocurricular experiences that

- Allow you to develop leadership and helping skills (e.g., leadership retreats, student government, college committees, peer counseling, or peer tutoring);
- Enable you to interact with others from diverse ethnic and racial groups (e.g., multicultural club or international club); and

- Provide you with out-of-class experiences related to your academic major or career interests (e.g., student clubs in your college major or intended career field).

Keep in mind that cocurricular experiences are also résumé-building experiences that provide solid evidence of your commitment to the college community outside the classroom. Be sure to showcase these experiences to prospective employers.

Also, the campus professionals with whom you may interact while participating in cocurricular activities (e.g., the director of student activities or dean of students) can serve as valuable references for letters of recommendation to future employers or graduate and professional schools.

Pause for Reflection

What do you predict will be your best work products in college—those that are most likely to appear in your portfolio?

Why?

Personal Portfolio

You may have heard the word "portfolio" in reference to a collection of artwork that professional artists put together to showcase or advertise their artistic talents. However, a portfolio can be a collection of any materials or products that illustrates an individual's skills and talents or demonstrates an individual's educational and personal development. For example, a portfolio could include such items as:

- Outstanding papers, exam performances, research projects, or lab reports;
- Artwork and photos from study-abroad, service learning, or internships experiences;
- Video footage of oral presentations or theatrical performances;
- CDs of musical performances;
- Assessments from employers or coaches; and
- Letters of recognition or commendation.

You can start the process of portfolio development right now by saving your best work and performances. Store them in a traditional portfolio folder, or save them on a computer disc to create an electronic portfolio. Another option would be to create a Web site and upload your materials there. Eventually, you should be able to build a well-stocked portfolio that documents your skills and demonstrates your development to future employers or future schools. You can start to develop an electronic portfolio now by completing Exercise 14.2 at the end of this chapter.

Personal Résumé

Unlike a portfolio, which contains actual products or samples of your work, a résumé may be described as a listed summary of your most important accomplishments, skills, and credentials. If you have just graduated from high school, you may not have accumulated enough experiences to construct a fully developed résumé. However, you can start to build a skeletal résumé that contains major categories or headings (the skeleton) under which you'll eventually include your experiences and accomplishments. (See **Box 14.4** for a sample skeleton résumé.) As you acquire experiences, you can flesh out the résumé's skeleton by gradually filling in its general categories with skills, accomplishments, and credentials.

Take Action!

Constructing a Résumé

14.4

Use this skeletal résumé as an outline or template for beginning construction of your own résumé and for setting your future goals. (If you have already developed a résumé, use this template to identify and add categories that may be missing from your current one.)

Name (First, Middle, Last)

Current Addresses:
Postal address
E-mail address
Phone no.

Permanent Addresses:
Postal address
E-mail address
Phone no.

EDUCATION: Name of College or University, City, State
Degree Name (e.g., Bachelor of Science)
College Major (e.g., Accounting)
Graduation Date, GPA

RELATED WORK   Position Title, City, State
EXPERIENCES:
(List skills used or developed.)

Start and stop dates
(Begin the list with the most recent
position dates held.)

VOLUNTEER (COMMUNITY SERVICE)
EXPERIENCES:
(List skills used or developed.)

NOTABLE COURSEWORK:
(e.g., leadership, international, or interdisciplinary courses)

COCURRICULAR EXPERIENCES:
(e.g., student government or peer leadership)
(List skills used or developed.)

PERSONAL SKILLS AND POSITIVE QUALITIES:
(List as bullets. Be sure to include those that are especially relevant to the position for which you're applying.)

HONORS AND AWARDS: (In addition to those received in college, you may include
those received in high school.)

PERSONAL INTERESTS: (Include items that showcase any special hobbies or talents
that are not directly related to school or work.)

Letters of Recommendation (a.k.a. Letters of Reference)

Personal letters of recommendation can be a powerful way to document your strengths and selling points. To maximize the power of your personal recommendations, give careful thought to:

- Who should serve as your references;
- How to approach them; and
- What to provide them.

Strategies for improving the quality of your letters of recommendation are suggested in **Box 14.5**.

!

Take Action!

The Art and Science of Requesting Letters of Recommendation: Effective Strategies and Common Courtesies

14.5

1. **Select recommendations from people who know you well.** Think about individuals with whom you've had an ongoing relationship, who know your name, and who know your strengths; for example, an instructor who you've had for more than one class, an academic advisor whom you see often, or an employer whom you've worked for over an extended period.

2. **Seek a balanced blend of letters from people who have observed your performance in different settings or situations.** The following are settings in which you may have performed well and people who may have observed your performance in these settings:
   - The classroom—a professor who can speak to your academic performance
   - On campus—a student life professional for a cocurricular reference who can comment on your contributions outside the classroom
   - Off campus—a professional for whom you've performed volunteer service, part-time work, or an internship

3. **Pick the right time and place to make your request.** Be sure to make your request well in advance of the letter's deadline date (e.g., at least 2 weeks). First ask whether the person is willing to write the letter, and then come back with forms and envelopes. Do not approach the person with these materials in hand because this may send the message that you have assumed or presumed the person will automatically say "yes." (This is not the most socially sensitive message to send someone whom you're about to ask for a favor.) Lastly, pick a place where the person can give full attention to your request. For instance, make a personal visit to the person's office, rather than making the request in a busy hallway or in front of a classroom full of students.

4. **Waive your right to see the letter.** If the school or organization to which you're applying has a reference-letter form that asks whether or not you want to waive (give up) your right to see the letter, waive your right—as long as you feel reasonably certain that you will be receiving a good letter of recommendation. By waiving your right to see your letter of recommendation, you show confidence that the letter to be written about you will be positive, and you assure the person who reads the letter that you didn't inspect or screen it to make sure it was a good one before sending it.

5. **Provide your references with a fact sheet about yourself.** Include your experiences and achievements—both inside and outside the classroom. This will help make your references' job a little easier by providing points to focus on. More importantly, it will help you because your letter becomes more powerful when it contains concrete examples or illustrations of your positive qualities and accomplishments. On your fact sheet, be sure to include any exceptionally high grades you may have earned in certain courses, as well as volunteer services, leadership experiences, special awards or forms of recognition, and special interests or talents that relate to your academic major and career choice. Your fact sheet is the place and time for you to "toot your own horn," so don't be afraid of coming across as a braggart or egotist. You're not being conceited; you're just showcasing your strengths.
6. **Provide your references with a stamped, addressed envelope.** This is a simple courtesy that makes their job a little easier and demonstrates your social sensitivity.
7. **Follow up with a thank-you note.** Thank your references about the time your letter of recommendation should be sent. This is the right thing to do because it shows your appreciation; it's also the smart thing to do because if the letter hasn't been written yet the thank-you note serves as a gentle reminder for your reference to write the letter.
8. **Let your references know the outcome of your application** (e.g., your admission to a school or acceptance of a job offer). This is the courteous thing to do, and your references are likely to remember your courtesy, which could strengthen the quality of any future letters they may write for you.

Summary and Conclusion

In national surveys, employers rank attitude of the job applicant as the number one factor in making hiring decisions; they rate this higher in importance than such factors as reputation of the applicant's school, previous work experience, and recommendations of former employers (Education Commission of the States, 1995; Institute for Research on Higher Education, 1995). Graduating from college with a diploma in hand may make you a more competitive job candidate, but you still have to compete by documenting and selling your strengths and skills. Your diploma doesn't work like a merit badge or passport that you flash to gain automatic access to an ideal job. Your college experience will open career doors, but it's your attitude, initiative, and effort that will enable you to step through those doors and into a successful career.

Pause for Reflection

Have you met a faculty member or other professional on campus who knows you well enough to write a personal letter of recommendation for you?

If yes, who is this person, and what position does he or she hold on campus?

Internet-Based Resources for Further Information on Careers

For additional information related to the ideas discussed in this chapter, we recommend the following Web sites:

Career Descriptions and Future Employment Outlook: **www.bls.gov/oco**

Internships: **www.internships.com**
www.vaultreports.com

Personalized Career Plan:
www.mapping-your-future.org

Position openings:
www.monster.com

Salaries Associated with Specific Positions:
www.salary.com

14.1 Conducting an Information Interview

To learn accurate information about a career that interests you, interview working professionals in that career—a career-exploration strategy known as information interviewing. An information interview enables you to:

- Learn what a career is really like;

- Network with professionals in the field; and

- Become confident in interview situations and prepare for later job interviews.

1. Select a career that you may be interested in pursuing. Even if you are currently keeping your career options open, pick a career that might be a possibility. You can use the resources cited on **pp. 288–289** in this chapter to help you identify a career that may be most appealing to you.

2. Find someone who is working in the career you selected and set up an information interview with that person.

    To help locate possible interview candidates, consider members of your family, friends of your family members, and family members of your friends. Any of these people may be working in the career you selected and may be good interview candidates, or they may know others who could be good candidates. The Career Development Center on your campus and the Alumni Association (or the Rotaract Club) may also be able to provide you with graduates of your college, or professionals working in the local community near your college, who are willing to talk about their careers with students.

    Lastly, you might consider using the Yellow Pages or the Internet to find names and addresses of possible candidates. Send them a short letter or e-mail asking about the possibility of scheduling a short interview. Mention that you would be willing to conduct the interview in person or by phone, whichever would be more convenient for them.

    If you do not hear back within a reasonable period (e.g., within a couple of weeks), send a follow-up message; if you do not receive a response to the follow-up message, then consider contacting someone else.

3. Conduct an information interview with the professional who has agreed to speak with you. Consider using the following suggested strategies.

Suggested Strategies for Conducting Information Interviews

- **Thank the person for taking the time to speak with you.** This should be the first thing you do after meeting the person—before you officially begin the interview.

- **Prepare your interview questions in advance.** Here are some questions that you might consider asking:

1. How did you decide on your career?

2. What qualifications or prior experiences did you have that enabled you to enter your career?

3. How does someone find out about openings in your field?

4. What steps did you take to find your current position?

5. What advice would you give to beginning college students about things they could start doing now to help them prepare to enter your career?

6. During a typical day's work, what do you spend most of your time doing?

7. What do you like most about your career?

8. What are the most difficult or frustrating aspects of your career?

9. What personal skills or qualities do you see as being critical for success in your career?

10. How does someone advance in your career?

11. Are there any moral issues or ethical challenges that tend to arise in your career?

12. Are members of diverse groups likely to be found in your career? (This is an especially important question to ask if you are a member of an ethnic, racial, or gender group that is underrepresented in the career field.)

13. What impact does your career have on your home life or personal life outside of work?

14. If you had to do it all over again, would you choose the same career?

15. Would you recommend that I speak with anyone else to obtain additional information or a different perspective on this career field? (If the answer is "yes," you may follow up by asking: "May I mention that you referred me?") This question is recommended because it's always a good idea to obtain more than one person's perspective before making an important choice or decision, especially one that can have a major influence on your life—such as your career choice.

- **Take notes during the interview.** This not only benefits you by helping you remember what was said; it also sends a positive message to the person you're interviewing by showing that the person's ideas are important and worth writing down.

If the interview goes well, you could ask whether it might be possible to observe or shadow your interviewee during a day at work.

Self-Assessment Questions

After completing your interview, take a moment to reflect on it and answer the following questions:

1. What information did you receive that impressed you about this career?

2. What information did you receive that distressed (or depressed) you about this career?

3. What was the most useful thing you learned from conducting this interview?

4. Knowing what you know now, would you still be interested in pursuing this career? (If yes, why?) (If no, why not?)

14.2 Creating an Electronic Portfolio

Using Folio180, create an electronic portfolio of your accomplishments and activities. In this assignment, you will collect information related to the following four areas:

1. Interests

2. Work and professional experiences

3. Awards, honors, and commendations

4. Academic work

You will also have the opportunity to support your entries with documents (e.g., Word, Excel and PowerPoint files) as well as electronic photos, videos and recordings. When completed, you will have a professional-looking electronic portfolio that you can use to showcase in applications for jobs, internships, scholarships and admission to graduate and professional schools.

Detailed instructions for this assignment are found at http://www.folio180.com/customer/KH-Cuseo/Thriving2_11_portfolio1.htm. Just type in this URL in your Internet browser, and follow the instructions.

Career Choice: Conflict and Confusion

Josh is a first-year student whose family has made a great financial sacrifice to send him to college. He deeply appreciates the tremendous commitment his family members have made to his education and wants to pay them back as soon as possible. Consequently, he has been looking into careers that offer the highest starting salaries to college students immediately after graduation. Unfortunately, none of these careers seem to match Josh's natural abilities and personal interests, so he's conflicted, confused, and starting to get stressed out. He knows he'll have to make a decision soon because the careers with high starting salaries involve majors that have many course requirements, and if he expects to graduate in a reasonable period, he'll have to start taking some of these courses during his first year.

Reflection and Discussion Questions

1. If you were Josh, what would you do?

2. Do you see any way that Josh might balance his desire to pay back his family as soon as possible with his desire to pursue a career that's compatible with his interests and talents?

3. What other questions or factors do you think Josh should consider before making his decision? "If you want to earn more, learn more."

References

Abbey, A. (2002). Alcohol-related sexual assault: A common problem among college students. *Journal of Studies on Alcohol, 14*, 118–128.

AC Nielsen Research Services. (2000). *Employer satisfaction with graduate skills.* Department of Education, Training and Youth Affairs. Canberra: AGPS. Retrieved October 25, 2006, from http://www.dest.gov.au/ty/publications/employability_skills/final_report.pdf

Academic Integrity at Princeton. (2003). *Examples of plagiarism.* Retrieved October 21, 2006, from http://www.princeton.du/pr/pub/integrity/pages/plagiarism.html

Acredolo, C., & O'Connor, J. (1991). On the difficulty of detecting cognitive uncertainty. *Human Development, 34*, 204–223.

AhYun, K. (2002). Similarity and attraction. In M. Allen, R. W. Preiss, B. M. Gayle, & N. A. Burrell (Eds.), *Interpersonal communication research* (pp. 145–167). Mahwah, NJ: Erlbaum.

Ainslie, G. (1975). Specious reward: A behavioral theory of impulsiveness and impulse control. *Psychological Bulletin, 82*, 463–496.

Ainslie, G. (1992). *Picoeconomics: The strategic interaction of successive motivational states within the person.* New York: Cambridge University Press.

Alkon, D. L. (1992). *Memory's voice: Deciphering the brain-mind code.* New York: HarperCollins.

Allport, G. W. (1954). *The nature of prejudice.* Cambridge, MA: Addison-Wesley.

American College Testing. (2009). *National college dropout and graduation rates, 2008.* Retrieved June 4, 2009, from http://www.act.org/news

American Heart Association. (2006). *Fish, levels of mercury and omega-3 fatty acids.* Retrieved January 13, 2007, from http://americanheart.org/presenter.jthml?identifier=3013797

American Obesity Association. (2002). *Obesity in the U.S.* Retrieved April 26, 2006, from http://www.obesity.org/subs/fastfacts/obesity_US.shtml

Amir, Y. (1976). The role of intergroup contact in change of prejudice and ethnic relations. In P. A. Katz (Ed.), *Towards the elimination of racism* (pp. 245–308). New York: Pergamon Press.

Andersen, P. A. (1985). Nonverbal immediacy in interpersonal communication. In A. W. Siegmean & S. Feldstein (Eds.), *Multichannel integrations of nonverbal behavior* (pp. 1–36). Hillsdale, NJ: Lawrence Erlbaum.

Anderson, J. R. (2000). *Cognitive psychology and its implications.* Worth Publishers.

Anderson, J. R., & Bower, G. H. (1974). Interference in memory for multiple contexts. *Memory and Cognition, 2*, 509–514.

Anderson, M., & Fienberg, S. E. (2000). Race and ethnicity and the controversy over the U.S. census. *Current Sociology, 48*(3), 87–110.

Anderson, L. W., & Krathwohl, D. R. (Eds.). (2001). *A taxonomy for learning, teaching, and assessing: A revision of Bloom's taxonomy of educational objectives.* New York: Addison Wesley Longman.

Applebee, A. N., Langer, J. A., Jenkins, L. B., Mullis, I. V. S., & Foertsch, M. A. (1990). *Learning to write in our nation's schools: instruction and achievement in 1988 at grades 4, 8, and 12.* Princeton, NJ: The National Arrow, K. J. (ed.) 1983. *Collected Papers of Kenneth J. Arrow, The Volume One: Social Choice and Justice.* Cambridge, MA: The Belknap Press of Harvard University Press.

Assessment of Educational Progress.

Appleby, D. C. (2008, June). *Diagnosing and treating the deadly 13th grade syndrome.* Paper presented at the Association of Psychological Science Convention, Chicago, IL.

Arnedt, J. T., Wilde, G. J. S., Munt, P. W., & MacLean, A. W. (2001). How do prolonged wakefulness and alcohol compare in the decrements they produce on a simulated driving task? *Accident Analysis and Prevention, 33*, 337–344.

Association of American Colleges & Universities. (2002). *Greater expectations: A new vision for learning as a nation goes to college.* Washington, DC: Author.

Astin, A. W. 1993. *What Matters in College: Four Critical Years Revisited.* San Francisco: Jossey-Bass.

Astin, A. W. (1993). *What matters in college?* San Francisco: Jossey-Bass.

Astin, A. W., Parrot, S. A., Korn, W. S., & Sax, L. J. (1997). *The American freshman: Thirty year trends, 1966–1996.* Los Angeles: Higher Education Research Institute, University of California.

Avolio, B. J. & Gardner, W. L. 2005. "Authentic leadership development: Getting to the root of positive forms of leadership." *Leadership Quarterly, 16(3),* 315–338.

Avolio, B. J. & Luthans, F. 2005. *The High Impact Leader: Moments Matter in Accelerating Authentic Leadership Development.* New York: McGraw-Hill.

Baer, J. M. (1993). *Creativity and divergent thinking.* Hillsdale, NJ: Erlbaum.

Baker, J. H. 2001. "Is Servant Leadership Part of Your Worldview?" *weLEAD Online Magazine.* Retrieved from http://www.leadingtoday.org/Onmag/jan01/hb-jan01.html.

Barker, E. (ed.) 1960. *Social Contract.* New York: Oxford University Press.

Bandura, A. (1986). *Social foundations of thought and action: A social cognitive theory.* Englewood Cliffs, NJ: Prentice Hall.

Bandura, A. (1994). Self-efficacy. In V. S. Ramachaudran (Ed.), *Encyclopedia of human behavior* (Vol. 4, pp. 71–81). New York: Academic Press.

Bandura, A. (1997). *Self-efficacy: The exercise of control.* New York: Freeman.

Bandura, A., & Cervone, D. (1983). Self-evaluative and self-efficacy mechanisms governing the motivational effects of goal systems. *Journal of Personality and Social Psychology, 45(5),* 1017–1028.

Barefoot, B. O., Warnock, C. L., Dickinson, M. P., Richardson, S. E., & Roberts, M. R. (Eds.). (1998). *Exploring the evidence: Vol. 2. Reporting outcomes of first-year seminars* (Monograph No. 29). Columbia: National Resource Center for the First-Year Experience and Students in Transition, University of South Carolina.

Bargdill, R. W. (2000). A phenomenological investigation of being bored with life. *Psychological Reports, 86,* 493–494.

Barker, L., & Watson, K. W. (2000). *Listen up: How to improve relationships, reduce stress, and be more productive by using the power of listening.* New York: St. Martin's Press.

Bartlett, T. (2002). Freshman pay, mentally and physically, as they adjust to college life. *Chronicle of Higher Education, 48,* 35–37.

Basadur, M., Runco, M. A., & Vega, L. A. (2000). Understanding how creative thinking skills, attitudes, and behaviors work together. *Journal of Creative Behavior, 34(2),* 77–100.

Bassham, G., Irwin, W., Nardone, H., & Wallace, J. M. (2005). *Critical thinking* (2nd ed.). New York: McGraw-Hill.

Bass, B. M. 1990. *Bass and Stogdill's Handbook of Leadership: Theory, Research and Management Applications* (3rd ed.). New York: Free Press.

Bates, G. A. (1994). *The next step: College.* Bloomington, IN: Phi Delta Kappa.

Baumeister, R. F., Heatherton, T. F., & Tice, D. M. (1994). *Losing control: How and why people fail at self-regulation.* San Diego, CA: Academic Press.

Bean, John C. "How Writing Is Related to Critical Thinking." In *Engaging Ideas,* 15–35. San Francisco: Jossey-Bass, 1996.

Bellah, R. N., Madsen, R., Sullivan, W. M., Swidler, A., & Tipton, S. M. (1985). *Habits of the heart: Individualism and commitment in American life.* Berkeley: University of California Press.

Benjamin, L. T., Jr., Cavell, T. A., & Shallenberger, W. R., III. (1984). Staying with initial answers on objective tests: Is it a myth? *Teaching of Psychology, 11,* 133–141.

Benjamin, M., McKeachie, W. J., Lin, Y. G., & Holinger. D. (1981). Test anxiety: Deficits in information processing. *Journal of Educational Psychology, 73,* 816–824.

Bennet, W., & Gurin, J. (1983). *The dieter's dilemma.* New York: Basic Books.

Benson, H., & Klipper, M. Z. (1990). *The relaxation response.* New York: Avon.

Bergen-Cico, D. (2000). Patterns of substance abuse and attrition among first-year students. *Journal of the First-Year Experience and Students in Transition, 12(1),* 61–75.

Berndt, T. J. (1992). Friendship and friends' influence in adolescence. *Current Directions in Psychological Science, 1(5),* 156–159.

Biglan, A. (1973). The characteristics of subject matter in different academic areas. *Journal of Applied Psychology, 57,* 195–203.

Bishop, S. (1986). Education for political freedom. *Liberal Education, 72(4),* 322–325.

Bjork, R. (1994). Memory and metamemory considerations in the training of human beings. In J. Metcalfe & A. P. Shimamura (Eds.), *Metacognition: Knowing about knowing* (pp. 185–206). Cambridge, MA: MIT Press.

Blakeslee, S. (1993, August 3). Mystery of sleep yields as studies reveal immune tie. *The New York Times,* pp. C1, C6.

Boekaerts, M., Pintrich, P. R., & Zeidner, M. (2000). *Handbook of self-regulation.* San Diego: Academic Press.

Bok, D. (2006). *Our underachieving colleges.* Princeton, NJ: Princeton University Press.

Bolles, R. N. (1998). *The new quick job-hunting map.* Toronto, Ontario, Canada: Ten Speed Press.

Booth, F. W., & Vyas, D. R. (2001). Genes, environment, and exercise. *Advances in Experimental Medicine and Biology, 502,* 13–20.

Boudreau, C., & Kromrey, J. (1994). A longitudinal study of the retention and academic performance of participants in a freshman orientation course. *Journal of College Student Development, 35,* 444–449.

Bowen, H. R. (1977). *Investment in learning: The individual and social value of American higher education.* San Francisco: Jossey-Bass.

Bourke, V. J. (ed.) 1960. *The Pocket Aquinas.* New York: Washington Square Press.

Bowen, H. R. (1997). *Investment in learning: The individual and social value of American higher education* (2nd ed.). Baltimore: Johns Hopkins Press.

Bowlby, J. (1980). *Attachment and loss: Vol. 3. Loss, sadness, and depression.* New York: Basic Books.

Boyer, E. L. (1987). *College: The undergraduate experience in America.* New York: Harper & Row.

Bradshaw, D. (1995). Learning theory: Harnessing the strength of a neglected resource. In D. C. A. Bradshaw (Ed.), *Bringing learning to life: The learning revolution, the economy and the individual* (pp. 79–92). London: Falmer Press.

Bransford, J. D., Brown, A. L., & Cocking, R. R. (1999). *How people learn: Brain, mind, experience and school.* Washington, DC: National Academy Press.

Braskamp, L. A. (2008). Developing global citizens. *Journal of College & Character, 10*(1), 1–5.

Bridgeman, B. (2003). *Psychology and evolution: The origins of mind.* Thousand Oaks, CA: Sage.

Brody, J. E. (2003, August 18). Skipping a college course: Weight gain 101. *The New York Times,* p. D7.

Brodsky, A. 2000. *Grover Cleveland: A Study in Character.* New York: St. Martin's Press.

Brown, R. D. (1988). Self-quiz on testing and grading issues. *Teaching at UNL (University of Nebraska–Lincoln), 10*(2), 1–3.

Brown, S. A., Tapert, S. F., Granholm, E., & Delis, D. C. (2000). Neurocognitive functioning of adolescents: Effects of protracted alcohol use. *Alcoholism: Clinical & Experimental Research, 24*(2), 164–171.

Brown, S. D., & Krane, N. E. R. (2000). Four (or five) sessions and a cloud of dust: Old assumptions and new observations about career counseling. In S. D. Brown & R. W. Lent (Eds.), *Handbook of counseling psychology* (3rd ed., pp. 740–766). New York: Wiley.

Bruffee, K. A. (1993). *Collaborative learning: Higher education, interdependence, and the authority of knowledge.* Baltimore: Johns Hopkins University Press.

Burka, J. B., & Yuen, L. M. (1983). *Procrastination: Why you do it, what to do about it.* Reading, MA: Addison-Wesley.

Burke, E. 1987. *Reflections on the Revolution in France.* J. G. A. Pocock (Ed.). Indianapolis: Hackett.

Burns, J. M. 1978. *Leadership.* New York: Harper & Row.

Burr, J. R. & Goldinger, M. 1984. *Philosophy and Contemporary Issues* (5th ed.) New York: Macmillan.

Bushman, B. J., & Cooper, H. M. (1990). Effects of alcohol on human aggression: An integrative research review. *Psychological Bulletin, 107*(3), 341–354.

Business/Higher Education Round Table. (1991). *Aiming higher: The concerns and attitudes of leading business executives and university heads to education priorities in Australia in the 1990s* (Commissioned Report No. 1). Melbourne, Australia.

Business/Higher Education Round Table. (1992). *Educating for excellence part 2: Achieving excellence in university professional education* (Commissioned Report No. 2). Melbourne, Australia.

Caine, R. N., & Caine, G. (1991). *Teaching and the human brain.* Alexandria, VA: Association for Supervision and Curriculum Development.

Calhoun, J. C. 1953. *A Disquisition on Government and Selections from the Discourse.* C. Gordon Post (Ed.), New York: Liberal Arts Press.

Cameron, L. (2003). *Metaphor in educational discourse.* London: Continuum.

Campbell, J. with Moyers, B. 1988. *The Power of Myth.* New York: Doubleday.

Campbell, T. A., & Campbell, D. E. (1997, December). Faculty/student mentor program: Effects on academic performance and retention. *Research in Higher Education, 38,* 727–742.

Caplan, P. J., & Caplan, J. B. (1994). *Thinking critically about research on sex and gender.* New York: HarperCollins College Publishers.

Carey, G. W. & J. McClellan (eds.) 2001. *The Federalist.* The Gideon Edition. Indianapolis: The Liberty Fund.

Caroli, M., Argentieri, L., Cardone, M., & Masi, A. (2004). Role of television in childhood obesity prevention. *International Journal of Obesity Related Metabolic Disorders, 28*(Suppl. 3), S104–S108.

Cates, J. R., Herndon, N. L., Schulz, S. L., & Darroch, J. E. (2004). *Our voices, our lives, our futures: Youth and sexually transmitted diseases.* Chapel Hill, NC: University of North Carolina at Chapel Hill School of Journalism and Mass Communication.

Cheney, L. V. (1989). *50 hours: A core curriculum for college students.* Washington, DC: National Endowment for the Humanities.

Chi, M., de Leeuw, N., Chiu, M. H., & LaVancher, C. (1994). Eliciting self-explanations improves understanding. *Cognitive Science, 18,* 439–477.

Chickering, A. W., & Schlossberg, N. K. (1998). Moving on: Seniors as people in transition. In J. N. Gardner, G. Van der Veer, et al. (Eds.), *The senior year experience* (pp. 37–50). San Francisco: Jossey-Bass.

Chronicle of Higher Education. (2003, August 30). Almanac 2003–04. *Chronicle of Higher Education, 49*(1).

Claxton, C. S., & Murrell, P. H. (1988). *Learning styles: Implications for improving practice.* ASHE-ERIC Educational Report No. 4. Washington, DC: Association for the Study of Higher Education.

Coates, T. J. (1977). *How to sleep better: A drug-free program for overcoming insomnia.* Englewood Cliffs, NJ: Prentice Hall.

Colcombe, S. J., Erickson, K., Scalf, P. E., Kim, J. S., Prakash, R., McAuley, E., et al. (2006). Aerobic exercise training increases brain volume in aging humans. *Journal of Gerontology: Medical Sciences, 61A*(11), 1166–1170.

Coleman, R. 1984. *Lennon.* New York: McGraw-Hill.

Collingwood, R. G. 1946. *The Idea of History.* New York: Oxford University Press.

College Board (2009). Economic challenges lead to lower non-tuition revenues and higher prices at colleges and universities. Retrieved November 4, 2009, from http://www.collegeboard.com/press/releases/ 208962.html

College Board. (2008). *Education pays 2007.* Washington, DC: Author.

Collins, A. M., & Loftus, E. F. (1975). A spreading activation theory of semantic processing. *Psychological Review, 82,* 407–428.

Collins, R. K. L. & Skover, D. M. 2002. *The Trials of Lenny Bruce: The Fall and Rise of an American Icon.* Naperville, IL: Sourcebooks MediaFusion.

Colombo, G., Cullen, R., & Lisle, B. (1995). *Rereading America: Cultural contexts for critical thinking and writing.* Boston: Bedford Books of St. Martin's Press.

Corbin, C. B., Pangrazi, R. P., & Franks, B. D. (2000). Definitions: Health, fitness, and physical activity. *President's Council on Physical Fitness and Sports Research Digest, 3*(9), 1–8.

Countryman, E. 1996. *Americans: A Collision of Histories.* New York: Hill & Wang.

Covey, S. R. (1990). *Seven habits of highly effective people* (2nd ed.). New York: Fireside.

Cowan, N. (2001). The magical number 4 in short-term memory: A reconsideration of mental storage capacity. *Behavioral and Brain Sciences, 24,* 87–114.

Coward, A. (1990). *Pattern thinking.* New York: Praeger Publishers.

Crawford, H. J., & Strapp, C. H. (1994). Effects of vocal and instrumental music on visuospatial and verbal performance as moderated by studying preference and personality. *Personality and Individual Differences, 16*(2), 237–245.

Cronon, W. (1998). "Only connect": The Goals of a Liberal Education. *The American Scholar* (Autumn), 73–80.

Crosby, O. (2002). Informational interviewing: Get the scoop on careers. *Occupational Outlook Quarterly* (Summer), 32–37.

Cross, K. P. (1982). Thirty years passed: Trends in general education. In B. L. Johnson (Ed.), *General education in two-year colleges* (pp. 11–20). San Francisco: Jossey-Bass.

Cude, B. J., Lawrence, F. C., Lyons, A. C., Metzger, K., LeJeune, E., Marks, L., & Machtmes, K. (2006). College students and financial literacy: What they know and what we need to learn. *Proceedings of the Eastern Family Economics and Resource Management Association Conference* (pp. 102–109).

Cuseo, J. B. (1996). *Cooperative learning: A pedagogy for addressing contemporary challenges and critical issues in higher education.* Stillwater, OK: New Forums Press.

Cuseo, J. B. (2003a). Comprehensive academic support for students during the first year of college. In G. L. Kramer et al. (Eds.), *Student academic services: An integrated approach* (pp. 271–310). San Francisco: Jossey-Bass.

Cuseo, J. B. (2005). "Decided," "undecided," and "in transition": Implications for academic advisement, career counseling, and student retention. In R. S. Feldman (Ed.), *Improving the first year of college: Research and practice* (pp. 27–50). Mahwah, NJ: Lawrence Erlbaum.

Cuseo, J. B., & Barefoot, B. O. (1996). A natural marriage: The extended orientation seminar and the community college. In J. Henkin (Ed.), *The community college: Opportunity and access for America's first-year students* (pp. 59–68). Columbia: National

Resource Center for the First-Year Experience and Students in Transition, University of South Carolina.

Dalton, J. C., Eberhardt, D., Bracken, J., & Echols, K. (2006). Inward journeys: Forms and patterns of college student spirituality. *Journal of College & Character, 7*(8), 1–21. Retrieved December 17, 2006, from http://www.collegevalues.org/pdfs/Dalton.pdf

Daly, W. T. (1992, July/August). The academy, the economy, and the liberal arts. *Academe*, pp. 10–12.

Daloz Parks, S. 2005. *Leadership Can Be Taught.* Boston: Harvard Business School.

Damrad-Frye, R., & Laird, J. (1989). The experience of boredom: The role of self-perception of attention. *Journal of Personality & Social Psychology, 57*, 315–320.

Daniels, D., & Horowitz, L. J. (1997). *Being and caring: A psychology for living.* Prospect Heights, IL: Waveland Press.

DeGregorio, W. A. 1984. *The Complete Book of the Presidents.* New York: December Books.

DeJong, W., & Linkenback, J. (1999). Telling it like it is: Using social norms marketing campaigns to reduce student drinking. *AAHE Bulletin, 52*(4), pp. 11–13, 16.

Dement, W. C., & Vaughan, C. (1999). *The promise of sleep.* New York: Delacorte Press.

Dement, W. C., & Vaughan, C. (2000). *The promise of sleep: A pioneer in sleep medicine explores the vital connection between health, happiness, and a good night's sleep.* New York: Dell.

Demmert, W. G., Jr., & Towner, J. C. (2003). *A review of the research literature on the influences of culturally based education on the academic performance of Native American students* Retrieved from the Northwest Regional Educational Laboratory, Portland, Oregon, Web site: http://www.nrel.org/indianaed/cbe.pdf

Dictionary.com Unabridged (v 1.1). Retrieved September 30, 2007, from http://dictionary.reference.com/browse/leadership.

Donald, J. G. (2002). *Learning to think: Disciplinary perspectives.* San Francisco: Jossey-Bass.

Dorfman, J., Shames, J., & Kihlstrom, J. F. (1996). Intuition, incubation, and insight. In G. Underwood (Ed.), *Implicit cognition.* New York: Oxford University Press.

Doyle, S., Edison, M., & Pascarella, E. (1998). *The "seven principles of good practice in undergraduate education" as process indicators of cognitive development in college: A longitudinal study.* Paper presented at the annual meeting of the Association for the Study of Higher Education, Miami, FL.

Druckman, D., & Bjork, R. A. (Eds.). (1991). *In the mind's eye: Enhancing human performance.* Washington, DC: National Academy Press.

Dryden, G., & Vos, J. (1999). *The learning revolution: To change the way the world learns.* Torrance, CA: Learning Web.

Dunn, R., Dunn, K., & Price, G. (1990). *Learning style inventory.* Lawrence, KS: Price Systems.

Dupuy, G. M., & Vance, R. M. (1996, October). *Launching your career: A transition module for seniors.* Paper presented at the Second National Conference on Students in Transition, San Antonio, TX.

Eble, K. E. (1966). *The perfect education.* New York: Macmillan.

Eckman, P., & Friesen, W. V. (1969). Nonverbal leakage and clues to deception. *Psychiatry, 32*, 88–106.

Education Commission of the States. (1995). *Making quality count in undergraduate education.* Denver, CO: ECS Distribution Center.

Education Commission of the States. (1996). *Bridging the gap between neuroscience and education.* Denver, CO: Author.

Edwards III, G. C. & Wayne, S. J. 1990. *Presidential Leadership: Politics and Policy Making.* New York: St. Martin's Press.

Ehrlich, T. 2000. *Civic Responsibility and Higher Education.* Westport, CT: The American Council on Education and The Oryx Press.

Einstein, G. O., Morris, J., & Smith, S. (1985). Note-taking, individual differences, and memory for lecture information. *Journal of Educational Psychology, 77*(5), 522–532.

Ellin, A. (1993, September). Post-parchment depression. *Boston Phoenix*.

Ellis, A. (1995). Changing rational-emotive therapy (RET) to rational emotive behavior therapy (REBT). *Journal of Rational-Emotive & Cognitive Behavior Therapy, 13*(2), 85–89.

Ellis, A. (2000). *How to control your anxiety before it controls you.* New York: Citadel Press/Kensington Publishing.

Engs, R. C. (1977). Drinking patterns and drinking problems of college students. *Journal of Studies on Alcohol, 38*, 2144–2156.

Engs, R., & Hanson, D. (1986). Age-specific alcohol prohibition and college students' drinking problems. *Psychological Reports, 59*, 979–984.

Entwistle, N. J., & Marton, F. (1984). Changing conceptions of learning and research. In F. Marton et al. (Eds.), *The experience of learning*. Edinburgh: Scottish Academic Press.

Entwistle, N. J., & Ramsden, P. (1983). *Understanding student learning*. London: Croom Helm.

Erickson, B. L., Peters, C. B., & Strommer, D. W. (2006). *Teaching first-year college students*. San Francisco: Jossey-Bass.

Erickson, B. L., & Strommer, D. W. (1991). *Teaching college freshmen*. San Francisco: Jossey-Bass.

Erickson, B. L., & Strommer, D. W. (2005). Inside the fist-year classroom: Challenges and constraints. In J. L. Upcraft, J. N. Gardner, & B. O. Barefoot (Eds.), *Challenging and supporting the first-year student* (pp. 241–256). San Francisco: Jossey-Bass.

Everly, G. S. (1989). *A clinical guide to the treatment of the human stress response*. New York: Plenum Press.

Ewell, P. T. (1997). Organizing for learning. *AAHE Bulletin, 50*(4), 3–6.

Family Care Foundation. (2005). *If the world were a village of 100 people*. Retrieved December 19, 2006, from http://www.familycare.org.news/if_the_world.htm

Feldman, K. A., & Newcomb, T. M. (1997). *The impact of college on students*. New Brunswick, NJ: Transaction Publishers. (Original work published 1969).

Feldman, K. A., & Paulsen, M. B. (Eds.). (1994). *Teaching and learning in the college classroom*. Needham Heights, MA: Ginn Press.

Festinger, L. (1954). A theory of social comparison processes. *Human Relations, 7,* 117–140.

Fidler, P., & Godwin, M. (1994). Retaining African-American students through the freshman seminar. *Journal of Developmental Education, 17,* 34–41.

Fisher, J. L., Harris, J. L., & Harris, M. B. (1973). Effect of note-taking and review on recall. *Journal of Educational Psychology, 65*(3), 321–325.

Fischer, L. 1954. *Gandhi: His Life and Message for the World*. New York: Mentor Books.

Fixman, C. S. (1990). The foreign language needs of U.S. based corporations. *Annals of the American Academy of Political and Social Science, 511,* 25–46.

Flavell, J. H. (1985). *Cognitive development* (2nd ed.). Englewood Cliffs, NJ: Prentice Hall.

Fletcher, A., Lamond, N., van den Heuvel, C. J., & Dawson, D. (2003). Prediction of performance during sleep deprivation and alcohol intoxication using a quantitative model of work-related fatigue. *Sleep Research Online, 5,* 67–75.

Flowers, L., Osterlind, S., Pascarella, E., & Pierson, C. (2001). How much do student learn in college? Cross-sectional estimates using the College Basic Academic Subjects Examination. *Journal of Higher Education, 72,* 565–583.

Ford, P. L. (Ed.). (1903). *The works of Thomas Jefferson*. New York: Knickerbocker Press.

Franklin, K. F. (2002). Conversations with Metropolitan University first-year students. *Journal of the First-Year Experience and Students in Transition, 14*(2), 57–88.

Frazier, J. G. 1922. *The Golden Bough*. New York: Collier Books.

Frost, S. H. (1991). *Academic advising for student success: A system of shared responsibility* (ASHE-ERIC Higher Education Report No. 3). Washington, DC: School of Education and Human Development, George Washington University.

Furnham, A., & Argyle, M. (1998). *The psychology of money*. New York: Routledge.

Gamson, Z. F. (1984). *Liberating education*. San Francisco: Jossey-Bass.

Gardner, H. (1983). *Frames of mind: The theory of multiple intelligences*. New York: Basic Books.

Gardner, H. (1993). *Frames of mind: The theory of multiple intelligences* (2nd ed.). New York: Basic Books.

Gardner, H. (1999). *Intelligence reframed: Multiple intelligences for the 21st century*. New York: Basic Books.

Gardner, P. D. (1991, March). *Learning the ropes: Socialization and assimilation into the workplace*. Paper presented at the Second National Conference on the Senior Year Experience, San Antonio, TX.

Gellner, E. 1983. *Nations and Nationalism*. Ithaca, NY: Cornell University Press.

George, B. 2003. *Authentic Leadership: Rediscovering the Secrets to Creating Lasting Value*. San Francisco: Jossey-Bass.

George, B. & Sims, P. 2007. *True North: Discover Your Authentic Leadership*. San Francisco: Jossey-Bass.

Gibb, J. R. (1961, September). Defensive communication. *Journal of Communication, 11,* 3.

Gibb, H. R. (1991). *Trust: A new vision of human relationships for business, education, family, and personal living* (2nd ed.). North Hollywood, CA: Newcastle.

Giles, L. C., Glonek, F. V., Luszcz, M. A., & Andrews, G. R. (2005). Effect of social networks on 10-year survival in very old Australians: The Australia longitudinal study of aging. *Journal of Epidemiology and Community Health, 59,* 574–579.

Gladwell, M. (2008). *Outliers: The story of success.* New York: Little, Brown.

Glass, J., & Garrett, M. (1995). Student participation in a college orientation course: Retention, and grade point average. *Community College Journal of Research and Practice, 19,* 117–132.

Glenberg, A. M., Schroeder, J. L., & Robertson, D. A. (1998). Averting the gaze disengages the environment and facilitates remembering. *Memory & Cognition, 26*(4), 651–658.

Goleman, D. (1992, Oct. 27). Voters assailed by unfair persuasion. *The New York Times,* pp. C1–C3.

Goleman, D. (1995). *Emotional intelligence: Why it can matter more than IQ.* New York: Random House.

Goleman, D. (2006). Social intelligence: The new science of human relationships. New York: Dell.

Gordon, L. (2009, Oct. 21). College costs up in hard times. *Los Angeles Times,* p. A13.

Gordon, V. N., & Steele, G. E. (2003). Undecided first-year students: A 25-year longitudinal study. *Journal of the First-Year Experience and Students in Transition, 15*(1), 19–38.

Gottman, J. (1994). *Why marriages succeed and fail.* New York: Fireside.

Graf, P. (1982). The memorial consequence of generation and transformation. *Journal of Verbal Learning and Verbal Behavior, 21,* 539–548.

Grannis v. Ordean, 234 U.S. 394 (1914).

Green, M. G. (Ed.). (1989). *Minorities on campus: A handbook for enhancing diversity.* Washington, DC: American Council on Education.

Greenberg, R., Pillard, R., & Pearlman, C. (1972). The effect of dream (stage REM) deprivation on adaptation to stress. *Psychosomatic Medicine, 34,* 257–262.

Greenleaf, R. K. 1977. *Servant Leadership: A Journey into the Nature of Legitimate Power and Greatness.* Mahwah, NJ: Paulist Press.

Greenleaf, R. K. 1995. "Servant Leadership." In J. T. Wren (Ed.), *The Leader's Companion: Insights on Leadership Through the Ages* (pp. 18–23). New York: Free Press.

Grunder, P., & Hellmich, D. (1996). Academic persistence and achievement of remedial students in a community college's success program. *Community College Review, 24,* 21–33.

Hagberg, J. 1994. *Real Power.* Salem, WI: Sheffield.

Hall, R. M., & Sandler, B. R. (1982). *The classroom climate: A chilly one for women.* Project on the Status of Women. Washington, DC: Association of American Colleges.

Hall, R. M., & Sandler, B. R. (1984). *Out of the classroom: A chilly campus climate for women.* Project on the Status of Women. Washington, DC: Association of American Colleges.

Halpern, D. F. (2003). *Thought & knowledge: An introduction to critical thinking* (4th ed.). Mahwah, NJ: Lawrence Erlbaum Associates.

Hamby, A. L. 1995. *Man of the People: A Life of Harry S. Truman.* New York: Oxford University Press.

Hamilton, E. 1942. *Mythology.* Boston: Little, Brown.

Harris, M. B. (2006). Correlates and characteristics of boredom and proneness to boredom. *Journal of Applied Social Psychology, 30*(3), 576–598.

Hart, B. H. L. 1970. *History of the Second World War.* New York: G. P. Putnam's Sons.

Hartley, J. (1998). *Learning and studying: a research perspective.* London: Routledge.

Hartley, J., & Marshall, S. (1974). On notes and note taking. *Universities Quarterly, 28,* 225–235.

Hashaw, R. M., Hammond, C. J., & Rogers, P. H. (1990). Academic locus of control and the collegiate experience. *Research & Teaching in Developmental Education, 7*(1), 45–54.

Hauri, P., & Linde, S. (1996). *No more sleepless nights.* New York: John Wiley & Sons.

Health, C., & Soll, J. (1996). Mental budgeting and consumer decisions. *Journal of Consumer Research, 23,* 40–52.

Heath, H. (1977). *Maturity and competence: A transcultural view.* New York: Halsted Press.

Heifetz, R. A. 1994. *Leadership Without Easy Answers.* Cambridge, MA: The Belknap Press of Harvard University Press.

Herman, R. E. (2000, November). Liberal arts: The key to the future. *USA Today Magazine, 129,* 34.

Hersey, P. 1984. *The Situational Leader.* Escondido, CA: Center for Leadership Studies.

Hersey, P. & Blanchard, K. H. 1995. "Situational Leadership." In J. T. Wren (Ed.), *The Leader's Companion: Insights on Leadership Through the Ages* (pp. 207–221). New York: Free Press.

Hersh, R. (1997). Intentions and perceptions: A national survey of public attitudes toward liberal arts education. *Change, 29*(2), pp. 16–23.

Hesselbein, F. 1999. "Introduction." In F. Hesselbein & P. M. Cohen (Eds.), *Leader to Leader* (p. xii). San Francisco: Jossey-Bass.

Higbee, K. L. (2001). *Your memory: How it works and how to improve it*. New York: Marlowe.

Higher Education Research Institute. 1996. *A Social Change Model of Leadership Development*. Los Angeles: University of California, Los Angeles.

Hildenbrand, M., & Gore, P. A., Jr. (2005). Career development in the first-year seminar: Best practice versus actual practice. In P. A. Gore (Ed.), *Facilitating the career development of students in transition* (Monograph No. 43, pp. 45–60). Columbia: National Resource Center for the First-Year Experience and Students in Transition, University of South Carolina.

Hill, A. J. (2002). Developmental issues in attitudes toward food and diet. *Proceedings of the Nutrition Society, 61*(2), 259–268.

Hill, J. O., Wyat, H. R., Reed, G. W., & Peters, J. C. (2003). Obesity and environment: Where do we go from here? *Science, 299*, 853–855.

Hobbes, T. 1996. *Leviathan*. Ed. R. Tuck. New York: Cambridge University Press.

Hobson, J. A. (1988). *The dreaming brain*. New York: Basic Books.

Hollenbeck, J. R., Williams, C. R., & Klein, H. J. (1989). An empirical examination of the antecedents of commitment to difficult goals. *Journal of Applied Psychology, 74*(1), 18–23.

Holmes, K. K., Levine, R., & Weaver, M. (2004). Effectiveness of condoms in preventing sexually transmitted infections. *Bulletin of the World Health Organization, 82*, 254–464.

Horne, J. (1988). *Why we sleep: The functions of sleep in humans and other mammals*. New York: Oxford University Press.

Howard, P. J. (2000). *The owner's manual for the brain: Everyday applications of mind-brain research* (2nd ed.). Atlanta: Bard Press.

Howe, M. J. (1970). Note-taking strategy, review, and long-term retention of verbal information. *Journal of Educational Psychology, 63*, 285.

Hughes R. L., Ginnett R. C., & Curphy G. J., 2006. *Leadership: Enhancing the Lessons of Experience*. New York: McGraw-Hill.

Hunter, M. A., & Linder, C. W. (2005). First-year seminars. In M. L. Upcraft, J. N. Gardner, B. O. Barefoot, et al. (Eds.), *Challenging and supporting the first-year student: A handbook for improving the first year of college* (pp. 275–291). San Francisco: Jossey-Bass.

Indiana University. (2004). *Selling your liberal arts degree to employers*. Retrieved July 7, 2004, from http://www.indiana.edu/~career/fulltime/selling_liberal_arts.html

Institute for Research on Higher Education. (1995). Connecting schools and employers: Work-related education and training. *Change, 27*(3), 39–46.

Internal Revenue Service. (2004). *Statistics of income 2001–2003*. Washington, DC: Author.

Jablonski, N. G., & Chaplin, G. (2002). Skin deep. *Scientific American* (October), 75–81.

Jakubowski, P., & Lange, A. J. (1978). *The assertive option: Your rights and responsibilities*. Champaign, IL: Research Press.

Janis, I. L. (1982). *Groupthink: Psychological studies of policy decisions and fiascoes* (2nd ed.). Boston: Houghton Mifflin.

Jemott, J. B., & Magloire, K. (1988). Academic stress, social support, and secretory immunoglobulin. *Journal of Personality and Social Psychology, 55*, 803–810.

Jenkins, J. G., & Dallenbach, K. M. (1924). Oblivescence during sleep and waking. *American Journal of Psychology, 35*, 605–612.

Johansson, J. (2005). *Death by PowerPoint*. Retrieved November 11, 2009, from http://articles.tech.republic.com5100-22_11-5875608.html

Johnsgard, K. W. (2004). *Conquering depression and anxiety through exercise*. New York: Prometheus.

Johnston, L. D., O'Malley, P.M., Bachman, J. G., & Schulenberg, J. E. (2005). *Monitoring the future national survey results on drug use, 1975–2004: Vol 2. College students and adults ages 19–45*. National Institute on Drug Abuse: Bethesda, MD: 2005. NIH Publication No. 05-5728.

Johnstone, A. H., & Su, W. Y. (1994). Lectures: a learning experience? *Education in Chemistry, 31*(1), 65–76, 79.

Joint Science Academies Statement. (2005). *Global response to climate change*. Retrieved August 29, 2005, from http://nationalacademies.org/onpi/06072005.pdf

Jones v. Van Zandt, 5 How (46 U.S.) 221 (1847).

Jones, L., & Petruzzi, D. C. (1995). Test anxiety: A review of theory and current treatment. *Journal of College Student Psychotherapy, 10*(1), 3–15.

Julien, R. M. (2004). *A primer of drug action*. New York: Worth.

Kadison, R. D., & DiGeronimo, T. F. (2004). *College of the overwhelmed: The campus mental health crisis and what to do about it*. San Francisco: Jossey-Bass.

Kagan, S., & Kagan, M. (1998). *Multiple intelligences: The complete MI book*. San Clemente, CA: Kagan Cooperative Learning.

Karabell, Z. 2004. *Chester Alan Arthur*. New York: Times Books.

Kaufman, J. C., & Baer, J. (2002). Could Steven Spielberg manage the Yankees? Creative thinking in different domains. *Korean Journal of Thinking & Problem Solving, 12*(2), 5–14.

Kearns, D. (1989). Getting schools back on track. *Newsweek* (November), pp. 8–9.

Kendall, J. C. and Associates. 1990. *Combining Service and Learning: A Resource Book for Community and Public Service, Volume 1.* Raleigh, NC: National Society for Experiential Education.

Kettner, J. H. 1978. *The Development of American Citizenship.* Chapel Hill: University of North Carolina Press.

Kielcolt-Glaser, J. K., & Glaser, R. (1986). Psychological influences on immunity. *Psychosomatics, 27,* 621–625.

Kiecolt, J. K., Glaser, R., Strain, E., Stout, J., Tarr, K., Holliday, J., et al. (1986). Modulation of cellular immunity in medical students. *Journal of Behavioral Medicine, 9,* 5–21.

Kiewra, K. A. (1985). Students' note-taking behaviors and the efficacy of providing the instructor's notes for review. *Contemporary Educational Psychology, 10,* 378–386.

Kiewra, K. A. (2000). Fish giver or fishing teacher? The lure of strategy instruction. *Teaching at UNL (University of Nebraska–Lincoln), 22*(3), 1–3.

Kiewra, K. A., DuBois, N., Christian, D., McShane, A., Meyerhoffer, M., & Roskelley, D. (1991). Note-taking functions and techniques. *Journal of Educational Psychology, 83*(2), 240–245.

Kiewra, K. A., & Fletcher, H. J. (1984). The relationship between notetaking variables and achievement measures. *Human Learning, 3,* 273–280.

Kiewra, K. A., Hart, K., Scoular, J., Stephen, M., Sterup, G., & Tyler, B. (2000). Fish giver or fishing teacher? The lure of strategy instruction. *Teaching at UNL (University of Nebraska–Lincoln), 22*(3).

King, A. (1990). Enhancing peer interaction and learning in the classroom through reciprocal questioning. *American Educational Research Journal, 27*(4), 664–687.

King, A. (1995). Guided peer questioning: A cooperative learning approach to critical thinking. *Cooperative Learning and College Teaching, 5*(2), 15–19.

King, J. E. (2002). *Crucial choices: How students' financial decisions affect their academic success.* Washington, DC: American Council on Education.

King, J. E. (2005). Academic success and financial decisions: Helping students make crucial choices. In R. S. Feldman (Ed.), *Improving the first year of college: Research and practice* (pp. 3–26). Mahwah, NJ: Lawrence Erlbaum.

King, P. N., Brown, M. K., Lindsay, N. K., & VanHencke, J. R. (2007, September/October). Liberal arts student learning outcomes: An integrated approach. *About Campus,* pp. 2–9.

Kintsch, W. (1968). Recognition and free recall of organized lists. *Journal of Experimental Psychology, 78,* 481–487.

Kintsch, W. (1970). *Learning, memory, and conceptual processes.* Hoboken, NJ: John Wiley & Sons.

Kintsch, W. (1994). Text comprehension, memory, and learning. *American Psychologist, 49,* 294–303.

Klein, S. P., & Hart, F. M. (1968). Chance and systematic factors affecting essay grades. *Journal of Educational Measurement, 5,* 197–206.

Knapp, J. R., & Karabenick, S. A. (1988). Incidence of formal and informal academic help-seeking in higher education. *Journal of College Student Development, 29*(3), 223–227.

Knoll, A. H. (2003). *Life on a young planet: The first three billion years of evolution on earth.* Princeton, NJ: Princeton University Press.

Knouse, S., Tanner, J., & Harris, E. (1999). The relation of college internships, college performance, and subsequent job opportunity. *Journal of Employment Counseling, 36,* 35–43.

Knox, S. (2004). *Financial basics: A money management guide for students.* Columbus: Ohio State University Press.

Kolb, D. A. (1976). Management and learning process. *California Management Review, 18*(3), 21–31.

Kolb, D. A. (1985). *Learning styles inventory.* Boston: McBer.

Kouzes, J. & Posner, B. 1995. *The Leadership Challenge.* San Francisco: Jossey-Bass.

Kramer, A. F., & Erickson, K. I. (2007). Capitalizing on cortical plasticity: Influence of physical activity on cognition and brain function. *Trends in Cognitive Sciences, 11*(8), 342–348.

Kristof, K. M. (2008, December 27). Hooked on debt: Students learn too late the costs of private loans. *Los Angeles Times,* pp. A1, A18–A19.

Kruger, J., Wirtz, D., & Miller, D. (2005). Counterfactual thinking and the first instinct fallacy. *Journal of Personality and Social Psychology, 88,* 725–735.

Kuh, G. D. (1993). In their own words: What students learn outside the classroom. *American Educational Research Journal, 30,* 277–304.

Kuh, G. D. (1995). The other curriculum: Out-of-class experiences associated with student learning and personal development. *Journal of Higher Education, 66*(2), 123–153.

Kuh, G. D., Douglas, K. B., Lund, J. P., & Ramin-Gyurnek, J. (1994). *Student learning outside the classroom: Transcending artificial boundaries.* ASHE-ERIC Higher Education Report No. 8. Washington, DC: George Washington University, School of Education and Human Development.

Kuh, G. D., Kinzie, J., Schuh, J. H., Whitt, E. J., et al. (2005). *Student success in college: Creating conditions that matter.* San Francisco: Jossey-Bass.

Kuhn, L. (1988). What should we tell students about answer changing? *Research Serving Teaching, 1*(8).

Kurfiss, J. G. (1988). *Critical thinking: Theory, research, practice, and possibilities.* ASHE-ERIC Report No. 2. Washington, DC: Association for the Study of Higher Education.

Kurfiss, Joanne G. *Critical Thinking: Theory, Research, and Possibilities.* Texas: Association for the Study of Higher Education, 1988.

Kurland, P. B. & Lerner, R. (eds.) 1987. *The Founder's Constitution.* Indianapolis: The Liberty Fund.

Ladas, H. S. (1980). Note-taking on lectures: An information-processing approach. *Educational Psychologist, 15*(1), 44–53.

Lakein, A. (1973). *How to get control of your time and your life.* New York: New American Library.

Langer, J. A., & Applebee, A. N. (1987). *How writing shapes thinking.* NCTE Research Report No. 22. Urbana, IL: National Council of Teachers of English.

Lankaster, L., & Stilman, D. (2002). *When generations collide.* New York: HarperCollins.

Latané, B., Liu, J. H., Nowak, A., Bonevento, N., & Zheng, L. (1995). Distance matters: Physical space and social impact. *Personality and Social Psychology Bulletin, 21*, 795–805.

Lay, C. H., & Silverman, S. (1996). Trait procrastination, time management, and dilatory behavior. *Personality & Individual Differences, 21*, 61–67.

Lehrer, P. M., & Woolfolk, R. L. (1993). *Principles and practice of stress management* (Vol. 2). New York: Guilford Press.

Leibel, R. L., Rosenbaum, M., & Hirsch, J. (1995). Changes in energy expenditure resulting from altered body weight. *New England Journal of Medicine, 332*, 621–628.

Levitin, D. J. (2006). *This is your brain on music: The science of a human obsession.* New York: Dutton.

Leuwerke, W. C., Robbins, S. B., Sawyer, R., & Lewin, K., Lippit, R., & White, R. K. 1939. "Patterns of Aggressive Behavior in Experimentally Created Social Climates." *Journal of Social Psychology, 10*, 271–301.

Hovland, M. (2004). Predicting engineering major status from mathematics achievement and interest congruence. *Journal of Career Assessment, 12*, 135–149.

Levine, A., & Cureton, J. S. (1998). *When hopes and fears collide.* San Francisco: Jossey-Bass.

Levitsky, D. A., Nussbaum, M., Halbmaier, C. A., & Mrdjenovic, G. (2003, July). *The freshman 15: A model for the study of techniques to curb the "epidemic" of obesity.* Annual meeting of the Society of the Study of Ingestive Behavior, University of Groningen, Haren, The Netherlands.

Levitz, R., & Noel, L. (1989). Connecting student to the institution: Keys to retention and success. In M. L. Upcraft, J. N. Gardner, et al. (Eds.), *The freshman year experience* (pp. 65–81). San Francisco: Jossey-Bass.

Lewin, K. (1935). *A dynamic theory of personality.* New York: McGraw-Hill.

Liebertz, C. (2005a). Want clear thinking? Relax. *Scientific American Mind, 16*(3), 88–89.

Light, R. J. (2001). *Making the most of college: Students speak their minds.* Cambridge, MA: Harvard University Press.

Linn, R. L., & Gronlund, N. E. (1995). *Measurement and assessment in teaching* (7th ed.). Englewood Cliffs, NJ: Prentice Hall.

Lock, R. D. (2000). *Taking charge of your career direction* (4th ed.). Belmont, CA: Wadsworth/Thomson Learning.

Locke, E. (1977). An empirical study of lecture note-taking among college students. *Journal of Educational Research, 77*, 93–99.

Locke, E. A., & Latham, G. P. (1990). *A theory of goal setting and task performance.* Englewood Cliffs, NJ: Prentice Hall.

Locke, J. 1960. *Two Treatises on Government.* Ed. P. Laslett. New York: Cambridge University Press.

Love, P., & Love, A. G. (1995). *Enhancing student learning: Intellectual, social, and emotional integration.* ASHE-ERIC Higher Education Report No. 4. Washington, DC: Graduate School of Education and Human Development, George Washington University.

Lucretius. 1951. *The Nature of the Universe.* Ed. R. Latham. Baltimore: Penguin Books.

Luotto, J. A., Stoll, E. L., & Hoglund-Ketttmann, N. (2001). *Communication skills for collaborative learning* (2nd ed.): Dubuque, IA: Kendall/Hunt.

Mackes (2003). Employers describe perfect job candidate. *NACEWeb Press Releases*. Retrieved July 13, 2004, from http://www.naceweb.org/press

Maddi, S. R. (2002). The story of hardiness: Twenty years of theorizing, research, and practice. *Consulting Psychology Journal: Practice and Research, 54*(3), 175–185.

Mae, N. (2005). *Undergraduate students and credit cards in 2004: An analysis of usage rates and trend.* Wilkes-Barre, PA: Nellie Mae.

Maes, J. D., Weldy, T. G., & Icenogle, M. L. (1997). A managerial perspective: Oral communication competency is most important for business students in the workplace. *Journal of Business Communication, 34*(1), 67–80.

Maguire, D. C. & Fargnoli, A. N. 1991. *On Moral Grounds: The Art/Science of Ethics.* New York: Crossroad.

Maier, N. R. F. (1970). *Problem solving and creativity in individuals and groups.* Belmont, CA: Brooks/Cole.

Malcolm, J. L. (ed.) 1999. *The Struggle for Sovereignty: Seventeenth-Century English Political Tracts.* Indianapolis: The Liberty Fund.

Malvasi, M., Rudowsky, C., & Valencia, J. M. (2009). *Library Rx: Measuring and treating library anxiety, a research study.* Chicago: Association of College and Research Libraries.

Maritain, J. 1951. *Man and the State.* Washington, DC: The Catholic University of America Press.

Marzano, R. J., Pickering, D. J., & Pollock, J. (2001). *Classroom instruction that works: Research-based strategies for increasing student achievement.* Alexandria, VA: Association for Supervision and Curriculum Development.

Maslow, A. H. (1954). *Motivation and personality.* New York: Harper & Row.

Matsui, T., Okada, A., & Inoshita, O. (1983). Mechanism of feedback affecting task performance. *Organizational Behavior and Human Performance, 31*, 114–122.

McCance, N., & Pychyl, T. A. (2003, August). *From task avoidance to action: An experience sampling study of undergraduate students' thoughts, feelings and coping strategies in relation to academic procrastination.* Paper presented at the Third Annual Conference for Counseling Procrastinators in the Academic Context, University of Ohio, Columbus.

McCoy, D. R. 1984. *The Presidency of Harry S. Truman.* Lawrence: The University Press of Kansas.

McGuiness, D., & Pribram, K. (1980). The neurophysiology of attention: Emotional and motivational controls. In M. D. Wittrock (Ed.), *The brain and psychology* (pp. 95–139). New York: Academic Press.

Mehrabian, A. (1972). *Nonverbal communication.* Chicago: Adline-Atherton.

Meiland, Jack W. *College Thinking: How to Get the Most Out of College.* New York: New American Library, 1981, 9–24.

Meilman, P. W., & Presley, C. A. (2005). The first-year experience and alcohol use. In M. L. Upcraft, J. N. Gardner, & B. O. Barefoot, & associates, *Challenging and supporting the first-year student: A handbook for improving the first year of college* (pp. 445–468). San Francisco: Jossey-Bass.

Middleton, F., & Strick, P. (1994). Anatomical evidence for cerebellar and basal ganglia involvement in higher brain function. *Science, 226*(51584), 458–461.

Miller, G. (1988). *The meaning of general education.* New York: Teachers College Press.

Miller, M. A. (2003, September/October). The meaning of the baccalaureate. *About Campus*, pp. 2–8.

Millman, J., Bishop, C., & Ebel, R. (1965). An analysis of test-wiseness. *Educational and Psychological Measurement, 25*, 707–727.

Milton, O. (1982). *Will that be on the final?* Springfield, IL: Charles C. Thomas.

Minninger, J. (1984). *Total recall: How to boost your memory power.* Emmaus, PA: Rodale.

Mitler, M. M., Dinges, D. F., & Dement, W. C. (1994). Sleep medicine, public policy, and public health. In M. H. Kryger, T. Roth, & W. C. Dement (Eds.), *Principles and practice of sleep medicine* (2nd ed.). Philadelphia: Saunders.

Moeller, M. L. (1999). History, concept and position of self-help groups in Germany". *Group Analysis, 32*(2), 181–194.

Molnar, S. (1991). *Human variation: race, type, and ethnic groups* (3rd ed.). Englewood Cliffs, NJ: Prentice Hall.

Montesquieu, Baron de. 1989. *The Spirit of the Laws.* Cohler, A. M., Miller, B. C., & Stone, H. S. (Eds.). New York: Cambridge University Press.

Motley, M. T. (1997). *Overcoming your fear of public speaking: A proven method.* Boston: Houghton Mifflin.

Multon, K. D., Brown, S. D., & Lent, R. W. (1991). Relation of self-efficacy beliefs to academic outcomes: A meta-analytic investigation. *Journal of Counseling Psychology, 38*(1), 30–38.

Murname, K., & Shiffrin, R. M. (1991). Interference and the representation of events in memory. *Journal of Experimental Psychology: Learning, Memory, & Cognition, 17,* 855–874.

Murray, D. M. (1993). *Write to learn* (4th ed.). Fort Worth: Harcourt Brace.

Myers, D. G. (1993). *The pursuit of happiness: Who is happy—and why?* New York: Morrow.

Myers, D. G., & McCaulley, N. H. (1985). *Manual: A guide to the development and use of the Myers-Briggs Type Indicator.* Palo Alto, CA: Consulting Psychologists Press.

Myers, I. B. (1976). *Introduction to type.* Gainesville, FL: Center for the Application of Psychological Type.

Nagda, B. R., Gurin, P., & Johnson, S. M. (2005). Living, doing and thinking diversity: How does pre-college diversity experience affect first-year students' engagement with college diversity? In R. S. Feldman (Ed.), *Improving the first year of college: Research and practice* (pp. 73–110). Mahwah, NJ: Lawrence Erlbaum.

Naisbitt, J. (1982). *Megatrends: Ten new directions transforming our lives.* New York: Warner Books.

Narciso, J., & Burkett, D. (1975). *Disclose yourself: Discover the "me" in relationships.* Englewood Cliffs, NJ: Prentice Hall.

National Association of Colleges & Employers. (2003). *Job Outlook 2003 survey.* Bethlehem, PA: Author.

National Resource Center for the First-Year Experience and Students in Transition (2004). *The 2003 Your First College Year (YFCY) Survey.* Columbia, SC: Author.

National Resources Defense Council. (2005). *Global warming: A summary of recent findings on the changing global climate.* Retrieved Nov. 11, 2005, from http://www.nrdc.org/global/Warming/fgwscience.asp

National Survey of Student Engagement. (2003). *Converting data into action: Expanding the boundaries of institutional improvement.* Bloomington, IN: Author.

Neustadt, R. E. 1980. *Presidential Power and the Modern Presidents: The Politics of Leadership from Roosevelt to Reagan.* New York: Free Press.

Newell, A., & Rosenbloom, P. S. (1981). Mechanisms of skill acquisition of the law of practice. In J. R. Anderson (Ed.), *Cognitive skills and their acquisition.* Hillsdale, NJ: Erlbaum.

Newton, T. (1990, September). *Improving students' listening skills.* IDEA Paper No. 23. Manhattan, KS: Center for Faculty Evaluation and Development.

Nichols, M. P. (1995). *The lost art of listening.* New York: Guilford Press.

Nichols, R. F. 1931. *Franklin Pierce: Young Hickory of the Granite Hills.* Philadelphia: University of Pennsylvania Press.

Niederjohn, M. S. (2008). First-year experience course improves students' financial literacy. *ESource for College Transitions* (electronic newsletter published by the National Resource Center for the First-Year Experience and Students in Transition), *6*(1), 9–11.

Niles, S. G., & Harris-Bowlsbey, J. (2002). *Career development interventions in the 21st century.* Upper Saddle River, NJ: Pearson Education.

Norman, D. A. (1982). *Learning and memory.* San Francisco: W. H. Freeman.

Nummela, R. M., & Rosengren, T. M. (1986). What's happening in students' brains may redefine teaching. *Educational Leadership, 43*(8), 49–53.

Obama, B. (2006). *The audacity of hope: Thoughts on reclaiming the American dream.* New York: Three Rivers Press.

Ober, W. (ed.) 1964. *Intellectual Origins of American National Thought: Pages from the Books Our Founding Fathers Read.* New York: Corinth Books.

Office of Research. (1994). *What employers expect of college graduates: International knowledge and second language skills.* Washington, DC: Office of Educational Research and Improvement, U.S. Department of Education.

O'Keefe, J., & Nadel, L. (1978). *The hippocampus as a cognitive map.* Oxford, England: Clarendon Press.

Onwuegbuzie, A. J. (2000). Academic procrastinators and perfectionistic tendencies among graduate students. *Journal of Social Behavior and Personality, 15,* 103–109.

Orszag, J. M., Orszag, P. R., & Whitmore, D. M. (2001). *Learning and earning: Working in college.* Retrieved July 19, 2006, from http://www.brockport.edu/career01/upromise.htm

Paivio, A. (1990). *Mental representations: A dual coding approach.* New York: Oxford University Press.

Palank, J. (2006, July 17). *Face it: "Book" no secret to employers.* Retrieved August 21, 2006, from http://www.washtimes.com/business/20060717-12942-1800r.htm

Park, O. (1984). Example comparison strategy versus attribute identification strategy in concept learning. *American Educational Research Journal, 21*(1), 145–162.

Pascarella, E. T. (2001, November/December). Cognitive growth in college: Surprising and reassuring findings from the National Study of Student Learning. *Change*, pp. 21–27.

Pascarella, E., & Terenzini, P. (1991). *How college affects students: Findings and insights from twenty years of research*. San Francisco: Jossey-Bass.

Pascarella, E., & Terenzini, P. (2005). *How college affects students: A third decade of research* (Vol. 2). San Francisco: Jossey-Bass.

Paul, R., & Elder, L. (2002). *Critical thinking: Tools for taking charge of your professional and personal life*. Upper Saddle River, NJ: Pearson Education.

Paul, R., & Elder, L. (2004). *The nature and functions of critical and creative thinking*. Dillon Beach, CA: Foundation for Critical Thinking.

Peigneux, P. P., Laureys, S., Delbeuck, X., & Maquet, P. (2001, December 21). Sleeping brain, learning brain: The role of sleep for memory systems. *NeuroReport, 12*(18), A111–A124.

Perry, A. B. (2004). Decreasing math anxiety in college students. *College Student Journal, 38*(2), 321–324.

Perry, W. G. (1970, 1999). *Forms of intellectual and ethical development during the college years: A scheme*. New York: Holt, Rinehart & Winston.

Peskin, A. 1978. *Garfield*. Kent, OH: Kent University Press.

Peter D. Hart Research Associates. (2006). *How should colleges prepare students to succeed in today's global economy?* Based on surveys among employers and recent college graduates. conducted on behalf of the Association of American Colleges and Universities. Washington, DC: Author.

Peterson, C., & Seligman, M. E. P. (2004). *Character strengths and virtues: A handbook and classification*. New York: Oxford University Press.

Pettigrew, T. F. (1998). Intergroup contact theory. *Annual Review of Psychology, 49*, 65–85.

Pew Internet & American Life Project. (2002). *The Internet goes to college: How students are living in the future with today's technology*. Retrieved January 30, 2005, from http://www. perinternet. org/reports/pdfs/Report1.pdf

Piaget, J. (1978). *Success and understanding*. Cambridge, MA: Harvard University Press.

Piaget, J. (1985). *The equilibration of cognitive structures: The central problem of intellectual development*. Chicago: University of Chicago Press.

Pinker, S. (1994). *The language instinct*. New York: HarperCollins.

Pintrich, P. R. (Ed.). (1995). *Understanding self-regulated learning* (New Directions for Teaching and Learning, No. 63). San Francisco: Jossey-Bass.

Pope, L. (1990). *Looking beyond the Ivy League*. New York: Penguin Press.

Porter, S. R., & Swing, R. L. (2006). Understanding how first-year seminars affect persistence. *Research in Higher Education, 47*(1), 89–109.

Potts, J. T. (1987). Predicting procrastination on academic tasks with self-report personality measures. (Doctoral dissertation, Hofstra University). *Dissertation Abstracts International, 48*, 1543.

President's Council on Physical Fitness and Sports. (2001). Toward a uniform definition of wellness: A commentary. *Research Digest, 3*(15), 1–8.

Pribram, K. H. (1991). *Brain and perception: Holonomy and structure in figural processing*. Hillsdale, NJ: Erlbaum.

Prince, Howard T. II. 2007. "Ethical Leadership." Retrieved August 24, 2007, from http://www. utexas.edu/lbj/research/leadership/slc2007/.

Pratt, B. (2008). *Extra credit: The 7 things every college student needs to know about credit, debt & cash*. Keedysville, MD: ExtraCreditBook.com.

Price, R. H., Choi, J. N., & Vinokur, A. D. (2002). Links in the chain of adversity following job loss: How financial strain and loss of personal control lead to depression, impaired functioning, and poor health. *Journal of Occupational Health Psychology, 7*(4), 302–312.

Purdue University Online Writing Lab. (1995–2004). *Writing a research paper*. Retrieved August 18, 2005, from http://owl.english.purdue.edu/workshops/hypertext/ResearchW/notes.html

Purdy, M., & Borisoff, D. (Eds.). (1996). *Listening in everyday life: A personal and professional approach*. Lanham, MD: University Press of America.

Putman, R. D. (2000). *Bowling alone: The collapse and revival of American community*. New York: Simon & Schuster.

Rader, P. E., & Hicks, R. A. (1987, April). *Jet lag desynchronization and self-assessment of business-related performance*. Paper presented at the meeting of the Western Psychological Association, Long Beach, CA.

Ramsden, P. (2003). *Learning to teach in higher education* (2nd ed.). London: RoutledgeFalmer.

Ramsden, P., & Entwistle, N. J. (1981). Effects of academic departments on students' approaches to studying. *British Journal of Educational Psychology, 51*, 368–383.

Randall, W. S. 1993. *Thomas Jefferson: A Life*. New York: Henry Holt.

Ratcliff, J. L. (1997). What is a curriculum and what should it be? In J. G. Gaff, J. L. Ratcliff, et al. (Eds.), *Handbook of the undergraduate curriculum: A comprehensive guide to purposes, structures, practices, and change* (pp. 5–29). San Francisco: Jossey-Bass.

Ratey, J. J. (2008). *Spark: The revolutionary new science of exercise and the brain*. New York: Little, Brown.

Reed, S. K. (1996). *Cognition: Theory and applications* (3rd ed.). Pacific Grove, CA: Brooks/Cole.

Reiff, J. Feb. 15, 2006. *Leadership Development Through Service Learning*. NSLC associates. Web Seminar.

Rennels, M. R., & Chaudhair, R. B. (1988). Eye-contact and grade distribution. *Perceptual and Motor Skills, 67* (October), 627–632.

Rennie, D., & Brewer, L. (1987). A grounded theory of thesis blocking. *Teaching of Psychology, 14*(1), 10–16.

Rhoads, J. (2005). *The transition to college: Top ten issues identified by students*. Retrieved June 30, 2006, from http://advising.wichita.edu/lasac/pubs/aah/trans.htm

Richmond, V. P., & McCloskey, J. C. (1997). *Communication apprehension: Avoidance and effectiveness* (5th ed.). Boston: Allyn & Bacon.

Riesman, D., Glazer, N., & Denney, R. (2001). *The lonely crowd: A study of the changing American character* (rev, ed.). New Haven, CT: Yale University Press.

Ring, T. (1997, October). Issuers face a visit to the dean's office. *Credit Card Management, 10,* 34–39.

Riquelme, H. (2002). Can people creative in imagery interpret ambiguous figures faster than people less creative in imagery? *Journal of Creative Behavior, 36*(2), 105–116.

Roffwarg, H. P., Muzio, J. N., & Dement, W. C. (1966). Ontogenetic development of the human sleep-dream cycle. *Science, 152,* 604–619.

Roos, L. L., Wise, S. L., Yoes, M. E., & Rocklin, T. R. (1996). Conducting self-adapted testing using MicroCAT. *Educational and Psychological Measurement, 56,* 821–827.

Rose, Mike. "The Politics of Remediation." In *Lives on the Boundary*, 167–204. New York: The Free Press, 1990.

Rosenberg, M. (2009). *The number of countries in the word*. Retrieved Nov. 18, 2009, from http://geography.about.com/cs/countries/a/number countries.htm

Rosenfield, I. (1988). *The invention of memory: A new view of the brain*. New York: Basic Books.

Rousseau, Jean-Jacques. 1973. *The Social Contract and Discourses*. C. D. H. Cole (ed.).

Rothblum, E. D., Solomon, L. J., & Murakami, J. (1986). Affective, cognitive, and behavioral differences between high and low procrastinators. *Journal of Counseling Psychology, 33*(4), 387–394.

Rotter, J. (1966). Generalized expectancies for internal versus external controls of reinforcement. *Psychological Monographs: General and Applied, 80*(609), 1–28.

Ruggiero, V. R. (2004). *Beyond feelings: A guide to critical thinking*. New York: McGraw-Hill.

Runco, M. A. (2004). Creativity. *Annual Review of Psychology, 55,* 657–687.

Rutland, VT: Charles E. Tuttle.

Sadker, M., & Sadker, D. (1994). *Failing at fairness: How America's schools cheat girls*. New York: Charles Scribner's Sons.

Saint Augustine. 1958. *City of God*. V. J. Bourke (ed.). New York: Image Books.

Sax, L. J. (2003, July–August). Our incoming students: What are they like? *About Campus,* pp. 15–20.

Sax, L. J., Astin, A. W., Korn, W. S., & Mahoney, K. M. (1999). *The American freshman: National norms for fall 1999*. Los Angeles: Higher Education Research Institute, Graduate School of Education & Information Studies, University of California.

Sax, L. J., Bryant, A. N., & Gilmartin, S. K. (2004). A longitudinal investigation of emotional health among male and female first-year college students. *Journal of the First-Year Experience and Students in Transition, 16*(2), 29–65.

Sax, L. J., Lindholm, J. A., Astin, A. W., Korn, W. S., & Mahoney, K. M. (2004). *The American freshman: National norms for fall 2004*. Los Angeles: Higher Education Research Institute, University of California.

Schacter, D. L. (1992). Understanding implicit memory. *American Psychologist, 47*(4), 559–569.

Schlosser, E. (2001). *Fast food nation: The dark side of the all-American meal*. Boston: Houghton Mifflin.

Schneider, W., & Chein, J. M. (2003). Controlled and automatic processing: Behavior, theory, and biological mechanisms. *Cognitive Science, 27,* 525–559.

Schunk, D. H. (1995). Self-efficacy and education and instruction. In J. E. Maddux (Ed.), *Self-efficacy, adaptation, and adjustment: Theory, research, and application* (pp. 281–303). New York: Plenum Press.

Secretary's Commission on Achieving Necessary Skills. (1992). *Learning a living: A blueprint for high performance. SCANS Report for America 2000.* Washington, DC: U.S. Department of Labor.

Sedlacek, W. (1987). Black students on White campuses: 20 years of research. *Journal of College Student Personnel, 28,* 484–495.

Segall, M. H., Campbell, D. T., & Herskovits, M. J. (1966). *The influence of culture on visual perception.* Indianapolis: Bobbs-Merrill.

Segal, E. (ed.) 1986. *Dialogues of Plato.* New York: Bantam Books.

Seligman, M. E. P. (1991). *Learned optimism.* New York: Knopf.

Service-Learning Faculty Manual. 2002. Colorado State University Service Integration Project Office for Service-Learning and Volunteer Programs: Fort Collins, CO.

Shanley, M., & Witten, C. (1990). University 101 freshman seminar course: A longitudinal study of persistence, retention, and graduation rates. *NASPA Journal, 27,* 344–352.

Shatz, M. A., & Best, J. B. (1987). Students' reasons for changing answers on objective tests. *Teaching of Psychology, 14*(4), 241–242.

Sheehan, C. A. & MacDowell, G. L. (eds.) 1998. *Friends of the Constitution: Writings of the "Other" Federalists.* Indianapolis: The Liberty Fund.

Shelton, J. T., Elliot, E. M., Eaves, S. D., & Exner, A. L. (2009). The distracting effects of a ringing cell phone: An investigation of the laboratory and the classroom setting. *Journal of Environmental Psychology,* (March). Retrieved October 25, 2009, from http://news-info.wustl.edu/news/page/normal/14225.html

Shirer, William L. 1979. *Gandhi: A Memoir.* New York: Simon & Schuster.

Sidle, M., & McReynolds, J. (1999). The freshman year experience: Student retention and student success. *NASPA Journal, 36,* 288–300.

Sidney, A. 1996. *Discourses Concerning Government.* Thomas G. West (ed.). Indianapolis: The Liberty Fund.

Singh, N. A., Clements, K. M., & Fiatarone, M. A. (1997). A randomized controlled trial of the effect of exercise on sleep. *Sleep, 20,* 95–101.

Smith, D. (1997). How diversity influences learning. *Liberal Education, 83*(2), 42–48.

Smith, D. D. (2005). Experiential learning, service learning, and career development. In P. A. Gore (Ed.), *Facilitating the career development of students in transition* (Monograph No. 43, pp. 205–222). Columbia: National Resource Center for the First-Year Experience and Students in Transition, University of South Carolina.

Smith, J. B., Walter, T. L., & Hoey, G. (1992). Support programs and student self-efficacy: Do first-year students know when they need help? *Journal of the Freshman Year Experience, 4*(2), 41–67.

Smith, P. 1962. *John Adams.* Garden City, NY: Doubleday.

Smith, R. L. (1994). The world of business. In W. C. Hartel, S. W. Schwartz, S. D. Blume, & J. N. Gardner (Eds.), *Ready for the real world* (pp. 123–135). Belmont, CA: Wadsworth Publishing.

Snyder, C. R. (1994). *Psychology of hope: You can get from here to there.* New York: Free Press.

Snyder, C. R., Harris, C., Anderson, J. R., Holleran, S. A., Irving, L. M., Sigmon, S. T., et al. (1991). The will and the ways: Development and validation of an individual-differences measure of hope. *Journal of Personality and Social Psychology, 60,* 570–585.

Sprenger, M. (1999). *Learning and memory: The brain in action.* Alexandria, VA: Association for Supervision and Curriculum Development.

Stark, J. S., Lowther, R. J., Bentley, M. P., Ryan, G. G., Martens, M. L., Genthon, P. A., et al. (1990). *Planning introductory college courses: Influences on faculty.* Ann Arbor: National Center for Research to Improve Postsecondary Teaching and Learning, University of Michigan. (ERIC Document Reproduction Services No. 330 277 370)

Starke, M. C., Harth, M., & Sirianni, F. (2001). Retention, bonding, and academic achievement: Success of a first-year seminar. *Journal of the First-Year Experience and Students in Transition, 13*(2), 7–35.

Staudinger, U. M., & Baltes, P. B. (1994). Psychology of wisdom. In R. J. Sternberg (Ed.), *Encyclopedia of intelligence* (Vol. 1, pp. 143–152). New York: Macmillan.

Stein, B. S. (1978). Depth of processing reexamined: The effects of the precision of encoding and testing appropriateness. *Journal of Verbal Learning and Verbal Behavior, 17,* 165–174.

Sternberg, R. J. (2001). What is the common thread of creativity? *American Psychologist, 56*(4), 360–362.

Strout, C. 1974. *The New Heavens and New Earth: Political Religion in America.* New York: Harper & Row.

Strommer, D. W. (1993). Not quite good enough: Drifting about in higher education. *AAHE Bulletin, 45*(10), 14–15.

Suárez, Francisco. 1994. *On Efficient Causality: Metaphysical Disputations 17, 18, and 19.* A. J. Freddoso (trans.). New Haven, CT: Yale University Press.

Sullivan, R. E. (1993, March 18). Greatly reduced expectations. *Rolling Stone*, pp. 2–4.

Sundquist, J., & Winkleby, M. (2000, June). Country of birth, acculturation status and abdominal obesity in a national sample of Mexican-American women and men. *International Journal of Epidemiology, 29*, 470–477.

Susswein, R. (1995). College students and credit cards: A privilege earned? *Credit World, 83*, 21–23.

Svinicki, M. D., & Dixon, N. M. (1987). The Kolb model modified for classroom activities. *College Teaching, 35*(4), 141–146.

Taranto, J. & Leo, L. (eds.) 2004. *Presidential Leadership: Rating the Best and the Worst in the White House.* New York: Wall Street Journal Books.

Ten Commandments of PowerPoint Presentations (2005). Retrieved November 15, 2009, from http://power-points.blogspot.com/2005/09/10-commandments-of-powerpoint.html

Thomson, R. (1998). University of Vermont. In B. O. Barefoot, C. L. Warnock, M. P. Dickinson, S. E. Richardson, & M. R. Roberts (Eds.). (1998). *Exploring the evidence: Vol. 2. Reporting outcomes of first-year seminars* (Monograph No. 29, pp. 77–78). Columbia: National Resource Center for the First-Year Experience and Students in Transition, University of South Carolina.

Tinto, V. (1993). *Leaving college: Rethinking the causes and cures of student attrition* (2nd ed.). Chicago: University of Chicago Press.

Tocqueville, Alexis de. 1990. *Democracy in America.* P. Bradley (ed.). New York: Vintage Books.

Torrance, E. P. (1963). *Education and the creative potential.* Minneapolis: University of Minnesota Press.

Truman, H. S. 1955. *Memoirs by Harry S. Truman, Volume One: Year of Decisions.* Garden City, NY: Doubleday.

Tyson, E. (2003). *Personal finance for dummies.* Indianapolis: IDG Books.

Underwood, B. J. (1983). *Attributes of memory.* Glenview, IL: Scott, Foresman.

University of Wisconsin, La Crosse (2001). *Strategies for using presentation software (PowerPoint).* Retrieved November 13, 2009, from http://www.uwlax.edu/biology/communication/Powerpoint Strategies.html

U.S. Census Bureau. (2000). *Racial and ethnic classifications in Census 2000 and beyond.* Retrieved December 19, 2006, from http://census.gov/population/www/socdemo/race/racefactcb.html

U.S. Census Bureau. (2004). *The face of our population.* Retrieved December 12, 2006, from http://factfinder.census.gov/jsp/saff/SAFFInfojsp?_pageId=tp9_race_ethnicity

U.S. Department of Education (1999). *The new college course map and transcripts files: Changes in course-taking and achievement, 1972–1993* (2nd ed.). Washington, DC: Author.

U.S. Department of Education, National Center for Education Statistics. (2002). *Profile of undergraduate students in U.S. postsecondary institutions: 1999–2000.* Washington, DC: Government Printing Office.

U.S. National Center for Health Statistics. (2003). *National vital statistics report*, Volume 51, No. 5.

Van Dongen, H. P. A., Maislin, G., Mullington, J. M., & Dinges, D. F. (2003). The cumulative cost of additional wakefulness: Dose–response effects on neurobehavioral functions and sleep physiology from chronic sleep restriction and total sleep deprivation. *Sleep, 26*, 117–126.

Van Overwalle, F. I., Mervielde, I., & De Schuyer, J. (1995). Structural modeling of the relationships between attributional dimensions, emotions, and performance of college freshmen. *Cognition and Emotion, 9*(1), 59–85.

Viorst, J. (1998). *Necessary losses.* New York: Fireside.

Vodanovich, Wallace, & Kass, (2005). A confirmatory approach to the factor structure of the boredom proneness scale: Evidence for a two-factor sort form. *Journal of Personality Assessment, 85*(3), 295–303, 305.

Voelker, R. (2004). Stress, sleep loss, and substance abuse create potent recipe for college depression. *Journal of the American Medical Association, 291*, 2177–2179.

Vogler, R. E., & Bartz, W. R. (1992). *Teenagers and alcohol: When saying no isn't enough.* Philadelphia: The Charles Press.

Voltaire. 1994. *Political Writings.* D. Williams (ed.). New York: Cambridge University Press.

Vygotsky, L. S. (1978). Internalization of higher cognitive functions. In M. Cole, V. John-Steiner,

S. Scribner, & E. Souberman (Eds. & Trans.), *Mind in society: The development of higher psychological processes* (pp. 52–57). Cambridge, MA: Harvard University Press.

Wabash National Study. (2007). Retrieved October 4, 2007, from http://www.liberalarts.wabash.edu/nationalstudy

Waddington, P. (1996). *Dying for information: An investigation into the effects of information overload in the USA and worldwide.* London: Reuters.

Wade, C., & Tavris, C. (1990). Thinking critically and creatively. *Skeptical Inquirer, 14,* 372–377.

Walker, C. M. (1996). Financial management, coping, and debt in households under financial strain. *Journal of Economic Psychology, 17,* 789–807.

Wall, R. 1977. *Ocean Liners.* London: New Burlington Books.

Walsh, K. (2005). *Suggestions from more experienced classmates.* Retrieved June 12, 2006, from http://www.uni.edu/walsh/introtips.html

Walter, T. W., Knudsbig, G. M., & Smith, D. E. P. (2003). *Critical thinking: Building the basics* (2nd ed.). Belmont, CA: Wadsworth.

Walter, T. L., & Smith, J. (1990, April). *Self-assessment and academic support: Do students know they need help?* Paper presented at the annual Freshman Year Experience Conference, Austin, Texas.

Webber, R. A. (1991). *Breaking your time barriers: Becoming a strategic time manager.* Englewood Cliffs, NJ: Prentice Hall.

Weschsler, H., & Wuethrich, B. (2002). *Dying to drink: Confronting binge drinking on college campuses.* Emmaus, PA: Rodale.

Weinstein, C. F. (1994). Students at risk for academic failure. In K. W. Prichard & R. M. Sawyer (Eds.), *Handbook of college teaching: Theory and applications* (pp. 375–385). Westport, CT: Greenwood Press.

Weinstein, C. F., & Meyer, D. K. (1991). Cognitive learning strategies. In R. J. Menges & M. D. Svinicki (Eds.), *College teaching: From theory to practice* (New Directions for Teaching and Learning, No. 45, pp. 15–26). San Francisco: Jossey-Bass.

Wesley, J. C. (1994). Effects of ability, high school achievement, and procrastinatory behavior on college performance. *Educational & Psychological Measurement, 54,* 404–408.

Wheelright, J. (2005, March). Human, study thyself. *Discover,* pp. 39–45.

Whittemore, R. C. 1964. *Makers of the American Mind: Three Centuries of American Thought and Thinkers.* New York: William Morrow.

Wiederman, M. (2007). Why it's so hard to be happy. *Scientific American Mind, 18*(1), 36–43.

Wilkie, C. J., & Thompson, C. A. (1993). First-year reentry women's perceptions of their classroom experiences. *Journal of the Freshman Year Experience, 5*(2), 69–90.

Wilhite, S. (1990). Self-efficacy, locus of control, self-assessment of memory ability, and student activities as predictors of college course achievement. *Journal of Educational Psychology, 82*(4), 696–700.

Williams, Joseph M. and McEnerney. *Writing in College: A Short Guide to College Writing.* September 1, 1995. http://writing-program.uchicago.edu/resources/collegewriting/high_school_v_college. htm (April 12, 2004).

Willingham, W. W. (1985). *Success in college: The role of personal qualities and academic ability.* New York: College Entrance Examination Board.

Wilson, W. 1903. *History of the American People.* New York: Harper & Brothers.

Winsor, J. L., Curtis, D. B., & Stephens, R. D. (1997). National preferences in business and communication education: A survey update. *JACA, 3* (September), 170–179.

Woodward, B. 1987. *Veil: The Secret Wars of the CIA 1981–87.* New York: Simon & Schuster.

Wright, D. J. (Ed.). (1987). *Responding to the needs of today's minority students.* New Directions for Student Services, No. 38. San Francisco: Jossey-Bass.

Wyckoff, S. C. (1999). The academic advising process in higher education: History, research, and improvement. *Recruitment & Retention in Higher Education, 13*(1), 1–3.

Yerkes, R. M., & Dodson, J. D. (1908). The relationship of strength and stimulus to rapidity of habit formation. *Journal of Neurological Psychology, 184,* 59–82.

Young, K. S. (1996, August). *Pathological Internet use: The emergence of a new clinical disorder.* Paper presented at the annual meeting of the American Psychological Association, Toronto, Ontario, Canada.

Zeidner, M. (1995). Adaptive coping with test situations: A review of the literature. *Educational Psychologist, 30*(3), 123–133.

Zimbardo, P. G., Johnson, R. L., & Weber, A. L. (2006). *Psychology: Core concepts* (5th ed.). Boston: Allyn & Bacon.

Zimmerman, B. J. (1995). Self-efficacy and educational development. In A. Bandura (Ed.), *Self-efficacy in changing societies*. New York: Cambridge University Press.

Zinsser, W. (1988). *Writing to learn*. New York: HarperCollins.

Zull, J. E. (2002). *The art of changing the brain: Enriching the practice of teaching by exploring the biology of learning*. Sterling, VA: Stylus.